# The Fight for Dublin, 1919–1921

ALSO BY JOSEPH MCKENNA
AND FROM MCFARLAND

*Voices from the Easter Rising: Firsthand Accounts
of Ireland's 1916 Rebellion* (2017)

*The IRA Bombing Campaign Against Britain,
1939–1940* (2016)

*The Irish-American Dynamite Campaign:
A History, 1881–1896* (2012)

*Guerrilla Warfare in the Irish War of Independence,
1919–1921* (2011)

British Ships in the Confederate Navy (2010)

The Fight for Dublin, 1919–1921

Urban Warfare in the Irish Struggle for Independence

JOSEPH MCKENNA

McFarland & Company, Inc., Publishers
Jefferson, North Carolina

LIBRARY OF CONGRESS CATALOGUING-IN-PUBLICATION DATA

Names: McKenna, Joseph, author.
Title: The fight for Dublin, 1919–1921 : urban warfare in the Irish struggle for independence / Joseph McKenna.
Other titles: Urban warfare in the Irish struggle for independence
Description: Jefferson, North Carolina : McFarland & Company, Inc., Publishers, 2021 | Includes bibliographical references and index.
Identifiers: LCCN 2021023900 | ISBN 9781476684413 (paperback : acid free paper) ∞
ISBN 9781476642062 (ebook)
Subjects: LCSH: Ireland—History—War of Independence, 1919–1921. | Political violence—Ireland—Dublin—History—20th century. | Ireland—History—War of Independence, 1919–1921—Military intelligence. | Intelligence service—Ireland—Dublin—History—20th century. | Espionage, British—Ireland—Dublin—History—20th century. | Dublin (Ireland)—History, Military—20th century. | BISAC: HISTORY / Military / Wars & Conflicts (Other) | HISTORY / Europe / Ireland
Classification: LCC DA962 .M478 2021 | DDC 941.5082/1—dc23
LC record available at https://lccn.loc.gov/2021023900

BRITISH LIBRARY CATALOGUING DATA ARE AVAILABLE

ISBN (print) 978-1-4766-8441-3
ISBN (ebook) 978-1-4766-4206-2

© 2021 Joseph McKenna. All rights reserved

No part of this book may be reproduced or transmitted in any form or by any means, electronic or mechanical, including photocopying or recording, or by any information storage and retrieval system, without permission in writing from the publisher.

Front cover image: A photo purported to be the Cairo Gang who conducted intelligence operations against prominent members of the IRA. Most of these men were assassinated by the IRA on November 21, 1920, in a planned series of simultaneous strikes engineered by Michael Collins (Wikimedia Commons).

Printed in the United States of America

*McFarland & Company, Inc., Publishers
Box 611, Jefferson, North Carolina 28640
www.mcfarlandpub.com*

For my grandfather and all the other unsung heroes
who likewise fought, who likewise died.

Table of Contents

Acknowledgments   ix

List of Abbreviations   x

Preface   1

Introduction   3

1. Preparing for War   17
2. British Intelligence in Ireland 1914–1918   24
3. Establishing an Irish Intelligence Service   30
4. Eliminating the G Men   50
5. Special Branch Strikes Back   78
6. Military Intelligence and the Paramilitaries   91
7. Winter Arrives   111
8. Dublin Special Branch—The Murder Gang   123
9. Bloody Sunday, November 21, 1920   147
10. Hardy, King and Igoe   174
11. IRA Active Service Units   205
12. Burning the Custom House   216
13. The Road to Peace   232

Appendix I—Intelligence Staff and The Squad   239

Appendix II—Known or Suspected British Agents   241

Table of Contents

Appendix III—Known or Suspected Touts   243

Appendix IV—British Secret Service Men and Others Assassinated or Wounded on November 21, 1920   246

Appendix V—Members of G. Division, Dublin Metropolitan Police, Shot and Killed by The Squad   249

Chapter Notes   251

Bibliography   265

Index   269

Acknowledgments

My thanks to all the staff of the British Newspaper Library at Colindale Avenue. Thanks also to the staff of the National Archive at Kew. My thanks, too, to the staff at the Bureau of Military History for downloading the Witness Statements of the many people that I have quoted. Last, but not least, I would like to thank David Grant, who has done an unbelievable job in collecting source material and uploading it to the Internet. His contribution is immeasurable.

List of Abbreviations

ADRIC   Auxiliary Division of the Royal Irish Constabulary
ASU   Active Service Unit
DMP   Dublin Metropolitan Police
DORA   Defence of the Realm Act
GAA   Gaelic Athletic Association
G.H.Q.   General Headquarters
GPO   General Post Office
IRA   Irish Republican Army
JP   Justice of the Peace
K.C.   King's Council (a senior lawyer)
MC   Military Cross
M.I.   Military Intelligence
MI5   British Intelligence (Internal)
M.P.   Member of Parliament (British)
NCO   Noncommissioned Officer
I.O.   Intelligence Officer
RIC   Royal Irish Constabulary
ROIR   Restoration of Order in Ireland

Preface

The war fought out in Dublin lacked the glamor of the war fought by the flying squads in the west of Ireland. There, out in the countryside, ambushes of but a few men developed from 1919 to 1921 into something approaching what would be recognized as a battle, with 100-plus Irish Volunteers taking on the British Army and the paramilitary police force of the Auxiliaries and the Black and Tans. The war in Dublin was nothing like that. It was a dirty little war of betrayal and assassination—out-and-out murder, brutality and torture by both sides. It was a desperate war, lacking in humanity, with one nation seeking to retain its empire while the other sought to gain its freedom. There were undoubtedly brave men on both sides, doing what they believed was their duty, but there were also men who seemed to delight in the brutality that ensued.

The futility of the Easter Rising, idealists led by dreamers, showed how not to conduct an urban war against Britain. Men and women had been placed in concentrated static positions, waiting for the enemy to come and annihilate them. This was how the British wanted to confront the rebels, to encircle and destroy them. A new realistic form of fighting, fitted to the urban environment, resulted in the rise of the Active Service Units, whose men engaged in brief hit-and-run attacks, wearing down the resistance of the enemy. The response to this was British brutality against the population, driving them into active support for their national army, the IRA.

Success in winning such a war also lay in the gathering of and the denial to the other side of intelligence. The intelligence war fought out in Dublin between 1919 and 1921 was rather like a game of chess. The ultimate prize was Ireland. One side would make a move; the other side would counter. Pawns were taken, but each pawn reflected the death of a human being. In some cases, death was incidental; in others, it was significant. Neither side succeeded in achieving a checkmate, but Irish Intelligence came very close.

The main sources for this study from the British point of view are *A*

Record of the Rebellion in Ireland in 1920–21 and *A Report on the Intelligence Branch of the Chief of Police, Dublin Castle from May 1920 to July 1921*. In addition, material in the National Archive at Kew, in London, usually Home Office or War Office papers, was also sourced as was material in the library of the Imperial War Museum. The Bibliography gives details of secondary sources, which include diaries, biographies of senior officers and politicians, and later works of analysis.

From the Irish perspective, my primary source of information has been the Witness Statements deposited with the Bureau of Military History (now online). These are in the main the statements of men and women working in Irish Intelligence, the Active Service Units, and The Squad. Also included is material from the standard histories and biographies of the time.

Because this work has been set out like a game of chess—attack and counterattack—chapters occasionally overlap each other with regard to time frames. This perhaps is better than chopping and changing and, in the process, confusing the reader.

Introduction

As the defeated and exhausted remnants of the Irish Republican Army lay huddled on the green sward before the Rotunda concert hall at the end of the Easter Rising, members of G. Department, the political section of the Dublin Metropolitan Police, moved amongst the prisoners.[1] They scanned the faces of the defeated, pulling out the people they recognized. There was the old man, Tom Clarke, who kept a tobacconist shop in Great Britain Street. He was well known to them; a Fenian, his crimes went back as far as the 1880s. He was a convicted dynamiter who had served fifteen years for his offenses. Then there was Sean MacDiarmada, a man crippled by polio. They pulled him from the crowd and threw away his walking stick. There was no need to do that; it was petty and spiteful.[2] Through the ranks they proceeded, pulling out the known people. The G. men had files on all those chosen. The young man, a 25-year-old staff captain who had fought in the General Post Office during the Easter Rising, watched as the police did their work. They knew what they were doing. Their actions were intelligence-led. One of the police numbers, Edward Broy, recounted:

> Immediately on the Rising being finished, the senior political detectives went to Richmond Barracks to identify and classify the prisoners, selecting those who were best known as leaders for immediate trial by courtmartial. It was then that the political record books in the Detective Office were brought into use. The books were taken to the Castle and, I believe, subsequently to Richmond Barracks.
>
> The records might show, for example, that Michael O'Hanrahan met Thomas McDonagh in Grafton St. three months before and had a conversation of some minutes' duration....[3]

Such was the minutiae gathered by the detective force and then assembled into a file on each man. Civil servant Thomas Markham detailed how the information was gathered:

> The Constable records everything in his diary. What he frightens from the child and coaxes from the cailin. What he hears, sees, infers. The sergeant

transfers the constable's report, never abbreviating. It is not his part to select. The policeman moves in a social atmosphere, he writes down everything, gossipy servants, what the retired RIC pensioner says. A "someone" whose name is never written down. He's a "reliable source." He could be the publican. The rail spy could be the inspector.

The road to the castle is paved with anonymous letters, deriving from the besetting Irish sin, jealousy. The depth and widespread nature of this treachery would make a good Irishman despair. The local loyalist could have a good post and be merely a disreputable spotter ... what was said at a Volunteer meeting; where arms are kept; the eavesdropping prison warder; the opening of letters in the post.[4]

It was all gathered together, enabling the police to identify the Volunteer leaders. They were led off to execution. The senior Volunteer officers were deported to English prisons, and the remaining prisoners were sent to Frongoch internment camp in North Wales.

The young staff captain who had watched the G Men at work was Michael Collins. He was born near Clonakilty, in West Cork, in October 1890, the youngest child of Michael and Marianne Collins, and was educated at Lisavaird National School. Having passed the Post Office examinations in July of 1906 at the age of 15, Collins was offered a job in the Post Office Savings Bank in West Kensington, London, the heart of the British Empire. Collins stayed with his sister Hannie at 5, Netherwood Road, West Kensington. Here he remained for the next nine years in lower-middle-class comfort. He threw himself into the numerous Irish clubs and societies that existed in the British capital, joining the London branch of the Gaelic Athletic Association. In November 1909, at Barnsbury Hall, Islington, London, he was sworn in as a member of the secret Irish Republican Brotherhood by fellow post office worker Sam Maguire. Ambitious by nature, Collins went on to become treasurer of both the IRB in London and the GAA for London and the South of England. In 1910, Collins left the Savings Bank for a job with the stockbroking firm of Horne & Co. of 23, Moorgate Street. At the time he was also studying for the Civil Service exam at evening classes at King's College with a view to entering the Board of Trade, which he joined on September 1, 1914.

The Irish National Volunteers was formed at the Rotunda Concert Hall in Dublin on November 25, 1913, in defense of Irish Home Rule. In English cities with Irish Roman Catholic populations, the Volunteer movement took off, growing out of such organizations as the Gaelic League and the Gaelic Athletic Association. In London, three branches of the Volunteers were established. The young Michael Collins attended the inaugural meeting of the Volunteers in North London, which was

Introduction

held in the German Gymnasium, Pancras Road, near King's Cross Station. He was enrolled on April 25, 1914, into No. 1 Company of the London Volunteers by his cousin, Sean Hurley. Collins was a very determined young man, as fellow Volunteer Joe Good relates:

> I enlisted in the Volunteers at a place called the German Gymnasium near King's Cross, London, some time early in 1914. When I joined, the only person I saw that I knew really well was Michael Collins. He was in the ranks with me the first night I joined up and the following week he was section leader.
> My first impression of Michael Collins as a man was that he recognised ability in a rival, and I had no doubt as to his competence to lead. Obviously this man, Michael Collins meant to be in command.[5]

On August 4, 1914, the German Army invaded Belgium. World War I had begun. The Home Rule Bill, which promised Ireland a degree of independence, was shelved. There was the possibility that it would be shelved completely and something less, or nothing at all, would be offered in its place at the end of the war. In the British Parliament it was believed that the people of Ireland would put their differences aside in order to see the defeat of Germany and her allies. The Ulster Protestant leaders pledged to call off their Home Rule opposition for the duration. John Redmond, the Irish Nationalist leader in Parliament, being lost in the euphoria of it all, offered the support of the Irish Volunteers as a demonstration of loyalty. He had convinced himself that when the guns fell silent this support would be rewarded. His pledge, without consultation, split the Volunteer movement in Ireland. The IRB Provisional Committee called a meeting to repudiate Redmond's statement and to maintain the reason for the establishment of the Volunteers in the first place—the defense of Home Rule. The Volunteer movement broke in two. The National Volunteers, as they became known, gave their support to Redmond and fell in their thousands in Flanders' fields. The Irish Volunteers who remained were now a much smaller organization but remained true to the ideals of the founding movement.

In London the Redmondite split also affected the Volunteers there. In North London at the German Gymnasium, the Volunteers sided with Redmond. Loyal to the Republican cause Michael Collins, Joe Good and others, were obliged to travel south of the river to continue their training. By 1915, with conscription in the air, the English-based Volunteers were summoned back to Dublin. At the Sinn Fein rooms at 6, Harcourt Street, Nellie Gifford, assisted by the Countess Markievicz, found work for the young men who had returned. Miss Gifford found work for Michael Collins with her future brother-in-law, leading IRB man

Joseph Plunkett. Collins was now at the very heart of the Republican movement. The Easter Rising story has been too often told to require detailing here. It was a magnificent failure—a blood sacrifice. It was an example to all of how not to take on the British Empire.

The British crushed the insurgents with overwhelming might. The rebel leaders were executed, the senior officers imprisoned, and the rank and file were interned in Frongoch in northern Wales. It was true that the Rising had little support amongst the majority of the people of Ireland. The insurgents had no electoral mandate, and with the Rising's failure, that could have been an end to any further insurgency for a generation. From a British perspective, with all opposition crushed, it was difficult to see how the Government could ever be persuaded to revert to that thirty-two-county concept on which every previous Home Rule Bill had been based.

With the unwarranted executions of the leaders of the Rising, the mind-set of the people of Ireland changed. Following the defeat of the Boers in the South African War, Britain had been magnanimous. Only one of the Boer leaders were hanged; the remainder, after brief imprisonment or exile, had been pardoned. Yet following the Rising in Dublin, sixteen men were shot or hanged, including the wounded James Connolly, who had been brought from a hospital bed to the place of execution. They had been executed for no valid reason other than expediency. Even arch-Unionists like Sir Edward Carson, a man bitterly opposed to Home rule, asked for the executions to stop—but they did not. As a consequence of these judicial killings, the emotions of the people of Ireland changed that year from apathy to sympathy and finally to support for Sinn Fein and the Volunteers who had fought for Irish independence. Margaret Skinnider, who herself had fought alongside her Citizen Army colleagues as a sniper at St. Stephen's Green during the Rising, recalled:

> When I went back to Dublin in August, it was to find that almost everyone on the streets was wearing republican colours. The feeling was bitter too—so bitter that the British soldiers had orders to go about in fives and sixes, but never singly. They were not allowed by their officers to leave the main thoroughfares, and had to be back in barracks before dark—that is, all except the patrol. The city was still under martial law, but it seemed to me the military authorities were really nervous persons.[6]

That same August the first batch of released prisoners arrived back at Kingstown (Dun Laoghaire). One of the released, Seamus Daly, also sensed the change that had come about:

> At the time we left [after the failure of the Rising] there was no mistake, the people of Dublin were definitely hostile to us, to the whole thing. But now we sensed change. There was one particularly dour little tram conductor

who would never be civil to us before the time. When I got on the tram, he had been chatting on the front platform with the driver. The driver and he came round and shook hands with us heartily, and gave us a welcome home. When we got to Clontarf, there was quite a number of people there, and each shouting to the other, "The boys are coming home." They gave us a friendly reception.[7]

At the beginning of 1917, the political climate to which the prisoners had returned had changed dramatically. There was support, but for what? Views on the political way forward were at variance. Somehow there could be no return to the past. The Irish Parliamentary Party now seemed irrelevant. Many preferred a return to the Sinn Fein orthodox constitutional doctrine of pre–Rising days. Then there were the reformed Volunteers—what of them? What was to be their function? Some preferred that they should revert to being a defense force as previously represented by Eoin MacNeill.

The Irish Republican Brotherhood knew exactly what they wanted. The secretive, but highly organized, IRB, overhauled in Frongoch, moved in to quell the indecision and to fill the political and military void. Returning IRB man Richard Mulcahy, a hero of the Battle of Ashbourne, rejoined his old Volunteer company. Almost immediately he became captain of C Company, and within a short time O/C of the 2nd Battalion. Michael Collins, who had risen through the ranks of the IRB, now sat on its central committee. Collins also became secretary of the newly founded National Aid Association. It was an institution that the widow of the executed Tom Clarke had set up as a charity to aid the relatives of executed and dead Volunteers and former internees. With his forceful personality Collins was soon running the concern. He began networking and establishing contacts.

With the death of J. J. Kelly, the old member of Parliament for Roscommon, the opportunity arose to clarify the political situation. Count Horace Plunkett, a Papal count and father of the executed Joseph Mary Plunkett, was persuaded to stand as the Sinn Fein candidate in the forthcoming by-election in February 1917. The result was better than expected. The Irish Parliamentary Party candidate received 1,078 votes—Plunkett received 3,022. The people had shown their support for Sinn Fein. As a successful candidate Plunkett then announced that he would abstain from sitting in the British Parliament. He had decided that his place was beside the people in their own country. In his abstentionism from the imperial government, he set in train an alternative rival government in Ireland. A week after the first anniversary of the Easter Rising, an Irish Assembly was convened at the Mansion House in Dublin. Over 1,200 delegates attended. The conference began with the affirmation that Ireland was a separate nation and asserted her right to freedom from all foreign control, denying the authority of the British Parliament in Ireland. It was heady stuff. In Britain they called it treason.

A second by-election was called at South Longford in May 1917. Sinn Fein put up Joseph McGuinness as its candidate. At the time he was an unknown prisoner in Lewes Jail in England. McGuinness was a Republican and was reluctant at first to stand for a party advocating Home Rule under a dual monarchy, such as existed in Austro-Hungary, an ideal extolled by Arthur Griffith. Fellow prisoner Thomas Ashe, now head of the IRB, persuaded him to stand on the basis that a victory would allow Republicans to change Sinn Fein policy from within. McGuinness agreed to stand. The Republican slogan for his election was "Put him in to get him out." The largely unknown McGuinness defeated his Irish Parliamentary Party rival Patrick McKenna by the narrow margin of 37 votes. It was a tiny majority, but the *Manchester Guardian* (May 10, 1917) astutely picked up on its significance, declaring that it was "the equivalent of a serious British defeat in the field."

The following month, June 1917, Major Willie Redmond, brother of John Redmond and the member of Parliament for East Clare, was killed at Messines in France. Only a few days before, the Rural District of Ennis main town of Clare had passed a resolution calling upon John Redmond and all the other Nationalist M.P.s to "resign their seats in Parliament as they no longer represent the views and wishes of the Irish people at home or abroad."

But did Sinn Fein represent the aspirations of the people of Ireland? For the forthcoming by-election, the party put up Eamon de Valera, the last surviving (but still imprisoned) commandant of Easter Week. The very day after it was announced that he would stand, de Valera was included in a general amnesty of the remaining 117 officer-prisoners of Easter Week. Returning to Ireland, de Valera went on the stump, protected from police interference by a detachment of the Volunteers. The Redmondite candidate in the by-election was a popular local man, Patrick Lynch, K.C. He put forward a strong case for continuing the struggle for Home Rule through the Parliamentary process. He pointed out the failure of the insurrection of Easter Week and the cruel loss of young Irishmen. Uncompromisingly, de Valera declared that he stood for an independent Irish Republic. Nothing else would do. In support the Volunteers participated in de Valera's campaign, marching through the streets, maintaining order and guaranteeing by their presence that their candidate would be heard. They became, in Richard Mulcahy's words, "the operative part of the election machinery for the new party."[8] The people of Clare agreed with de Valera. He received twice as many votes as Lynch—5,010 to Lynch's 2,035. Eighty-seven percent of the eligible electorate had voted. Sinn Fein now had three members of Parliament. A fourth by-election, this time in Kilkenny, consolidated Sinn Fein's position. Candidate William Cosgrave, a veteran of the Easter Rising, was returned with a majority of two to one. All four men insisted that they would only sit in an Irish Parliament, Dail Eireann.

On July 4, 1917, Sinn Fein, the Volunteers, Cumann na mBan (the women's movement), and the Gaelic League were all proclaimed by the British as dangerous associations. In August a small group of Volunteer leaders met secretly to plan a Volunteer convention. Among those present were Eamon de Valera, now by common consent the leader of the army; Cathal Brugha, Thomas Ashe, Diarmuid O'Hegarty, Diarmuid Lynch, Michael Staines and Michael Collins (now a member of the Supreme Council of the IRB). The Army convention, it was agreed, would take place in October under the cover of the Sinn Fein convention.

As the Volunteers began openly asserting themselves once more, the G Men of Dublin Castle struck. Following a demonstration at Ardfert to commemorate the anniversary of Roger Casement's execution, Austin Stack was arrested and sentenced to two years imprisonment for wearing an unauthorized uniform—that of an IRA officer. Thomas Ashe, a hero of the Easter Rising, was arrested following a speech he delivered at Longford. Other arrests followed. Imprisoned, the captives went on hunger strike in order to gain political status. In the force-feeding that followed, Thomas Ashe died. The Coroner's inquest that followed condemned the force-feeding as "inhuman and dangerous." At his funeral, three volleys were fired over the grave by a Volunteer firing party. Then the former young staff officer, Michael Collins, stepped forward and delivered a short funeral oration:

> Nothing additional remains to be said. That volley which we have just heard is the only speech which is proper to make over the grave of a dead Fenian.

The funeral brought the hitherto unknown figure of Michael Collins to the public's attention. He was, by now, well known to G. Department of the DMP, though. He had a political file, and his arrest was well overdue.

The Sinn Fein political convention was held at the end of October 1917. It drew some 2,000 delegates. In the election for the presidency, two of the major candidates, Count Plunkett and Arthur Griffith, stood down to allow Eamon de Valera to be appointed unopposed. In accepting the nomination, de Valera, with an eye to the promised post-war Peace Conference to be held in Paris, was conciliatory. He declared that Sinn Fein's aim was "at seeing the international recognition of Ireland as an independent republic, and having achieved that status, the people might by referendum, choose their own form of government, when they would deny the right of the British, or other foreign government to legislate for Ireland." With no suggestion of an armed struggle, Sinn Fein won the support of the Roman Catholic Church in Ireland.

Under cover of the Sinn Fein Convention, the Volunteers met at the Gaelic Athletic Association's ground at Jones Road, Drumcondra. Eamon de Valera was elected as President, thus bringing the two main thrusts of Irish Republicanism, political and military, under the control of one man. Cathal Brugha was appointed Chief of Staff, Richard Mulcahy was made Director of Training, and Michael Collins became Director of Organisation. Six of the twenty members elected that day to the Volunteer national executive were also members of the Sinn Fein executive, thus creating a strong military-political relationship. In order to better coordinate the work of the various Volunteer units around the country, a General Headquarters Staff was formed, based in Dublin. Richard Mulcahy was appointed Chief of Staff. Michael Collins was appointed Director of Organisation and Adjutant General. Collins's role was non-defined, allowing him to engage in a myriad of activities. That suited him. Sean MacMahon was appointed Quartermaster-General; Rory O'Connor became Director of Engineering; and Dick McKee became Director of Training, and, as Mulcahy's successor, O/C of the Dublin Brigade. At this time there was apparently no suggestion, in Mulcahy's mind, of fighting a war of aggression, let alone a guerrilla war. He was following the pre–Rising doctrine of passive resistance. For some, though, the idea of raising an army and not fighting was an anathema. Their views started coming through in *An tOglach,* the journal of the Volunteers.

While the Republicans were holding their conventions, the old Irish Parliamentary Party had been in negotiations with the Ulster Unionists, who were opposed to Home Rule. As the convention started coming to its inevitable end, the Parliamentary leader, John Redmond, fell ill. After a short illness and an operation, he died in London in March 1918. His death brought about a by-election in Waterford. Sinn Fein put forward a candidate, and expectations were high. The people of Waterford remained true to Redmond, though. His son, who campaigned in his British Army officer's uniform and wore a black armband in remembrance of his dead father, won the seat by 478 votes. The result showed that Sinn Fein could not take the support of the people for granted. Sinn Fein held rallies around the country. Michael Collins was briefly arrested in County Sligo following a speech deemed "likely to cause disaffection." He was released on bail to await trial. Looking at a possible two years in prison, Collins went to ground.

On the greater stage, with the collapse of the Russian Army following the October Revolution of 1917 and the signing of the Brest-Litovsk Treaty, the German Army on the Eastern Front was moving rapidly to the west. In April 1918, General Erich Ludendorff launched a major offensive against the Allies in the hope of destroying the British and French armies before the American Expeditionary Force entered the lines. For three weeks the British Army in France sustained an all-out assault on a front of fifty miles. The Channel ports themselves were threatened. Faced with this crisis, the British Government prepared to enforce conscription in Ireland in order to raise an army of half a million men to reinforce its soldiers in France. The Conscription Bill came before the House of Commons for discussion. The Irish Parliamentary Party was totally opposed to it. They voted against it on April 16, but nonetheless the bill became law by 301 votes to 103. In protest the Irish Party left the House of Commons and returned to Ireland to garner resistance. At a conference at the Mansion House in Dublin on April 18, an anti-conscription proposal was drafted. It was to be signed in every parish in the country on the following Sunday. On April 23, a General Strike in opposition to subscription was held throughout Ireland—with the exception of the Unionist stronghold of Belfast. Pressure mounted on the British administration as the Roman Catholic bishops of Ireland issued a joint statement opposing conscription. They declared, "We consider that Conscription forced in this way upon Ireland is an oppressive and inhuman law which the Irish people have a right to resist by every means that are consonant with the law of God." This decision by the clergy removed the last barrier against full-hearted support for Sinn Fein by the Irish people. Thousands of young men rushed to join the Volunteers.

At the beginning of May 1918, both the Viceroy to Ireland, Lord Wimborne, and Henry Duke, the Chief Secretary of Ireland, resigned their posts. They were replaced by Field Marshal Lord French as Governor of Ireland and Edward Shortt as Chief Secretary. Walter Long was appointed Colonial Secretary and Sir Bryan Mahon, a Roman Catholic, was replaced in Military Command by General Sir Frederick Shaw. According to Field Marshal Sir Henry Wilson, knowing that another insurrection was now inevitable, "Lloyd George impressed on Johnny [French] the necessity of putting the onus for first shooting on the rebels."[9]

A by-election was called in East Cavan. Sinn Fein put up Arthur Griffith as its candidate. Success was far from assured, though, in this mixed Ulster county. To complicate matters, within five days of his arrival in Ireland as Viceroy, Lord French declared that there was a

"German Plot" and that Sinn Fein had been in treasonable communication with the German enemy. The evidence was dubious to say the least. Joseph Dowling, a member of Casement's ill-fated Irish Brigade, was captured following his landing from a German U-boat. Under interrogation in London, he revealed that his mission was to persuade the Volunteers to rise in support of Germany. They were to be provided with arms, artillery, machine guns and German troops. It was more a case of German intention than reality. Nevertheless, it gave Britain the excuse it needed to make mass arrests and, in the process, to destroy the anti–conscription campaign. A spy within Dublin Castle reported to Irish Intelligence Chief Eamon Duggan regarding the intended arrests:

> In the case of the German Plot arrests in May 1918, a large list of names and addresses of those to be arrested in Dublin came into my hands. There were continual additions to the list but, finally in May 1918, the list was complete, and several copies were made.
> On the day of the proposed arrests—as far as I recollect it was Friday—I met Tracy [Patrick Tracy, his contact with Duggan] and told him: "Tonight's the night. Tell O'Hanrahan [another contact] to tell the wanted men not to stay in their usual place of abode and to keep their heads."[10]

Duggan warned the wanted men, including de Valera, that they were about to be arrested. Weighing up the situation, de Valera realized the impact the arrests would have on world opinion, particularly in America. He made no attempt to evade the round-up. Seventy-three of Sinn Fein's leading activists were arrested. Collins, Boland, Mulcahy and Brugha, likewise warned, evaded arrest. With so many leading activists in prison, a power vacuum was created. Into this void stepped the IRB in the shape of Michael Collins and his close friends Harry Boland and Richard Mulcahy, who had come to realize that Ireland must fight. Collins immediately set about contacting the leading political and military personnel throughout the country, men he knew who would support him. Within a short time, the whole movement, Sinn Fein and the Volunteers, came under his control. The result was to create a more militant underground leadership under Collins.

Collins was a driven man. West Cork guerrilla leader Tom Barry described him, faults and all: "The man was without a shadow of doubt, the effective driving force and the backbone at GHQ of the armed action of the nation against the enemy. A tireless, ruthless, dominating man of great capacity he worked like a Trojan in innumerable capacities to defeat the enemy."[11]

The by-election in East Cavan eventually took place on June 19. With their candidate still in prison, Sinn Fein again adopted the slogan,

"Put him in to get him out." When the result was declared, it was found that Griffith had won by a majority of 1,204.

The conscription crisis abated when the advance of the German army was checked. On August 8, 1918, a counter-offensive was launched by the Allies, and by September 28, with the German Army pushed back, General Ludendorff conceded defeat. His assault had failed. The war was lost, and an Armistice was signed. In December 1918, a month after the cessation of hostilities with Germany, a General Election was called throughout the United Kingdom. This was what Sinn Fein had prepared for, the democratic legitimization of an Irish Republic by the will of the people. The greatest danger now was that Britain would cancel the election in Ireland if there were any disturbances. As head of the IRA, Mulcahy ordered that nothing should be done to jeopardize the situation.

The election was held in Ireland as throughout the rest of Great Britain. Quite a few of the Irish candidates held dual Sinn Fein/Volunteer status. In the subsequent election, eleven of the twenty-two members of the Volunteer Executive were elected members of the Irish Parliament. Included in that number were Mulcahy, elected for Clontarf, Boland for Roscommon, and Collins for South Cork. In all, in the General Election held on December 14, 1918, Sinn Fein triumphed at the polls. They won 73 of the 105 seats. The Irish Nationalists gained 6 seats; the Unionists, 26. The people of Ireland had voted for an Irish Republic by a majority of 73 percent. The London *Times* reported on January 17, 1919, "The General Election in Ireland was treated by all parties as a plebiscite and admittedly Sinn Fein swept the country."

In the face of Sinn Fein's democratic success, Brigadier-General Joseph A. Byrne, Inspector General of the RIC, advocated that the British Government should negotiate with the party. It would split the moderate politicians in the Irish movement from the firebrands, he contended. Such a democratic notion was beyond the understanding of the military mind. Lord French was appalled at such a suggestion. It would be viewed as a sign of weakness, he maintained. French sent Byrne on a "gardening leave" from which he did not return.

Sinn Fein, the Irish Parliamentary Party and Labour refused to sit in the Westminster Parliament and instead formed their own parliament, Dail Eireann (Assembly of Ireland). They met as (Teachtai Dala) T.D.s for the first time in the Round Room of the Dublin Mansion House on January 21, 1919. On arrival they took an oath of loyalty:

> I hereby pledge myself to work for the establishment of an independent Irish Republic; that I will accept nothing less than complete separation from England in settlement of Ireland's claims; and that I will abstain from attending the English Parliament.

Of the possible 105 members of the new Irish Parliament, 33 Republicans were in prison. A 34th member had died in prison, a victim of the influenza pandemic then sweeping through the world. The names of the elected T.D.s were called out, and they responded with pride. When the names of the imprisoned were called out, the Clerk announced in Irish that they were "prisoners of the English." Someone else answered when the names of Collins and Boland were called. They had slipped quietly away, and at the beginning of February, they spirited Eamon de Valera and two others out of Lincoln Gaol and back to Ireland. On March 7, in a face-saving gesture, the British Government made a general release of its remaining untried political prisoners.

The Paris Peace Conference first met on January 20 on, 1919. This was the conference upon which the Republicans had pinned their hopes for recognition of Ireland as an independent nation. American President Woodrow Wilson had made known his position: the ending of colonial empires and the granting of independence to small nations. Expectations ran high in Ireland. In the world of realpolitik, though, Ireland's appeal for independence was already lost. The Great Powers at the conference had pledged against interference in each other's internal affairs. Under international law Ireland was unquestionably an internal affair for Britain. Instead, the Conference concerned itself with the minorities of the defeated powers of Germany and Turkey. To Irish eyes, and to many others, too, it was democracy betrayed. Never was the name Sinn Fein more appropriate—We Ourselves, or perhaps, We Alone—for no one else was going to help Ireland to achieve its independence.

At the beginning of 1919, Nationalist Ireland had a democratically elected political assembly, Dail Eireann. It was the expression of the will of the people. The Volunteers were its army. Under international law Dail Eireann claimed that its army had the right to defend that nation against its enemies.

On the evening of January 21, 1919, as representatives of the Dail began collecting up their papers in preparation for the departure, news arrived that two policemen had been killed in County Tipperary. It was the following morning before details of what had happened reached Cathal Brugha and Richard Mulcahy. Two constables, James McDonnell and Patrick O'Connell, who were escorting a cart carrying gelignite to a quarry at Soloheadbeg in county Tipperary, were set upon by masked Volunteers and shot dead at point blank range. The Volunteers stripped the bodies of their carbines and ammunition and made off with these and the gelignite. The men responsible were Sean Treacy, Dan Breen, Seaumus Robinson and Sean Hogan. It was an unauthorized action and is generally credited as being the opening shot of the War of

Independence. Brugha's emotions were mixed. He was well aware that the hotheads in the Volunteer movement were becoming impatient. Dan Breen justified himself and others: "but of what use, we asked ourselves, are men who are toy soldiers? Of what use are guns that have been oiled and cleaned but never fired."[12]

Brugha knew that the Volunteers were not yet ready for war. They were not well-ordered, and they were not yet armed. There was no clear vision of an armed struggle for independence. His deputy, Richard Mulcahy, was of the opinion that the people had to be educated and led gently into open war. The shootings at Soloheadbeg changed all that. The response to the murders was predictable. In pulpits all over Ireland the deaths of two policemen, both Catholics, was condemned as a crime. McDonnell, aged 56, was a father of seven children. They were now orphans. There was concern that the killing of two policemen at this early stage of the struggle would have an adverse effect on public support for the Volunteers. Brugha summoned Treacy and Breen to Dublin. In the meantime, he called a meeting of the Volunteer Executive. The war had begun. There was no going back. Now was the time to be pragmatic. The Executive agreed upon a stance. There was to be no apology. They would take the moral high ground. Piaras Beaslai, the editor of *An tOglch*, issued Brugha's statement in justification of the Volunteers' action in Tipperary:

> Every Volunteer is entitled, morally and legally, when in the execution of his military duties, to use all legitimate methods of warfare against the soldiers and policemen of the English usurper, and to slay them if it is necessary to do so in order to overcome their resistance. He is not only entitled but bound to resist all attempts to disarm him. In this position he has the authority of the nation behind him, now constituted in concrete form.[13]

Following the Soloheadbeg ambush, attacks on the police became more common. Between March and October 1919, the RIC recorded 144 "outrages," including, between May and December, the deaths of twenty-one policemen.

On April 1, de Valera was present at the opening of the second session of the Dail. He was formally appointed President. He, in turn, appointed Michael Collins as Minister of Finance and Richard Mulcahy as Chief of Staff of the Irish Republican Army. Collins was given full power to raise a national loan "without further reference to the Dail." This clause allowed Collins to secretly divert money to the military and to intelligence. At this session, the Dail passed a resolution that called upon the Irish people to ostracize the RIC. Its intention was to discourage recruitment into the police force and to encourage the resignations of those who were members. In May 1919, de Valera sailed to America to highlight Ireland's case for independence and to campaign for funds. In his absence, Cathal Brugha was nominally Minister for Defence and leader of the Volunteers. His deputy Richard Mulcahy, as well as Michael Collins and Harry Boland, IRB men all, now had a free hand in conducting the war. As James Gleeson pointed out, "Collins … knew the gun to be but a propaganda weapon, its power of destruction a headline, its detonation a slogan."[14]

From the British perspective, Prime Minister David Lloyd George sought to downplay the forthcoming war as acts of criminality. He declared to his cabinet that the "Irish job was a policeman's job…," adding, "You do not declare war against rebels." Any individual actions were then classed as criminal acts, to be dealt with by the existing police force. Information was not collated; interpretation of events was not considered. Several valuable months were lost to British Intelligence, and in particular to Military Intelligence, while this pretense continued.

1

Preparing for War

From as early as 1917, arms had been smuggled into Ireland piecemeal from Britain and the USA by using friendly sailors and stewards. Customs officers and the police were on a constant lookout to disrupt the import and distribution of these arms. It was a cat-and-mouse game, as Nicholas Laffan, an officer with G Company, 1st Battalion of the Dublin Brigade, testified in his Witness Statement:

> About a week earlier [the first week in October 1917] we were instructed to collect rifles from a house in Lower Baggot Street, the men selected for the job being Joe O'Reilly, Tom Burke, P. Kelly and Joe Dodd, prior arrangements having been made with the 3rd Battalion of the Dublin Brigade in whose area the house was located. When the rifles were being collected, the house was surrounded by 15 DMP men and 2 detectives, but the men selected for the collection of the rifles had entered the house by the back. In order to get the rifles safely away, it was decided that Dodd and Burke would put the rifles in two sacks while the other two men would leave by the rear and walk into the main thoroughfare, thereby attracting the attention of the police. The ruse succeeded. Burke and Dod walked out with the rifles, the other men keeping between the police and the men carrying the weapons. The two detectives followed as far as Michael's Lane, off Winetavern Street, where they stopped. As the lane was so narrow, the men with the rifles were too far ahead for the police to get near them and they succeeded in taking them to Tom Burke's house in Monmouth Street, off Chancery Place.[12]

Arms were also purchased from hard-up soldiers stationed in Ireland. It was a safer billet than being posted to Flanders for them. The Paddies were, after all, British. What was the problem in selling them guns? Nicholas Laffan again:

> In April 1918, the Company succeeded in getting 4 rifles and about 150 rounds of .303 ammunition from Islandbridge Barracks. The rifles were hid in a military car coming out one at a time, for which the driver was paid £3.

George Fitzgerald, a member of A Company, 1st Battalion, Dublin Brigade, recalled a similar story of purchasing arms from British soldiers in his 1952 Witness Statement:

In the Company we had three brothers called Coles. Although these men didn't parade frequently like the majority of the Company members they proved themselves of estimable value by being able to contact soldiers. One day one of the Coles went to a Wippet Meeting at Shelbourne Park. There he met a British soldier and, in the course of conversation, the soldier said to Coles: "I fancy a certain dog for the next race. Unfortunately, I haven't anything to put on it because I have been losing all day." He told Coles to back it. Coles backed it both for himself and for the soldier. The dog won and this cemented their friendship. Out of that Coles broached the subject of getting arms out of Wellington Barracks where the soldier was stationed. This soldier according to himself was in the army against his wishes. He had no intention of fighting, if he possibly could avoid it, and as he had lost his business he had made up his mind he was going to make money anyway he could. This gave Coles the opportunity he was looking for. He put it up to the soldier to supply rifles at a price.... A short time later word came through that he would be in a position to deliver rifles to us on a certain night. On that night a number of us went down the canal and at an appointed time the soldier handed over a couple of rifles. On the next evening money for the rifles was given to Coles who passed it on to the soldier. Following the first delivery many more rifles were procured in this way. I cannot say how many in all we got from the soldier but the number was quite considerable.[3]

Sometimes it was a close-run thing when the Army authorities discovered what was happening, as Volunteer Edward Dolan pointed out:

On one occasion I was sent with Tommy McCrane, a member of C Company, to Phil Shanaghan's public house in Foley Street to purchase a rifle from a deserter from the British Army. The purchase was being arranged by Paddy Hughes, also a C Company member, and a [Dublin] Corporation employee. While waiting in Shanaghan's, the deserter was spotted by two Red Caps [the British military police] who chased him through the public house. The rifle had, however been handed over to Hughes who, in turn passed it to me. It was a long Ross rifle and projected quite a lot below the hem of my overcoat, but we managed (McCrane and I) to get it safely to his (McCrane's) house in Middle Gardiner Street.[4]

Arms were also gained by sheer audacity. Fitzgerald again:

Information reached us ... that two rifles could be got easily if we acted quickly, in the house of a Mr.----, at Donnybrook—that this man was very pro–British and that he believed that he was going to hand the rifles into the Police Barracks on the following day for safe custody. Three of us drove to the house of the man on a side car, Peadar Breslin dressed as a Military officer. Peadar and myself adopted the pose of G. men. When we called at the house we were invited in and explained to the owner that we had come to collect the rifles as we thought that if they were left with him any longer they would be raided by the Sinn Feiners, and told him we were now there to take them into safe custody. He received us very well and his housekeeper went down to the kitchen and brought up the two rifles in a sack and put them on the dickey of the jaunting car that we hired. We told the owner that if he called at the Police Barracks at Donnybrook in the morning he would get a receipt.

Storage of hard-won arms was a constant worry for Volunteer quartermasters. The police were ever vigilant, especially the G. men, the political wing of the Dublin Metropolitan Police. In many cases, they were aware of the names and addresses of Volunteers in the area. At Easter time 1918, the quartermaster Jimmy Murray of A Company, 3rd Battalion, was stopped near his home for not having a light on his bicycle. Despite all his protests and giving his name and address, the DMP men took Murray and his bicycle off to the local police station. This gave the authorities the opportunity of searching Murray's home and its outbuildings. The British Army supplied three companies of soldiers, some armed with machine guns, to investigate the area. After an eight-hour search, they found what they were looking for—A Company's arms dump. Within it they discovered 43 single-shot Martini-Henry rifles, one BSA 22-caliber rifle, two hundredweight of gelignite, guncotton, revolvers, Mills grenades and cases of .303 ammunition.

The 3rd Battalion had other arms dumps. One in particular was in a yard off Christchurch Place. Joe O'Connor, Battalion O/C, was concerned that in their search the police might have discovered the address. Orders went out that it had to be cleared at once and a new dump provided. Tom Scully, a squad leader (the equivalent of a corporal), was tasked with the job. He took with him Kit Farrel and Christy Murray, a brother of the now-imprisoned Jimmy Murray. The new dump was to be in the cellar of Pierce Walsh's provision shop. Now came the problem of transporting the arms. Scully turned down the idea of using a car, in case it might draw attention in a city that still much depended upon the horse. Instead, he hit on the idea of using a builder's handcart. Handcarts were a common sight around Dublin. A woman known to be friendly to the Republican cause was having repairs done to her house. She was persuaded to obtain the loan of a cart, complete with a ladder and some building materials to give authenticity. The cart was wheeled up to the old dump and 43 Martini-Henry rifles and a hundredweight of gelignite were loaded aboard. On the second trip, Lee-Enfield rifles and accompanying .303 ammunition were taken away. The third and final trip proved to be something of a nightmare, as Scully relates:

> Our third and final journey was nearly a failure, for we got stuck in a traffic jam at the Grafton Street corner of Nassau Street. One of the hand-cart wheels had a tendency to come off and, to make matters worse, the policeman on point duty became very abusive and, as we moved away, shouted after us that he would report our boss (the builder) for employing kids to do

men's work. The names this cop called us and our employer would lift the hair from your head, and, of course we had to grin and bear it. Here we were with a load of war materials, which included slabs of gun-cotton and Mills grenades, and a hand-cart with one wheel doing its damnedest to come off. Well, anyone with an elementary knowledge of explosives will agree that the other traffic and our poor selves would have been in a bad way had this hand-cart's wheel succeeded in its object, for gun-cotton, coming into contact with hand-grenades or paving stones, is likely to make one hell of a mess of surrounding objects.[5]

The cart eventually arrived at the new dump and its contents were safely unloaded and hidden.

This piecemeal collecting of arms was all very well, but what was required, the Volunteer Convention agreed, was the acquisition of arms on a much larger scale. Given the difficulty of importing arms with an ever-vigilant Customs Service, the best, if perhaps the more dangerous, source was to seize or steal from the British Army. In between the two sessions of the Dail, in January and April, an audacious raid was made on a British Army arsenal at Collinstown Aerodrome in West Meath. At the time, a number of the Volunteers were employed on constructional work at the airfield, including Gary Houlihan, a veteran of the Easter Rising. He discovered that the base had an arsenal of weapons and reported to IRA GHQ, giving details of the strength and layout of the position. Michael Collins agreed to the plan Houlihan submitted and gave the go-ahead. A number of Volunteers from A. and F. Companies of the 1st Battalion, Dublin Brigade, were selected to carry out the raid. A final reconnoiter of the aerodrome revealed that, in addition to the soldiers guarding the aerodrome, there were also two large guard dogs. From experience the Volunteers knew that the dogs barked at anyone not in British Army uniform. The dogs, it was decided, would have to be silenced. Reluctantly, as Houlihan and George Fitzgerald (who was also in the raiding party) revealed, there was no alternative but to poison them, which they did on the afternoon before the attack. The raid took place on the night of the March 19–20. Houlihan recorded:

> As we left for the aerodrome at about 11.30 p.m., we were troubled to notice that there was a glorious moon, a silent enemy, which would greatly increase our difficulties in approaching the aerodrome unnoticed. According to plan we were to divide forces about four miles from Collinstown, and I appointed the party which was to attack the rear to Peadar Breslin, I myself taking command of the party which was to attack the front, the total number of those engaged being about twenty-five. The party which I was commanding had to reach the front of the guardroom without detection, so we had to crawl, lying flat on the ground, for about two miles. Peadar's squad had orders not to attack in the rear, until my squad was already in action in the front.[6]

The party with Breslin also experienced difficulty, as George Fitzgerald records:

> We had to advance over 200 yards practically in the open. As we advanced we could see the lighted guardroom window which faced us. Had any one of the guards been looking out that window at that particular time I am afraid there would be few of us left to tell the tale.[7]

For whatever reason, the poison had not worked very effectively on the dogs. As Fitzgerald entered through a wicket gate, one of the dogs ran at him. Not losing his nerve, Fitzgerald, who was dressed as a British officer, reached out his hand and petted the dog. The guard dogs were trained not to attack anyone in uniform, and this undoubtedly saved the situation. The dog turned around and, growling quietly to itself, returned to its kennel.

In Houlihan's party, Volunteer Tom Merrigan, had been detailed to deal with the sentry outside the guardroom. He waited until the sentry was at the point farthest from the room, then rushed at him from behind. The sentry was taken completely by surprise, disarmed, and led towards the guardroom. Both teams were under strict instructions to keep conversation to a minimum and under no circumstances to address each other by name. Both IRA parties now entered the guardroom simultaneously. Fitzgerald entered through the back door, dressed as a Staff Officer. Upon seeing him, the guard immediately got to their feet and saluted him. The room was then filled with civilians, the combined IRA parties. Completely surprised, and perhaps confused, the guards were rushed and overpowered. They were made to lie down on the floor, where they were tied up. As this was being done, their rifles and ammunition, as well as the arms in the arsenal, were gathered up and taken outside to now-waiting cars. The operation was completely successful, and no one was injured. Before they left, the Volunteers went over to the military garage, where, using sledgehammers, they damaged the engines of at east twenty cars and trucks to prevent any pursuit. The Volunteers captured seventy-five rifles and some thousands of rounds of ammunition. The rifles and ammunition were driven to North County Dublin where they were received by local Volunteers. Subsequently, A Company received twenty-five of the seized rifles. The next morning, the IRA men who worked at the aerodrome turned up as usual. They were surprised to see their recent British captives being taken away under escort. In the security investigation that followed, all the civilian workers were dismissed from their jobs. It was a classic case of shutting the stable doors after the horse had bolted.

The aerodrome raid was followed by another breathtaking

operation, this one engineered by Michael Collins. Twenty prisoners, including Piaras Beaslai, editor of the Volunteer paper *An tOglach*, climbed over the wall of Mountjoy Prison with a rope ladder in broad daylight and escaped, to the obvious delight of passers-by. At this time, even though there was an arrest warrant out on him for failure to surrender to his bail, Collins was still moving about Dublin untroubled. When the body of Pierce McCann, who had died of influenza in Gloucester Jail just before the general amnesty, arrived back in Dublin, Collins was there to receive the coffin. With him there were about 500 Volunteers, part of a funeral cortege, many in uniform. Collins helped to carry the coffin. Unable to interfere due to the number of armed Volunteers, G. men noted Collins's actions and updated their files with a view to a future arrest.

Sometime in early 1919—no specific date is given by Evelyn Lawless, but it was sometime after the first meeting of the Dail—there was a police raid upon 6, Harcourt Street. The multi-storied premises housed several Sinn Fein departments. The G. men were looking, Miss Lawless indicated, "for wanted men." On the day of the raid, Michael Collins, Fintan Murphy and Diarmuid Hegarty, the Secretary of the Dail, were present dealing with detail regarding the Dail Loan. Ginger O'Connell, former Volunteer O/C in Frongoch, was just leaving the upper floor office as the police dashed into the building. As he left the room, he failed to close the door, which now lay half open. As Evelyn Lawless got up to close to it, she saw a policeman standing on guard outside. She shut the door and warned Collins that a raid was taking place:

> At that stage we discussed what we were going to do. I think only Mick was armed. If any of the others were the girls took the arms from them. I stuck Mick's revolver down my stocking and anything else incriminating we girls took charge of. The police seemed to start the raid systematically from the bottom up thus giving us time to take these precautions. When they arrived we had disposed of everything and they found nothing of any importance. They searched the men but not us.
>
> We had contemplated every possibility of escape for Mick whom we thought they were looking for, as it had been published that there was a large reward for anyone who helped to find him. There was no means of escape, however, as the military had occupied the narrow entrance in the back as well as the front. Mick said: "We are caught like rats in a trap and there is no escape." He remained seated at his desk, quite calm and collected until they came in.
>
> One of the police inspectors—I think Love was his name—had a special commission to capture Collins, but it was Inspector McFeeley who came to our rooms, looking a little bit frightened. He went round searching the different desks and seemed desperately anxious to finish his task and get out.

Mick sat casually on his desk with one leg swinging and told him in no measured terms what sort of work he was engaged on. He was scathing in his remarks about it. "What sort of legacy will you leave to your family, looking for blood money. Could you not find some honest work to do, &c.?"[8]

Meanwhile, at the office across the corridor, prominent Sinn Feiner Ernest Blythe was discovered hiding in a cupboard and was recognized. He was arrested and taken away. Collins, convinced that the police would return, slipped up the stairs and escaped through a skylight. Sure enough, the police did return. This time the party was led by Inspector Love, who, apparently from McFeeley's description of the man who had spoken to him so roughly, recognized that it was probably Collins. Love burst into the office, but his quarry had eluded him. He scanned the faces of those present in the office, then, without questioning anyone, he left. A short time later, Collins came down from the roof, and, returning to his desk, continued with the work in hand.

The Dail Loan was a tedious business upon which Collins, as Minister of Finance, was obliged to work, along with his other duties. It lacked any glamor, but it was essential to the maintenance of the Irish Government and the financing of a war of liberation. The initial funding was for £1,000,000. Of this, £500,000 was offered to the public in the form of bonds for immediate subscription. Bonds to the value of £250,000 were issued at home; £250,000, abroad. Collins handled the prospectus, all advertising, funds collection, and the issue of receipts. Within a year, he was able to announce to the Dail that £357,000 had already been raised in Ireland alone. The British Government declared the loan to be illegal and made periodic raids on banks in the hope of discovering where the money was—but it had no success. Rather than keeping the money together and risking the loss of all of it, should it be discovered, Collins deposited the funds in small accounts in banks all over the country. Small businesses secretly added money to their accounts, withdrawing it when called upon. From time to time, police raids discovered paperwork and lists of subscribers and how much they had given, but the loan itself remained safe. Salaries were paid and arms purchased. As 1919 turned into 1920, the war began.

2

British Intelligence in Ireland 1914–1918

At the outbreak of World War I, senior RIC officer Inspector Ivon Price was appointed Intelligence Officer to the British Army's Irish Command with the rank of major. His two principal sources of information were those supplied by the two police forces in Ireland, the Royal Irish Constabulary and the Dublin Metropolitan Police. Price was also put in contact with Colonel Kell of MI5 and given access to postal, cable and telephonic communications that were intercepted by government censors. Though reports from Military Intelligence in Ireland were available, little of any consequence was received by him.

The DMP had infiltrated the Irish Volunteers at a low level, and information that had trickled down from March 1916 indicated that something was in the offing. However, following the cancellation of the mustering of the Irish Volunteers on Easter Sunday 1916, the Rising on the following day came as a complete surprise to the British authorities in Ireland. Mitigating that surprise had been the capture on April 21st of the German arms ship *Aud* off the coast of Kerry and the detention by a RIC patrol of three men landed by a German submarine in Tralee Bay. By Easter Saturday, one of the prisoners was identified as Sir Roger Casement, who was sent to London for interrogation.

A commission of enquiry was later set up to establish the causes of the failed Rising. The blame was laid at the door of the Chief Secretary for Ireland, Augustine Birrell. The failure, it was concluded, was not down to the lack of intelligence. After all, intelligence had reported that *Aud* was bringing in arms, but Birrell had failed to act. Basil Thomson of Scotland Yard was asked to prepare a report on intelligence gathering in Ireland. His conclusion found a lot of overlap in intelligence gathering, which was linked to a lack of coordination and, as a consequence, unnecessary expense. Information gathering in Ireland was obtained, he discovered, by five autonomous bodies: the Admiralty, the

War Office (MI5), Irish Command, the Royal Irish Constabulary and the Dublin Metropolitan Police. In addition, in America, the Home Office, the War Office, the Foreign Office and Royal Irish Constabulary were also supplying information regarding Irish groups based there. All this information, though, was not necessarily being transmitted to the Irish Government. Thomson made a series of recommendations regarding the provision and passing on of information. Perhaps the greatest weakness in intelligence gathering in Ireland, he found, lay in the unwillingness of Intelligence chiefs in London to share vital information with the Irish authorities, and their failure to accept what was reported to them by the other organizations regarding the true state of Ireland. The Intelligence view from London was that they knew best; consequently, few of Thomson's measures regarding integration were, in fact, adopted.[1]

The perceived apathy of the Irish public towards the Easter Rising and the lack of any military threat thereafter encouraged the British Government to believe that it was an isolated outbreak of violence. Matters continued as they had before. Ireland remained ruled by mild coercion. The British Government failed to understand the real effect of the Rising. The Commander-in-Chief in Ireland, Sir John Maxwell, who had put down the Rising, noticed, barely three months later, the change in public feeling by the people in Ireland. Reporting to Prime Minister Herbert Asquith, he wrote that there was now "a disposition to demonstrate on every possible occasion in favor of Sinn Feinism or republicanism." He pointed out that these incidents were in the main trivial "but if permitted will shortly embarrass the police."[2] Maxwell's insight was ignored in favor of milder coercion. The advice listened to was that the enforcement of military conscription into the British Army would settle the Irish question.

With Ireland seemingly pacified, pressure grew on the British Government to release the rebels involved in the Easter Rising, especially those held without trial in Frongoch internment camp in Wales. Gradually during the summer of 1916 prisoners began to be released, with the remainder being freed at Christmas as a seeming gesture of goodwill. In the process, and without due process of intelligence gathering, the more militant prisoners were released along with the less militant ones. Very soon intelligence was coming into the British authorities in London that two senior members within the Republican movement who had escaped detection were organizing further militant action.[3] On the ground, the Irish police were not so sure. The men who mattered, as far as they were concerned, were still in prison as convicted felons. There was no sense of a further rising, and besides, the reinforcement of troops in Ireland weighed heavily against such a rising. The "evidence" for a further rising emanated from America. Royal Navy Intelligence had broken the German codes, and messages sent by the Irish American organization, Clan na Gael, to Germany were decoded. Additionally, following a raid by the police on the San Francisco offices of Clan na Gael, papers seized suggested that Germany was about to arm the insurgents in Ireland. In truth, it was no more than an aspiration by the San Francisco branch; it was hoped that the Germans could be persuaded to send more arms. Furthermore, there was no indication that the Republicans in Ireland knew of the American plans. Nevertheless, with the unsubstantiated material they possessed, the British Secret Service issued a warning to the Irish administration without going into detail as to its source. Given the warning, and coming from MI5, the authorities in Ireland reacted to the supposed threat. A number of prominent Sinn Feiners were deported to England even though no charge could be proved against them.

In 1917 the United States declared war on Germany. All telegraphic communications between the two countries ceased. As such, there were to be no more intercepts and decrypts. MI5 was in the dark and from then on had to rely upon colorful gossip and innuendo regarding Ireland. An informant within the Irish administration in Dublin, codename "Z," informed MI5 that the Germans had landed machine guns and other arms along the west coast of Ireland. Another report was that the Sinn Feiners had established contact with Germany through the seminary of Maynooth and the Vatican. It was all nonsense. Unable to check out the information, MI5 nevertheless passed on sanitized versions of the story to the Dublin authorities, confirming "Z's" original speculative story. Dublin felt obliged to react.[4] Some prominent Sinn Feiners and Volunteers were arrested without charge. Following on from this, a number of imprisoned Volunteers went on hunger strike to obtain political status. On September 25, 1917, one of these hunger strikers, Thomas Ashe, the leader of the Volunteers at the Battle of Ashbourne, died in Mountjoy Prison after forcible feeding. Following a public outcry, the Government weakened and released all the remaining Republican prisoners. This was to the total frustration of British Military Intelligence. One Army Officer wrote: "As it is now evident to the parties concerned that they have only to hunger-strike for a couple of days in order to get out of gaol, whether convicted or untried, it is really very little use arresting them."[5]

Realistically, the Irish police forces, while having failed to penetrate the higher echelons of Sinn Fein or the Volunteers, were very much aware of the day-to-day situation in Ireland. With the return of the Frongoch internees, the people of Ireland who, in pre–Easter 1916, had been somewhat indifferent now began taking a keener interest in Sinn Fein, the aspiration of which had moved from establishing a dual-monarchy as displayed in the division of Austro-Hungary to one of attaining complete independence. In an effort to thwart this political evolution towards Republican independence, Captain Reginald Hall, Director of Naval Intelligence, and Basil Thomson of the Special Branch of the Metropolitan Police launched a black operation, the "German Plot," to discredit the leaders of Sinn Fein. This was an advancement on the earlier Clan na Gael plot. It was more cleverly thought out. Supposedly, an agent of Thomson's had secreted a powerful Dictaphone in the secret meeting room of the Sinn Fein executive at the time of the Irish Convention in 1917. The information gathered, which linked Sinn Fein to Germany, was typed out and passed on to British politicians and to the Dublin authorities. Hall and Thomson declined to reveal their sources in order to protect those who had supplied the information.

Then, unbelievably, the "German Plot" developed a life of its own. The RIC arrested a man on April 12th on the coast of County Clare. He was Corporal Joseph Dowling, a former prisoner of war in Germany who had joined Casement's Irish Brigade. Taken to London for interrogation, he openly admitted that he had been landed from a U-boat in order to make contact with Sinn Fein. His mission was to "ascertain the true state of affairs" in Ireland and to sort out details for the landing of arms, artillery, machine guns and German troops. Major Price, the British Army's senior intelligence officer in Ireland, was understandably alarmed. Lord French, who was due to become Viceroy, as well as W. V. Harrell, the head of the Admiralty's intelligence network, dismissed Dowling's statement as a fabrication. British Intelligence in London, however, saw this as a golden opportunity to arrest the leading players in the Republican movement. Following MI5's report, which was presented to the Prime Minister, the arrest of the leading members of Sinn Fein was ordered. On the night of May 17–18, 1918, there was a widespread roundup of suspected "plotters." Almost the entire leadership of Sinn Fein, some 150 people, was arrested and interned in English jails. In Parliament, M.P. Walter Long emphasized the need for the arrests, complaining that his cabinet colleagues had not fully "realized the dangerous state of things in Ireland—especially the prevalence of German intrigue."[6] Forewarned of the arrests, Michael Collins and the leadership of the IRB went into hiding. British Intelligence succeeded in arresting the moderates while the militants escaped. The militants therefore filled the vacuum of leadership provided by those arrests, thereby pushing the movement inevitably towards war.

It became clear that the British Secret Service, when pressed, could not produce any real evidence of a "German Plot." Admiral Reginald Hall of British Intelligence appeared before a cabinet committee of enquiry, which established that while some material "provided ample evidence of German designs," there was no evidence "of Sinn Fein complicity." Following on from that statement, most of those arrested were released. The British politicians at the time had been all too ready to accept the Secret Service's "plot." Some of them sincerely thought that the threat was real, particularly those Unionists who believed that the Germans were manipulating the Irish for their own ends. In reality, Sinn Fein was now a popular movement and not dependent on Germany for support. The very concept that the Republicans espoused was that they, and they alone, could achieve independence. This concept was summed up in their choice of name—Sinn Fein—We Ourselves. On the face of it, the movement had progressed from the military sacrifice of the Easter Rising towards the democratic process and democratic elections. Behind the scenes, however, the IRB were preparing for further armed conflict should democracy fail.

As noted before, following the unexpected German offensive of March 1918, in which the Allies were driven back, the British Cabinet took the decision to apply conscription to Ireland to raise further troops. It was something they had previously hesitated to do in order to avoid any political consequences. At the outbreak of the war, some 250,000 Irishmen, Unionists and Nationalists, had volunteered to fight for Britain. Some 50,000 of them were killed. The Nationalists joined on the back of some vague promise that Ireland would be given Home Rule when the war was over. Now, with the proposal to introduce forced conscription, the Irish did what the British Government had feared. Irish National M.P.s at Westminster voted against it. Having lost the vote by 103 to 301, they returned to Ireland to oppose the move. Sinn Fein gave anti-conscription its full support; importantly, and without any threats of violence by the nationalists, the Roman Catholic Church gave its support, too. Perhaps because of this support, the people threw their efforts into opposing conscription. When the German advance failed, forced conscription in Ireland was no longer necessary, and the notion of conscription was quietly dropped.

With the scare diminished, and the possibility of the war ending soon, there was every prospect of a General Election in which Sinn Fein was expected to do well. Home Rule, cancelled because of the war, was expected to be implemented. With the inevitable formation of a Nationalist Irish Government, brought about through the democratic process, political surveillance of Sinn Fein was scaled back. British Military Intelligence, however, continued their undercover work. A new organization, "Q," was established, with links to MI5. It was supposed to relay information to Major Price but failed to give him anything that his own the police forces had not already provided. Soon after the staff of "Q" were withdrawn.⁷

The General election of December 1918 saw a complete victory for Sinn Fein. The party won 73 of the 105 seats. General Byrne of the RIC suggested that, as Sinn Fein had become a majority party and was ready to form a government, the British administration should now deal with the party. This, he believed, would separate them from the reemerging physical force of republicanism. His views were at loggerheads with the ruling clique in Dublin Castle. For stepping out of line, Byrne was sent on indefinite leave—gardening leave as it was euphemistically called. The British, upon the advice of Dublin Castle, continued to treat Sinn Fein as a hostile and subversive organization indistinguishable from the Volunteers. Their view of the combination of the two seemed confirmed by a report to the Government by Military Intelligence, which had this reassuring rider:

> The Sinn Fein party has not yet sufficient arms of military value, or stores, has no artillery, and therefore without aid ... can never raise an armed force that cannot be dealt with at once by the troops already in this country.⁸

The use of the word *never* was a grave error.

Walter Long, First Lord of the Admiralty, was perhaps a little more astute in his analysis of Sinn Fein. On the last day of December 1918, in a comment to the Secretary of State for the Colonies, Long wrote:

> I have watched the rise and fall of every political party in Ireland for the last forty years, and I think that the present movement [Sinn Fein] is much the most difficult and dangerous of any the Government have had to deal with and for this reason.
>
> Their leaders are brave and fanatical and do not fear imprisonment or death; they are not to be influenced by private negotiations with Bishops or Priests, or captured by getting the patronage of appointments, which have been the favourite instruments of the Irish Government since 1905. Neither do they care a straw for the press.

3

Establishing an Irish Intelligence Service

The acquisition of intelligence, and its denial to the enemy, was the key to winning the war for Ireland's independence. Michael Collins grasped the reality of the above statement when he wrote,

"Without her spies England was helpless. It was only by means of their accumulated knowledge that the British machine could operate. Without their police throughout the country, how could they find the man they wanted? Without their criminal agents in the capital how could they carry out that removal of the leaders that they considered essential for their victory?"

In May 1918, an Intelligence Department was set up by Volunteer GHQ. Eamon Duggan, a lawyer with offices in Dame Street, was appointed Director of Information and Intelligence.[1] His principal intelligence assistant was Christopher Carbery. Learning as they went along, the two men operated out of the New Ireland Assurance Company offices in Bachelors Walk, the same building used by the Dail Loan scheme.[2] A lot of the material Duggan acquired was freely available to him and his small team, in the form of various publications. The newspapers and society magazines gave details of appointments and transfers of RIC officers and their attendance at social functions. Photographs were cut out and pasted onto cards. Senior British Army officers were traced through *Who's Who* and the *Army List.* Details of their addresses and clubs, their interests and other social pursuits were noted. Details were also kept on hotels and restaurants and sports meetings where police, British Army and British Secret Service agents gathered.

At an early stage, Duggan had incredibly good fortune in obtaining the services of a number of disillusioned members of G. Division, the political section of the Dublin Metropolitan Police. Included in that number was the 60-year-old detective Joseph Kavanagh. He, in his turn, recruited another detective, James McNamara, the confidential clerk to

3. Establishing an Irish Intelligence Service

the Dublin Metropolitan Police's Assistant Commissioner. The two men communicated with Duggan through an intermediary, Thomas Gay, the librarian of the Dublin Corporation Library in Capel Street. Duggan was supplied with information from the two policemen regarding arrests, intended police raids, and messages smuggled out by prisoners. Duggan then acquired a third source within G. Division, Eamon Broy. Broy had joined the force in 1911when Home Rule seemed imminent. Broy was transferred to G. Division in 1915. The salary was better, but he was not happy about political work. Then came the Rising, and following its failure, Home Rule seemed so far away. Disillusioned, Broy decided to offer his services to Irish Intelligence. He contacted a relative by marriage, Patrick Tracy, a member of Sinn Fein. Tracy put him in touch with Harry O'Hanrahan, brother of Michael O'Hanrahan, who had been executed in 1916. As Broy notes, "From then on, every secret and confidential document, police code, etc. that came to my hands was sent through Tracy and O'Hanrahan," to Irish Intelligence.[3]

In de Valera's reshuffle of the Irish Cabinet, on April 2, 1919, Michael Collins was appointed as Minister of Finance. Though the Dail records do not show it, he also became Director of Intelligence. He officially took over from Duggan on May 17, 1919.[4] His appointment to the new post was much welcomed. He was seen as a dynamic and a positive force, as opposed to Duggan's somewhat plodding manner. Volunteer Joe Leonard noted his arrival:

> Mick Collins, through necessity, had taken on three Dail Departments and as Director of Intelligence had, some time since, started our Intelligence Department with brilliant success and had been affectionately named the "Big Fellow." We now had first-hand knowledge of enemy movements, documents, photographs, which helped us a lot to counter their brutal assaults, shootings and reprisals on harmless, inoffensive people.[5]

The G Men also noted Collins's arrival. The Dail met at the Mansion House in Dublin in May to welcome the Irish American delegation who were on their way to Paris to put forward Ireland's case for independence. As Minister of Finance, Collins had just delivered a lengthy and powerful case against British exploitation of the taxation system in Ireland when it was discovered that the building had been surrounded by armed soldiers and G Men. They were led by Detective Daniel Hoey, and they were looking for Collins. As was usually the case, there were Volunteer watchers outside. As the British arrived, word was quickly sent in to warn the politicians. Collins, the obvious target, was whisked away up the stairs and escaped over the roof to an adjoining building. After some three hours, Hoey at last called off the search, and he and his men withdrew. Then, with a sense of theater,

Collins returned—in full Volunteer officer uniform. It became part of the Collins legend.

In his capacity as Director of intelligence, Collins began reorganizing the department on a larger and more proactive scale. He decided that intelligence was so important in countering enemy activities that he resigned most of his other positions to give it his full attention. Collins had long realized that England's power in Ireland lay in the efficiency of her Secret Service. Without her spies, England was helpless. He had witnessed the use of the detectives of the political branch of the Dublin Metropolitan Police and the Royal Irish Constabulary men who were brought in from the country districts to identify the leaders of the failed Easter Rising. If Dail Eireann was to function—if Dail Eireann was to survive—then Britain's control over intelligence must be broken. Collins gathered around himself a group of men of proven ability. He co-opted Liam Tobin from the management team of the New Ireland Assurance Company and appointed him as deputy director of intelligence. Collins worked his men hard. Some two years later David Neligan described the toll that the job had taken on Tobin:

> Tall, gaunt, cynical, with tragic eyes, he looked like a man who had seen the inside of hell. He walked without moving his arms and seemed emptied of energy. Yet this man was, after Collins, the Castle's most dangerous enemy.[6]

Briefly in the autumn of 1920, Tobin, no doubt with the constant anxiety and worry, did suffer a nervous breakdown. Somehow, he did recover and went back to work.

Tom Cullen was appointed Volunteer Assistant Quartermaster General. He was very astute and quick-witted, and Neligan describes him as one of Collins's "best intelligence men." In July 1919, Frank Thornton, the Volunteer organizer in Longford, was the transferred to Intelligence. The 28-year-old Thornton was from Drogheda. In 1912, members of his family had moved to Liverpool, where Thornton found work as a painter in the shipyards. He joined the Irish Volunteers soon after its inauguration and was sworn into the IRB by Collins himself. During the Easter Rising, Thornton commanded the little garrison in the Imperial Hotel. Returning to Ireland after Internment, Thornton joined Tobin in establishing the New Ireland Assurance Society. From there he was summoned by Collins to join Irish Intelligence. Thornton recalled:

> I was very happy about this transfer to Intelligence as I liked Michael Collins. I was a great admirer of him. I recognised at an early stage, even as far back as my first contact with him in Liverpool that he was a dynamic type of individual.... He was full of the exuberance of life and full of vitality.[7]

3. Establishing an Irish Intelligence Service 33

To this team Collins later added men who had experience of Intelligence work at company level within the Dublin Brigade. These were men who knew Dublin intimately. They tended to be drawn from the Drumcondra-based 2nd Battalion of north Dublin. Charles Dalton lists the initial Intelligence team:

> Michael Collins was Director of Intelligence. He operated from his own personal office in the daytime and saw his lieutenants at night. Liam Tobin was Deputy D.I., and Tom Cullen was Assistant D.I.
> The staff consisted of Frank Thornton, Joe Dolan, Joe Guilfoyle, Paddy Caldwell, myself, Frank Saurin, Charlie Byrne, Peter McGee, Dan McDonnell, Ned Kellegher, James Hughes, Con O'Neill, Bob O'Neill, Jack Walsh, and Paddy Kennedy.
> Inter-communication was maintained by [Collins'] special messenger, Joe O'Reilly.[8]

Dalton recalled his interview for a place in the Intelligence team:

> …one of the Squad called on me and asked me to accompany him. "The assistant director of intelligence wants to interview you," he told me.
> He brought me into the city and through a number of side streets to Crow Street, an alleyway off Dame Street, quite close to Dublin Castle…. When we came to a small printer's shop he beckoned me up the stairs, and on the second floor he knocked on the door. On the door was fixed, with the words in printed letters "Irish Products Coy."
> Sitting at the table was a tall young man, with dark hair brushed back very smoothly. He had the look of a dominant personality. I recognized him as a Volunteer whom I had seen occasionally when there was something very important on hand. He was Liam Tobin, the assistant director of intelligence, working immediately under Michael Collins…. After we had exchanged a few commonplace remarks, he asked me if I would like to become a member of his staff. There was nothing on earth I wished for more, but I had looked upon it as an honour far above my reach, and I was hard put to it to hide from him my eagerness … so I replied as composedly as I could that nothing would please me better.[9]

Paddy Kennedy also recalled his interview in his Witness Statement to the Bureau of History:

> About the middle of 1920 my Company O.C., Paddy Moran, sent for me and informed me that I had been selected as a suitable man for GHQ Intelligence work. He took me to Oriel Hall in Oriel Street and there introduced me to Tom Cullen, Liam Tobin and Frank Thornton. They informed me that I had been selected for Intelligence work. They pointed out how dangerous and secret this work was, and that if I was prepared to undertake it I would have to leave my employment as it would be full time work. I told them that I understood the conditions and that I was quite willing to take on any duties allotted to me.[10]

Writing in 1948, Piaras Beaslai also makes reference to the people who worked in the background of Irish Intelligence:

> Office work was almost as important as outside work. The co-ordination of the information obtained, the systematic and carefully planned filing of information, documents, photographs, the accumulation of a mass of information, readily accessible when required, with regard to any person or thing, which was likely to be of value to the IRA in their struggle with their enemies—this work was as essential in its way as the more picturesque work of outdoors.[11]

These were the people who collated information relating to the homes and workplaces of the enemy Intelligence men, their means of transport into and from work, and what they did for leisure pursuits, if any. They cross-indexed material coming in from disillusioned policemen, men who felt discriminated against because of their Roman Catholic religion. There were also clerks, shopkeepers, waiters, bar staff and transport workers. They all contributed snippets in regard to individual enemy Intelligence agents that eventually, when sorted, amounted to a biography. Not unsurprisingly, most of the Irish Intelligence officers were IRB members, largely recruited through IRB man Dick McKee from the Dublin Brigade.

Having brought his team together, Collins established Irish GHQ Intelligence in an office over Fowler's shop in Crow Street, a little road off Dame Street, just south of the river Liffey. It was not that far away from British Intelligence in Dublin Castle. In the late summer of 1920, another office, administered by Frank Thornton, was opened in the rooms above the old Antient Concert Rooms in Great Brunswick Street (now Pearse Street). A brass sign was placed outside the entrance hall door of the new premises. It read "O'Donoghue & Smith, Manufacturing Agents." Samples of wares were put on display in the outer office to complete the illusion. Thornton had his office at the front of the building, facing down onto the street, so that he could see what was going on.

Upon taking up his post at the original Crow Street headquarters, Thornton, who had experience as a Volunteer organizer, was now tasked with ordering intelligence within the various Brigades throughout the country:

> Each Company appointed an Intelligence Officer for its own area. The Intelligence Officer was responsible for setting up a system for the collection of information of all sorts through the medium of agents acting within, and outside the ranks of the enemy forces. He employed people in all walks of life, special attention being paid to movements of troops and location of enemy spies, and the securing of positions in enemy centres for our own agents where possible.

3. Establishing an Irish Intelligence Service

The next step was the appointment of the Battalion Intelligence Officer in this area. He received continuous reports from all Company I/Os and sifted all the information as it came through. He passed on what was useful to his Brigade I.O. In this way every area was covered by a network of agents. The system proved extremely useful as the war developed. If information on any particular point was required by Brigade Headquarters or GHQ it was easy to secure, so many and varied were these agents. The Brigade Intelligence Officer was always in touch with both his own Intelligence Staff and the GHQ Intelligence Branch.[12]

Intelligence gathering, as a whole, was divided into two main subjects. The first, which applied mainly to the countryside, related to the movement of British forces from one area to another. This included arrivals and departures and the numbers involved. The second function was the acquiring of intelligence on the activities of British Agents, be they Secret Service men or Military Intelligence Officers, and later, Auxiliary Intelligence Officers.[13] Alongside this was the need to check up on all people, women as well as men, who were discovered to be sympathetic to or constantly in the company of members of the British Establishment in Ireland. Frank Saurin was attached to the second category of intelligence gathering and gives details of what was undertaken:

> Each member was given a number to cover his identity for reference in correspondence and to sign reports. Each I.O. had his own field of work. Mine covered hotels, restaurants, sports meetings and such other places where the Auxiliaries and British Secret Service agents foregathered—Jammets, The Wicklow, The Shelbourne, Fullers, The Moira, The Central, etc. We had contacts in these hotels and restaurants, who passed on any information concerning enemy agents that might be of use to us. Through our agents I was enabled to get to know by sight a number of enemy personnel—the object being their extermination if and when the opportunity offered.[14]

Meanwhile, with his team in place, Collins examined the assets bequeathed to him by Duggan. One of them was the G. Man Eamon Broy. He was an underused asset in Collins's eyes. Duggan had failed to direct the policeman in the acquisition of targeted material. Broy later reflected:

> During the whole time of my association with Tracy and O'Hanrahan, I did not know who ultimately handled the documents I transmitted. I knew nothing about Michael Collins. I knew Miss Maire Smart (now Mrs Michael Foley). We had many talks about Sinn Fein, the insurrection and national activities, and we both solemnly agreed that violence was the only method. One day she said to me "You should meet Mick Collins."
>
> I was deeply intrigued to know who or what this man Collins was like, because whoever was to handle the information I was giving directly would have to trust me, first of all; would have to understand the significance of the

information; would need to have control of the Volunteers and be able to think and act quickly.¹⁵

The policeman was invited to the home of Michael Foley at 5, Cabra Road:

> I was filled with curiosity ... looking up the police record book to see what was known about him, I discovered that he was a six footer, a Corkman, very intelligent, young and powerful. There was no photograph of him at that time in the record book.... I saw Michael at the door, before he had time to walk across and shake hands, I knew he was the man.... The Foleys went away and I had a long talk with Mick from about 8 p.m. until midnight. He thanked me for all the documents I had sent and all the information, and said it was of the utmost assistance and importance to them.¹⁶

Broy himself was described during the Truce negotiations by British civil servant Tom Jones, secretary to Lloyd George. He appeared:

> ...a strongly-built, broad-shouldered, stiff-backed man entering the room. I found it difficult to believe that this gauche, ill-at-ease, obsequious person was Ned Broy, the famous "G" man who had turned traitor and wilily double-crossed his British masters. But not for long: soon I was convinced that his hard, cruel, green eyes were indicative of his character.¹⁷

When Broy first saw Collins, the Irish Chief of Intelligence was wearing breeches and leggings. He stood out, rather than blended in. His apparel gave the observer the impression that the wearer had some sort of military connection. "You'll have to change your clothes," Broy reportedly said to Collins. After explaining, Collins took the comment on board. Thereafter, the Director of Irish Intelligence dressed more like a company director, with suit, clean collar and tie. After the change, he just did not look like a terrorist. Terrorists do not wear neatly pressed grey suits and ride around on Raleigh bicycles. Better still, Collins adopted the notion that if he did not think of himself as being on the run, then he was not a fugitive. Much to Broy's satisfaction, the policeman later saw Collins out and about in Dublin:

> I remember one morning about a quarter past nine I went to keep an appointment with Tommy Gay in the vicinity of Tara Street. I was casually watching the traffic coming from the direction of Butt Bridge and going along Tara Street, when who should I see but Michael Collins cycling in the stream of traffic. As I had no direct business in talking to him at that precise moment, I did nothing to attract his attention. Such a proceeding, in any case, would have been risky in drawing attention to him and myself. He did not notice me and passed on. He wore a high quality soft hat, dark grey suit, as usual, neatly shaved and with immaculate collar and tie, as always, seeming to be ready for the photographer. His bicycle was of first class quality and fitted with a lamp and many other accessories. He looked like a bank clerk

or stockbroker or "something in the city" and cycled on as if he owned the street.[18]

Guerrilla leader from Cork's No. 3 Brigade, Tom Barry, was summoned to Dublin to report. He confirms that the leadership had taken up Broy's advice:

> The way of life of those GHQ officers was in great contrast to that of the West Cork IRA. Dressed like business men, carrying brief or attaché cases, with their pockets full of false papers to support their disguise, they travelled freely to their "business" offices and to keep their various appointments. To a great extent those GHQ men kept regular business hours at those offices, but after closing hours often worked late into the night at some other venue.[19]

A sartorial tradition had grown up amongst the Volunteers. Charles Dalton, who was sent to meet James MacNamara, one of Collins's contacts within the Castle, explains:

> We walked together further down the badly lighted street till we came to a dark spot where any passer-by who knew the detective would not become suspicious.
> Mac's first words to me were: "Why have you got on that hat? The sooner you get rid of it the better."
> It was a black velour hat which I had only bought that evening. I had been rather pleased with it, but as soon as Mac spoke I realized my indiscretion. I never wore it again. Among the Black and Tans there was an idea that it was traditional for Volunteers to wear black hats—a sort of distinguishing mark by which they were known to each other.[20]

So, change came about there, also, especially for the men of Irish Intelligence. Do not stand out; blend in with the populace.

Collins had a number of "business" offices from which he took up the issues of government and warfare. For a long time, his principal office was Vaughan's Hotel in Parnell Square—the logic being that guerrillas simply did not use what might be considered middle-class establishments. Later he used an upper room in Devlin's public house in Parnell Street, just off Upper O'Connell Street. The idea behind this was that as a public house no one would really notice the comings and goings of so many people, whereas they would if the meeting place was a private house.

Though no date is quoted for Broy's first meeting, it was certainly prior to Collins officially taking over the Intelligence Department at the start of May 1919. Piaras Beaslai and Tim Pat Coogan both agree that in the month prior (April), Collins made a daring midnight visit to the headquarters of G. Division in Brunswick Street (now Pearse Street). It had to be carefully arranged for when Broy was on night duty:

> So, meeting Mick one night in April 1919, I was able to tell him that I would be on duty the following night from 10 p.m. to 6 a.m. We arranged that, at twelve o'clock he would ring up to make certain that it was I who was on duty, as there were frequently last minute changes. He was to use the name "Field," and my name was to be "Long."[21]

On duty that night, Broy had to tactfully get rid of a uniformed colleague, Sergeant Kerr of the Carriage Office. He went off eventually to the single men's dormitory. At midnight Collins telephoned, and at about 12:15 a.m. he arrived with Sean Nunan. Both men were armed, with guns and truncheons, as instructed. Broy let them in and showed them to the small semi-circular secret room up on the first floor. They used the back entrance through the yard. Broy had managed to get an extra key cut to gain access. The room which held the books and documents was without electric light. Collins was obliged to work by candlelight.

Then panic set in as a stone came crashing through the window. Instructing them to go back into a dark passage, Broy went to investigate. On looking out onto Great Brunswick Street he saw a British soldier in the custody of a policemen. Enquiring as to what was going on, the policemen announced that the soldier was drunk. The policemen then took the drunk to the police station next door. Relieved that it was nothing more serious, Broy then led Collins and Nunan upstairs to the secrets room. Unlocking it, Broy handed Collins and Nunan candles and matches, and leaving the door unlocked, he went off. No sooner had Broy returned to his desk when the young policeman who had apprehended the drunk presented himself at the downstairs office door. He came enquiring as to the value of the window that was broken. Pulling a figure out of the air, the policeman went off to formally enter up the cost in the Day Book so that the drunken soldier could be fined accordingly.

In the secrets room, Collins searched through the reports, anxious to discover the background to the information supplied by Broy. He wanted to know just how much the Castle authorities knew concerning the Volunteers and Sinn Fein. He wanted to know who the British agents were, how many of them were known to Irish Intelligence, and who those were who were still unknown. Could he learn from the system adopted by British Intelligence? What were they good at? —What were they bad at? Collins searched, read and digested the information. He remained in the room from 12:15 a.m. to about 5 a.m., when Broy returned, now anxious to get him off the premises before anyone awoke. Collins was particularly amused when reading his own secret file. It began with the sentence, "He comes from a brainy Cork family."

Collins's ambition was to get at least one person who was prepared to work for Irish Intelligence in every British Government department.

Having secured agents, they were then instructed to look for others within the departments who were sympathetic to the Republican cause. Once identified, background checks were made on these individuals. Then a member from GHQ Intelligence approached them with a view to recruiting them to work for Irish Intelligence. No checking was necessary in the case of Nancy O'Brien, though. She was Michael Collins's cousin and worked for Sir James McMahon in Dublin Castle. He was Under Secretary in the British Administration of Ireland. One day McMahon called Nancy into his office. She was told:

> That in view of the worsening situation it was imperative that the Castle's most secret coded messages be in safe hands and that he was putting her in charge of handling these messages for him.[22]

It was an incredible lapse in security. As she had been recruited in England, there had been no in-depth check on her and her family connections before she was appointed to this senior secretarial post. When Collins found out, he reportedly said in disbelief, "In the name of Jesus how did these people ever get an empire?" The information she passed onto her cousin was brief, however. Lord French was always skeptical about McMahon, a Roman Catholic, and on December 11, 1919, effectively sidelined him, denying him access to important papers and documents. With McMahon's departure, Nancy was moved on to other duties.

Another of these Castle contacts was Lillie Mernin, who was employed as a typist in Command Headquarters of Dublin District. She worked in the Intelligence Branch under the control of Colonel Stephen Hill Dillon, Chief Intelligence Officer. Mernin was approached by her cousin, Piaras Beaslai, editor of *An tOglach*, the Volunteer's newspaper, to spy for Irish Intelligence. Collins, introduced as "Mr. Brennan," spoke to her personally, and she agreed to pass on information that might be of value, material that she came across in her normal, day-to-day duties. Her Witness Statement is brief, just seven pages in length, but it is very revealing:

> The Garrison Adjutant for Ship Street Barracks and Dublin District at the time was Major Stratford Burton. The work that he gave me to do was connected with Volunteer activities generally and, in addition, Courtmartial proceedings on Volunteers was also given me to type. These dealt with the strength of the various military posts throughout Dublin district. Each week I prepared a carbon or a typed copy, whichever I was able to get. Sometimes I would bring these to the [IRA] office placed at my disposal at Captain Moynihan's house, Clonliffe Road. He had a typewriter there and I typed several copies of the strength returns and other correspondence which I may have brought with me that I thought would be of use.[23]

In order to protect her identity, Michael Collins and the Intelligence team always referred to her as the "little gentleman," sometimes abbreviating it in writing to "Lt. G."[24]

Then one day Mernin presented Collins with the very thing that he most wanted:

> It was part of my normal duty to type the names and addresses of British agents who were accommodated at private addresses and living as ordinary citizens in the city. These lists were typed weekly and amended whenever an address was changed. I passed them on each week either to the address at Moynihans, Clonliffe Rd. or to Piaras Beaslai.[25]

As Mernin was led deeper and deeper into intelligence work, her mission became riskier:

> On various occasions I was requested by members of the Intelligence Squad to assist them in the identity of enemy agents. I remember the first occasion on which I took part in this work was with the late Tom Cullen in 1919. Piaras Beaslai asked me to meet a young man who would be waiting at O'Raghallaigh's bookshop in Dorset Street and to accompany him to Lansdowne Road. I met this man, whom I learned later was Tom Cullen, and went with him to a football match at Lansdowne Road. He asked me to point out to him and give him the names of any British military officers who frequented Dublin Castle and GHQ. I was able to point out a few military officers to him whom I knew.[26]

Once she came close to being discovered. There was a fellow typist in the same office, Lilly Dunne, the daughter of DMP Superintendent Dunne. She lived with her father and brother in Mount Street, just off Merrion Square. Stopping at the same address were a number of men. Every morning Miss Dunne would go into the office and tell her fellow typists about them. They kept strange hours she revealed. Her brother got into conversation with them, and he would tell her what they had said. One of the men was frequently under the influence of drink. He became indiscreet as a result. He revealed that he was a British officer. His name was McMahon. One of the other men he named as Peel. They talked of raids and arrests of wanted IRA men. Hearing this, Lillie Mernin told Tom Cullen. He encouraged her to pass on everything that she heard in the typing office. One morning, Miss Dunne came into the office and excitedly said that her brother was missing. She believed that he had been abducted by the IRA. Now with an audience in the typing pool, she began speculating—somebody in the office must have told the IRA about the conversations that had gone on. Mernin bluffed and suggested that perhaps her brother himself was to blame if he passed on the conversations to others. The brother turned up later that day; the crisis was over. With the departure of Miss Dunne soon after, through illness, any suspicion that Lily was involved with the IRA was eased. Mernin continued in her espionage work.

Collins was also interested in how British Intelligence worked—how its men were trained and the system of working within G. Department. His idea was to establish a counter-intelligence service using the experience that the enemy had gained and counter it. He was aided in this endeavor by another defecting detective, David Neligan. Neligan had joined the DMP in 1918. In the following year, with staff shortages, he transferred to G. Division. Neligan's job was escorting G Men in danger of being shot. When he fully realized the extent of the government's suppressive ways, he handed in his notice and retired to Tralee to spend time with his brother. When his Republican sympathies became known to the local Volunteer Intelligence Officer, Neligan was summoned back to Dublin by Michael Collins in June 1920. Collins persuaded Neligan to rejoin the police. Using the pretext that his life had been threatened out in the country, Neligan persuaded the Commissioner of the DMP, Colonel Johnstone, to take him back. He recalled:

> Broy, McNamara and Kavanagh, who were G Men, were working for Michael Collins. Inspector Bruton had taken over a special wing of the G. Division which was engaged in warring against Volunteers activities. As Broy and Kavanagh were attached to what was then known as Brunswick Street Detective Office and McNamara to the Assistant Commissioner's Office, this left the Castle Squad without any agent working for Collins. This was the vacancy I was intended to fill.
>
> I met Broy, MacNamara and Kavanagh, fellow G Men, on a new footing because they were working for Michael Collins. They told me so themselves and I was accepted with the same status. They had known for some time that I was friendly to the cause. The three of them and myself used to meet Collins every week after that at Tommy Gay's house, Haddon Road, Clontarf.[27]

One night, following one such meeting at Gay's house, Broy, McNamara, Neligan and Collins shared a taxi back into the city:

> We drove right into a cordon of British Tommies across the road. Collins got out of the car for a moment. He thought it was a trap but we persuaded him to get back in again. A young English Lieutenant came over to talk to us and we told him we were G Men. He told us to go by a roundabout way because a bomb had just been thrown at their lorry and he thought that it was us they were out to attack.[28]

Neligan later went on to become a member of the British Secret Service, right at the heart of British Intelligence in Ireland. Upon retirement, he drew a pension from British Intelligence, the DMP and the Irish Free State for whom he went to work after independence.

Irish Intelligence also turned a considerable number of uniformed policemen. Some were of senior rank. One of them was Peter Forlan, Head Constable of the RIC. He had first met Michael Collins way back when Collins as a teenager and was working for the GPO in London. Forlan's brother-in-law, Michael Barrett, also a policeman, was stationed in Clonakilty and was very friendly with Collins's sister Margaret and her husband, with whom the young Barrett had stayed while studying for his GPO entrance exam. In 1915 Forlan was considering retirement from the DMP. The work was becoming more and more politicized, with action being taken against those with nationalistic leanings. Michael McHugh, a compositor on the *Freeman's Journal,* and an important IRB man, persuaded Forlan to stay for the time being. Forlan was still there when the shooting of G Men commenced. These were dangerous times for political policemen:

> To make sure that I would be recognised and not molested by the IRA they had me photographed several times as I went along the street to my work in the Castle. I took out copies of secret documents. My method was to take shorthand notes of the documents on the files, translate them into longhand and pass the translations to them.
>
> On one occasion, I cannot remember the date, the military had collected the names of all the IRA on the north side of the city. The list ran into several pages. The military were to arrest everyone on the list that night between 12 o'clock and dawn. Knowing that I would not be able to give a complete list, I brought the file home with me inside my shirt. I then communicated with Father Paddy Flanagan in Aughrim Street. He gave us the loan of his room and we got a few typewriters and copied the whole list. Father Flanagan had a couple of girls to type it. In the meantime a number of friends were summoned and they went around every address warning the Volunteers to be out of their houses that night. The next morning I left the file back in its place. There was hell to pay in the Castle. The military had gone out in their lorries; they visited the nests but the birds had flown.[29]

Irish Intelligence also recruited policemen from the lower uniformed ranks of the DMP. Patrick Kennedy of Irish Intelligence recorded in his Witness Statement the names of Constables John Kennedy and Terry O'Reilly, just two of many undercover agents. Both were of Fitzgibbon Street Station, up near the North Circular Road. In mid–1920, Intelligence chief Frank Thornton, on Collins's instruction, met two other policemen, Sergeant Matt Byrne and Constable Patrick Mannix, at a private house in Rathgar Avenue, south Dublin. Both men had agreed to work for Irish Intelligence. Thornton instructed them in how they could help. Thornton was interested in enemy activities, particularly at night. As well as passing on information, the two men recruited other police officers to the cause. There was at least a dozen such policemen. They carried out invaluable work, particularly relating to the night-time

British raids. Invariably when a raid was to take place, the British would take a DMP man with them, one who was familiar with the raid's specific part of Dublin. In quite a lot of cases, the policeman was advised in advance of where the raid was to take place and whom the British were after. As a result, a warning was passed on to Irish Intelligence. If there was insufficient time to prepare, the policeman would cover for any IRA man, if the British happened to recognize him. Mannix describes one such raid:

> On a few occasions while accompanying the search parties, I saved the lives of men who were found in the houses that were being searched, as I informed the officers in charge that these men were law abiding citizens, although in each case they were much wanted men. The officer, relying on my information, then withdrew and the men got safely away. On one occasion I was with a search party, the officer in charge being Lieutenant Brookbank, who was attached to the Royal Irish Rifles. He knocked at the door of a certain house and when the door was opened I saw a number of men playing cards, one of whom I knew to be a very much wanted man. I informed the officer that they were all friends of my own and we retired, leaving the men to escape.[30]

A tremendous breakthrough for Irish Intelligence occurred when it gained access to the British secret code. While accepting that Irish Intelligence had access to the code—a cipher had been found on Cork's Lord Mayor Terence MacSwiney—British Military Intelligence was in denial that the code had been broken. The unpublished *Record of the Rebellion in Ireland* incorrectly recorded that "…there is no evidence that Sinn Fein had an efficient cryptographic branch."[31]

One of the members of Irish Intelligence's "cryptographic branch," as the British referred to it, was Charles Dalton. By the time he was appointed, transcribing was firmly established:

> I was next shown how to decode telegrams. Liam Tobin received copies of telegrams from some person he had working for him in the Central Telegraph Office. These were all in code and were addressed to district inspectors of the RIC throughout the country. We possessed the key word, so we had no difficulty in deciphering them…. The contexts of these messages usually referred to contemplated arrests and raids on Volunteers' houses. By communicating copies of these messages to the areas concerned, the police were frustrated. When the raiders arrived the men they were looking for were not at home.[32]

How Irish Intelligence broke the British codes is described by a number of participants. One was a schoolteacher Sean Kavanagh. He came into contact with a disillusioned County Inspector's chief clerk, Sergeant Maher of the RIC. Kavanagh reported the fact to GHQ Irish Intelligence, who instructed him to cultivate the policeman. Kavanagh was invited to Dublin, where he met Collins:

> Collins told me that the police had recently been issued with a new figure cipher and that he was most anxious to get hold of the key of it. He told me he had been trying to get it through other contacts but that, so far, he had not succeeded, and he asked me if I could do my best to get it for him. This cipher was used only for the more important telegraphed messages (a simple code being used for ordinary telegrams) and the experts had failed to crack it.[33]

Kavanagh persuaded Maher to obtain some examples for him; the message in cipher and then decoded. Using the two pieces of paper, Kavanagh was able to establish the current key. Subsequently, Maher supplied him with all the coded messages, and these he passed on to Michael Collins. Now risking torture and imprisonment if he were caught, Maher tried to get the cipher from his superior's safe:

> The County Inspector kept this cipher locked in his safe. After some time Maher succeeded in getting an impression of the key of the safe, and Collins got a duplicate made. Sergeant Maher had free access to the safe from then on, and, as a result, was able to bring me the "key" to the figure cipher each time a new one was issued, which occurred on an average about once a month.
> The police exercised the greatest precaution in passing this cipher from Dublin to the various County Inspectors throughout the country. Their method of delivery was to send police couriers in mufti by train. These were met at the different stations by local police couriers, who delivered the cipher into the hands of the County Inspector concerned. It often took a couple of days for the cipher to travel from Dublin to a distant county, and Collins frequently had the key of the cipher back in Dublin before it reached some of the County Inspectors.[34]

Liam Archer, a member of GHQ Intelligence, explained the cipher system in his 1953 Witness Statement:

> The cipher was very elementary, being a simple transposition. The key was a word in which no letter was repeated and having 10 or 11 letters but no more than 13. The word being written out was followed by the first letters of the alphabet which were not in it to bring the number of letters to 13 and the remaining letters of the alphabet written underneath, viz:-
>
> SWITZERLANDBC
> FGHJKMOPQUVXY
>
> Thus F-S or vice versa. As the new key word was sent out in the old cipher on the 1st of each month, we were automatically supplied. The cipher was so simple it could be broken without a key. Later a double transposition cipher using two key words was adopted. They operated as in the case of the single

3. Establishing an Irish Intelligence Service

word, the first key giving another cipher message, and the second converting this into plain language. Later, a complicated figure cypher was adopted. This provided for each letter from two to six double figures. Thus A could be represented by any of the following—16, 34, 23, 87; E by 41, 53, 69, 24, 76, 91; Z by 12, 29. The number of alternatives depended upon the frequency with which each letter is used in the English language—thus E had six and Z two.[35]

The British authorities also had a two-word code, one of the words changing every day and the other changing every week. This code was supplied to selected members of the RIC but not directly to G. Division of the DMP. One evening, when Eamon Broy, Collins's agent within G. Division went to see Collins.

> ...[H]e had the cipher of a former two-code message and was very anxious to get the decipher. He felt that, if he had it deciphered, he would learn who gave away, in the north of Ireland, the information that enabled the British to capture forty thousand rounds of .303 in J.J. Keane's Corn Store, Smithfield Dublin. We spent hours using the correct two words which we had, but without the instructions, in endeavouring to decode, but we failed.

Returning to the G. Division office, just after 10 o'clock that night, Broy's disappointment turned to joy. The G. man on duty in the office was pleased to see him:

> "Here's the man that will decipher this for us." I saw almost at a glance that it was a two word code message....
> The sender was apparently unaware that the G. Division were never supplied with the instructions concerning the two-word code. I told the man on duty that we had not got that code in the office upstairs and that the only people who had it were the RIC.... He asked me would I ever mind going up to the Castle and getting the decode.... The Head Constable took the message from me and brought it to an inner room to somebody else. The decipher was brought out to me after a couple of minutes, but this did not make me any wiser as to how the code was to be worked. The message that night was to the effect that Patrick "Somebody" was coming to Dublin. I asked the man on duty could it possibly be "Peter"? He replied, "I will take it in again." When he returned, he said, "The man inside wants you to come in and satisfy yourself." I went in and the man said to me, "There now is the code, there is the letter so-and-so—isn't that right?"—and so on, with the second code word. I, of course, saw instantly the method of decoding.... So, from that on, we had the solution of the two-word codes.

Another important access to British Intelligence was through the Post Office and Telegraphic services. Post Office workers were recruited by Irish Intelligence across the country. Sorters and telegraphic operators were arranged to collect copies of all enemy messages that were sent in code. Telephone Exchanges tapped calls to and from Dublin Castle. Letters addressed to particular people, who were on lists supplied by Irish Intelligence, were collected and handed to GHQ for examination, then carefully resealed and reposted. Outgoing letters from Dublin Castle were also checked. Frank Thornton recalled:

> It is amazing the amount of information which we secured by this method as enemy soldiers and agents were most indiscreet in the type of letters they wrote home to England.[36]

Sean Kavanagh was also tasked with acquiring the Dublin Castle post from the Dublin to Cork mail train. The mail was taken under armed guard from the Castle to the station. Once put aboard though, the guard withdrew. Kavanagh revealed, "The sorting staff on the train were most co-operative, and whenever I asked for the Castle mail bag they simply handed it over to me." Most of the time, Kavanagh revealed, there seemed to be little of any importance, but Collins reassured him, "… what appeared to me to be of little importance might turn out to be very useful." This would be when cross-referenced to other material.

Pat Moynihan, a postal official based at the sorting office at the Rotunda Rink, was Collins's principal agent within the central post office service in Dublin. Moynihan was a captain in GHQ Intelligence and was given the code number "118." He passed on information of concern. Patrick Kennedy recalled one such message from him:

> I remember on one occasion he sent out word that bundles of "An tOglach" which were being sent by Piaras Beaslai to country districts had been seized and collected within the Rink. We retaliated immediately by going into the Rink armed, holding up the staff and taking the bundles of "An tOglach" from them.[37]

The importance here was the names and addresses of the intended recipients. Had British Intelligence had got hold of them, they could have decimated whole county Brigades. Another similar incident involved the Dail Loan. Without that money, both the Irish Government and its army would have been in dire financial straits:

> [Captain Moynihan] gave information to Collins that covering letters from the Dail Bonds were in the Rink and that the British military were coming to take them away. He told us that the letters were in a basket in the Rink, gave us the location of the basket, and said that it should be taken away immediately at all costs.
>
> Paddy Kennedy, Dan McDonnell and myself were detailed to go and seize the basket, which we were to hand to one of our own messengers. We went to the Rink, went straight to where the basket was and whatever officials were there we kept them covered and held them up. I gave the basket to the

young messenger, who ran out of the Rink with it. It was brought to Mary Street.

Just as we were leaving the Rink a double turret armoured car arrived to take away the letters. It was a lightning raid, and if we had been a minute later getting away we would have been captured.[38]

Another of their agents at the Rotunda Rink was Charles McQuaille. He dealt with military correspondence:

Letters received into the Post Office did not indicate the location of the officer or soldier; they simply gave the number, rank and name of the individual and serving somewhere in Ireland. It was my job to endorse the address of the unit to which the officer or soldier belonged. In that way I was in possession of a complete list of all the military units and their locations throughout the country. This information I passed on to Michael Staines.[39]

Post vans were intercepted on the street when it had been impossible to secure mailbags in the post office. One particular raid took place on a post van in Dublin in February 1920. The van, carrying the day's official correspondence for Dublin Castle, was held up in Parnell Square, Dublin. On another morning in Cathedral Street at about 8 a.m., Vinnie Byrne and Tom Keogh of The Squad held up another mail van carrying Dublin Castle post:

We pulled our guns and told the driver to halt. There was only one bag and, of that, we had already been informed. I went to the back of the van to open it up.... After getting the bag out, Tom Keogh told the driver to go ahead to Amiens St. Station and not to say a word to anybody on the way there; if they did, it would be worse for both of them. We had [a] bicycle with us.... It was arranged that I should take the mail bag to the [Squad's] dump, which was in Upper Abbey St.[40]

Off Vinnie Byrne set on his own, precariously cycling down the road, one hand on the bicycle handle, the other holding the mail bag. He cycled into O'Connell Street and took a shortcut by Nelson's Pillar over to Henry Street near the still-damaged General Post Office. As he did, the bag slipped to one side:

...down came the bag, nearly bringing me with it. I was in a right jam now, for there, standing with his back to the GPO was a peeler [a policeman]. However, the only thing to do was to act as if I were an auxiliary postman. Leaving the mails where they fell, I stood the bike at the edge of the path and got ready to mount again. Just then a man turned the corner of the GPO and I asked him would he mind giving me a hand with the bag. He obliged and lifted the bag on my back. Off I went again down Henry St., Mary St., and was in the act of turning into Stafford St. when down came the bag again. By this time the bag was getting very heavy. So I had to carry out the same thing again, stand the bike at the kerb, but there was no one around near me to call to my assistance. With a great effort I mounted the bicycle, gripped the bag, pulled it up on my back and off I went. I had not very far to go now, for if I had, I'm afraid I would never have made it.

Byrne eventually arrived at The Squad's headquarters without further incident. Later in the day the mail bag was transferred to Irish Intelligence's Crow Street address, for an examination of its contents.

Patrick Kennedy recalled another similar incident in which he was involved:

> I remember one occasion when the Director of Intelligence, Michael Collins, instructed me, through Frank Thornton, that a particular letter was going through the post from the British military headquarters in Parkgate Street, and that it was to be intercepted before it reached the Rink. I knew the number of the post office van going from Park Street, and, accompanied by Pat McCrae, we held it up at the junction of Parnell Square and Parnell Street. We seized all the mails in the van. I was informed later that we had succeeded in our mission, as the wanted letter was amongst the many seized.[41]

From the summer of 1920, the British, learning by experience, dispatched and collected all "State" mail by armored car. They did not, however, deal with mail stolen from within the central post office.

IRA Intelligence man Liam Archer related:

> After this, the mails were carried by armoured car but in mid-summer (June-July) it was decided to seize them from the Rotunda Rink. I drew a detailed plan of the building and pin-pointed the location of the wanted mails and the alarm signal. I went over this plan with McKee and advised as to how the raid should be carried out within the building. The result was that Oscar Traynor [Brigadier, Dublin Brigade] found the task a simple one.[42]

For their part the IRA operated an alternative postal system in Dublin. Phil Sheerin's Coolevin Dairies, situated under the loopline bridge in Amiens Street, close to the railway station, was used by railway employees bringing in messages from IRA leaders out in the countryside. Then there were "sub-post offices." Harry Boland's tailoring shop in Middle Abbey Street was one; The Bookshop in Dawson Street with Susan Killeen was another. Nancy O'Brien's flat in Glasnevin was yet a third. Eveleen Lawless, Collins's personal secretary recalled more "post offices" in her Witness Statement of May 1951:

> Most of the correspondence that reached us was not addressed to the office. It was addressed to private addresses in various parts of the city which we called covering addresses. Joe O'Reilly, myself and some other people called daily to these addresses to collect the correspondence which was then taken by Joe to Mick, who was seemingly the key man for all activities connected with the Dail and Volunteers. His ability to deal with them was recognised by all. A man called Flanagan—"The Rabbit" Flanagan—in Camden Street was

one address that I called to regularly. Keogh's, the photographers, in St. Stephen's Green, where Miss Quinn, a sister-in-law of Diarmuid Lynch, worked, was another.[43]

Everywhere in Dublin there was a rival, alternative Irish Republican system of administration running in parallel to the British system. By the late summer of 1919, Collins and the men and women who worked so closely with him had successfully created a rival Intelligence service in Ireland. Its agents stretched from shopkeepers, cleaners and barmen right up to agents within Dublin Castle itself, at the very heart of the British Administration in Ireland. More importantly, as British repression increased, so too did the support of the people for their fledgling nation. Intelligence chief Frank Thornton put their support into words:

> ...the ordinary "five-eight" common citizen was marvellous. Time after time when our men were watching houses, watching individuals, or watching for ambushes, men and women came along and quietly told them to look out that there was somebody watching them from a door or a street corner, and even after ambushes, we had women who were out shopping virtually grabbing grenades and revolvers from men who were in danger of being captured and coolly walking through the enemy lines. This spirit prevailed right through the country, but here in the citadel of British Imperialism the assistance given by the ordinary man and woman was simply marvellous and was responsible in the main for the success of our fighting services.[44]

With an intelligence service in place, Collins now decided to strike back at the British Administration. He had watched, studied, and prepared for this moment. He knew that "[w]ithout her spies England was helpless. It was only by means of their accumulated knowledge that the British machine could operate. Without their police throughout the country, how could they find the man they wanted? Without their criminal agents in the capital how could they carry out that 'removal' of the leaders that they considered essential for their victory?" He decided to eliminate Dublin's political police spies, the men of G. Department—the G Men.

4

Eliminating the G Men

Back in the early days, when Duggan was in charge of Irish Information and Intelligence, Dick McKee, O/C of the Dublin Brigade, was also gathering information. He identified the G Men as the principal enemy and had them followed. More ruthless than Collins at this date, his intention was to remove them and the threat that they posed. The British could replace a detective, but the replacement could not step into the dead man's shoes and his knowledge. Barney Byrne of the resurrected D Company of 1st Battalion, Dublin Brigade was to comment:

> Sometime prior to the Armistice in 1919 what I believe to have been the first real effort to establish military intelligence as such, in the IRA was made at 44, Parnell Square under the direction of Dick McKee. Leo Henderson, to the best of my recollections, was his assistant. Our attention was chiefly directed to the necessity for recording the movements and hostile activities of members of the DMP. Selected representatives from the various Companies of the Brigade were asked to attend a conference at which Dick McKee presided. He gave us an outline as to where we should direct our energies and activities henceforth, that is, as already stated, to observe the movements of DMP men who made themselves obnoxious to the Volunteer organisation. He gave us copy-books to take away with us, in which we were to record their movements.[1]

Dick McKee, an IRB man, having identified the most active of the G Men, now wanted to take action against them. He put forward the idea of an assassination team. In the Spring of 1919, Dick Mulcahy, Chief of Staff of the IRA, called a meeting at 44, Parnell Square to discuss the matter. Invited to take part were Dick McKee himself, to explain his proposal, Peadar Clancy, Director of Munitions, Michael Collins, Director of Organisation, and Mick McDonnell, Brigade Quartermaster. Mulcahy put forward McKee's proposal, which, with some reservation, was accepted. Collins expressed some concern, as Broy indicated:

> Collins was extremely anxious as to what effect the shooting of detectives would have on the Volunteers themselves and on the Sinn Fein movement generally, and how it would be taken by the public.[2]

Public opinion had to be taken into account. Would the public support the killing of policemen? Would they consider it to be murder? Public support was crucial. A compromise was reached. The detectives would first be warned. Then, if they continued in their actions against Dail Eireann and the Volunteers, they would be shot. McDonnell, upon his own request, was appointed to lead The Squad—the men who would undertake the assassinations.³ He began recruiting men for his team. Likely candidates for The Squad were invited to a house at 35, North Great George Street, off Parnell Street, in mid–July. One of those invited was James Slattery:

> I received instructions to proceed to a house in North Great George Street, I think it was No.35. On arriving there I found a fairly big number of Volunteers present. Dick McKee and Mick McDonnell were there, and they picked out a number of us and took us to an inner room. Dick McKee addressed those of us who had been selected and asked us if we had any objection to shooting enemy agents. The greater number of Volunteers objected for one reason or another. When I was asked I said I was prepared to obey orders.
>
> Some of the Volunteers who accepted the proposition put to them that night were Tom Ennis, Tom Keogh, I am not sure if Mick Kennedy of Ballybough was there then, Paddy Daly, Tom Kilcoyne and Joe Leonard.⁴

Initially six men were chosen, with more recruited in the following months, bringing the number up to twelve. The Squad, with a sense of black humor, became known as the "Twelve Apostles." It comprised Mick McDonnell, (nominally in charge), his brother-in-law Tom Keogh, Joe Leonard, Sean Doyle, Jim Slattery, Bill Stapleton, Pat McCrae, James Conroy, Ben Barrett, Vinnie Byrne, Mick Kennedy and Paddy Daly (who later replaced McDonnell as leader). McKee became the liaison officer between The Squad and Michael Collins. They were originally based in an office of the Antient Concert Room in Brunswick Street, with an arms dump at a stable converted into a lock-up garage in Mountjoy Court, off Great Charles Street, near Mountjoy Square. The garage belonged to Mick McDonnell, who kept his motorcycle and side car there. Additional dumps were established at O'Rourke's bakery in Parnell Street and a builder's yard in Denzille Lane, off Holles Street, south of the river. Later The Squad established themselves and their arms dump at premises in Middle Abbey Street, facing Stafford Street. Squad man Vinnie Byrne described it:

> This was known as Moreland's, Cabinet making and Upholstering, the name being painted in very large letters on the gates, one with a wicket opening. The area of the premises was about 75' long by about 12' wide, flanked on each side by a high wall. The ground floor was used as a cabinet-making shop, which was only a blind of course. The second floor consisted of two

> large stores, one of which had a glass roof, with an opening window, which was very useful in case of a raid; in the other store, facing the entrance and commanding the passage, was a very large window, which opened on hinges, the bottom portion being sheeted with timber. Behind this, we built a concrete wall, 4'6" high by 9" thick. This was to act as a barricade. It was also intended to mine the passage, but the laying of the mines was never carried out. Some pretence at cabinet-making had to be shown, and for that purpose we needed tools. I was detailed to go to Messers. Booth, Stephen Street, and get a kit. On receiving the tools from the assistant, I handed him a note—"Taken in the name of the IRA." The first job done was the making of a bench. The next thing was to have plenty of shavings around to give the impression that work was being done. I was the decoy—wearing overalls and looking like a workman.[5]

Guns were kept in an old lavatory in the yard, its ground-floor entrance was bricked up. Access was gained from a secret trapdoor in the lavatory on the floor above. One of the joists had a 6-inch nail driven into it. Attached to it was a string which was used to haul up an old mail bag which contained the guns.

Bill Stapleton added to Byrne's account:

> …we had to put on a show of being Cabinet Makers at George Moreland's and I often thought it very funny that we would amuse ourselves playing with bits of timber, making small shelves and unmaking them, dressed up in our white aprons, and that underneath these aprons we were usually heavily armed. However, one member of the Squad, Vincent Byrne, was a Cabinet Maker by trade, and put his spare time to more practical use as he actually brought in pieces of furniture which he had to repair and actually repaired them in the workshop. In the early days of Morelands I amused myself by painting the front gate and it was actually I who painted the name in white letters on the gate…. I remember standing on a ladder painting the gate … when a British Military patrol moved along on both sides of the street at about twenty paces intervals. Sometimes they stopped and searched pedestrians or looked into shops. All this time I was painting the gate. I was not interfered with.[6]

The headquarters and the dump went undiscovered right through the conflict, though The Squad did suffer at least one fright. One evening in early 1920, they were relaxing by playing cards while waiting for instructions. Suddenly down below, they heard a burst of grenades and revolver fire. They thought that they were under fire and about to be raided. The Squad prepared to evacuate the premises through the skylight, but then all went silent. Tom Keogh urged Byrne to go down and investigate. He proceeded down to the yard and opened the wicket gate, to all and purposes a working carpenter. Popping his head out, he saw a British soldier and asked him what all the shooting was about. "Those bloody Shinners ambushed us," came the reply. Byrne sympathized with him over his plight, then told him that he would have to get back to work otherwise he would be in trouble with his boss. It turned out that an IRA Active Service Unit had ambushed the lorry load of soldiers at the corner of Swift's Row and Ormond Quay.

Later more men were added to The Squad. Patrick Lawson, 2nd Lieutenant in the 1st Battalion, and company I/O was recruited into The Squad in 1921—by which time it had expanded in numbers, as he relates:

> Early in March 1921, the Battalion O/C., Paddy Holohan, instructed me that I was being transferred in a higher rank to the Headquarters Squad and that I was to report to Paddy Daly at 10, Upper Abbey Street, known as the Oddfellows Hall. I met Paddy Daly as instructed, and he gave me an outline of my duties. He told me that the Squad was formed to carry out individual shootings of enemy agents and spies, and that in future I was to act under his command.
>
> I reported the following morning at Morelands. The strength of the Squad at that time was eighteen, and with three new additions, including myself, the strength was brought up to twenty-one. With this strength the Squad was divided into three groups, one under Joe Leonard, one under Tom Keogh, and one under Jimmy Slattery. Paddy Daly was [by then] in charge of the entire Squad.
>
> The duties of the Squad were so arranged that six men were always standing-to, ready for action at Morelands. Generally our tour of duty was for about six hours daily. There were occasions when the entire Squad stood-to.[7]

The revised Squad were appointed as full-time operatives and had to make themselves fully available at all times. To facilitate this, they were obliged to leave their daytime jobs and homes and to live in groups at safe houses. They were paid a weekly wage of £4 10s a week—the first unit of the Irish Army to be paid a salary. Squad member Bill Stapleton defined their purpose:

> While the main function of the Squad was the elimination of enemy agents and spies it was, nevertheless, very active in general raids, arrests of suspected spies for interrogation by GHQ and attacks on the enemy, even to the extent of interrupting the ration supplies to Dublin Castle and other military barracks, also with raids on the North wall for arms and general military equipment.

Having established a task force known as The Squad in mid–July 1919, Collins and McKee now set out to destroy the intelligence capability of the DMP. Lists of the members of the G. Department were distributed to the Dublin Brigade. Frank Henderson of F Company 2nd Battalion relates:

> ...in all the Battalion areas these junior detectives were rounded up on the same night close to their homes or lodgings as they were returning from duty, taken down quiet laneways and beaten until they solemnly promised to take no further part in such treacherous work against the country's efforts to regain freedom. They were told that if they did not keep their promise they would be shot but that they would not be prevented from doing detective work against criminals. This action had the desired result and drove in the outer ring of police spies.[8]

One of that number was Detective Denis O'Brien. They tracked him down and confronted him. As per the compromise reached with Collins, he was simply warned. What exactly happened was relayed to Collins by his police spy, Eamon Broy:

> He was tied to a railing. O'Brien, who was a native of Kanturk, had been more than usually active observing and shadowing Volunteers and Sinn Feiners, making a particular set on the Corkmen and other Munster men. O'Brien was warned during the tying up that, if he continued on the same lines, there would be no mercy shown to him next time. When O'Brien was released and taken to Dublin Castle, the Superintendent asked him why he had allowed himself to be tied up. This annoyed O'Brien very much and he said, "I would like to know what anyone else would do in the same circumstances." He said to some of us afterwards, "They were damned decent men not to shoot me, and I am not doing any more against them."[9]

Some G Men would not be intimidated as easily as O'Brien, as Broy discovered. Included in that number were Detective Sergeants Daniel Hoey, Patrick Smyth and John Barton. Divisional Detective Johnny Barton was a formidable character as fellow police officer David Neligan relates:

> Cadaverous, immensely tall with weird clothes and farmer's boots he looked like a rustic from an Abbey play. Anyone would take him for a simpleton but it would be a major error. He was easily the best detective in these islands, had plenty of touts working for him and was known to be well-off financially.[10]

They were indeed dangerous men. On the information provided by their informers, they made night-time raids on suspected Volunteers' and Sinn Fein politicians' homes, searching for suspects or arms. The home of Liam Archer, later to join Irish Intelligence, was raided early in 1918 by four detectives:

> I was not at home when they called, and though they made a close search of my room they did not open a locked drawer which, besides two revolvers, contained a lot of very incriminating papers. From the description I concluded the "Dog" Smyth, Hoey and Coffey were in the party.[11]

4. Eliminating the G Men

Unable to scare off the other G Men, McDonnell reported back to McKee and Collins and was given the go-ahead to act against them. Bernard Byrne outlined the procedure:

> We were directly responsible to Collins and received our orders from him, usually through the medium of Liam Tobin or Tom Cullen, who had their offices in Crow Street, in the forenoon of each day, where he would be either given instructions in relation to an immediate task or else forewarned as to some impending event. Making reports following incidents was, in fact, scarcely necessary, as newspapers invariably carried headlines if we were successful, and silence on the matter indicated that no action had taken place. The question of whether we would or would not carry out a job at any precise time or place was never the subject of discussion or even adverse comment. The decision as to whether we would do a particular task at any particular time was a matter for our own determination.[12]

Byrne goes on to explain how they operated:

> We had nothing to do with the initial tracking or locating of enemy agents, this being strictly a matter for Intelligence, who, having determined on the object of their interest, proceeded to get all the necessary information as to movement, whereabouts, times, etc. The selection as to the ultimate location of where the individual was to be eliminated was left to ourselves to determine.[13]

In an almost clinical description, Vinnie Byrnes describes how the members of The Squad became inured to the task:

> Perhaps the method used in carrying out these operations should be explained. First of all, the men selected for Squad work were brought on a few jobs and shown how they were carried out; secondly, each man had to prove his mettle, and was detailed to do an actual job; thirdly, there was always two men detailed, and fourthly, the remainder of the Squad would take up positions to act as a guard around them.[14]

Squad member Bill Stapleton described the procedure for a killing:

> Two or three of us would go out with an Intelligence Officer walking in front of us, maybe about ten or fifteen yards. His job was to identify the man we were to shoot.... The Intelligence Officer would then signal to us in the following way. He would take off his hat and greet the marked man. Of course we did not know him. As soon as he did this we would shoot. We had to accept that GHQ knew the right men to shoot.[15]

They began their work with an audacious attempt on the life of Assistant Inspector-General Albert Roberts of the RIC, on June 22, 1920. As his chauffeur-driven car was passing along the quay in front of the Custom House, three Squad men opened rapid fire. Both Roberts and his driver were wounded, but with great pluck the driver put his foot down and the car sped away to safety.

The first two targets within G. Department of the DMP, were Sergeants Smyth and Hoey. On July 24, The Squad went after them. Two groups of two began looking for them. One group under Paddy Daly was tasked with shooting Detective Sergeant Daniel Hoey. James Slattery, who headed the other group, was given Detective Sergeant Patrick Smyth as his target. McDonnell, in briefing Slattery, informed him where he could locate his quarry. On his way home from Dublin Castle, Smyth invariably caught the tram up to Drumcondra, getting off at Botanic Avenue. From there he walked across the bridge over the little river Tolka to his home in Millmount Avenue. Slattery and his group waited on their target for five evenings, but he did not show. Then, on the sixth evening, a man appeared, but they were not sure that it was Smyth. They watched as the man passed them. He approached the Avenue but did not turn down it. Slattery's emotions were mixed. He was convinced that he had nearly shot an innocent man. They continued watching. The man then turned down a narrow lane that ran along the back of Millmount Avenue and entered his house at the rear entrance. It was Smyth, and he had escaped them.

The operation was postponed for a week, to avoid any suspicion. Then on July 31, Slattery, Mick McDonnell, Mick Kennedy and Tom Keogh returned. Slattery described the killing:

> We came back again to the bridge and after about a week we shot Smith. We had .38 guns and they were too small. I thought that the minute we would fire at him he would fall, but after we hit him he ran. The four of us fired at him. Keogh and myself ran after him right to his own door and I think he fell at the door, but he got into the house. He lived for about a fortnight afterwards.[16]

The weapons were not heavy enough for a clean kill. McKee ensured that after that the men were issued with .45 caliber revolvers. G. Man Eamon Broy, now working for Irish Intelligence, recommended that they should have two types of handguns on an operation:

> I advised Collins that his men should not depend on automatic pistols, that, while these arms were very attractive and efficient when they worked, the Germans had been let down in the trenches very often, attempting to use automatic pistols against the British Webley revolver, and that each of his men should have both an automatic pistol and a revolver when going on a job. I also advised him that, where they were coming up against the police, either in the city or country, not to rely entirely on firearms, but to pick men of good physique as well, in view of the many things that could go wrong in such operations.[17]

Thereafter each member of The Squad carried two guns, an automatic and a short Webley on operations. There was a preference for the Colt .45 Automatic.

As Collins had suspected, Smyth's assassination was condemned in all the newspapers and from the pulpits. The Bishop of Galway declared, "There was no justification for murder and outrage."[18] Yet curiously, not all the clergy held the same view as the bishop, as Tim Pat Coogan discovered while talking to Vinnie Byrne years later:

> Byrne for example, remembered going to confession to "a great priest," Father Moriarty of South William Street. I told him: "I shot a man, Father." "Did you think you were doing right? Had you any qualms about it?" he asked me. I told him I didn't have any qualms, I thought I was doing right, and he said, "Carry on with the good work," and gave me absolution.[19]

As a punishment for the death of Smyth, the Government banned Sinn Fein. It was a ludicrous thing to do given that the party were democratically elected as the Government of Ireland. On September 12, Sergeant Hoey led a raid on the now illegal Sinn Fein headquarters at 6, Harcourt Street. Collins was very nearly caught. Hoey was becoming too dangerous to live. Orders went out that Hoey was to be shot. That evening a team from The Squad was assembled. Mick McDonnell, James Slattery and Tom Ennis went looking for Hoey. Slattery recalled:

> Mick [McDonnell] said he thought that Detective Hoey would be getting off duty at about ten o'clock, and he did get off. Hoey crossed over from College Street towards the police headquarters in Brunswick Street [now Pearse St.]. I asked Mick if he was sure that this man was Hoey, and he said, "I am not quite sure, but we will go after him." We intended that if he went straight to the door of the building we would shoot him, but instead of going there he went down Townsend Street nearly as far as Tara Street. We passed him by when he was looking at a window and Mick said, "It is Hoey all right." He went into a shop and we passed back up to the corner of Hawkins Street. When we saw him approaching again, we crossed over to his side of the street, which was at the back of the barracks, and we shot him at the door of the garage.[20]

Mortally wounded, Hoey managed to drag himself back to Headquarters. Fellow officer David Neligan was there:

> We were about to go on duty the night of 13th September 1919 at 10 p.m. when there was a rattle outside the door as if someone were running a stick across iron railings. On going out we saw a man lying in the street. He had been shot. He was detective Sergeant Hoey whom I'd often seen at S.F. meetings. He was a smart-looking fellow of thirty, flashily dressed. Engaged in a race for promotion with Detective Sergeants Smyth and Bruton (not to be confused with Barton), he now met his end.[21]

About that time a policeman had been killed in County Tipperary. The reaction to his death must have reflected on public opinion on the recent killings carried out in Dublin. In a passionate outburst, a parish priest demanded:

Who has authorised a small band of unknown, ignorant persons to meet in secret and decide that the life of a fellow human being may be taken lawfully.... The Irish people will not approve of bloodshed, and the freedom of martyred Ireland will not be achieved by midnight assassinations.[22]

This concern regarding public opinion saved the life of Detective Sergeant Bruton. The G. Man was very aware that his life was at risk. He was very cautious in his detective work, never venturing outside the Castle unless at night and with a strong back-up of soldiers. Irish Intelligence desperately wanted him out of the way. The only reasonable opportunity of catching him off guard was when he left the Castle to attend early Sunday Mass at Clarendon Street Church. Tom Keogh and Vinnie Byrnes were allocated the task of shooting him. Cautious as he was, Bruton had a group of minders to escort him to and from the church. Any attempt at assassination on the street would have led to a blood bath. Keogh decided that, as Bruton's escort left him at the church, he would follow the G. Man inside, where he would shoot him. Hearing of the new plan, Collins was horrified. Such a murder would bring down the wrath not only of the Church authorities but also of every decent, civilized man and woman—not only in Ireland but also across the world. Bruton survived the war, but as Squad man Bernie Byrne relates, "fate finally intervened and he finished his career as an inmate of Portrane Mental Hospital."

Soon after Hoey's death, the G Men made a series of raids in Dublin, looking for Michael Collins. In one, a raid on the Sinn Fein offices at 6, Harcourt Street, a mixed party of G Men and military were led by the newly promoted Inspector Neil McFeely. He was there on the orders of Inspector Love, who was in charge of political duties. McFeely had a list of names of people to be arrested. Curiously, Michael Collins's name was not on that list. No one thought for one moment that he would be there. In a room upstairs, Collins, Diamuid Hegarty, Fintan Murphy, Jenny Mason and Eveleen Lawless were at work. They heard the noise downstairs. It was a raid. Lawless clearly remembered the incident:

> We had contemplated every possibility of escape for Mick whom we thought they were looking for, as it had been published that there was a large reward for anyone who helped to find him. There was no means of escape however, as the military had occupied the narrow entrance in the back as well as the front. Mick said, "We are caught like rats in a trap and there's no escape. He remained seated at his desk, quite calm and collected until they came in."[23]

McFeely entered the room. He went round searching the different desks. Collins got up, and sat on the edge of his desk, almost defiantly. He was sure that he was at the point of being arrested and that the policeman was toying with him. But McFeely did not know Collins, and he evidently believed that someone working up there could not be anyone of any significance. He walked over to the desk where Collins was working and picked up a file of papers and began reading them. Collins seized the initiative. He snatched the file from McFeely and threw it on the fire. Then turning to the G. Man, he said, "What sort of a legacy will you leave to your family, looking for blood money. Could you not find some honest work?" This completely threw McFeely. Unsure of himself and not used to being spoken to in such a manner, he turned and left the room.

The raid did have its success, however. Ernest Blythe was discovered hiding in a cupboard and led away with another prisoner. Triumphant, the police proceeded down the stairs but only momentarily. McFeely must have said something to his boss. A group of G Men, led by Inspector Love, dashed back up the stairs, but Collins had made good his escape up to the top of the building. Love and his men entered the room. He knew what Collins looked like. Love briefly scanned the occupants, then left without questioning anybody.

Still withering under the personal attack, McFeely later complained to a colleague. Broy was present to hear what he said and playfully reported to Collins that evening:

> "He met a very determined young man, a clerk, in 6, Harcourt St., and if they are all as extreme as he is there is plenty of trouble coming." I told this to Mick, making it "junior clerk." Mick was highly amused.[24]

The problem of discovery was also one faced by the members of The Squad after a "job." Bill Stapleton emphasized the precautions they took:

> ...all of us carried fictitious papers of one sort or another.... Each man was left to his own devices to have whatever paper or story to suit himself and thus enable him to answer questions without hesitation if held up by the enemy and searched. It was no uncommon thing for the members of the Squad, having safely disposed of their guns, to be held up by the enemy advancing on the site of a recent execution. I was held up on several such occasions and I posed as a house-painter. I had a lot of house-painters' old Union cards and a few letters addressed to me as "T. Smith." I knew a lot of people in the house-building and painting line, as my father was a small building contractor, and I found it easy, if cross-examined, to discuss and explain my assumed trade in detail. Another member of the Squad was a cabinet maker, and Charles Dalton, Intelligence Officer, who had been a clerk, posed as a law student.[25]

A month later, on October 19, 1919, Constable Downing was shot and killed in Dublin. There is no mention in the witness statements of The Squad members as to who was responsible and why he was shot, other than that he was a G. Man.

Detective Sergeant Wharton was the next G. Man to be targeted for assassination. His assailants were Paddy Daly and Joe Leonard. On November 10th, the two men, having received an Intelligence report, set off to intercept him in Harcourt Street. Failing to find him, the two Squad men spent some time wandering around College Street but in the end gave up. Leonard wandered off to catch a tram home to Ranelagh. Walking away, with the intention of going home himself, Daly then saw Wharton walking up Grafton Street with three other detectives. He followed them as far as Harcourt Street, on the other side of St. Stephen's Green. With a good idea of Wharton's beat, Daly, who was unarmed, dashed off to find Leonard. The two men returned and met up with the detectives on the corner of Cuffe Street, on the western side of the Green. Daly recognized one of the three detectives as working for Irish Intelligence. Daly now had a gun:

> I fired at Wharton. The other detective turned around but seemed to make very little effort to draw a gun. I discovered then that the parabellum I had was choked and I could not fire the second shot. I kept my eyes on the other three detectives as we made for Cuffe Street, and I noticed that the friendly detective walked between me and the other two detectives. I saw the gun in his hand but I did not hear him fire it. I think he tried to get between the other detectives and myself in order to prevent them firing.[26]

Though he had fallen to the ground, Wharton was only wounded. The bullet hit him in the back of the right shoulder, passed through the right lung, and exited in the front, carrying on to strike a glancing blow on the scalp of a young female student, Gertrude O'Hanlon. Joe Leonard, the other participating Squad man, makes little of the episode other than to make this enigmatic comment:

> This action was carried out by two men with only one weapon between them and this wonderful machine got jammed on the first shot, when it became evident that hasty leg movement would be called for and a few blocks away from there would make a wonderful difference.[27]

Upon recovering, Wharton very wisely retired from the police force.

About this time, many of the Sinn Fein departments removed to larger premises at 76, Harcourt Street. The comings and goings of so many people soon drew the attention of G. Department. Early on the morning of November 11, 1919, soon after the offices were opened, a number of T.D.s arrived for a meeting connected with Dail business. These members of the Irish parliament were meeting quite openly as a way of asserting their right to meet as a government and to legislate for the people of Ireland—in open defiance of the British Government, which had declared the Dail to be an illegal institution.

Suddenly the building was surrounded by a large party of G Men and military. They dashed into the building, arresting the T.D.s and all male members of staff. Collins was in his office upstairs. Hearing the raiders coming in, Diamuid Hegarty dashed upstairs to warn Collins. Downstairs, aware that Collins was on the premises, the staff did their best to delay the political police. By a well-practiced drill, Collins escaped through a skylight and onto the roof, crossing a number of premises before reaching the Standard Hotel, then dropping down onto an upstairs landing and escaping. For greater safety, Collins thereafter opened a new office at 5, Mespil Road, on the other side of St. Stephen's Green, taking a secretary, Jenny Mason, with him.

In November 1919, Volunteer Vinnie Byrne, who had been out in 1916, was invited down to Mick McDonnell's home. When he arrived, he found fellow F Company Volunteers James Slattery and Tom Keogh there. After the preliminaries, McDonnell came to the point:

> "Would you shoot a man, Byrne?" I replied, "It's all according to who he was." He said, "What about Johnnie Barton?" "Oh," I said, "I wouldn't mind"— as he had raided my house. So Mick said, "That settles it. You may have a chance." He told me to come along the following evening to College Green at about 5.30 or 6 o'clock. Jimmy Slattery and myself worked together at the cabinet-making in Anthony Mackay's "The Irish Woodworkers," No.3, Crow Street. Jimmy said to me, "You had better bring in your gun after dinner," which I did.[28]

Barton was a notorious G. Man. He had helped to identify the defeated leaders of the Easter Rising, pulling them out from the dejected prisoners on the green sward before the Rotunda. He had also tried to make informers of some of the younger Volunteers. In short, he had made himself "obnoxious to the Volunteers." Bernard Byrne, "Barney," a younger brother of Joe Byrne, imprisoned after the Easter Rising, was regularly visited in his home by Barton and another G. Man, Detective Gibney:

> It was not unusual even as early as 1917 to have what might be termed weekly unofficial visits from these two detectives. They invariably timed their arrival for about midnight. The family were always very civil, one might almost say courteous, to them, invariably inviting them to partake of whatever was going in line of supper, but the two detectives were equally steadfast in their refusal to partake of same.
>
> Barton apparently concluded that because of my youth I would be a useful person to cultivate, hoping thereby to derive some information which would bring him closer contact with [Michael] Collins.[29]

On November 30, 1919, after finishing work for the day, Byrne and Slattery met up with Mick McDonnell and Tom Keogh. From previous observations McDonnell knew that Barton regularly walked a certain route around south Dublin during the evening. At 5:30 p.m. he would be somewhere along Grafton Street, walking up to St. Stephen's Green. Byrne and Slattery set off. Within a short time, Byrne spotted him:

> "There he is on the far side of the street." We followed him along up Grafton St. He was walking on the left-hand side, and we were on the right. Somehow I think he had second sight, for, from time we had seen him, he would just walk a few paces and, if possible, look into a mirror in the shop windows and then give a quick glance across to the right hand side. Perhaps he was not looking across at us, but somehow that was the impression both Jimmy and myself got. We tracked him up to the top of Grafton St. where he stopped for a few moments looking into a bookshop, then crossed the road and started walking down Grafton St. carrying out the same actions as he had done on his way up. We kept a fair distance behind him, at the same time keeping him under cover, until we came nearly to the bottom of Grafton St. when he vanished as if into thin air. I said to Jim, "Oh, we have lost him." We carried on to the corner of College Green. When we looked back, Barton appeared coming into the hallway. He crossed the street at the narrow part over to Trinity College side.[30]

At this point, the two Volunteers were rejoined by McDonnell and Keogh. The four followed Barton as he walked along by the railings of Trinity College. This was a busy road junction, and at a time when most finished work for the day, it was very crowded. Occasionally, when people crossed in front of them, they lost sight of Barton momentarily. Then he would reappear just in front of them. Now they were very close. He stopped at the curb in order to cross. Then they were upon him:

> Fire was opened on him. He went down on his side, falling to the right slightly. Then he turned towards the left and raised himself a little on his right knee and said, "Oh, God, what did I do to deserve this?" With that, he pulled his gun and fired up College St. I cannot say how, or in what direction, the remainder of my party or the other party went. Mick McDonnell and myself cleared up College St. on the right hand side and, as we came to the corner of College St. and Westmoreland St. a peeler tried to stop Mick. I drew my gun and let a shout at him. What I said, I do not know; but we got round the corner, and so to safety.[31]

Detective William Gibney, who often worked with Barton, was apparently not happy with political work. Nor was he happy with the prospect of being killed by the IRA. One day Barney Byrne was proceeding along Great Brunswick Street along with Tom Keogh. Each of them was transporting a number of handguns to a new arms dump. Byrne tells what happened next:

> We were about half-way across the road and directly opposite College Street police station when four Auxiliaries emerged from that building. They saw us and had evidently just determined that we were likely suspects when Gibney

appeared immediately behind them, apparently in their company and presumably having been called upon to act as guide or some such capacity. As soon as I saw Gibney I shouted to him, "Hullo Bill, any chance of getting out of here without being held up all day?" and he immediately replied, "If you are not afraid to walk along with us everything will be O.K." We walked down by the Royal, Gibney keeping Keogh and myself behind the three Auxiliaries. Then Gibney said to the Auxiliaries, "You go to your right here and I'll see these lads past the corner." He was as good as his word, but when he got Keogh and I away from the immediate vicinity of the three Auxiliaries his language was anything but civil and certainly not fit for recording. My association with Gibney thus served a good purpose, because were it not for his lucky intervention on that occasion both Tom Keogh and myself would have been taken by the Auxiliaries, complete with our arms.[32]

As a consequence of this, and other backtracking of his political work, Gibney was never targeted for assassination. Indeed, he was rewarded. With the establishment of the Irish Free State, he was promoted to the rank of sergeant in the new police force, the Garda, for which he was duly grateful.

G. Man Eamon Broy, who was working for Irish Intelligence, was mistakenly identified for assassination. It was the custom for Broy, as part of his duties, to go and pay local suppliers for produce provided for the Departmental mess. One day a member of the Volunteers was approached by a van man who worked for Byrne's the butchers at 91, Camden Street. Broy himself tells the story:

This van man went to a Volunteer he knew and said, "Don't youse Volunteers want to shoot G Men?" On the Volunteer replying in the affirmative he said, "Well, there's one comes at 4 o'clock every Thursday to pay the ould lad I work for and there should not be much difficulty in shooting him." I was the man referred to. So, in due course, the matter reached the local Volunteer Intelligence Officer, thence the Battalion Commandant, probably the Brigadier, and finally, the Director of Intelligence, Michael Collins himself, who ordered, "No action without my prior sanction!"

Shortly after, when I met Michael, he rubbed his hand over his mouth, a sure sign of something that amused him, and said, "I see where you pay your butcher very promptly." Then he told me the whole story, which duly gratified his never failing love of anything humorous.[33]

In December 1919, Detective Constable Walshe, a clerk in G. Division, was fired upon, but escaped.

Cardinal Logue, the Catholic Primate of All Ireland, felt compelled to speak out formally against the long sequence of killings in Dublin and elsewhere:

Holy Ireland, the land of St. Patrick, shall never be regenerated by deeds of blood or raised up by the hand of the midnight assassin.... It is hard to believe that the intelligent and reasonable members of any Christian political party could sanction or sympathize with crime.... Among the body of the people those crimes inspire horror, contempt and reprobation. Their sympathies are with the unfortunate and innocent victims, not with the cowardly assassins.[34]

Naturally, his comments had an effect on members of The Squad. They were all practicing Roman Catholics. To be thus condemned was not taken lightly. There were doubts as to the righteousness of their actions. Their only consolation was that in their doing wrong, they were overcoming a greater wrong, the occupation and exploitation of Ireland by a foreign nation. If the hierarchy of the Church condemned them, surprisingly, many of the younger clergy were very supportive, and this was reassuring.

Even as Cardinal Logue was preparing his letter to the Faithful on December 19, a mixed party of Volunteers and Squad members were preparing their most daring assassination attempt to date—on no less a person than the Viceroy, Lord French himself. On the previous evening, Vinnie Byrne was in the Sean Connolly Sinn Fein Club in North Summer Street, just off the North Circular Road. There were a number of members sitting around the fire chatting. One of their number, Paddy Sharkey, a member of E Company, 2nd Battalion, got up to leave. It was about 9 p.m. Byrne asked him, "What's your hurry? Have you a date or something?"

"Oh, nothing like that," he answered, "I have got to get the father's basket ready." It was a puzzling response, and Byrne was intrigued. Sharkey told him that the basket was for his father who was a guard on the railway that was going down to Roscommon, "to bring ould French back to Dublin tomorrow morning."

Here was an opportunity not to be missed. Byrne asked him what time his father would be back in Dublin. The response was, about eleven or twelve o'clock. Sharkey made his way home. Byrne made his way to Mick McDonnell's house in Richmond Crescent. McDonnell needed time to prepare. He dismissed Byrne and told him to report back about ten o'clock in the morning.

The next morning Vinnie Byrne reported to Mick McDonnell as ordered. There were a number of men present, including Paddy Daly, Joe Leonard, Tom Keogh and Martin Savage. There was also a group of men Byrne did not know. McDonnell introduced them. They were Dan Breen, Seumas Robinson, Sean Treacy and Sean Hogan—the "Soloheadbeg Gang," as the British authorities were now calling them.[35] Armed with handguns and grenades, and with McDonnell in charge, the men cycled up to Ashtown. It was a quiet little hamlet, and in order not to raise suspicion, they split up into three groups and went into Kelly's pub.

4. Eliminating the G Men

At the time most of them did not drink alcohol. They ordered mineral waters as they waited. Kelly's was a noted handball house, with a court out back. To allay suspicion, they pretended to be rival handballers and challenged one another to a game on the following Sunday. McDonnell had a quiet word with Byrne and instructed him to cycle over to the station and see if there was any sign of a train. He had got about one hundred yards down the road when he was overtaken by a fleet of cars. They were to be French's military escort heading up towards the railway station to collect him. Byrne wheeled around and rode back to Kelly's.

The three teams went to their agreed ambush sites. Daly, Leonard, Treacy, Robinson and Hogan went into the back yard of the pub and into the field where they took up a position overlooking the road. The second group took up positions on the corner of the main Navan Road, and the road leading to the station. McDonnell, Dan Breen and Tom Keogh rushed into the yard and started to pull a big farm cart out onto the road, but it got stuck in the side ditch. To complicate matters, an inspector and constable arrived to hold up traffic and ensure that French's party had right of way. The inspector went off, leaving the constable standing in the middle of the road to direct traffic.

Then they heard the four cars approaching. The general consensus was that French would be travelling in the second car. As the cars approached the ambush site, the IRA opened rapid fire and threw their grenades. The first car was a dark blue one. Sitting beside the driver was Detective Sergeant Nicholas Halley, who opened fire in response. As the car cleared the corner, Byrne lobbed a grenade, which hit the back of the car and exploded. The second car passed by the men behind the hedge. It was an enclosed car, khaki green in color. The third car was a box Ford with a canvas roof, and the fourth was an open Sunbeam car. It was manned by two soldiers, a driver and a sergeant who was lying across the back of the car firing from a rifle. Byrne described the brief, but bloody, combat, as the fourth car moved past them at speed:

> Where we were standing, we were an open target for them. In fact you could hear the bullets whizzing by, finding a billet in the wall behind us. As this car was disappearing around the bend of the road leading to the Ashtown gate of the Phoenix Park, I heard Martin Savage saying something, and it sounded like this, "Oh lads. I am hit." The next moment, he was dead, lying on the road.
>
> All this time, Dan Breen, who had been hit in the leg, did not notice it. Then he said, "I am hit in the leg." As we had only bicycles, we could not get Martin Savage's dead body away. The next thing was we were told to get back into town and to travel in twos. I was about to get away, when I was told to act rearguard action to Dan Breen who, after mounting his bicycle, had to lean on Paddy Daly's shoulder.[36]

Lord French was travelling in the first car. Though badly shaken, he was unhurt. He was less than complimentary towards the Dublin Metropolitan Police, who were responsible for his security. The sheer audacity of the attack on French forced change in the Castle administration. Assistant Commissioner Fergus Quinn was retired and replaced by Dennis Barrett.

The young Volunteer Charles Dalton, who was only sixteen years old, espied a Volunteer from another area cycling in his neighborhood. He thought it was curious. Then it became all too clear when he met a newsboy shouting "Stop Press." Dalton bought a copy of the newspaper. It was all about the attack on Lord French at Ashtown. The Volunteer had obviously been part of the ambush party. Impressionable, and perhaps not having the common sense to know that such activities were dangerous, Dalton set about joining those engaged in such special work. Sometime later Dalton approached the Volunteer, and after some temerity, announced that he would like to join him in his unit. The other man made no promises but said that he would see what he could do. Checks were obviously made, and one evening soon after, Dalton was invited to visit the home of the quartermaster of his battalion, Mick MacDonald. He gave him an address to which he was invited to attend the next morning. Arriving punctually, Dalton found:

> There met several men who were present, and now for the first time I met, to speak to, the famous Squad who worked under Dick McKee and Michael Collins, and whose achievements never failed to produce "Stop Press" editions.
>
> They were having breakfast, with home-made bread, and they asked me to join them, which I did with the greatest pleasure. I could hardly believe it possible that I was sitting at the same table with such fearless men, whom I had long admired, though till now I had never met them, or known them by name.

Young Dalton joined The Squad and took part in a number of their missions. One that must have pleased him was the robbery of Dublin Castle mail. He became part of that evening's "Stop Press–Sensational Coup. Robbery of Castle Mails." He relates:

> There followed detailed descriptions by "eye-witnesses" which greatly surprised me as they were quite erroneous. In the trams there was no other conversation. I could hear scraps of the news exchanged. "French's mail seized!" "A wonderful coup!" "Such remarkable intelligence work!" And here followed an imaginary story, so that I had trouble not to interrupt and tell them what lies they were talking.
>
> But we had to keep our mouths sealed. Not a word could we drop even to our dearest friends. Silence and success went hand in hand.[37]

4. Eliminating the G Men

With Lord French's angry response to the lack of security provided for him, Dublin Castle sent for a capable Belfast police inspector by the name of W.C. Forbes Redmond. He was appointed Second Assistant Commissioner, responsible for G. Division. His instructions were to "take care of political crime." Redmond brought with him his own team of detectives from northern Ireland. They were plain-clothed and lived about the city as civilians. Dave Neligan recorded his first meeting with Redmond:

> All the G-men were ordered to parade one night in November 1919, in Brunswick Street. We were addressed by Redmond. He was a neatly-built man of about forty, nattily dressed and wearing a bowler. He looked more like a stockbroker than a policeman. He gave us a pep talk. It was extraordinary, he said, that we, who knew Dublin so well, could not catch Michael Collins, whereas a man who had only just arrived from England had managed to meet him more than once.[38]

This set alarm bells ringing amongst the G Men present who were working for Collins. Amongst them was James McNamara, whom Redmond had selected as his guide around Dublin. Liam Tobin, deputy head of Irish Intelligence, was informed of what had been said. He quickly deduced who the British agent was. As the suspected spy was temporarily in England, little could be done until his return. Tobin now turned his attention as to what was to be done about Redmond. He needed a photograph of Redmond for identification purposes. Frank Thornton was sent up to Belfast to obtain one:

> I met Sean Heuston who introduced me to a Sergeant McCarthy from Kerry who was stationed at Chichester Street Police Barracks of the RIC in Belfast. By arrangement, I went to the Barracks the following evening as a cousin of his from the country and stayed the night in the Barracks with him. The object of the visit was to secure a photograph of Redmond. On this particular night the Police Amateur Boxing Championships were taking place at the Ulster Hall and practically all the Police Force off duty were in attendance, including the District Inspector, in whose office was a photograph of Redmond. Getting my direction from McCarthy I had no trouble in slipping into the D.I.'s office and annexing the photograph, which I brought back to Dublin the following day.[39]

Now knowing what Redmond looked like, a team from The Squad, led by Mick McDonnell, set out to kill him. Collins had given the order to "oggs him." Their first attempt was on January 30, 1920. Redmond left Dublin Castle each evening between 5:30 and 6 p.m. He usually proceeded along Dame Street to the Dublin Bread Company restaurant for his evening meal. The restaurant was situated on the right-hand side looking towards College Green, just facing Fownes Street. The team followed on behind but were not quick enough. Redmond entered the restaurant. McDonnell and his men waited for two hours, but Redmond did not reappear. Taking precautions, he had apparently left by a back door. Redmond was security minded. As insurance, he also wore a bullet-proof waistcoat.

Later that same night, Redmond was involved in the stakeout at a Dublin house in what proved a futile vigil in his search for Collins. The Castle authorities were offering a reward of £10,000 for information leading to his conviction or death. Among those present that night was Detective MacNamara, one of Collins's men in G. Section.

Meanwhile, The Squad were planning their own execution. IRA Intelligence Officer Joseph Dolan, who was in the assassination team, recorded:

> We were after Redmond for about a fortnight, trying to get him on his way from the Castle to the Standard Hotel. We could have got him in the morning on his way to the Castle from the Standard, but at that period Collins did not want any daylight shootings. I used to be watching for him outside the Castle. I had his description and more or less knew him. He was a tall man and used to wear a hard hat and a black coat with a black velvet collar. He had two overcoats; the second was a grey one. He was easily identified and could not be mistaken on the street.
>
> One evening I saw Redmond coming down from the Castle but he turned back and went in again. Paddy Daly, Tom Keogh, Vinny Byrne and myself were waiting and Redmond came out again. Tom Keogh turned to Vinny Byrne and myself and told us to cover them off. Redmond went straight up Dame street, Grafton Street and Harcourt Street, and we followed him. Just as he came as far as Montague Street Paddy Daly pulled out his revolver and shot him under the ear and Tom Keogh pulled out his revolver and shot him in the back. Daly and Kehoe carried out the execution, and Byrne and myself acted as a covering party.[40]

With Redmond dead, his leaderless team returned to Belfast. During February 1920, the killing of the G Men ruthlessly continued. Detective Constable Walshe was again targeted. Out on patrol with Detective Constable Dunleavy, the two policemen came under sustained fire. This time Walshe was killed, and Dunleavy was wounded.

Collins was now faced with a case of treachery, a case that would have seen him being murdered in his own county of Cork. The instigator was a man to whom Collins had shown kindness when he came to him for help. His name was Henry Quinlisk. Eveleen Lawless was present when the story came to a crisis. It was November 1919:

> One evening about 6, when we were preparing to leave the office [at 46, Harcourt Street], Mick had come in about 5 that evening—Bob Conlon

4. Eliminating the G Men

answered a ring at the door and found a man inquiring for Mick. Bob went upstairs to inquire whether Mick would see him, leaving the man, who was a doubtful looking character, standing on the steps outside. I had a glance at the man. He was of medium height, looking fairish in complexion—not in any way impressive or good looking in appearance—rather mean-looking with shifty eyes. He looked like a "toucher." He said in an impudent kind of way: "I want to see Mick." Contrary to advice and our expectations, Mick said he would come down and see him. He knew who he was—an ex-British soldier whom he suspected of double-crossing.... Mick brought him into the hall and told him what he thought of him. He gave him the chance to clear out before appropriate action would be taken, adding "If you don't get out quick, I'll kick you down the steps."[41]

Henry Quinlisk was a former corporal in the Royal Irish Regiment, who, as a German prisoner of war, had enrolled in Casement's Brigade. Upon his return to Ireland Collins not only gave him money to support himself, but also paid for a new suit. Quinlisk kept coming back for more hand-outs until, in the end, Collins lost his temper with him. In anger, Quinlisk offered to betray Collins. He decided to write to the authorities in Dublin Castle offering to tell "all I know" of Sinn Fein and of "that scoundrel Michael Collins" who had "treated me scurvily." Quinlisk was invited to G. Division headquarters in Brunswick Street for an interview. His statement was given to Eamon Broy to type up. He sent a copy to Michael Collins. Before it reached him, however, the police staged a raid on the Harcourt Street offices from which Collins was known to operate. Eveleen Lawless continues:

> The following evening at about the same time, when there was no one in the office except myself, who had remained to fill in cheques that had already been signed by Mick Collins, and Sean Hyde, who had come in with Loan Certificates for registration, Tom Cullen arrived, saying he had imitated the "big fellow's" walk coming across from the lane into Harcourt St. as they suspected there would be a watch placed by the British near the house at the same hour as Mick had been in the office the day before. This was intended to be a test of the ex-British soldier whom Tom said he had seen standing about the Standard Hotel corner.
> Sure enough, before 10 minutes had elapsed, the cars drove up and the military who were accompanied by Inspector McFeely started hammering at the door. I opened it and McFeely asked me in a very truculent way where was Mick Collins. I replied that I did not know.

A search was made of the premises but to no avail. The next day when told of the raid Collins put it down to chance circumstance. Then he received the report from Broy. In the meantime, Quinlisk approached Arthur Griffith, asking if he knew where Michael Collins was. Feeling uneasy over the encounter, Griffith went to see Collins. He decided that

Quinlisk had become too dangerous, but first of all, he wanted proof of his treachery. In a round-about way, Quinlisk discovered that Collins would be at the Wren's Hotel, Cork, on a certain day. As a consequence, a coded message was sent from Dublin Castle to the RIC District Inspector in Cork to that effect. Liam Archer, a Post Office telegraphist working for Irish Intelligence intercepted it:

> I abstracted a copy of a lengthy cipher message from Inspector General RIC to Co. Inspector, Cork. On leaving the office, I went to the Keating Branch and there started to decipher it. While at this Sean O'Muirthuile joined me. The message informed the Co. Inspector that Collins would be in a hotel in Cork the following night, that he would probably be armed, was dangerous, and should be captured dead or alive. When O'Muirthuile saw this he got very excited and then told me that a man named Quinlisk had got in touch with Collins and had almost convinced him of his sincerity. O'Muirthuile was not convinced and induced Collins to set a trap for him by telling him he was going to Cork and where he would stay.... Later that night Collins came to the Keating Branch and when he read the message he commented: "That ... has signed his death warrant."[42]

The avaricious Quinlisk traveled to Cork himself, to be on hand to collect the £10,000 reward. Irish intelligence in Cork were informed by Dublin. Quinlisk was picked up by them and shot. His dead body was found the next day, February 18, 1920, lying in a ditch.

In March 1920, Michael Collins formed a new Squad to implement the work of the Intelligence Department. He took over the old Squad, formerly under the control of Dick McKee, and introduced his own personnel into what became known as the "Official" Squad. Mick McDonnell was replaced by Collins's own nominee, Paddy Daly, a decision not universally approved of amongst the old Squad members. The new team were told that they were now operating directly under Collins and were solely responsible to him, and him alone.

Detective Constable Henry Kells, a plainclothes G. Man, was killed on April 14th. Kells had been a member of the DMP for twenty years but only a member of the G. Division for a few months. In is short period of time, he had come to the attention of Irish Intelligence for his pursuit of prominent Republicans. On the morning of his death there was a General Strike in Dublin. His assailants, led by Paddy Daly, had traced him to his home at 7, Pleasants Street, a five-minute walk away from St. Stephen's Green. On the day of his assassination, the day of the strike, there were no trams running. Daly reckoned that he would make his way to work walking along Camden Street. On the way, the three-man team picked up a fourth man, Hugo MacNeill, the nephew of Eoin MacNeill, the first president of the Irish Volunteers. With four men, Daly split his team into two groups of two each, with Joe Leonard leading the second group. Leonard and MacNeill found Kells. There were two shots, and another G. Man was dead. A short time later Daly saw MacNeill sauntering down Pleasants Street and asked about the shooting. "Kells is up there if you want him," MacNeill responded, "on the footpath." A passing car stopped to take Kells to Meath Hospital, but he was dead upon arrival. In his Witness Statement, dictated some thirty years later, Leonard is almost flippant in his account of Kells' death: "Constable Kells left off all earthly worries about this time—not lost but gone before." His comment was callous. The Squad had become inured to killing.

A week later, on April 20, Detective Constable Laurence Dalton, who had just been transferred to G. Division, was assassinated. Dalton was a popular figure amongst his fellow police officers. David Neligan described him:

> Dalton was also from West Limerick and a stout man of about thirty. A charming fellow of mild disposition, he never raised a finger against Sinn Fein, except for one incident. G Men went to the house of a well-known Sinn Feiner named J.J. Walsh in Dublin to arrest him. Dalton was sent to the rear. Walsh ran out of the back door and tried to persuade Dalton to let him go, but he would not.[43]

His intransigence was to cost him his life. A team from The Squad was sent after him. Liam Tobin of Irish Intelligence pointed him out to members of the team the evening before he was shot. The assassination team the following day comprised Mick McDonnell in charge, Tom Keogh and Jim Slattery, with Vinnie Byrnes and Joe Dolan providing cover. At about 12.30 on the afternoon of April 20, Dalton, accompanied by Detective Constable Robert Spencer, made his way up to Broadstone Station to meet the 1:10 p.m. train from the west. Dalton's task was to watch the incoming trains and arrest known IRA men from Mayo and Galway. As the two policemen crossed Mountjoy Street and approached the Black Church in Dorset Street, the three-man Squad team struck. Dalton was shot by Slattery and Keogh. Though he wore a steel waistcoat, it was not enough to protect him. He was shot in the head. Badly wounded, he was taken to the Mater Hospital, where he died at 3:00 p.m.

Detective Sergeant Denis Coffey was a G. Man of long standing. He was one of those G Men that Collins saw picking out the leaders of the Rising. Coffey knew many of the older Volunteers by sight. Perhaps out of revenge for his past activity, and certainly because he presented a current danger, his name was put forward for assassination. Intelligence discovered his home address. It was Kenmare Parade, off the North Circular Road. Vinnie Byrne, who was one of the back-up team, now tells the story:

The two men detailed to carry out the operation were stationed at the corner. We had not very long to wait when Coffey and his escort appeared, coming down Kenmare Parade. As the men on the corner were about to open fire, two women came over, stood very close to them and asked them something about the Salvation Army. In the meantime, Coffey and his escort got away up the N.C. Road.[44]

The following day The Squad tried again, and again Coffey was lucky. Word arrived that he was patrolling around the Dame Street area. At 5:30 p.m. the team located him in St. Andrew's Street. They followed him as he turned the corner into Trinity Street. When they turned the corner, there was no sign of him. He had disappeared completely. It may be that he became aware of his pursuers. Colleague Denis Neligan, who knew Coffey as a likable man, warned him that he had overheard a conversation in a public house that he, Coffey, was to be killed the next day. For his own safety Coffey and his family were moved into the greater safety of Dublin Castle.

On May 8, 1920, Detective Sergeant Richard Revelle was shot at seven times near his home. Though wounded, he escaped. Revelle worked out of an office in Dublin Castle. His hours of working, and patrolling, were both at irregular times. The only certain chance of killing him was as he left his home, situated along the first road on the left as one leaves the city by the Phibsborough Road. Vinnie Byrne was instructed to follow him and note down the details. On the day before the intended assassination Byrne waited for his target, but Byrne was new to the game. Lavelle, for his part, was a professional:

> On the morning before he was shot, I arrived at Phibsboro' Road at 9 a.m., unarmed, and took up a position about fifty yards from Connaught St. on the right-hand side coming from the city. I was standing there, I would say, about half an hour, when he came out of Connaught St. I tried to look as innocent as I could. He walked down Phibsboro Road towards the city on the right-hand side. As he came right opposite to me, he stopped and stared very hard over at me. Whether I showed any signs of watching him, I did not know. He moved off at a smart pace. I let him have a few yards start on me and then I commenced to follow him. He disappeared in a flash; and then I saw him standing behind a tramway standard and looking towards me. I halted and pretended to look at my watch. Looking up and down the road he moved off again. I made no further attempt to follow him, as I could see that he had me under cover. The next thing, he went over to the policeman, who was on point duty at Phibsboro' and had a conversation with him. I said to myself, "It's about time I made myself scarce." I boarded a tram going towards Glasnevin, got off it at Lindsay Road and proceeded to Mick McDonnell's house to make my report.[45]

With Mick McDonnell was Intelligence chief Liam Tobin. The choice now facing them was to either postpone the shooting for a week or so or to go ahead and do it the following morning. They decided to risk it and do it the next day, May 8th. The Squad took up their positions the next morning along the Phibsborough Road. They did not have to wait long. Revelle appeared riding a bicycle. The two men tasked with shooting the G. Man were standing about twenty-five yards away from Connaught Street, facing the oncoming traffic. As Revelle approached to within a few feet of them, they stepped out onto the road and began firing. Revelle was hit, and he and the bicycle veered across the road before finally careering over. Convinced that he was dead—they had pumped five bullets into his body—The Squad men withdrew. Further down the road the policeman on point duty dashed up towards Connaught Street, revolver in hand. He saw Revelle's assailants disappear towards Cross Guns Bridge and set off after them. As he got to the flour mill near the bridge, he called out to the crowd who had gathered to stop the men. But they did not. As one of them said to the policeman, "Do you want us to get the same as the fellow got down there?"

Revelle did not die. He was wearing body armor. The impact of the bullets had knocked him off the bike, but save for a few grazes, he was safe. That evening he gave an interview to the press. Of his assailants he announced, "I would know one of them very well, as I had seen him the previous morning." Byrne was safe from identification, though. Revelle never left the Castle after that.

Perhaps emboldened by the presence of the Auxiliaries and the Black and Tans on the streets of Dublin, G Men in groups of four or five began patrolling the streets of Dublin once more in the autumn of 1920. The order went out to dispatch them. Dan Breen, now recovered from his wounds, took part in a number of Squad actions against them:

> During my stay in Dublin Sean Treacy and myself had many adventures in the company of Mick Collins' most trusted men, Liam Tobin and Tom Cullen. Special jobs were often assigned to the four of us by Collins. Liam and Tom were dare-devils and brave to a fault. Liam was ice-cool in a crisis, Tom was of an impetuous nature, a very fine character but a very bad shot.
>
> One night I was taken by Tobin and Cullen on a very urgent mission. They hoped to have the pleasure of an encounter with a particularly obnoxious "G" man. The plan was to decoy him along to Exchange Street. Cullen and I were instructed by Tobin to stand in the archway leading to the *Evening Mail* office. While we were there a big powerful man stopped under the arch to take shelter from a heavy shower and got into conversation with us chiefly about the weather. After a few minutes he looked furtively up and down the street. "I don't think it will clear at all. I'll be off," he said and made a hasty departure. Up came Tobin. "What delayed you?" we asked with impatience. "You promised to send along that 'G' man."

"Weren't you talking with him ten minutes!" he said in exasperation. But we had no clue as to the man's identity.[46]

There is an unattributed story of one of the last G Men to be assassinated, told in James Gleeson's account of Bloody Sunday:

> One of the leaders of the "G" Division was an IRA man. His commanding officer called him one day and said, "There is an IRA spy among us—I am convinced of it."
>
> "Well," said the spy, "it can only be you or I or one of the fifteen others—what shall we do about it?"
>
> "I have just had information," answered the Chief, "that the IRA leaders are meeting at a house in Merrion Square at twelve o'clock today. Now only you and I know, and only you and I will go and arrest them."
>
> The spy knew that his Chief's information was correct, and that Collins, Cathal Brugha and many of the other leaders would be at the house mentioned.
>
> The Chief told him to change his clothes and get his pistol and he remained with him as he did so. Then having arranged for reinforcements to be at hand the two men left the Castle.
>
> As they walked through the streets a shot rang out and the Chief dropped dead. His companion lay on the ground and "returned" the fire until his ammunition was gone, then he took the revolver from the dead body beside him and continued to fire that. Troops arrived on the scene, the body was removed and the spy returned to his duties. He said afterwards, "I was sorry I could not tell the Chief who the spy was before I had to shoot him."[47]

It became known that on Sunday mornings certain G Men went to mass as a group, either at St. Michael's or St. John's churches, not far from the Castle. In early October members of The Squad, supplemented by the Tipperary men—Breen, Treacy, Hogan and Robinson—and led by members of the Intelligence Department lay in wait. The took up positions in Essex Street outside the rear entrance to the church. A group of ten to twelve men approached. They were recognized as G Men. Then suddenly someone from Irish Intelligence arrived, and the mission was aborted. Amongst the group was Dave Neligan, one of Collins's men, who was acting as a minder. The next week the mission was also called off. News had been received that Terence McSwiney, on hunger strike in Brixton Prison, might well be released. Collins had decided that the killing of the G Men would jeopardize that opportunity. During the following week McSwiney died. The operation was back on, and on Sunday morning the team was back in place. Then, perhaps to their dismay, one of the newspaper boys who stood outside the church called out to them, "Misters! They're not here today!"[48] The team realized that they were now in danger themselves. If a young lad had identified them, so

4. Eliminating the G Men

also might others. The attempt was given up, and the remaining political G Men survived the war.

The assassination of the G Men was one of expediency. The killing of Captain Lea-Wilson was one of revenge. It was a retribution dating back to the end of the Easter Rising. Back in 1916, the defeated Republicans were assembled in Sackville Street (now O'Connell Street) and marched to the front of the Rotunda Hospital where they were made to sit down on the little grassy lawn before it. Four hundred prisoners were crowded together in the small place. Amongst them were nurses Julia Grenan and Winifred Carney, who squatted alongside Sean McDermott. With no sanitation provided, men, to their great embarrassment, had to relieve themselves on the grass, in the presence of the women. In the early hours, the junior officer on guard duty was relieved by the 31-year-old Anglo-Irishman, Captain Percival Lea-Wilson of the 5th Battalion Royal Irish Regiment. Volunteer prisoner Desmond Ryan later wrote of him:

> He strides around looking for looters and threatening to have us all shot and telling us not to smoke, not to stand up, and not to lie down and, if we want lavatories, use the [flower] beds provided and lie down in both. He roars madly at his own men and issues contradictory orders. Rushes at this man and shouting he'll have them shot. Strikes matches and holds them in the faces of the men and shouts, "Anyone want to see the animals?" He bends over Plunkett and snatches a document from his inner pocket: "Ah, his Will! He certainly knew what he was coming out to get!" He yells at [Tom] Clarke: "The old bastard is the Commander-in-Chief. He keeps a tobacco shop across the street. Nice general for your ------- army."[49]

Liam Tobin also observed Lea-Wilson:

> He wore a smoking cap with a fancy tassel hanging out of it. He kept walking round and round, stopping now and again to speak to his soldiers saying, "Whom do you consider worst, the Boche or the Sinn Feiners?" and of course they all answered that we were the worst. With the number of us lying in the small area of grass we were cramped for space, and it was damp and uncomfortable so that I got cramp in my legs. As Lea-Wilson was passing Piaras Beaslai said to him, "There's a young fellow here who is not well," explaining what was wrong and asking if I could stand up. Lea-Wilson said, "No let the so and so stay where he is." Those of us who wanted to relieve ourselves had to do so on the grass lying alongside our comrades; we had to use the place where we lay.[50]

Later Lea-Wilson selected some of the prisoners to humiliate. He had them stripped and searched. Amongst those whom he chose to humiliate was Tom Clarke. Eamon Dore, a Volunteer from Limerick, witnessed the cruelty:

The second incident I remember was seeing a British Army Captain, Lea-Wilson take Tom Clarke, Sean MacDiarmadha and Ned Daly and search them. Clarke had an old pre–Rising bullet wound in the elbow which healed partly, making it difficult to flex the elbow. Wilson, finding it difficult to take off Clarke's coat because of the stiffness, just forcibly straightened the arm and so reopened the wound, causing terrible pain. Not satisfied with this he stripped all three to the skin in the presence of us and, being broad daylight, in the presence of those nurses etc. looking out windows.[51]

Seeing the old man so badly mistreated, junior Volunteer officer Michael Collins swore to avenge the cruelty that had been shown to Clarke.

In June 1920, Irish Intelligence succeeded in tracking down Lea-Wilson. He had retired from the British Army and was then a District Inspector of Police at Gorey in county Wexford. He proved to be his own worst enemy. He came to the attention of IRA Intelligence:

Reports had been received in Enniscorthy of Lea Wilson's aggressive attitude towards people who were forced to remain on the street even under rain when frequent and unnecessary raids were carried out for the sake of upsetting the household.[52]

Early on the morning of June 15, members of The Squad and the Intelligence Department travelled down to Gorey. Previously, a member of the Intelligence Department had located their target. From their car they watched as Lea-Wilson approached. They pretended to be fixing a problem with their car; its bonnet was open. Lea-Wilson had emerged from the police station. He had bought a newspaper from the little shop by the railway station and was walking along the road reading it. He walked up towards the group of men. It was 9:30 a.m. A shot rang out, and Lea-Wilson was hit. He staggered on but was shot again. Then he fell to the ground. Two members of The Squad fired a further two bullets to the head, killing him. The bonnet to the car was closed, and the five men drove away. Frank Thornton, Deputy Assistant Director of Intelligence, in his Witness Statement gives a detached account of the shooting:

The shooting of Captain Lea Wilson was carried out by GHQ Intelligence personnel from Dublin, and Wilson was shot because of brutal treatment of IRA leaders during 1916, the treatment of Cumann na mBan prioners whom he herded with the men like sheep up on the Rotunda Gardens, and finally because of his renewed activity in the Gorey district in 1920.[53]

Curiously, no member of The Squad writes of having taken part in the shooting, and perhaps they did not. Edward Balfe, Acting O/C of Wexford Brigade of the IRA, ambiguously indicates that the senior officers of Irish Intelligence were involved:

15th June. Percival Lea Wilson, D.I., RIC, shot dead in Gorey under the direction of GHQ officers, viz: Frank Thornton and Liam Tobin. Joseph

McMahon and Jack Whelan also took part in the shooting and Liam O'Leary was one of the scouts.[54]

The elimination of the G. men—and out in the country the IRA's ruthless attacks upon the Royal Irish Constabulary—denied police forces the collection of political intelligence. By contrast, the Dublin Metropolitan Police, who were mostly unarmed and less widely employed on "political" duties, were left alone. This was a reality pointed out to the British Cabinet by the Chief Commissioner of the DMP:

> With regard to the moral effect of [IRA] outrages on the DMP ... on the whole force this was negligible, but ... in regard to the Political Section ... which consisted of ten men only, it was having an effect which was not surprising in view of the fact that out of this small number, two men had been killed, one dangerously wounded, and two had had attacks made upon them.[55]

Military Intelligence agreed with this summing up. The *Record of the Rebellion,* as drawn up by the Army dismissively declared, "G. Division ceased to affect the situation, and the force did little more than point duty during the years 1920–21."

5

Special Branch Strikes Back

At the opening of 1920 Michael Collins had achieved his objective. G. Department of the Dublin Metropolitan Police had been neutered. Five out of ten G Men were dead, and one who had narrowly escaped, sought safer work in England. The remainder were holed up within Dublin Castle, having ceased their political work. David Neligan, Collins's man in G. Department, recalled this atrophy:

> Often I was sent on duty with an elderly detective inspector and detective sergeant. They were supposed to be investigating the killing of Barton, Smyth and Hoey. They spent each day on a pub-crawl and did no investigating as they wanted to stay alive. They drank steadily from 10 a.m. until 6 p.m.—all whiskey—with an interval for lunch.[1]

In exasperation at the failure of British Intelligence, General French, the new Viceroy of Ireland, who had narrowly escaped an assassination attempt upon himself due to what he considered to be police incompetence, wrote to Lord Londonderry on January 3, 1920:

> Our Secret Service is simply non-existent. What masquerades for such a Service is nothing but a delusion and a snare. The DMP are absolutely demoralised, and the RIC will be in the same case very soon if we do not quickly set our house in order.[2]

The existing Intelligence Service in 1920, military and police, was headed by Major S.S. Hill Dillon, a British Army GHQ staff officer. He had replaced the wartime Coordinator of Intelligence, Major Ivon Price, in 1919. Hill Dillon cleared out Intelligence Officers who were mainly policemen and staffed his section with junior army officers who were sent for training in England. This new situation was beset by problems, as an intelligence report indicated:

> At first, intelligence officers were changed far too frequently. This was inevitable because suitable officers were not always selected. Once, however, a suitable officer is appointed and knows his area, he should not be changed

5. Special Branch Strikes Back

save in most exceptional circumstances and, even if his battalion is transferred to another station, it may be desirable for him to remain.[3]

This observation was endorsed by a subsequent police intelligence chief, Ormonde de l'EpeeWinter:

> The building up of an efficient Intelligence Service is not a task that can be accomplished in a day, a week or a month.... The ramifications of the Sinn Fein organisation were multiple and to create a service to counter these requires an intimate knowledge of their constitutions, methods and resources.... It is necessary to become saturated with the knowledge of the leading rebels' activities, personalities and histories. It follows, therefore, of necessity, that some delay occurred between the end of May, 1920, the formulation of the scheme and the bringing of that scheme into operation.[4]

Even when the intelligence services of the armed forces and police were in operation, and while there was frequent overlapping of intelligence, there was often little exchange of information. Each service jealously guarded its own interests. Throughout 1917 and 1918, Ivon Price had looked for links between Sinn Fein and the Germans in order to make mass arrests of Sinn Fein members and destroy opposition to conscription. In the process, he virtually ignored the military wing of Republicanism, the IRA, which he believed had been destroyed in 1916. Coming into the job, his successor Hill Dillon, was initially forced to rely upon the very same DMP and RIC men for information supplied to Price until he could get his men trained up. Precious time was wasted.

The whole thing was a shamble, as French had pointed out. Dillon and his advisors decided that a new service should be formed under the direction of the head of British Intelligence, Sir Basil Thomson, and be based in London. To his credit, Thomson was familiar with the state of Irish affairs. After the Easter Rising, he had compiled a report on the failure of British Intelligence in Ireland. Thomson, the son of an Archbishop of York, had been appointed Assistant Commissioner (Crime) in 1913 and in 1919 had become Director of Intelligence at the Home Office. He worked alongside Captain Vernon Kell of the military-based Secret Service Bureau, later to become MI5, which was responsible for counterespionage. Thomson also ran the Scotland Yard-based Special Branch, which was often used as the physical arm of the Secret Service.

Special (Irish) Branch, as it was formerly known, had been created in 1883 at the height of the Fenian dynamite campaign in Britain. Its men had originally been drawn from the Royal Irish Constabulary, with some of its men based permanently in England. Quite often, to the annoyance of many a Chief Constable, the Special Branch acted independently of the local police and were not above fabricating evidence.[5]

At the time, they were very knowledgeable concerning Irish affairs and had men imbedded within the various Nationalist groups. Now, in 1920, the Special Branch operated from new headquarters at Scotland House, directly opposite Scotland Yard. Its personnel were mainly English, and its new enemy was the rise of international communism. With the departure and retirement of so many of its old Irish policemen, a lot of knowledge was also lost. While Thomson could teach spy craft, knowledge of what was going on in Ireland would have to be relearned.

As early as December 1919, Lord French set up a secret committee to "place matters in Dublin and the country on a proper footing."[6] It consisted of the Chief Commissioner of the DMP, the Acting Inspector General of the RIC, the Assistant Under Secretary Sir John Taylor, and Alan Bell, a resident magistrate and former RIC intelligence officer who was experienced in political crime. They found that "an organized conspiracy of murder, outrage and intimidation has existed for some time past with the object of … rendering useless the Police Forces." An addendum was added to this that "Dublin City is the storm center and the mainspring of it all." The report recommended infiltrating IRA Intelligence through other Republican organizations:

> This might be speedily obtained [they believed] if an accredited agent, already closely connected with the organization in America were to come to this country and ingratiate himself with the extreme section here and learn their plans. Such a person should not be known to any member of the Police Forces in Ireland. He ought to be able to give … information which would lead to the capture of intending assassins and the breaking up of the criminal organization. It might also be possible to find men skilled in trades who could be sent to Dublin, being engaged for a regular salary, to ply their trade, join their appropriate Union and mix with the artisans who would be their fellow workers. Such men should be capable of gaining valuable information.[7]

The report further recommended

> …sending to Dublin members of the RIC, young active men of courage and determination, good shots and preferably men accustomed to city life. These men should be lodged in pairs in various localities in the City. Their presence should not be made known to either the DMP or the RIC. Having made themselves acquainted with the members of the "G" Division as regards their appearance they might very occasionally follow at a distance behind them so as to be ready to take action should anything occur…. We are inclined to think that the shooting of a few would-be assassins would have an excellent effect. Up to the present they have escaped with impunity. We think this should be tried as soon as possible.

Commander Mansfield George Smith-Cumming of MI1c was responsible for the training of these new agents. Under Sir Basil Thomson, he set up a school of espionage at the Cavalry Barracks at Hounslow, west London (now home to the 1st Battalion, Irish Guards). Some 60–80 serving and demobilized ex-army officers were recruited for training in January 1920. Half that number, about 40, were eventually chosen for work in Ireland. In addition, Thomson also organized a unit of ethnic Irish agents. They worked at a fairly low level and in IRA terms would be described as "touts"—men supplying information to the intelligence service for money.[8]

In overall charge of this new intelligence service in Ireland was Lieutenant-Colonel Ralph Heyward Isham, a man with a proven track record in espionage. Born in New York in July 1890, Isham attended both Cornell University and Yale College, where he studied law. Very much an Anglophile, he sailed for England in 1916 and joined the British Army to fight against Germany. His talents were quickly recognized, and he was inducted into Military Intelligence. Isham was seconded to A-2 GHQ to investigate disaffection and mutiny within the army. His brief was extended in 1918 under Field Marshall William Robertson to investigate Bolshevism and prevent strikes amongst servicemen. With the end of the war and the demobilization of the conscripted men and their return to civilian life, the problem was dissipated. A-2, complete with its personnel, was then subsumed within the Home Office. Isham now came under the control of Thomson.

In March 1919 Captain Isham was promoted to Lieutenant-Colonel while being "specially employed" and dispatched to Dublin, where, for a time, he established himself at the Shelbourne Hotel. He was unknown in Ireland and apparently did not make himself known to the Irish police. As a consequence, his presence went undetected by the detectives working for IRA Intelligence within G. Department of the DMP. With Isham in place, the British then began to infiltrate Dublin with secret-service men. Some were civilians, some serving officers, some ex-officers and NCOs, and some, like Isham, professional agents. Most were English or Anglo-Irish.

Upon instruction, Isham made contact with Belfast Inspector W.C. Forbes Redmond, as previously mentioned. The Inspector, who took over G. Division of the DMP in early November 1919, brought with him his own team who appear to have worked in isolation from the other members of G. Division to the extent that even their clerical work was done in-team. Redmond, a Northern Unionist, believed that he had been summoned down to the capital to show the lazy Dubliners how to do their job. Redmond became fully conversant with Isham and his team of intelligence men, which included John Charles Byrne. Redmond boasted about how good they were. In a pep talk to the men of

G. Department, attended by Michael Collins's man David Neligan, he revealed, as previously quoted:

> It was extraordinary, he said, that we, who knew Dublin so well, could not catch Michael Collins, whereas a man who had only just arrived from England had managed to meet him more than once.[9]

This shook Neligan to the core. British Intelligence had seemingly penetrated the IRA at its highest level. At his earliest opportunity, Neligan reported to Tom Cullen of Irish Intelligence. Cullen knew at once who the British agent was and had expressed his suspicions to Collins about the "Crooked Englishman," as he had called him. This new British agent was John Charles Byrne, alias John Jameson. He was being run by Alan Bell of MI5. Born in London of Irish descent, Byrne had enlisted in the Territorial Army in 1908, and, at the outbreak of World War I, was made a sergeant in the British Army. He served in Salonika during the war and, at its end, was recruited by Thomson as an agent in A2, Military Intelligence.[10] Like Isham, he investigated Bolshevism in the British Forces, to the extent that he became General Secretary of the Sailors', Soldiers' and Airmen's Union (SSAU), acting as an agent provocateur. Byrne also spied on the British Socialist Party, which had connections with the Soviet Union, a fact that he later used to his advantage.

Byrne was instructed to infiltrate the Irish Republican movement, which he had succeeded in doing by December 1919, with a view to arresting or killing Michael Collins. To accomplish this, he first had to ingratiate himself into the upper echelons of the Gaelic League in London. He indicated that he could supply the IRA with weapons from the Soviet Union, via the British Socialist Party. With a letter of introduction from Sean McGrath in London, Byrne sailed for Dublin, using his continued alias of John Jameson. Frank Thornton of Irish Intelligence observed of him:

> He posed as one of those fiery communistic speakers who appeared on the platform in Hyde Park every Sunday morning and at that time the communistic platform was erected next to the Irish Self-Determination League platform at the same venue.... On numerous occasions they handed over arms and ammunition to Sean McGrath and Art O'Brien.... It evidently impressed the London leaders because they contacted Michael Collins who agreed to meet Jameson in Dublin.[11]

They did meet and seemed to get on quite well. Collins was intrigued. They even had lunch together at the home of Batt O'Connor and his wife in Brendan Road, Donnybrook. Thereafter Collins asked Liam Tobin, Tom Cullen and Frank Thornton to take over any further proceedings. From the start, Cullen took a dislike to Byrne. Besides, who had ever heard of an Englishman bearing gifts? Physically he was the ideal spy, as Thornton observed, "Plump, sharp-featured, middle-aged, of average height, his knee-length boots were the only distinguishing thing about the man known as Jameson."

It was decided to test the Englishman out. As a show of goodwill Byrne had brought with him a portmanteau containing a number of Webley revolvers, which he alleged he had smuggled into the country. Tobin told him that they would hide them in an IRA arms dump. The two men took the bag down to the New Ireland Assurance Society building at 56, Bachelors Walk, on the corner of O'Connell Street. At the ground floor entrance, the two met Frank Thornton, who took the portmanteau from them. As Byrne watched, Thornton walked along the hall and down the steps to the basement of the building. Byrne was thanked and dismissed, with the promise of a further meeting with Collins. With Byrne gone, Cullen then proceeded down to the basement and took the portmanteau away to 32, Bachelors Walk, which was the IRA Quartermaster General's stores. Before all this, Thornton had meanwhile contacted Jim McNamara, their man in G. Division, and asked him to let him know if he heard of any forthcoming raids. About midday McNamara got back to him. A raid on the New Ireland Assurance Society's premises was planned for three o'clock. Naturally, the British did not want the guns getting into the hands of the IRA and being used against them. Thornton, Tobin and Cullen met up at McBirney's on the far side of the river just before 3:00 p.m. to await developments. At three o'clock precisely a large force of military and police arrived by tenders and cars and surrounded the building. A party of them dashed into the building and down into the basement, which they ransacked in the search for the portmanteau—but to no avail.

Soon after, Batt O'Connor's house, where Byrne had enjoyed a meal with Collins, was raided by Detective Inspector Redmond. Fortunately for Collins, who would have been there, Redmond had picked G-Man James McNamara as his guide. McNamara sent out a word of warning to Collins of the intended raid. Thornton concludes, "Suffice it to say that following other incidents which happened it was finally decided that Jameson was a spy and as such would have to be shot."

For the time being that had to be postponed. Both Byrne and his handler, Isham, briefly returned to London. Isham had been recalled and, on February 2, was, perhaps surprisingly, dismissed from his post. From that date he was no longer "specially employed."[12]

In the dark world of espionage, not everything is certain, but it appears that Isham was replaced by a triumvirate in Dublin headed by Alan Bell. He was a Resident Magistrate from Portadown and a former

RIC Intelligence Officer. Bell had previously been seconded to Dublin Castle to inquire into the Dail Fund and had met with some success. In a report to Lord French, sometime in January 1920, Bell wrote, "...in the course of their moving about my men have picked up a good deal of useful information which leads to raids."[13] As a result of a number of raids, he successfully confiscated over £71,000 from the Republicans. Not so well known was the fact that, as a member of a secret three-man committee, his function was in identifying and having killed leading Volunteers and members of Sinn Fein. He appears to have been the unofficial head of intelligence (MI5) for the British administration in Ireland. On the inside cover of his notebook, now held in the Public Record Office in Kew, is written in his own hand, "The Director of Intelligence, Scotland House, London SW1."[14] One entry refers to him being "on the track of one of the S.F. who escaped from M'joy [Mountjoy Prison]." Another entry refers to information received from a "Mr. Quigley," relating to the ambush of Lord French at Ashtown. Following the assassination of William Redmond, Assistant Commissioner of the DMP, brought in to track down Michael Collins and the senior Irish Intelligence Officers, Bell, in a note to Lord French, wrote of his regret of the death, "Through him I was able to make inquiries which I should not care to entrust to the 'G' Division." This surely goes beyond his official remit of tracking down the Dail Fund.

Byrne returned to Dublin on February 28. Curiously, as G. Man David Neligan reported, Collins "seemed strangely reluctant to kill him, even though it was plain as a pikestaff that he was a spy and furthermore an agent provocateur." Instead, Collins warned his men to keep away from Byrne. When researching a biography of Michael Collins, Frank O'Connor was introduced to Joe O'Reilly, Collins's messenger and general factotum. O'Connor asked the question, "How did Collins behave when he had to have someone shot?" This was a difficult one. Some needed to be shot; others had to be shot. Collins clearly differentiated between the two. O'Reilly, ever loyal to his former leader:

> Then he suddenly jumped up, thrust his hands in his trouser pockets and began to stamp about the room, digging his heels in with a savagery that almost shook the house. Finally he threw himself on to a sofa, picked up a newspaper, which he pretended to read, tossed it aside after a few moments and said in a coarse country voice, "Jesus Christ Almighty, how often have I to tell ye?" It was no longer Joe O'Reilly who was in the room. It was Michael Collins, and for close on two hours I had an experience that must be every biographer's dream, of watching someone I had never known as though he were still alive. Every gesture, every intonation was imprinted on O'Reilly's brain as if on tape.[15]

5. Special Branch Strikes Back

Unfortunately for Byrne, that same evening, of the February 28, 1920, he espied Joe O'Reilly and demanded that he arrange a meeting for him with Collins. O'Reilly said he would do so and reported back to Collins. He became angry. He was now forced into a decision and decided that something would have to be done. He scribbled a note to Liam Tobin. Tobin read the note and organized the shooting of Byrne. He arranged for a junior member of the Intelligence unit, Joe Dolan, to be in d'Olier Street at a certain time, there to identify the man to be shot. When Dolan arrived, he saw Tobin talking to the target. Dolan described the procedure:

> I went along and saw the man and I made sure I would know him again. I took particular note of him. Two days after that Tobin told me he was going to be done in. On 1st March 1920, Dolan met Paddy Daly [from the Squad] by arrangement.... We both had bicycles. We were to go out to Ballymun and pick out a place where we would shoot him. We cycled out to Ballymun and picked out a place in Lovers Lane. Paddy Daly, Tom Kilcoyne and Ben Barrett were to carry out the execution.[16]

On the evening of March 2, 1920, Dolan, Kilcoyne and Barrett cycled out to Ballymun to the place of execution, as prearranged. Joe O'Reilly met with Byrne and told him that Collins had agreed to see him at a secret location. Daly and Joe Dowling would take him there. They caught the tram to the terminus at Ballymun. Then they proceeded to the rear of Albert College, where the others were waiting. Daly told him that he was an identified British spy and that he was to be shot. Byrne was searched. They took all his documents, which proved to be incriminating. At the moment of his death, he tried to bluff his way out of it. "If you shoot me, you shoot one of your best boys." Then, accepting his fate, he admitted he was an agent, saying, "That's right. God bless the King. I would love to die for him."[17] Daly obliged, and Byrne was shot. In Byrne's room in the Granville Hotel, more incriminating effects were discovered. Dolan adds the postscript: " It was told afterwards, that Sir Basil Thomson said when Jameson was shot, that he had lost one of his best men."[18]

Michael Collins was not the only target for Thomson's agents. By now British Intelligence was aware of Liam Tobin, Tom Cullen and Frank Thornton. One day Tobin was introduced to a man by Batt O'Connor. The man claimed that he was a British Intelligence operative but wanted to help the Republican cause. His name, or the name he gave, was Brian Fergus Molloy.[19] He admitted working for Colonel Hill Dillon, Assistant Chief of GHQ Intelligence Staff in Dublin Castle. Tobin was probably fully aware of who, and what, Molloy was before he met him.

Irish Intelligence's man in British Intelligence, David Neligan, had previously met the would-be double agent:

> Mulloy [sic] was a red cap, or military policeman or soldier clerk stationed in Dublin Castle. Of course this may not have been his true role as those fellows are like actors, playing many parts and possessing numerous cover stories. I imagine an ordinary red-cap would not display the form that Mulloy showed. He sought out Sinn Fein, especially Volunteer contacts, and offered to help in any way possible.[20]

Tobin met up with Molloy for a chat. As a show of good faith Molloy promised to get Tobin, Thornton and Cullen into the records room of Dublin Castle where they could copy out secret documents. All three men expressed the concern. If they got in, could the get out? Was it a trap? Tobin asked for proof of his sincerity—that Molloy bring along a secret document to their next meeting. Joseph Dolan of Irish Intelligence went along with Tobin to meet Molloy at the Grafton Bar in Grafton Street. Molloy was supposed to have brought some information of importance, but he did not. Dolan describes the dapper British agent, "Coming out in the evenings he was always unusually well dressed in civilians." The suggestion in Dolan's mind was that he was more than just a private in the British Army. Dolan reported:

> I left him in the Grafton Street Bar and then I followed him to see where he went. These were my instructions. I discovered he went back to Parkgate Street.[21]

Parkgate was British Military GHQ. It was later used by the Black and Tans as their headquarters. As a test of good faith, Molloy, in his second meeting with Irish Intelligence, was asked if he would assist in the assassination of Hill Dillon. At the time the Assistant Chief of Intelligence lived out in a Dublin suburb. Very soon after the interest expressed in him, Hill Dillon moved into the greater safety of the Castle. It might have been a coincidence, but for the fact that Lily Mernin, who was working as Hill Dillon's secretary, was able to inform Collins of what had transpired within British Intelligence. Molloy, or whatever his name was, was dangerous and had to be shot. On March 23, 1920, Frank Saurin met Molloy and took him to Café Cairo in Grafton Street, ostensibly to discuss his meeting with Michael Collins. In reality, it was so that he could be identified by Vinnie Byrne, a member of the Irish Intelligence staff:

> I took a chair at the next table. Frank Saurin turned to me and said: "Hello, so-and-so." Then, turning to Molloy, he had a few words with him and he invited me to join them, which I did. I was introduced to Molloy. After a little while, Frank said: "Our friend is very anxious to meet Liam Tobin and I am

sure you could arrange it." I said: "I will see," and then agreed. Molloy mentioned something about the great help he could be to the movement. After having tea, I made arrangements to meet him the following evening at 5.30 p.m. at the corner of South King St. and Grafton St. and that we would each wear a flower on our coats, so that we would know one another.[22]

The watchers saw Molloy, complete with flower in his buttonhole, turn up on time for his meeting the next day. He stood there waiting, but there was no sign of Tobin or the man he had met in Café Cairo. Waiting unidentified on the other side of the road were four men, Mick McDonnell and Tom Keogh, who were detailed to shoot him. With them were Joe Guilfoyle and Joe Dolan, who were to act as a covering party. Tobin had failed to turn up. After waiting for about three-quarters of an hour, Molloy moved off down Grafton Street, closely followed by the four. The street was busy with people, and The Squad's men could not risk firing at him for fear of hitting an innocent person. Molloy turned down Wicklow Street. His pursuers had to act fast now. Just beyond Wicklow Street was the Central Hotel in Exchequer Street, then occupied by the British military. Dashing forward, the two Squad men opened fire, killing the British agent—one bullet to the body, one to the head. That was their trademark.

There was a postscript to Molloy's death, as Collins's man in the Castle, David Neligan, relates:

> ...Mulloy [sic] had left a will in the Castle, in which he stated that if he was shot, Liam Tobin was the man who would do it. That I learnt from another red-cap, a friend of Mulloy's, who told me he had often shadowed him when he went to meet Tobin. My informant was an Englishman with a rough, coarse face—my private name for him was Bulldog Drummond. I warned Tobin that this man was on the lookout for him and he lay low for a while, and a hunt began for my informant. The red-cap disappeared from the castle soon afterwards and I never saw him again.[23]

Collins and his senior intelligence men now turned their attention towards Molloy's operations chief, Alan Bell. He had initially been brought in to investigate Sinn Fein funds, known as the Dail Loan, and had achieved some success. In March 1920, he was given special powers under an ancient statute, known as the Crimes Act, to interrogate bank managers and others in order to lay his hands on that money. To avoid losing the funds, Collins devised a scheme whereby he lodged the money in the bank accounts of a number of Sinn Fein supporters. Bell, who was now also running Thomson's agents as well, had become a dangerous man. The order went out to assassinate him.

With information supplied by Irish Intelligence—that, on a particular day, Bell would be in a chauffeur-driven car going to the Four Courts from Dublin Castle—Squad members Vinnie Byrne and Mick McDonnell waited at the corner of Chancery Street and Ormond Quay. An Irish Intelligence Officer was posted on Gratton Bridge to signal the approach of Bell's car. As the car passed by the agent, he waved a handkerchief, and the two Squad men, standing outside of the Four Courts, prepared to act as Bell dismounted from the car. They waited in readiness, with a hand grenade which they intended to throw at him. Instead, the car did not stop, but continued on at speed. Instinct, or training, had saved Bell's life. The mission was aborted.

Determined to get Bell, Vincent Byrne and James Slattery waited for him outside the Empire Theatre in Dublin on the following day. He passed by there most evenings on his way home to Monkstown in south Dublin. Byrne espied a man leaving Dublin Castle. They could not be sure from that distance that it was Bell. The man looked all around him for suspicious persons. He gave Slattery and Byrne a hard look before setting off. Amidst the crowds of home-going commuters, Bell proceeded along Dame Street heading towards College Green, then turned into George Street. The two Squad men began to follow. Then, to their frustration, the quarry reentered the castle. The two waited. After a few minutes the man reappeared, accompanied by another man, a minder. Killing him was now made more difficult without a running fight.

The Squad men decided to abort the mission. As they moved off, to their consternation, they now discovered that they had become the quarry. The Castle men began to follow them. Slattery and Byrne proceeded down Crow Street and headed towards the Ha'penny Bridge, which they crossed. The two detectives followed on behind. The IRA men decided to confront their stalkers at the North Lotts, on the other side of the river. Looking back, they saw that their pursuers had stopped in the middle of the bridge, then turned back. They were not prepared to follow any further for fear of being lured into an ambush. The Squad men reported back to Tobin.

Shooting Bell in the city center was proving a challenge. Intelligence then decided to shoot him as he left his home in Monkstown. In their box Ford van, six members of The Squad drove to Monkstown to survey the situation. When they arrived, they saw another car outside Bell's house, and standing around were five or six G-men. Any shootout would turn into a blood bath. The plan was again aborted. A few days later news came in that Bell was coming in to work by tram. Arriving in the city center he dismounted at Grafton Street. Waiting for him was a G. Man to escort him safely into the Castle. It was decided that Bell would have to be killed en route. One final check, and all was ready. Squad member Tom Keogh cycled out to Monkstown, and from a distance, watched as Bell boarded a tram. As it moved off Keogh followed on his bicycle. Further along the route at the Ailsbury Road tram stop, more members of The Squad waited. Cycling behind, Keogh identified the tram to the team. As it came to a halt, members of The Squad boarded it. Some went upstairs; others stayed down below. As the tram approached Simmonscourt Road, just before the Royal Dublin Showground, Bell was pulled off the tram by the shoulder. Squad man Mick McDonnell informed him, "We want you!" Bell briefly resisted but was dragged off the tram and shot dead on the pavement. Two of Basil Thomson's triumvirate, Redmond and Bell, were dead. The third man, Frank Brooke, remained.

The order went out from Collins himself that Brooke was to be killed. Squad man Vinnie Byrne relates, "I believe the 'big Fella' Michael Collins—was getting very uneasy on account of same. So a big drive was made to get him, no matter where."[24] Brooke had stepped up his mission to capture or kill Collins. It had now become a personal duel. Based at the Castle, Brooke proved very illusive. He never ventured out without a sizable escort. An alternative site had to be found. Brooke lived in a big country house in County Wicklow called Coolattin and travelled into the city each day with an armed DMP escort. Three of The Squad, Tom Keogh, Jim Slattery and Vinnie Byrne, were ordered to go down to Coolattin to see if it was possible to get him there. They cycled to County Wicklow and based themselves at Tom Keogh's family home. Byrne relates, "It was in the summer time. The weather was glorious and we were in no hurry to end a grand chance of spending a few days in the country." There was work to be done, though. The following morning, they cycled out to Coolattin. They went unarmed. To the casual observer they were a group of Dubliners out for a day's cycling. A public road ran through the grounds of Brooke's home. As they cycled along it, they expected to be stopped by the police, but no, there was no one there—not even Brooke. He was in Dublin.

After a few days The Squad men were summoned back to the city. They were only back a day or two when news was received from one of their police agents in the Castle that Brooke would be at a certain office in Westland Row belonging to the railway company. Ostensibly he was working for that company. With an Intelligence man leading, a three-man team, comprising Paddy Daly, Tom Keogh and Jim Slattery, went over to Westland Row. They entered the hallway beside the station and went upstairs; one man was left in the hallway as a guard. Amidst the background noise of a train entering the station, with a hissing of steam and a calling out of destinations, the three men entered the office. Brooke was sitting at his desk. As he rose from his seat, they shot him. No one heard the shooting above the noise of the trains. As they departed down the stairs, Daly said to Slattery:

> "Are you sure we got him?" I said I was not sure, and Daly said, "What about going back and making sure?" Keogh and myself went back. When I went into the room I saw a man standing at the left of the door and I fired a shot in his direction, at the same time looking across at Brooke on the floor. I fired a couple of shots at Brooke and satisfied myself that he was dead. Although I did not wound the other man who was in the room, I was informed afterwards that it would have been a good job if he had been shot, as he too was making a nuisance of himself.[25]

The other man was Arthur Cotton, who, when the assassins entered the room, dived for cover under a desk. How deeply he was involved in the Secret Service is unknown. Noting the death of Brooke in his diary for July 31, 1920, senior civil servant in Dublin Castle Mark Sturgis wrote:

> Yesterday at about 12.30 Frank Brooke was shot dead in his office—a dirty cold blooded senseless murder. London will react badly against anything that looks like truckling now and small blame to them. The only line for peace, which is true, is that the gun man element want to smash DHR [Dominion Home Rule.][26]

Many of those who had made up the Castle administration lived openly in and around Dublin. The deaths of Bell and Brooke changed that. No one was quite safe. The order went out in August 1920 for the more important members of that administration to move into Dublin Castle for greater safety. As conditions worsened, more and more officers and their families entered the Castle. The British administration in Dublin became an administration under siege. The military were confined to Park Lodge, a heavily protected building close to army headquarters in Phoenix Park. Lord French himself rarely ventured forth, and when he did, it was with an armored car in support. While The Squad operated during the day time, Dublin at night was left to British Intelligence, who used the Auxiliaries as its foot soldiers.

6

Military Intelligence and the Paramilitaries

At the opening of 1919, Military Intelligence in Ireland was woefully lacking. In the whole of Ireland there were just three Military Intelligence officers, designated one G.S.O. 2, one G.S.O. 3, and one clerk. At the battalion level, the appointment of Intelligence Officers was "encouraged rather than ordered," depending on whether the battalion commanders considered it necessary. Where they did exist, the Intelligence Officers were ordinary regimental officers without specialized training. All too often they had to fit their intelligence work around their general duties. The attitude prevailing was that such work was really the job of the Secret Service.

Following the surrender of the rebels at Easter 1916—between then and 1918—the emphasis of MI5 in England, and both military and police intelligence in Ireland, had been on seeking out a German connection with Sinn Fein. To a great extent this permitted the growth of the IRA to go on largely unchecked.

G. Division of the DMP had been concerned with the collecting of personal, and local, knowledge rather than on organization and methodical recording. In the failure to connect and coordinate this material, they saw only the smaller picture. The clerical section of G. Department had been pitifully inadequate to the task that would have been required. It consisted of just three RIC sergeants and a constable. Their sole duties were to register, file, and index cards. At no stage did they analyze the material collected to see the bigger picture. With the decimation of G. Department, coupled with the assassination of so many of Thomson's Special Branch agents, the British intelligence system in Ireland was virtually destroyed. In February 1920 attempts were made in Dublin to organize a new intelligence section, Dublin District Intelligence, using a combination of a few junior army officers, men due for demobilization, remnants of G. Division, and a few plain clothes RIC officers. The organization was haphazardly funded by the Chief Commissioner of the DMP. It was suggested that the formation of this new unit "immediately bore fruit. Information became available and gave objectives for raids."[1]

At the end of January 1920 on one particular day—and acting upon information supplied by Military Intelligence—sixty suspected persons were arrested throughout Ireland. Fifty-four were in Leinster and Munster, and eight were in the city and suburbs of Dublin. Much of this success stemmed from IRA "paper-trails," lists of names and addresses discovered during raids. In February 1920, the military raided Michael Collins's temporary headquarters at Cullenswood House in the south Dublin suburb of Ranelagh. Richard Mulcahy and his wife also lived here in an upstairs flat. All three managed to get away. However, papers and files were discovered by the raiders. Included was the complete roll of names and addresses of 3,000 members of the Dublin IRA Brigade. While many were warned and escaped, arrests followed. The fault was very much with Michael Collins and his unnecessary retention of paperwork, the result of his youthful clerical training.

In April, British Intelligence had a major coup when a further 317 arrests were made. This followed a raid and seizure of receipts relating to *An t'Oglach*, the journal of the IRA. Having arrested and court-martialed their suspects, their details were entered both regionally and with Military Intelligence in Dublin. The prisoners were then transferred to the civil authorities and interned. In response, the prisoners went on hunger strike. To the dismay of the Military Intelligence, on April 14, all the prisoners were released by the Castle authorities. All the work of the previous months by Military Intelligence had come to nothing. On the positive side, Military Intelligence knew who the released men were. On the negative side, those released were able to identify the plainclothes British agents who had interrogated them.

In late March 1920, Prime Minister Lloyd George reshuffled the Irish Executive. Chief Secretary Ian McPherson was replaced by Sir Hamar Greenwood, a Canadian Liberal M.P. In the new scheme of things, Lord French was side-lined and found himself as Lord Lieutenant, reduced to little more than a figurehead. Selected to assist Greenwood was the Chairman of the Board of Inland Revenue, Sir John Anderson, who took over administration. It was said of him that he was "the greatest administrator of his time, perhaps of any time in the country's history."[2] He was ably assisted by his deputy, Alfred "Andy" Cope, an ex-customs detective, appointed directly by the Prime Minister, David Lloyd George. Cope worked to instructions from Lloyd George and inaugurated secret discussions with Sinn Fein to bring about a peace. This was not generally known by his superiors in Ireland. Lloyd George's

6. Military Intelligence and the Paramilitaries 93

idea was to separate the politicians from the IRA. The two administrators were joined by a third senior civil servant, Mark Beresford Sturgis, who came to act as Joint Assistant Under Secretary with Cope. The new triumvirate had their offices in Dublin Castle, but resided at the Royal Marine Hotel in Kingstown. As an astute man, Anderson and his team quickly realized that a British military victory would be difficult to achieve unless it resorted to out-and-out brutality. This the government in London would not permit—certainly not openly, with the eyes of the world upon Ireland. Major (later Field Marshal) Bernard Montgomery was of the same opinion as the new Dublin ministers, one he expressed when he wrote to his former Sandhurst colleague Major Percival:

> My own view is that to win a war of this sort you must be ruthless. Oliver Cromwell, or the Germans, would have settled it in a very short time. Nowadays public opinion precludes such methods, the nation would never allow it, and the politicians would lose their jobs if they sanctioned it.[3]

The IRA, starved of arms, ammunition and men, was equally unable to deliver a decisive blow. Some sort of compromise was inevitable. Against that day, Anderson, along with Cope, put out peace feelers to the more moderate elements of Sinn Fein.

In order to counter Republican propaganda—which was very successful in influencing opinion, not only in Ireland and the USA, but also in Britain—a rival British propaganda machine was established. It was known as the Public Information Branch and was based in Dublin Castle under the direction of Basil Clarke. Unfortunately, it lacked the sophistication of its Irish equivalent run by Erskine Childers. Its most notable failure was a short news item shown in Dublin cinemas before the main feature. This was the so-called British success at the "Battle of Tralee," of November 12, 1920. This propaganda film was made some 175 miles or so away from the battle scene—along the Vico Road, Dalkey, County Dublin. It was a view recognized by most of its Dublin audience. The item was greeted with laughter and derision by the audience when seen. It was clear to all who watched that the IRA "prisoner" held by the Auxiliaries was undoubtedly a fellow Auxiliary in mufti, right down to his regulation highly polished shoes.

On the military/police side of the restructuring in Ireland, the Army Commander in Chief, Sir Frederick Shaw, was replaced by the former Commissioner of the Metropolitan Police in London, General Nevil Macready, a former Royal Artillery officer. He was offered the joint command of both army and police. Macready was reluctant to take on the combined post but eventually agreed on the proviso that two new posts be created under him: one officer to take command of the army; the other to command the joint police forces. The post of "Police Advisor to the Irish Government" was given to Major-General Hugh Tudor, a former artillery officer. Macready then brought in Major S.S. Hill Dillon to take over command of Military Intelligence, acting under the direction of Brigadier General J.E.S. Brind, based in London. To the post of Chief of Police, to coordinate all intelligence, Macready appointed Lieutenant-Colonel Ormonde de L'Epee Winter, yet another artillery man. An analysis of the situation in Ireland was then prepared for Macready by Major-General Hugh Jeudwine. He looked at communications and transport and particularly at intelligence, which he found most wanting.

Under the new establishment the Military/Police structure was:

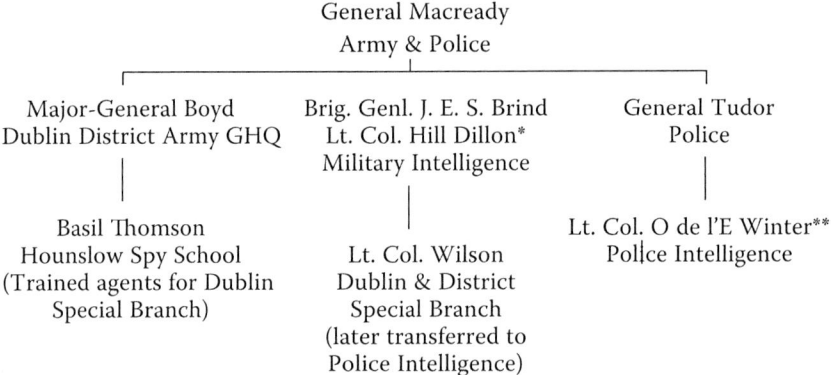

*Lt. Col. Hill Dillon was formerly of MI5.
**Winter was appointed Deputy Chief of Police, and Director of Intelligence, in May 1920.

Within the army structure, under Major-General Boyd, was Colonel Herbert Edward Rawson. It would appear that he dealt with day-to-day matters. Michael Noyk, the Republic's solicitor working on official business, was introduced to him at British Headquarters at Parkgate Street, Phoenix Park:

> ...[W]e gathered that we were to meet someone very important. We were not mistaken. We were ushered into a room—a special office—and there we were approached and greeted most courteously by a gentleman in mufti with a monocle. He introduced himself as Colonel Rawson and was very pleased to meet us.... He then proceeded to talk generally and some of his remarks were very interesting. "It is extraordinary," he said, "how well organized these people are. They are just like our own Army—Brigades, Battalions, Companies, etc."[4]

The new consortium, the Dublin District Special Branch (later D. Branch), was originally put under the command of Military Intelligence rather than the police. In April, a plainclothes section was formed to collect both military and police information. The unit was divided into six areas within the city. Each was in the charge of a head agent who controlled a number of sub-agents, who in turn obtained information from within their areas. By and large, these sub-agents were Irishmen—informers, whom the IRA derisively called "touts." Kenneth Strong, Company Intelligence Officer with the Royal Scots Fusiliers was paid £5 a month for paying his touts:

> My agents were not of a very high calibre. Sometimes a railway porter who noted suspicious train travellers; sometimes a shopkeeper who might report unusual purchases of food or medical supplies; a bartender who had noted the arrival of strangers in the neighbourhood.... To get a rendezvous I would disguise myself, usually as the owner of a small donkey cart, but my English accent was against me and I had several narrow escapes.[5]

Tudor, when appointed Chief of Police in May 1920, found that intelligence gathering was a shamble. There was little information they possessed that could not be garnered by reading the local nationalist press. In the light of this, Tudor conferred with Macready that a branch of his Chief of Police's office should be made responsible for reorganizing the intelligence system. Macready agreed, and on May 11, police and Military Intelligence were united under a single leadership, that of policeman, Brigadier-General Ormonde Winter. This was to prove a source of bitter contention with Military Intelligence.

The reformed Dublin and District Special Branch, based at the Royal Barracks, now came under police administration. It began with just seven officers plus what remained of Thomson's agents. After training at Hounslow, the group had grown to fifty-one by July 1920, peaking at ninety-seven by November 21st of that year.

The "Spy School," based at the Royal Fusiliers Depot at Hounslow Barracks in London, was run by Charles A. Tegart, a counterterrorism expert formerly based in India, and his Singapore-based colleague, Godfrey C. Denham, on behalf of MI5. It was set up in June 1920. The official World War I history of the Royal Fusiliers (perhaps disingenuously) indicates that the 10th Royal Fusiliers, based at Hounslow, was merely an administration section, employing former Scotland Yard officers and others with language and translation skills. The Hounslow "Spy School" also appears to have had an adjunct office based at the Horse Guards Annexe, at 12, Carlton House Terrace, London, SW1. At the time, 1919–20, the premises were listed in *Kelly's Directory* as occupied by "The London District Headquarters." All correspondence appears to have passed through an administrator, one Captain Harper. Captain R.D. Jeune, who was a graduate of the "Spy School," wrote:

> A rather hastily improvised Intelligence Organisation was formed, of which I was a member, and after a short course of instruction at Hounslow, we were sent over to Dublin in the early summer of 1920. The first batch were instructed to pose initially as R[oyal] E[ngineer] officers, but this rather futile procedure was soon dropped and the work consisted of getting to know the town thoroughly, tailing "Shinners," and carrying out small raids, with a view of collecting all possible information which would lead us eventually to stamping out the revolt.[6]

Instructions in their military personnel files were clear that their names should not be included in the Army List. They were not paid through the normal military channels but rather through the army's agents, Cox & Co., of Charing Cross, London. By the second half of 1920 there was an influx of "sleuths" into Dublin. They worked undercover, in plain clothes and roamed the streets looking for the IRA and Republican leaders. Some of the men, trained by Basil Thomson, were army officers of Irish extraction and others on loan from the Indian Secret Service. The new organization quickly became as ruthless as The Squad. They did not always operate within the law. IRA suspects were shot, and prisoners were tortured for information.

While Brigadier General Winter expected results from his new team, right from the start, Tegart warned that success would not be instantaneous. It had taken him five years to suppress the Indian revolutionary movement. He informed the authorities that he needed a dedicated team to collect together and compile a card index file on what was already known of the Irish organization. After just four months, and with nothing to show for it, Winter confronted the two experts over their lack of success. Following harsh words, Tegart and Denham left Dublin and resumed their former duties. Their role was taken over by William Francis Jeffries, formerly of the Royal Dublin Fusiliers, then a Secret Service man in Ireland, and the somewhat flawed Major Cecil Aylmer Cameron.[7]

Out in the countryside, the RIC had also been intimidated regarding their political work. Discretion was preferred to valor. A substantial number of resignations took place. In fact, over ten per cent of the force left the service. During the first six months of 1920, sixteen operational RIC barracks were attacked and destroyed and twenty-nine damaged in IRA attacks. Another 424 abandoned barracks were also destroyed. On April 4, IRA volunteers raided the tax offices in Dublin, Cork, and elsewhere, destroying the tax records for most of Ireland. They also burnt down more than 300 local government buildings, including courthouses. The attacks were so successful that from that date the British legal system in Ireland ceased to function, and the collection of income tax ceased.

6. Military Intelligence and the Paramilitaries

The British Government was determined that something had to be done to restore law and order. In August 1920, the Restoration of Order in Ireland Act was passed. It built on the old Defence of the Realm Act (D.O.R.A.). The new regulation did not impose martial law as such, but it gave the authorities extra powers. Importantly it gave power to "the competent Military Authority, the powers, previously vested in the police authorities and magistrates." The British Army was no longer shackled to what they believed had been an incompetent police service. Criminal Courts were replaced by Military Courts, and Military Courts of Inquiry replaced Coroner's Courts. Previously, IRA suspects had evaded conviction in the civil courts through sympathetic juries or juries afraid to testify against the prisoners. Also, in the past, Coroner's Courts had publicly named and shamed the security forces where they were responsible for the deaths of civilians. These comments often appeared in the newspapers to the embarrassment of both the military and the British Government.

During a cabinet meeting to discuss the troubles in Ireland, the Secretary of State for Defence, Winston Churchill, supported by fellow politicians Arthur Balfour and Lord Birkenhead, suggested the formation of a "Special Emergency Gendarmerie which could become a branch of the Royal Irish Constabulary." Churchill's proposal was initially rejected, but with the situation deteriorating, Tudor agreed to its use in Ireland on the basis that it would take too long to reinforce the RIC by ordinary means. By the end of April 1920, some 400 English recruits had joined the new service. By late September their numbers had risen to 2,000, reinforcing the 8,000 Irishmen still in the regular Royal Irish Constabulary. The new recruits were joining at the rate of 200 per week. Eventually, the number was established at about 7,000. A base for training these new police force was established at Gormanstown, just outside of Dublin. As there was a shortage of the traditional dark bottle-green RIC uniforms, the new force wore a combination of khaki tunics and dark green trousers. Where this occurred in county Limerick, they were promptly nicknamed the "Black and Tans," after a famous local pack of hounds. The name caught on nationally. Derogatory to the Irish, this disparity in uniform was picked up as a positive piece of "jingoism" in the Dublin Castle-produced *Weekly Summary* for August 27:

> They did not wait for the usual uniform. They came at once. They were wanted badly, and the RIC welcomed them. They know what danger is. They have looked death in the eyes before, and did not flinch. They will not flinch now.
>
> They will go on with the job—the job of making Ireland once again safe for the law abiding, and an appropriate hell for those whose trade is agitation, and whose method is murder.

The men that joined the new service were demobilized ex-soldiers. They had to produce their discharge papers, and, it was said, that no man was eligible unless he could show that he was of "good character." The pay was £3.10s. a week, rising to £4.15s. These new recruits were veterans of the trenches. They were, in many cases, "damaged" by the War. Many had failed to settle down when they returned home. So, they joined up for an adventure. In Flanders, they had known who the enemy was; in Ireland, the situation was altogether different. The enemy did not wear uniforms. They were indistinguishable from other civilians. As their comrades came to be killed in ambushes, the difference between civilian and insurgent became blurred in the minds of the Black and Tans. Drunkenness out of boredom and violence out of frustration developed.

Major General Douglas Wimberley of the Cameron Highlanders, stationed in Ireland, remarked of the Black and Tans:

> They were totally undisciplined, by our regimental standards, and members of this curious force undoubtedly committed many atrocities, and, in retaliation, dreadful atrocities were, in turn, committed on them by the Sinn Fein bands roaming the countryside.
>
> They seemed to make a habit of breaking out of their barracks at night, illicitly, and killing men they thought were suspect rebels, and in this way the habit spread surreptitiously even to a few Army officers and men. So undisciplined were some of the auxiliary policemen, who had been recruited to reinforce the remnants of the Royal Irish Constabulary, most of whom had by this time been killed, that whenever some of them accompanied me, on any search, patrol or foray, in which I was in command, my first action was always to detail two or three of my Jocks simply to watch over them, and see that they did not commit any atrocities such as unlawful looting or burning houses, when they were acting under my command, or even shooting prisoners, on the grounds that they were attempting to escape.[8]

Corroboration of Wimberley's account of their brutality was recorded by a British "Tommy," Private J. P. Swindlehurst of the Lancashire Fusiliers, based in Dublin:

> We heard whilst on guard that a party of Sinn Feiners ambushed a car containing Black and Tans, threw a bomb in amongst them, and then shot them down one by one as they tried to get clear. As a reprisal the Black and Tans set out and cleared a whole street of inmates who were known to harbour Sinn Fein, any man who showed his displeasure at being turned out, was next in turn for a box [a beating]. It will always be a mystery how many went under, incidents like this are not published.... The Black and Tans have their grilling room, they are at it night and day, knocking information out of suspects and prisoners alike, and then carting them off to Mountjoy more dead than alive.[9]

6. Military Intelligence and the Paramilitaries 99

Lloyd George chose not to interfere amidst the tales of police brutality, preferring to let these new police have their heads in "unauthorized" reprisals. In Ireland, this brutality was encouraged, as was instanced in one notable event, recorded by a policeman who was present. Divisional Commissioner Lieut. Col. S.F. Smyth, in the presence of his superior, General Tudor, in an encouraging speech at the RIC barracks at Listowel in Munster on June 17, 1920, exhorted:

> Well, men I have something to tell you, something I am sure you would not want your wives to hear. Sinn Fein has had all the sport up to the present and we are going to have it now.... We must take the offensive and beat Sinn Fein at its own game. Martial Law, applying to all Ireland, is to come into operation immediately. In fact we are to have our scheme of amalgamation completed on 21st June. I am promised as many troops from England as I require, thousands are coming in daily....
>
> If a police barracks is burnt, or if the barracks already occupied is not suitable, then the best house in the locality is to be commandeered, the occupants thrown out into the gutter. Let them lie there, the more the merrier. Police and military will patrol the country at least five times a week. They are not to confine themselves to the main roads, but make across the country, lie in ambush and when civilians are seen approaching shout "Up hands." Should the order not be obeyed at once, shoot and shoot to kill. If the persons approaching carry their hands in their pockets, or are in any way suspicious looking, shoot them down. You may make mistakes occasionally, and innocent persons may be shot, but that cannot be helped and you are bound to get the right person sometime.
>
> The more you shoot the better I shall like you and I assure you that no policeman will get into trouble for shooting a man.[10]

This was seen as a carte blanche for murder, not only of IRA personnel, but indeed of any civilian slow to react to an order. A verbatim account of the speech was sent to Collins. He ordered Smyth's execution as an example to others. On July 17, 1920, as Smyth was relaxing at Cork's County Club, a six-man IRA team entered the smoking lounge and shot him dead.

The Black and Tans were supplemented by additional men. They were the Auxiliary Division of the RIC (ADRIC) and were a more formidable force than the Black and Tans. The new, autonomous service acted independently of the RIC. It was formed of ex-officers who were well-educated and intelligent. Many were war heroes. Included in their number were some ex-Scotland Yard members, who acted as Intelligence Officers. The new force, advertised as a Corps d'Elite, came into being on July 27, 1920, eventually reaching 1,500 in number. In the main, the men were British, but in addition they also included Americans, Canadians and South Africans. James Mackay, in his 1996 biography, *Michael Collins: A Life*, described the Auxiliaries:

They wore their medal ribbons with fierce pride and included many a Military Cross and Distinguished Service Order. They were the product of the finest English public schools and a good percentage of them came from old Anglo-Irish families; but otherwise they differed only from the Black and Tans in their ruthlessness and ferocity, utterly fearless, especially when cornered, they often earned the respect of their opponents, but they also included a sinister sprinkling of sadists and psychopaths who delighted in devising ever more fiendish methods of torture, mutilation and death.

In August 1920 General Tudor, in overall command of the police force, appointed Brigadier-General F.P. Crozier as commandant of the newly established Auxiliary Cadets. They soon adopted the nickname, amongst themselves, of "Tudor's Toughs"—and this they soon proved to be. The Auxiliary Cadets began arriving in Ireland in September of that year. They were permitted to wear their old Army officers' service uniforms (without badges of rank), with the addition of a dark Glengarry cap. Pay for them was £1 a day plus allowances. The Auxiliaries elected their own officers, usually by former senior rank. Each "Auxie" carried two .45 Webley revolvers strapped to his thighs, cowboy fashion, a rifle, pouches and a bandolier full of ammunition. They were walking arsenals. Five of the thirteen Auxiliary companies were based in Dublin, with F Company based in Dublin Castle itself. F Company formed a plainclothes Intelligence section, with a police intelligence officer to liaise with the Crimes Special Branch.

The Auxiliaries adopted a no-nonsense approach, "out-terrorizing" the terrorists and in the process developing a bad reputation for torture and murder. Anyone interrogated by them was almost certain to be in for a bad time. The two most feared of the interrogators were Captains Hardy and King. Captain William Lorraine King, who commanded F Company, was a former officer in the South African Infantry. He was a big man, over six feet tall, with a reputation for brutality. Captain Jocelyn Lee Hardy, formerly of the Connaught Rangers, was a decorated, but flawed, war hero. G. Man, David Neligan, in his autobiography, *The Spy in the Castle*, apparently refers to Hardy when he writes, "They had numerous so-called intelligence officers but these were really terrorists, most wore steel waistcoats, and one definitely had a slate off."

At first, the Auxiliaries rode around the country with impunity, inspiring awe and terror. On November 28, 1920, at Kilmichael in County Cork, Tom Barry and his guerrilla column deliberately targeted the Auxiliaries and destroyed the myth that they were invincible. Eighteen Auxiliaries were killed in the ambush. In the towns, ambushes on this scale were impossible. The circumstances between town and country were altogether different. In the city there were too many British

6. Military Intelligence and the Paramilitaries 101

garrisons, all close to hand, who could send reinforcements at a minute's notice. There could be no large-scale operations without the IRA's suffering severe losses. Ambushes were scaled down to hit-and-run attacks. The IRA engaged in brief, three-minute attacks, lobbing hand grenades, using handguns, then disengaging. It was slow attrition. Night was the time when the Auxiliaries were most effective. It was then, following curfew, that they conducted nighttime raids. In Dublin, one unnamed Auxiliary was to write:

> Raids we also found very different from in the country. We received orders to search such and such addresses. These searches had to be carried out very thoroughly, with no regard to the niceties, regardless of the time of night or the situation of the occupants. Everyone must be got out of bed, beds being favored hiding places for arms. No notice was taken of age or sex, or of their night wear or lack of it. All men found had to give a good account of themselves, backed by proof, or come along with us to be lodged in the jail until such time as they could prove themselves to be reliable citizens.[11]

This "rose-colored spectacles" account of the treatment of prisoners was very much at odds with reality. Private J. P. Swindlehurst of the Lancashire Fusiliers, then based in Dublin, recalled in his diary:

> 16th January [1921]: ... Secret Service men and detectives kept us on alert to admit them.... Prisoners were brought in occasionally, a few looked about all in, covered in blood, minus teeth, and numerous other injuries. After a grilling in one of the upper rooms, we could hear groans and curses coming down the stairway, a dull thump indicated someone had taken a count, they took them off to Mountjoy Prison on the outskirts.[12]

IRA Staff Captain Tony Woods, who was caught in a raid with others, was taken to Dublin Castle. The prisoners were placed in a small room in the Lower Yard. Woods had every reason to be afraid:

> We were each separately interviewed by a man in RIC uniform, a fine looking man about six foot two inches tall, who I afterwards discovered was, was the famous Sergeant Igoe. Major Hardy came in, took one look at us and went out again. He, evidently, was not going to bother with us unless Igoe decided that we were important. Hardy was a slight man and walked with a limp, but he could be deadly. He had interrogated Ernie O'Malley only a few months before. He was a brave but desperate person who never spared himself or others. He was responsible for the shootings, tortures and beatings which took place in the Castle, but he reserved himself only for the most important fish which was a relief to us.[13]

Ernie O'Malley, as indicated, was one such "important fish." An IRA organizer, using the alias of Bernard Stewart as Woods relates, he was arrested and questioned by Hardy and Major King in December 1920. In the English published edition of his book, *On Another Man's Wounds*, the names of his interrogators were censored. O'Malley had been arrested by an Auxiliary raiding party while in Kilkenny, and a gun was found in his possession. He was sent to Dublin Castle for further questioning. O'Malley was taken into the interrogation room:

> There were two men in the room; one was in civilians, the other in khaki. The man in the uniform of the Connaught Rangers was medium-sized and slight in build. He walked with a limp. His face was pale, the pupils of his eyes were large and black, around them was a thin rim of blue. He worked his lower lip. The other man was over six feet; well built, with an air of command, the lines on his forehead were drawn together when he spoke. He was Major King; the other Captain Hardy. They had both been concerned in the murder of prisoners.[14]

During the interrogation, O'Malley was badly beaten—to the extent that he was unrecognizable at its end. Escorted back across the yard to his cell, he was approached by two young women who had been visiting other prisoners. One of them was an old friend, Aine Malone. Her companion was a sister of Dick McKee. "Aine don't you know me?" O'Malley asked under his breath. She hesitated at first, then exclaimed, "My God Earnan. Is it you? I did not know you. Oh! Who did that to you?"

O'Malley's torturer, William Lorraine King, was the commandant of F Company of the Auxiliaries, based in Dublin Castle. Hardy was its Intelligence Officer. In another interrogation by King and Hardy, the badly beaten-up prisoner Christopher Carberry was allegedly made to lick up his own spilt blood, which had fallen onto the floor of the interrogation room. Michael Collins was determined to assassinate these torturers.

Eventually, through the agency of a rogue Auxiliary Officer, Major John Shaw Reynolds, Irish Intelligence penetrated the Auxiliaries and discovered the names of these torturers. Reynolds supplied information through a friend of his, Brighid Foley, whom he first met during a raid. There is perhaps a suggestion of romance between the two, but whatever, Reynolds agreed to pass on information. Frank Thornton records Reynolds' first interview with Irish Intelligence:

> Very shortly after the arrival of the Auxiliaries in Dublin, Dick Foley [Brighid's brother] contacted Michael Collins and suggested that it would be possible to get an Auxiliary named Reynolds who was a major in F Company to work for us. It was arranged, therefore that I would meet Reynolds with Foley and as a result Reynolds decided to act as one of our agents. I met Reynolds regularly in different public houses and gave him certain jobs to do, which he did successfully. At the beginning, however, we were not too satisfied about his trustworthiness, and on every occasion that I met Reynolds either Joe Dolan or Joe Guilfoyle was conveniently nearby and were armed.

6. Military Intelligence and the Paramilitaries

However, as time went on, Reynolds became more useful and secured quite a lot of valuable information in the form of photographs of the Murder Gang—F Company, Q Company and other Companies of Auxiliaries.[15]

One photograph in particular gained by Irish Intelligence was group photograph of some of the F Company plainclothes men whom they had named "The Special Gang." Patrick Kennedy of Irish Intelligence recalled:

> Reynolds supplied us with group photographs and individual photographs of Auxiliaries in "F" Company in the Castle. We also had photographs of Hardy and King. In group photographs the individuals that we were interested in were usually marked with an "X," and our Intelligence officers were instructed to study them closely so that they would be in a position to identify them.[16]

There are a number of copies of one of these photographs. Probably the most informative is that in the Piaris Beslai Collection in the Irish National Library. Each of the men depicted is numbered and named. Additional information has been appended. Perhaps surprisingly, two, possibly three of them, were Irish:

1. R. Dentieth, ADRIC* No. 101. Wounded March 14, 1921.
2. A. F. Fletcher, ADRIC No. 890, Irish.
3. F. Moore, ADRIC No.1393, Irish.
4. S. D. Swaffer, ADRIC No. 1234.
5. C. B. Dove, ADRIC 667.
6. L. G. Appleford, ADRIC 589. Section Leader, shot June 24, 1921.
7. H. F. Gorman, ADRIC 625.
8. A. Winch, ADRIC No. 888. Later Intelligence Officer F Company.
9. D. F. McClean, ADRIC No. 588.
10. G. A. Stapley, Military Medal, ADRIC No. 33.
11. Unknown man, sitting behind them in civilian clothes, only his legs are shown. Could this be Hardy?

ADRIC–Auxiliary Division Royal Irish Constabulary

Appleford, listed above, aged 27, and George Gerald Warnes, aged 29, were shot repeatedly by members of the 2nd Battalion, Dublin Brigade's Active Service Unit, near 98, Grafton Street, outside of Café Cairo. This may well explain the name later given to the group, "The Cairo Gang."[17]

Thornton, of Irish Intelligence, had a second Auxiliary working for him. He was an Irishman named McCarthy, also of F Company. He was a distant cousin of a Volunteer in A Company, 4th Battalion of the Dublin IRA. McCarthy met up with Liam Tobin at Hannan's public house in Abbey Street and agreed to work for Irish Intelligence—for money. McCarthy supplied documents, and on occasion files, which Irish Intelligence were able to copy and return. All went well for a time. McCarthy earned his pay. There was always a suspicion, though, that McCarthy was playing a double game. It was the habit of Liam Tobin, Tom Cullen and Frank Thornton to have lunch every other day at the La Scala Restaurant, attached to the La Scala Cinema. One day, sporting a brand-new brown suit, Liam Tobin and the other two, looking across the room from their table, saw McCarthy with two other men they could not identify. Neither the Intelligence men nor McCarthy made any indication that they knew each other. A few days later, Liam Tobin was called away, and at the last moment, so too, was Tom Cullen. Thornton, now a little later than usual, went to lunch on his own at La Scala. On the way, he noticed a large enemy convoy of vehicles pass him. When he reached the restaurant, he realized that a raid was taking place. He quietly walked on. A waitress at the restaurant later told Thornton that the British officer in charge went straight to the table where the three intelligence men always sat and demanded to know where they were. He described all three to her, including the tall thin man wearing a new brown suit. All the customers were held for up for two hours while they were questioned, and the restaurant was ransacked. McCarthy was a double agent. To avoid retribution, he left Dublin soon after. Thornton ruefully remarked, "When dealing with men of the McCarthy type, who after all were only working for the pay they received, well, one possibly couldn't expect anything else to happen, and we can only congratulate ourselves that we escaped so luckily on occasions like this."

Michael Collins's operative within Dublin Castle, Lily Mernin, came into contact with the Auxiliaries based there. It became important, Collins stressed, for her to identify and name those men involved in aggressive questioning. Mernin wrote in her Witness Statement:

> When I got to know the Auxiliaries better, I accompanied Frank Saurin (known as Mr. Stanley) to various cafés where I identified for him some of the Auxiliaries whom I knew.
> The Auxiliaries organized smoking concerts and whist drives in the Lower Castle Yard. I was encouraged by Frank Saurin, a member of the Intelligence Squad, to give all the assistance I could in the organization of these whist drives for the sole purpose of getting to know the Auxiliaries and finding out all I possibly could about them. Frank Saurin had arranged with me that should any of the Auxiliaries see myself or any of the girls of the Castle home, he would have members of his squad hanging around Dublin Castle to identify them.[18]

6. Military Intelligence and the Paramilitaries

By the summer of 1920, Dublin was full of policemen and British Intelligence Officers. Kathleen Napoli McKenna witnessed their presence one Sunday morning in July:

> ...citizens were thronging to hear Mass through streets filled with British Regulars carrying rifles with fixed bayonets, Auxiliary Cadets, Black and Tans and, here and there, broad-shouldered plain-clothes men distinguishable as members of the G. Division of the Dublin Metropolitan Division engaged in political espionage.[19]

As in the majority of its colonial conflicts, Britain was reluctant to describe the insurrection in Ireland as a war. It was decided to call it a police action. This meant, to the frustration of the Army, that it was forced to give precedence to the police. In May 1920, the office of Chief of Police was created, and it was felt by the British Government to be more logical for the main intelligence branch to come under the direction of that Chief of Police. Putting on a brave face, for they were reluctant to lose control of intelligence gathering, the Army announced that it supported the build up of "a system in which it was believed that the military authorities could rely upon." As a sop to an aggrieved military, a senior British officer was attached to the staff of the Chief of Police, in order to coordinate intelligence-led actions. The result, however, was an extraordinarily complex organization. The problem, Military Intelligence identified, was that "Moreover, as the officer in question [the new Chief of Police, Ormonde de l'Epee Winter] had no previous experience of intelligence duties, the organisation he controlled was not purely an Intelligence Branch; it undertook other duties; with the result that both they and intelligence suffered by not being carried out systematically and thoroughly."[20]

Effectively, the appointment of a Chief of Police meant that the Army lost control of its counter-insurgency strategy in Dublin. All intelligence thereafter was obliged to be submitted to and distributed through G. Division. The work of the previous months was discarded in deference to new ideas about how to tackle the IRA. No longer playing an important part in intelligence gathering, Military Intelligence in Dublin gradually decreased its intelligence staff, and henceforth was obliged to depend upon the police for information. From then on, Army Intelligence shifted its concentration to gathering information on the IRA out in the countryside, beyond Winter's influence. In November 1920, however, the pendulum swung the other way following the collapse of Winter's Intelligence Service. Military Intelligence once again asserted itself in the Irish capital. The author of *A Record of the Rebellion*, in constrained rebuke, diplomatically pointed out their seven-month period of frustration:

It follows therefore, of necessity, that some delay occurred between the end of May 1920, the formulation of the scheme and the bringing of that scheme into operation. This and the accommodation difficulty postponed any direct assumption of control to November of that year.[21]

Military Intelligence now enjoyed a period of success based on careful information gathering. Records of eight Dail Eireann departments were seized in raids by them, thus acquiring valuable information. The office of IRA Chief of Staff Richard Mulcahy's was discovered and raided, with Military Intelligence carrying away a number of important files and documents. In another raid, Military Intelligence came very close to arresting Austin Stack, Minister for Home Affairs in the Republican Government. At the time he was Acting President in de Valera's absence. The compiler of *A Record of the Rebellion in Ireland* summed up the importance of such raids:

> In Dublin both the military and the police agreed that their most important sources of information were captured documents. This was natural seeing that the chief offices both in Sinn Fein and the Irish Republican Army were in Dublin. These documents were not only the foundations on which the IRA List and Order of Battle were built, but each seizure usually led to further raids and the capture of more documents until GHQ, IRA, were almost entirely demoralised.[22]

Investigations into Austin Stack's escape revealed the name of an informer—Mrs. Maud Walsh. Colonel Garde, second in command to General Tudor, occasionally stayed in the Shelbourne Hotel overlooking St. Stephen's Green. When he did, he was accompanied by a Captain Walsh, who acted as his aide-de-camp. Unknown to these British officers, the Shelbourne Hotel telephonist was working for Irish Intelligence. She tapped all telephone calls going through the Shelbourne switchboard. One of these was a call from a Mrs. Maud Walsh to Captain James Walsh (no relation). She told him that while riding in a tram she had seen Austin Stack riding a bicycle in Dublin. She then asked if she could discover more information, would she be able to share part of the reward offered for his capture, then put at £2,000? There had been previous suspicions of her activities, and she was known to Irish Intelligence as a possible British agent. Frank Saurin was put on the case to secure more proof of her treachery. First of all, he wanted to identify her, and to that end he visited her home in Morehampton Road, Donnybrook, posing as an insurance agent. Irish Intelligence officer George Fitzgerald was then ordered to follow her. She had obviously been given some training in losing a pursuer, as he recalled the mission in his Witness Statement:

> One of my jobs was to observe the movements of people who went in and out of a certain house in Morehampton Road. I was told, in particular, to watch out for a red haired lady who was believed to be a contact or a secretary to Colonel Hill Dillon, at that time Provost Marshal at the Royal Barracks (now Collins Barracks), Dublin. I watched the house for a couple of mornings and noted that a few strange people went in. One morning this red haired lady appeared, came out, walked up Morehampton Road. Suddenly she decided to board a tram which was coming. She travelled on this tram as far as Baggot Street. I was on a bicycle and I followed the tram. I saw she got off the tram near Baggot Street Bridge and walked past the tram stop; suddenly turned back and boarded another tram going into the city. I followed this second tram and noticed she got off at Nassau Street. She turned up Dawson Street. I hung around and after about half an hour she came out carrying some papers. She came down Dawson Street, boarded the tram again at Nassau Street and went as far as O'Connell Bridge. She got off the tram and there took another tram to Parkgate Street. I followed to Parkgate Street and there discovered she went into the Royal Barracks.[23]

Fitzgerald followed her over the next few days. In one instance, she met Colonel Hill Dillon, who gave her a letter. This and other evidence confirmed Irish Intelligence's opinion that she was a British spy. Saurin was all for having her executed, but Collins stepped in to prevent it. He was well aware of the bad publicity, the killing of a woman, would engender in the British press. So, she was saved. Ironically in the post-war period, following the establishment of the Irish Free State, Maud Walsh was elected a Councilor of Dublin Corporation. Her namesake, Captain Walsh, became a solicitor in Dublin and practiced law in the Irish Courts.

In May, the British Cabinet in London discussed the introduction of more repressive laws into Ireland. Lloyd George's representative, Andy Cope, who had now begun talking to members of Sinn Fein, was fearful that more military measures could only worsen the chances of a final settlement. In this he was supported by Sir Warren Fisher, head of the civil service in Ireland. Both men objected most strongly to the Government of Ireland Bill and the coercive measures proposed by the Irish Chief Crown Solicitor. He had proposed the suspension of trial by jury and the introduction of tribunals composed of three judges. The efforts of Cope and Fisher came to naught.

In August 1920, the British Parliament passed the Restoration of Order in Ireland Act (ROIR), which gave the military more draconian powers: the right to impose night-time curfews; to disarm, arrest and intern; and to imprison suspects without trial. It also allowed them to try cases of murder by court-martial, without the benefit of juries. The Act also gave the British Army the right to hold military courts in place of Coroners' Court Inquests and to censor details of unofficial reprisals and murders from the public at large.

Lloyd George, in his support for Cope, had sought to separate the two wings of republicanism. He would talk to politicians, but to talk to the gunmen would smack of weakness, he declared. He saw the disarming of the IRA as an essential condition for negotiations. In this he was out of touch with reality, for Sinn Fein politicians saw the IRA as their national army.

In his bid to break the gunmen, Lloyd George gave his tacit support for the methods of counterterrorism then being practiced by the Auxiliaries and the Black and Tans. In a private meeting with Major General Tudor on June 6, Lloyd George assured him of his full support. The following day in conversation with Lt. Colonel Wilson, Chief of Dublin District Special Branch, Lloyd George expressed the opinion that "counter-murder was the best answer to IRA killing."[24] On July 23rd, Law advisor to Dublin Castle W.E. Wylie urged the British Cabinet not to refuse to talk to "murderers," for the IRA "were not committing outrages through blood-lust, but because they believed that they had been tricked by the British Government, and the only way to focus the eyes of Europe on their cause was the adoption of [these] methods."[25] In contrast, Walter Long was totally opposed to any negotiations, declaring, "We have no intention of entering into negotiations with ... men who have been guilty of these awful murders."

By August 1920, Macready began to express his concern about the actions of the ADRICS. The problem was one of indiscipline. His deputy, Major-General Tudor, reflected this concern in a memo to his men, but it was issued not as an order but as an instruction for "Information and Guidance." This softly-softly approach was taken up by Sir Hamer Greenwood, the Chief Secretary for Ireland, who stressed the positive action of the Auxiliaries. The employment of "energetic young men full of fight" was improving the RIC. He inferred that the upsurge of retaliation by them was "unfortunate" but perhaps understandable.

When captured, IRA men were interned in prison camps run by the military. Camps were established at Ballykinlar, County Down, and at Bere and Spike Islands, Cork. British Intelligence officers were based at the camps to gather information, but the intelligence gleaned was mixed. The British officers were handicapped by a lack of local knowledge. This prevented them from interrogating many of the prisoners successfully. One lesson they did learn, however, was that prisoners should be interrogated alone by one intelligence officer. This usually established a rapport between the two men. At first the questions would be innocuous, concerning the weather, sport, farming, or other points

6. Military Intelligence and the Paramilitaries 109

of common interest. Then gradually, questioning would lead on to more local matters, such as the village or neighborhood the man came from and details of the more prominent local people. This led on to political and military matters. This softly-softly approach was lost on the Auxiliary Intelligence Officers, who simply beat up prisoners to extract information and confessions. The censorship of internees' letters proved to be disappointing to Military Intelligence as a source of information. They were generally censored first of all by their own IRA leaders within the camps. By the time they had finished, there was very little of interest. Greater success was achieved by waylaying the "secret post." These were letters from the IRA officers smuggled out of the camp by released prisoners. These proved useful over time, allowing for the detailing of the structure of the local IRA Brigades and their officers.

Military Intelligence, as the Army's *Record of the Rebellion in Ireland* concluded, was gradually expanded to extend training to "a large number, suitable and available, in the ranks of the Auxiliary companies." More could have been done, but jealousy remained between the Army and the police. The author of the *Record of the Rebellion in Ireland... (Intelligence)* bitterly remarked, regarding Army Intelligence Officers, "They would have achieved even more had they been given clear and definite instructions as to their duties and had senior police officers had any conception as to what intelligence meant." This undoubtedly was another dig at Ormonde Winter.

By 1921, freed from police control, analysis by Military Intelligence showed that while British casualties were rising, those of the IRA out in the country, were proportionately greater. The IRA was losing by attrition. In Dublin, something similar was happening. Following the Custom House debacle (detailed in Chapter 10), some seventy members of the IRA were captured. Following a number of further raids leading on from that, more than 100 IRA men were also arrested in the capital and interned.[26]

If left to its own devices, Military Intelligence could have been more successful. The major setback to their success, the failure to arrest Michael Collins aside, was ill-advised government interference. This was coupled to the double system of police and Military Intelligence, which continued to involve in its loss of efficiency the failure of the police to pass on information quickly enough. As an example of the inefficiency between military and police, the author of *A Record of the Rebellion* points out the processing of captured documents:

> All documents captured by the troops are forwarded to the Brigade Headquarters. All documents captured by the police are forwarded to the local centre at the District Commissioner's office. It was duplication, and in the

process, delay. Each section typed up its findings, and distributed it to the other section, often consisting of over a hundred typed pages.... This meant that every branch had to read the whole of every epitome and then, where necessary, ask for a copy of the original.... This procedure could have been simplified.

A final reproach to the dual intelligence service is the comment by the compiler of *Records of the Rebellion*: "If all intelligence and all operations in the City had been controlled from one office better results might have been achieved and a great deal of friction and irritation would certainly have been avoided."

7

Winter Arrives

On May 11, 1920, as previously stated, the British Cabinet approved General Macready's proposal that all Irish intelligence should be put under a single Director of Intelligence. The man chosen for the job was Brigadier Ormonde de l'Epee Winter, who became known as "O." After completing his training at Sandhurst in 1894, Winter was seconded to the Royal Artillery. He spent two years in Ireland, from 1903 to 1905, but most of his service was spent in India. During World War I he served in Gallipoli in command of a battery, and later, in France, he commanded an artillery brigade. He was decorated and promoted and by 1920 was a full colonel. As newly appointed Chief of Police Winter was given the task of reorganizing an intelligence system. Assistant Under Secretary at Dublin Castle, Mark Sturgis, duly noted the arrival of Winter in his diary:

> "O" is a marvel—he looks like a wicked little white snake and can do everything! He is an Artillery Colonel and commanded a Division of artillery in France: in India, they say, he was tried for murder for a little escapade when doing secret service work.... He is clever as paint, probably entirely non-moral, a first class horseman, a card genius, knows several languages, is a super sleuth, and a most amazing original.[1]

Others, perhaps with hindsight, were not so sure. In an article published at the end of the war in *Blackwood's Magazine* in August 1922, the author, G. C. Duggan, Assistant Under Secretary for Ireland, under the penname "Periscope," wrote:

> Passing under the archway that pierces a block of buildings the Upper Castle Yard is entered. Who is this so lightly tripping, so debonair, his breast a blaze of medals won with the gunners in France and other fields? It is Colonel Winter, the Chief of Intelligence. That his only training is war, that he lacks any first-hand knowledge of Secret Service methods is irrelevant. He is a brave man, and one cannot cope with a secret society that holds life cheap without a stout heart. At first sight one would imagine him the typical colonel of light comedy—slight and small, dapper, delicate of speech, eyeglass

set in eye. He is one whom men would follow even to the cannon's mouth; perhaps not the best man for his present job, but hard-working, earnest and just.²

"Periscope" underestimated Winter's ability. True, he was a strange choice of appointment. He was a Royal Artillery officer, lacking any real experience in intelligence work prior to his appointment; but he did possess good organizational and analytical skills, and he was innovative. Winter, a slightly built, monocle-wearing 45-year-old, set about his new task with a will. When he came to the job, his primary sources of intelligence were the RIC and DMP weekly reports, plus whatever information that had been gained from Basil Thomson's Special Branch men before they had been assassinated. With the G Men of the DMP effectively neutered, there was little up-to-date information to go on. Winter analyzed the situation as to what was required and how he believed it could be obtained. In his 1955 autobiography, *Winter's Tale*, he set out his intentions as to how to progress:

1. Agents obtained by local Police and through the agency of Local Centres.
2. Agents recruited in England and sent to Ireland.
3. Dublin Special Branch.
4. Persons friendly to the Police volunteering information.
5. Those persons who give information whilst under arrest or in prison, with a view to escaping the punishment of their crimes.
6. Captured documents.
7. Information from ordinary Police sources based on observation.
8. "Moutons" [infiltrators—informers] placed either in prisons or in detention cells with rebel prisoners.
9. Listening sets.
10. Interrogation of prisoners.
11. Censorship of letters of prisoners in jail.
12. The establishment of Scotland House, London [the address to which anonymous letters were to be sent].

Though his brief was to coordinate intelligence for Ireland as a whole, he concentrated his energies in Dublin in the belief that if he cut off the snake's head in the capital, resistance in the rest of Ireland would collapse. General Macready was not so sure. He doubted that Winter had the organizational ability, but time would tell. Despite Macready's reservations, General Tudor promised Winter complete operational independence.

7. Winter Arrives

Winter began by recruiting 150 female staff as clerical workers. Unlike Military Intelligence, Winter ensured that they were English and that their backgrounds were checked. The male staff he employed, all educated, were former army and navy officers. His agents were experienced and ruthless men. They included men who had served in a similar capacity in India, Egypt, and Russia. They were not all murderers by any account, as some writers have indicated, but their experience and expertise made them a grave risk to the men of Irish Intelligence, for information indicated that their mission was to locate and destroy them.

Winter now looked at the sources of information available to him. With the virtual elimination of the G Men in Dublin and the isolation of the RIC out in the country, that aspect of information had dried up. As a stopgap measure, and until new agents could be trained up, Winter used the services of the paramilitary police, the Auxiliaries, of which he had some fifty Auxiliary Intelligence Officers seconded to him. At the end of the first six months, the RIC, in the shape of these "irregulars," had begun once more to assert the police presence, albeit in a more brutal fashion. Winter also reactivated former police touts. By a process of elimination, though, Irish Intelligence identified and executed them. As a consequence, this source of information also dried up.

Winter introduced a system to identify prisoners. In most cases, the prisoners would use an alias when captured. While the principal interrogators Hardy and King would do their best to beat it out of them, Winter sometimes used a more subtle method, in line with his stated intentions, as captured IRA man Bill Stapleton experienced:

> I was interrogated twice and brought before an identification parade on two occasions. This parade was organized in this way. A large canvas screen was outstretched across the corner of the quadrangle with holes cut here and there, and behind this screen individuals peered through at a prisoner, in this case myself, who was instructed to walk up and down, turn round, stand, bend down, speak, etc. We had no knowledge of the people behind this curtain except to hear them whisper.[3]

Meanwhile, Winter had set up a secret recruiting office for agents in England with the aid of Basil Thomson and Major C.A. Cameron, formerly head of the wartime British spy network in Holland and Belgium. Some sixty agents were recruited and trained at the spy school at Hounslow. Included in this number were men from the Military-run Dublin District Special Intelligence Branch. Others were ex-British officers and some civilians recruited on the "Old Boy" network.[4] The training of these men cost £15,000 a year, which a contemporary Military Intelligence report suggested was a waste in money:

The information which came through this source was always 24 to 48 hours delayed and this militated against its usefulness. Moreover, owing to the police office system it was never clear from what source their secret information came and no adequate arrangements for criticism by the expert branches were ever made. This of course is a fundamental necessity with secret service.[5]

There is a sense of interdepartmental rivalry, even frustration, here. The Army report goes on to point out that the efforts "of the police intelligence were concentrated on Dublin, where, however, the vicious plan of allowing parallel systems of secret service to work simultaneously in the same area, was encouraged." The Chief of Police, for his part, defended the overlapping of competing agencies because it preserved, in his own words, "police autonomy and kept up police morale." The problem of rivalry had arisen because the British Government, in a face-saving gesture, had decided that the insurrection should be dealt with as a police action rather than, as it really was, a war.

Winter's agents, once trained, started arriving in Dublin. They found accommodation in hotels and guest houses and were equipped with suitable cover, such as, in Winter's own words, taking up occupations such as "shop assistants, garage hands, and similar occupations." The more successful agents, though, became travelling sales representatives, positions which gave them the opportunity of moving around the country and establishing contacts.

One of Winter's less successful agents, as even he himself admitted,[6] was Frank Digby Hardy. He was an ex-convict, a man who lived on his wits. In many ways he was an ideal spy. Trained at the London Spy School he arrived in Dublin in July 1920. He established contact with Irish Intelligence by a roundabout route. Hardy promised all sorts of things if only he could become part of Irish Intelligence. He admitted that he was a British agent but wanted to change sides. Unfortunately, his mail was intercepted by Irish Intelligence agents within the Post Office. Hardy was trailed by Vinnie Byrne, and Tom Cullen had his room searched. Rather than "oggs him," it was decided to play him and expose British Intelligence and its use of agents provocateur. It was arranged that he should meet the heads of the IRA, but instead he was taken before a group of Irish and English journalists. Arthur Griffith was present at the meeting, held on September 16th, to lend greater authenticity. Hardy admitted that he was a British agent but had developed a bitter hatred for his mentor, Basil Thomson, who was "the man responsible for all the dirty work in Ireland." Hardy was induced to say what he could do to help the Irish cause, even to committing a murder. He completely incriminated himself. Then Griffith produced a copy of his criminal record and exposed him for what he was—an agent provocateur for British Intelligence. Hardy was publicly exposed for what he was, an incompetent British spy. He was ordered to leave Ireland. The next day the story was published in a number of Irish and British newspapers—"An English Spy Unmasked." British Intelligence was held up as a farce. An embarrassed Winter was not best pleased.

One of Winter's successes, brought about by a seemingly random raid, was the discovery of the offices in Molesworth Street, Dublin, of the outlawed newspaper *The Irish Bulletin*. The British seized the typewriter, duplicating machine, all the paper, and the names and addresses of the recipients, who included known politicians, journalists, and establishment figures in Britain, America, and on the Continent. Winter's intelligence team came up with the idea of forging and distributing copies to show the IRA in a bad light. The ruse lasted for about a month. What they were unaware of was that the *Bulletin* was also produced from another address. The recipients were thus receiving two copies of the newssheet. The typeface was the same, as was the edition numbering. The compilers of the "official" copy realized what was going on and announced the raid in their copies. When Winter's team missed a day of publication, and their sequential numbering differed, people were able to distinguish the forgery from the real thing. The enterprise was then dropped.

Raids and the searches of private houses and other buildings formed the bulk of military operations. Their objective was the arrest of wanted men and the seizure of arms and written or typed material to be evaluated later. Raids were conducted on the basis of information obtained by the police or the public. A high percentage of searches ended in failure—sometimes because the information was old and sometimes because details were leaked prior to a raid. Learning from their failures, the Army negated the second option by not revealing details until the last possible moment of a raid. Raiding parties learnt by the experience of failure. On the ground they learnt too that it was better to halt some distance away from the target and proceed quietly on foot, wearing rubber-soled and -heeled shoes to avoid detection. They also then began surrounding the house prior to entry to capture anyone attempting to escape once the raid had begun.

From the day of his arrival Winter was a marked man. Irish Intelligence sources within the Castle were quick to inform Collins about the selection and arrival of the new British Intelligence coordinator. Collins ordered his immediate assassination. Bernard Byrne from The Squad was in the initial ambush party:

Captain Kitton[7] and Colonel Winters were coming over to Dublin with a great record behind them for Intelligence work. Our information was that they were arriving at Kingstown by the evening mail-boat and would proceed to Dublin Castle by army transport. It was decided by our headquarters that a serious effort should be made to get these men on their journey into town on the day of their arrival in Ireland.

After much consideration it was agreed that that section of the road outside Blackrock Park and in line with Merrion Avenue would be the most suitable place for our attack to take place.

As far as I can recollect this was the first time that the Squad carried hand grenades with a view to using them against British agents listed for execution. So great was our aversion to grenades that before proceeding on the job we actually drew lots to determine who would carry and throw the grenades.

We arrived at our selected positions, some by tram and others by a small van which carried the bulk of our arms. The van was in a position in Merrion Avenue, with a view to providing us with a quick getaway.

This was another case where we were crediting our enemy with too little intelligence, because, while our attention was concentrated on the Blackrock-Kingstown route, a convoy consisting of two double-turret cars, one whippet and two armoured Lancias, was proceeding from Dublin to meet the boat. Ned Kellegher had by some extraordinary process become aware of the fact that this new feature had entered into the programme, and arrived with all haste to tell us to call off the job.[8]

Thereafter opportunities of killing Winter were scarce. He rarely ventured out of Dublin Castle during daylight hours. At night, when he did venture forth on some special mission, it was usually with a party of armed Auxiliaries and men from Dublin District Special Branch. Curiously, when he did go out on raids at night, he seems to have been in disguise. Whether it was theatricals on his part or something more sinister is debatable. Mark Sturgis noted in his diary entry for October 26, 1920:

> "O" came in this evening in a chestnut moustache and wig, trench coat, flannel trousers and bowler hat—looking the most complete swine I ever saw—He had been pinching M.C's [Michael Collins] "War Chest" from the Munster and Leinster Bank—quite illegally I expect—brought in about £4,000, £1,500 more to come. Hardly his job? And a bad make up at that.[9]

Certainly Winter seemed to have adopted a more hands-on approach than his predecessors. IRA Staff Officer Ernie O'Malley, later subject to brutal questioning, suggests that Winter was himself involved in questioning prisoners:

> The castle murder gang prowled around the guardroom. Colonel Winters [sic], known as the "Holy Terror," began the new interrogation with the added menace of Captain Hardy, both of whom the two other [IRA] officers knew by reputation and through photographs.[10]

Senior civil servant Mark Sturgis hints at something more sinister in Winter's questioning as he noted in his diary for May 19: "another poor devil has committed suicide in 'O's' office—this is the fifth—there seems to be a curse on the place.[11] In his comment there is perhaps a suggestion that while one suicide might be considered a tragedy, five deaths suggests that the men in custody might have been beaten to death for information.

Nighttime from 11:00 p.m., during curfew, was the time when British Intelligence was at its most active. It was then that Auxiliaries and Black and Tans made their raids and arrests. Sometimes in their seemingly random raids they would stumble upon something of interest, which when analyzed led on to specific targets. A nighttime curfew had been introduced in Dublin on February 20, 1920. Thus, the streets of the capital were mainly empty save for those engaged in essential work. Uniformed officers of the DMP patrolled the nighttime streets of Dublin. Among these policemen were men working for Irish Intelligence. From time to time, they would stop plainclothes British agents and demand to see some form of identity. Having examined their identity passes, the policemen would make a mental note of their details, then pass on the information to Michael Collins. Eventually, a list of these "hush-hush" men was compiled by Irish Intelligence.

It would seem that in particular cases British Secret Service men acted alone. As such, they were just as likely to become the prey. British "Tommy," Private J.P. Swindlehurst, stationed in Dublin, recorded in his diary:

> The nights have been full of alarms, shots, and bombs awakened the echoes, mostly after midnight. Early this morning I was on sentry at the main entrance [of Jury's Hotel, in Dame Street, commandeered by the British] behind the iron gate, when the noise of a motor and running footsteps caused my pal and I to look out for trouble. We got it, the runner was a secret service man being pursued by Sinn Feiners in a car.
> They dropped him with a fusilade of shots, when he was about two yards from the doorway. His impetuous roll, knocked us into the hall, when we were going to reply to them. In a few seconds they were gone, leaving a bomb in the roadway which failed to explode. The victim was luckily only slightly wounded, one through the leg and another through his hand. We don't know where he had been but a big party of men moved out armed to the teeth at dawn, so he must have got some information which was acted upon.[12]

A second opportunity eventually arose to kill the spymaster, who by then was assumed by Irish Intelligence to be deeply involved in the British "Murder Gang." These were the men who had killed Sinn Fein loan organizer John Lynch and shopkeeper Peter O'Carroll. The job of killing

Winter was given to the Active Service Unit of the 4th Battalion, some eight men in total. Two of the ASU, Joe McGuinness and George Nolan, give brief accounts of the attack. McGuinness relates an incident in 1921:

> We received information one morning that a touring car would be coming from Dublin Castle via Thomas Street to the Viceregal lodge and that some important person would be travelling in it. We got instructions that we were to attack this car. The section took up positions between Francis Street and Meath Street, and George Nolan and myself took up positions in Wright's butcher stall. Other members of the section were spread out below and above our position. We were not long in position when a member of the section fired a shot. We knew then that the car we were awaiting was approaching our position. When the car approached the butcher's shop where we were standing, we rushed out and opened fire on it with revolvers. The car zig-zagged then, and the man who was sitting in the back fell forward. The occupant of the car, we learned later, was a Major Winters who, I believe, was a member of the Auxiliaries in Dublin Castle.[13]

Nolan adds briefly to McGuinness's account:

> We opened fire on the car immediately with revolver and grenade with the result that we wounded the military officer.[14]

Winter was indeed wounded in the hand and suffered minor superficial glass cuts during the assault. It shook him up but did not put him off. Mark Sturgis puts the date of the attack as June 2. In his diary of the following day, he notes:

> Friday 3rd June: Yesterday afternoon Ormonde was wounded in the hand in an attack on his car in Dublin. I went and saw him in the evening in George V Hospital. Still cheerful, he expressed regret on two heads (1) that his hand hurts damnably (2) that he hadn't killed the man who shot him. The street was full of people at the time and both "O" and Lockhart who was with him said that the street seemed to empty by magic when the shots and a bomb or two began to fly.[15]

Winter returned to the job determined to implement his 12-point policy to defeat the IRA. He established a central office in Dublin for the collecting, dissecting and passing on of intelligence material. A second bureau, under MI5's Vernon Kell, was established in London. It passed on to Winter all information it received relating to Irish matters. Out in the countryside, RIC police stations and Auxiliary barracks each appointed an Intelligence Officer, who likewise passed on information to the central office in Dublin. In the capital, F Company of the Auxiliaries, based in the Dubline Castle, formed an intelligence section later to be known as the "Cairo Gang."

In September 1920, Winter, in accordance with his plan and in collaboration with police headquarters at Scotland Yard, set up a scheme to obtain information by correspondence. Anyone with information was invited to pass on that information by sending an anonymous letter to an address in London, Scotland House, just across the road from Scotland Yard. This scheme was a nonstarter. It foundered because of IRA infiltration of the postal system. Irish Intelligence intercepted these letters and either destroyed them or doctored them, implicating Loyalists as IRA supporters. Winter soon came to understand that the post offices had been penetrated. He writes that "[t]he ineffectiveness of the postal service led to the necessity of conducting all correspondence either by courier or by aerial mail, which frequently caused delay and handicapped the transmission of intelligence." Not even this proved safe. The IRA frequently halted motorcycle couriers and relieved them of their mail.

Perhaps Winter's most successful policy was the setting up of the Central Raid Bureau in October 1920. Winter's team, all screened by Scotland Yard, were responsible for:

> Filing all reports on raids.
> Receiving all documents, arms and articles seized in such raids by both the military and the police. Filing and safeguarding them so that at a future date they may be used as evidence against the owner if arrested.
> Epitomizing such documents and distributing the epitomes to all concerned.

The initial number of raiding parties, twelve, rose to twenty by October 1920. By December G.O.C. Dublin District claimed:

> 1. Owing to the courtesy shown by troops, civilians are beginning to realize that, when innocent, they have nothing to fear from a military raid.
> 2. Owing to the frequent Military and Police raids, the rebel leaders are continually on the run.
> 3. Owing to the experience gained from such affrays as at Fernside and Talbot St., and the sound tactical Principles displayed by military raiding parties, ill-disposed civilians now hesitate to conceal dangerous rebels.

Point 1 of the above list was greatly influenced by the use of women searchers and questioners. The searching of women by men was extremely controversial. From an early stage, Winter engaged the use of female officers from the Women Police Service at Eccleston Square in London. Miss M.S. Allen in *The Pioneer Policewomen* relates that they were obliged to hold themselves in readiness, at any hour of the day or night, to accompany the Crown forces on raiding expeditions, whenever the presence of uniformed women was considered desirable. They were to assist in the search for firearms, military dispatches or any letters or papers likely to contain information useful to the Crown.[16]

By the Truce of July 1921, as Winter himself testifies, the Central Raid Bureau had made 6,311 raids in the greater Dublin area[17]:

> In 1921 nearly all the officers of the Dublin Brigade, IRA were known and a good percentage of them had been arrested, including the IRA Director of Intelligence, the head of their secret service and four battalion I[intelligence] O[fficer]s. There were trained agents on most of the boats coming to Dublin and Kingstown. Eight of the principal departments of Dail Eireann and the IRA had been raided successfully and three [arms] dumps had been taken. Twice was the GHQ of the IRA raided, on one occasion the Chief of Staff's personal office and plans being captured, and only three days before the Truce the office of the IRA police was taken.[18]

The success of the raids lay in the documents discovered. These inevitably produced a paper trail which led to other raids and other successes. In the three months from November 1920 to February 1921, 1,745 arrests were made. Winter was obliged to bring in further Scotland Yard-vetted, outside staff from England to read through and correlate the material seized.

In the raids, key personnel in the IRA structure came very close to capture. Several times IRA Chief of Staff Richard Mulcahy was almost captured. The British raided a number of the twenty hideouts and offices, scattered in and around Dublin, that Mulcahy used.

As noted previously, Winter's men also came very close one night to capturing Michael Collins himself when they raided Cullenswood House, Oakley Road, in the south Dublin suburb of Ranelagh. This was Patrick Pearse's old home, now converted into flats. Mulcahy and his wife lived here, on the upper floor, and Collins maintained an upstairs office. All three fled the premises but left behind some important papers. Included were the complete rolls and addresses of 3,000 members of the Dublin IRA Brigade. By March 1920, a fair proportion of those listed had been arrested. The fault here was directly linked to Collins himself. To reprise, Richard Bennett noted of Collins:

> He had a fastidious mania for documentation; it seemed that his training as a filing clerk in the City would not allow him to destroy any papers.[19]

The documents provided the British with further paper trails both in Dublin and out in the country regarding IRA structures and operations. Also secured were a number of checkbooks that led to the confiscation

7. Winter Arrives

of about £3,000 of Sinn Fein money, funds that were lodged in various private accounts. The checkbooks also contained the names and addresses of the account holders, which led to further raids and at least one murder.

One of Winter's most successful raids was carried out on New Years Eve, December 31, 1920. It was on the flat of Miss Eileen McGrane at 21, Dawson Street. Miss McGrane was a prominent Sinn Feiner and lecturer in the National University. Eamon Broy indicated that the address was believed to have been given to the Castle authorities by a Loyalist who spotted Tom Cullen, a former neighbor in Wicklow, entering the house. Amongst the papers discovered was a sizeable portion of Tom Cullen's secret papers, which included reports from the political section of the DMP. These included documents that eventually led to the arrest of Eamon Broy. Some of the documents found had obviously been typed by him. Collins acted immediately. He contacted Broy's superior and warned him that he would be killed if he acted against Broy. Not wishing to be assassinated, the superior destroyed all the evidence he could find that implicated Broy. Next Collins persuaded another detective, who shared Broy's office, to disappear suddenly out of the country. His trip to America was paid for by Irish Intelligence. When the war was over, the detective returned to Ireland and was awarded promotion within the new police service. Also discovered amongst the papers was the secret headquarters of Cumman na mBan. It was situated just across the road from Miss McGrane's flat. It too was raided, and papers were taken away. Miss McGrane was interrogated by Winter himself over an hour and a half period, but he got nothing from her. With a suggestion of intended violence towards her, a colleague of Winter also interrogated her, but with the same result. Though she refused to talk, Winter's men were getting closer to their overall object—the capture or death of Michael Collins.

On April 1, 1921, Winter's men raided Collins's headquarters at 5, Mespil Road. The raid discovered a hoard of important papers. Miss Eileen Hoey, Collins's assistant, who was present, was arrested and suffered ill-treatment during interrogation. She gave nothing away and was eventually released.

More could have been achieved by the British had the handling of captured papers been dealt with more efficiently—a point Military Intelligence made more than once. There was always a delay in passing on information, and much to the frustration of Military Intelligence, seized documents were not passed on in full but summarized. As a result, on occasion, vital information was omitted. If there was anything of interest, then Military Intelligence had to request the complete document to be sent to them. This created delays as the author of the Army's *Record of the Rebellion* indicates in his report.

Winter's Intelligence failure was that, in promoting himself and police Intelligence, he locked himself into the old British Intelligence failure of internecine rivalry between the competing intelligence agencies. Perhaps an equal error was in underestimating the enemy. He failed to appreciate either the brains or the purpose behind IRA Intelligence. In his official account of the intelligence war, *A Report on the Intelligence Branch of the Chief of Police,* Winter sums up:

> It has been said that no European can fathom the mind of an Oriental, and it might equally well be said that no Englishman fully grasp the inner psychology of the Irish rebel character.
>
> Two things tend to make this rebellious movement remarkable: one is that it has, up to the present, produced no great man, and the other is that, for the first time in history, the Irishman has not succumbed to the temptation of gold. The former is, possibly due to the fact that, with one or two exceptions, the heads of the rebel organisations are recruited from a low and degenerate type, unequipped with intellectual education, the latter to the fact that a surfeit of terror has replaced an appetite for gain.[20]

His denial of the capability of the IRA and its Intelligence Department is, in fact, a reflection of his own failure. He simply could not understand the Irish mentality as he himself pointed out. In modern parlance, he could not get his head around how they had succeeded, especially when British Intelligence had all the advantages:

> Much has been said of the efficiency of the Sinn Fein Intelligence; it has even been eulogised in the Press, but, with the manifest advantages under which it worked, it is surprising that it has been better, and many instances could be cited in which it has been entirely at fault. In respect, however, to the class of information derived from captured documents, the Sinn Fein organisation was at a disadvantage compared with that of the Crown Forces.[21]

Yet despite Winter's measured success, General Macready was to write of him to Sir John Anderson, "[He] has not got the right method, and we here very much doubt whether he will ever get it."

At the end of the Intelligence dual between the rival systems, it has to be admitted that Irish Intelligence came out the winner. Perhaps if the politicians in London had not interfered so much and perhaps given another year with no holds barred, by sheer attrition Winter and his men might have won—eventually.

8

Dublin Special Branch— The Murder Gang

Dublin Special Branch, or Special Branch Dublin District, established in May 1920, was commanded by Lieutenant-Colonel Walter Wilson, a former General Staff officer. Though nominally under military control, it acted very much as an autonomous department. It was tasked with collecting and collating intelligence within the Dublin district. This included:

1. Secret Agents' reports.
2. Military Intelligence reports.
3. Informers' reports.
4. Documents discovered by members of "D" Branch and by military and police raids.
5. RIC and DMP reports.
6. Scotland House* reports (information sent by mail.)
7. Passing information to Registry, Chief of Police, for filing.

Home Office Directorate of Intelligence

Special Branch was initially staffed by ex-officers and Auxiliaries, though this was expanded to include others with specialist skills.[1] Dave Neligan, Collins's agent within the Castle, elaborated:

> The British flooded the place with secret service men. Some of these were civilians, some serving officers, some ex-officers and NCOs and some professional agents. Most were Anglo-Irish or British, though their head, Count Sevigne, may have been French and looked it. Of course these fellows had a different name and cover story for every day of the week.[2]

The department was based in Dublin Castle and used one of the offices allocated to General Boyd, Head of Army GHQ. From the start, the newly formed Special Branch operated as a plainclothes Secret Service unit. Its personnel were referred to by the Dublin Castle administration as the "hush-hush men." Taking up his position, Lt. Col. Wilson reviewed the situation and divided Dublin and its suburbs into six manageable areas. Each area, he decided, should be overseen by a trained senior agent. These officers recruited a number of sub-agents, men whom IRA Intelligence referred to as "touts." These men, many of them Irishmen, listened in pubs and restaurants, and trailed likely subjects. Arms dumps were raided, and IRA men were picked up. Often relying on brutality, the new organization began to achieve results. Irish Intelligence chief Frank Thornton could not help but admire what they achieved within a relatively short time:

> ...[T]hey decided to set up a full time Secret Service outside of the Army, working on proper continental lines with a Central Headquarters and other houses forming minor centres scattered all throughout the city in which they operated. In this way they built up quite a formidable organisation and were without doubt securing quite a lot of very valuable information.[3]

Writing in 1984, Eunan O'Halpin said of these new agents:

> In the violent circumstances of the time they did not operate within the law; suspects were sometimes shot, and prisoners tortured. The political repercussions of such behaviour probably outweighed the results gained, though it must be said that they made life a great deal harder for the IRA and scored some successes against them.[4]

One of the senior members of this new unit was Captain R. D. Jeune, a hero of the Great War. He had been in Ireland since January 1919 and had witnessed the assassinations or, in his eyes, the murders of the men of G. Department. In an account intended to have been published in the *Daily Telegraph* in the summer of 1972, he recalled his induction and training:

> A rather hastily improvised Intelligence Organisation was formed, of which I was a member, and after a short course of instruction at Hounslow, we were sent over to Dublin in the early summer of 1920. The first batch were instructed to pose, initially, as RE [Royal Engineer] officers, but this rather futile procedure was soon dropped and the work consisted of getting to know the town thoroughly, tailing "Shinners," and carrying out small raids, with a view to collecting all possible information which would lead us eventually to stamping out the revolt.[5]

Having been trained in the basics of spy craft and intelligence gathering, these agents were integrated into Dublin society according to their abilities and qualifications. By and large they lived outside the Castle in the environment in which they operated. While training in espionage in a classroom gave them the basics, the reality of life in Dublin was altogether different. These new intelligence officers lacked detailed knowledge of the enemy in the field. In many cases they lacked photographs of the wanted men they were seeking. They were also ignorant of Dublin, not only of its streets but also of its people and their quirky ways. As such, they were forced to use the services of the detectives and uniformed men of the DMP when going out on a raid. By this time, a number of the remaining G. men and uniformed officers were working for Michael Collins. When notified in advance of these raids, they were able to warn the intended subjects to hide. Like the men of Military Intelligence, the new arrivals were also greatly hampered in their Secret Service work by their own English accents, which gave them away as soon as they opened their mouths. For the moment, though, using paid informants and the nighttime curfew, they held sway during the hours of darkness. With the help of the Army, they sealed off city blocks and searched inside every building. It was hit and miss, but sometimes they struck lucky. Irish Intelligence was notorious for leaving paper trails. Captain Robert Dyne Jeune, in his account of his experiences in Ireland as a British spy, recalled a covert night-time burglary:

> I received orders to carry out a surreptitious night raid on the house of Arthur Griffith, the self-styled Vice-President of the Irish Republic. A successful and unobserved entry was effected, and a number of subversive documents were removed, which proved to be of considerable interest.
> On the following day, the local press published a report stating Mr. Griffith's house had been raided by "expert Cracksmen!"[6]

Jeune does not go into detail regarding the contents of the documents, but they may have included lists of Sinn Fein members and their duties. These would undoubtedly have included the national loan bankers and the small-time businesses who secretly hid money in their accounts. If so, this may well have influenced the murder of at least two men in the autumn of 1920.

In their raids the men of Special Branch soon developed a reputation for brutality. To what degree this was directed by senior Dublin-based officials like Lt. Col. Walter Wilson or Ormonde Winter, or, indeed, by London is unclear. What is evident, however, is that this new department, while collecting information, also acted as a death squad. Fifteen murders were committed in July, eleven in August, eighteen in September and twenty-three in the first eighteen days of November 1920. All were attributed to the Crown forces.[7] That Prime Minister Lloyd George was aware of what was going on, and indeed approved of the murders, is confirmed in the diary entry of Field Marshal Sir Henry Wilson, Chief of the Imperial General Staff, for September 1, 1920:

> I told Lloyd George that the Authorities were gravely miscalculating the situation but he reverted to his amazing theory that someone was murdering two Sinn Feiners to every loyalist the Sinn Feiners were murdering. I told him that this was not so, but he seemed to be satisfied that a counter murder association was the best answer to Sinn Fein murders.[8]

That there were British murder gangs operating in Ireland was confirmed later that month by Police Chief General Hugh Tudor to Sir Henry. In his diary for September 23rd, Wilson wrote:

> Tudor made it very clear that the police and the Black and Tans and the 100 Intell[igence] officers are all carrying out reprisal murders.... At Balbriggan, Thurles and Galway yesterday the local police marked down certain S[inn] F[einer]s as in their opinion the actual murderers or instigators and then coolly went and shot them without question or trial. Winston [Churchill] saw very little harm in this but it horrifies me.[9]

To disguise the fact that murders were taking place, coroners' inquests were abolished in favor of military inquiries. By the use of his agents within the Castle, Collins was able to show that a murder plot did exist and that the murderers had been given a free hand to operate. Patrick Kennedy from Irish Intelligence, through his contacts with corrupt Auxiliary cadets, was given details of these operations:

> I do remember the nature of the information that we received from Reynolds [an Auxiliary]. Reynolds reported the conversations of Auxiliaries describing how they carried out shootings, who carried them out and who the ring leaders were.[10]

As Frank Thornton reported in his Witness Statement:

> GHQ Intelligence got down to the job of tracking down and checking up on the activities of this new Secret Service Organisation almost at once and it was not long until we knew their Headquarters and their two Sub-Headquarters, and in actual fact we discovered that the caretaker of one of the houses from which they operated in Lower Pembroke Street was the sister of an old IRA man. You can imagine the rest, contact was made. It was soon managed to get an IRA man appointed as hall porter and gradually others were placed on the various staffs in the houses, resulting in very valuable information being collected from British Secret Service. In actual fact we had a key for the hall-door and keys of all the doors of all the rooms in these houses. We tracked down and got a complete detailed report on every individual. In this respect I would like to pay a very high tribute to the Intelligence Officers of the Dublin Brigade who rendered such very valuable service to GHQ in compiling that information.

As information started coming in, these men were identified both by name and from photographs. Their addresses were supplied by Lily Mernin. Watch was also kept on new arrivals. Intelligence Officer Joseph Kinsella relates:

We were continually on the watch for strangers moving in and taking up residences in the Battalion area. When it was reported to me that a stranger had moved into the area I instructed members of my staff who resided in the area to find out all they could about the stranger. This was usually through milkmen, maids and local shopkeepers. When I had sufficient information about the stranger I passed it on to the Brigade Intelligence Officer.[11]

Martin Finn of C Company, 1st Battalion of the IRA, identified one notorious Auxiliary Intelligence man closely linked to the Murder Gang. He was Captain William Lorraine King, who was staying at the hotel in Athboy, County Meath:

Captain King—well known subsequently as an active Intelligence Officer for the British—had been stopping in the local hotel for a period ostensibly engaged as sales representative for the Minimax Fire Extinguisher Company, an English company with headquarters in Dublin. He, apparently, used this as a means of travelling round the country with a view to obtaining information regarding the movements of the IRA.[12]

IRA Intelligence Officer Christopher Crothers, was alerted to a nest of British agents based in Dublin itself:

About the beginning of March 1920 a friend of my grandmother, a Miss Kate Murphy, was employed in a house numbered 15, Upper Fitzwilliam Street. Miss Murphy approached me one evening when she was visiting the house and told me that about twelve men had taken up residence in the house where she was employed. She thought that they were ex-British Officers because of the fact that one man to whom the others appeared to look up to was a man who had lost his arm in the Great War. He was known as Captain Bennett. I asked her if she was sure they were ex-officers and she said she could not be certain. She added they were all acting as Commercial Travellers. What they were travelling in she did not know, with the exception of Bennett who, she knew, was travelling for Irish horn beads. I asked her why she came to me with this story and she told me that while these men were supposed to be commercial travellers they never went out in the daytime; that the earliest they left the house was 5 o'clock in the evening and that they were not back when she was retiring.[13]

Other IRA Intelligence Officers searched their rooms, and a watch was kept on the house. In August Miss Murphy reported back to Crothers. The men were leaving. They had become aware that they were being watched. They suspected that Miss Murphy was involved, and upon leaving Bennett goaded her "that her friends would find it very hard to find them." The agents left, and later split up into ones and twos in their new accommodations.

No matter how often they changed their addresses, any change had to be notified at Special Branch headquarters. Here Lily Mernin, Collins's agent, typed up the new lists and passed on a copy each week to

Irish Intelligence. As noted previously, "The little gentleman" or "Lt. G." was her code name. The change from feminine to masculine gave her extra protection should any material be captured by the British. She further added to the information she provided:

> I was asked by the IRA Intelligence Squad to get what information I could about the movements of these officers. These were mainly descriptive particulars for the purpose of identification, where they resided, and where they frequented, also the registration numbers on motor cars used by them.... When I got to know the Auxiliaries better, I accompanied Frank Saurin (known as Mr Stanley) to various cafes where I identified for him some of the Auxiliaries whom I knew.[14]

The Castle authorities put together concerts and whist drives for its personnel, and this proved to be another source of identification. With a shortage of women, the girls of the typing pool were encouraged to bring along their friends to these social gatherings. Lily Mernin continues:

> On one occasion I asked Frank [Saurin] for a reliable girl, whom I could trust, who would come along to the whist drives with me, to enable her to get to know these Auxiliaries and so prove a further source of identification. He sent along Miss Sally McAsey, who is now his wife. She did her work very well.[15]

Having identified the names and addresses of other Secret Service men, and in the absence of photographs, Collins needed to put faces to these names. He arranged for Tom Cullen and Frank Thornton to meet with Neligan and Broy and pretend to be their touts. They met at Rabbiatti's saloon, one of the haunts of the "hush-hush" men. Frank Thornton recalled:

> ...as you know there are high-backed seats with a table in the middle and Tom and I found ourselves with three of these [British] touts sitting around a table having fish and chips. A general discussion was taking place when one of these fellows, who was an English man, turned to me and said—"Gor blimey, how did you learn the Irish brogue? We're here in Dublin for the last twelve months and we can't pick up any of it. You fellows seem to have perfected it." Of course, naturally we told them that there was an art in these matters, and just passed it over. Naturally men of this kind were very little use, but the British didn't realise that until it was too late.[16]

Having established themselves as touts, Thornton, Cullen and Frank Saurin began frequenting the Secret Service men's other haunts, at some considerable risk, it should be added:

> At that time most of the British Secret Service agents and British Intelligence Officers and Auxiliary Intelligence Officers met at a place which was well known in Dublin as Kidd's Buffet—Kidd's Back it was known—in

Grafton Street, and presently Jammets Back. Now here is where a lot of our information was picked up, and again it had to be picked up by taking a very big risk. Tom Cullen, Frank Saurin and myself were deputed to act with our two Secret Service friends who then frequented Kidd's Buffet with the Secret Service. We were introduced in the ordinary way as touts and eventually became friends of men like Major Bennett, Colonel Ames and a number of other prominent Secret Service Officers. Naturally Collins and all his staff and the whole activities of the organisation were discussed there daily. On one day, one of these officers turned suddenly to Tom Cullen and said, "Surely you fellows know these men—Liam Tobin, Tom Cullen and Frank Thornton, these are Collins' three officers and if you can get these fellows we could locate Collins himself." Needless to remark, if the ground opened and swallowed us, we could not have been more surprised, and for the moment we felt that we had walked into a trap, but that wasn't so at all. It was a genuine query to three Irishmen whom they believed should know all about the particular fellows they mentioned. The fact remains that although they knew of the existence of the three of us and they knew of the existence of Collins, they actually had no photograph of any of us, and had a very poor description of either Collins or the three of us.[17]

There were known photographs of Collins in the possession of British Intelligence from the time of his earlier arrest, but by the Autumn of 1920 the fresh-faced youth was now, with all his concerns and worries, anything but. The war had taken its toll.

The documents stolen from the house of Arthur Griffith by Captain Jeune would have been passed on to Colonel Winter, Chief of Police Intelligence. He, in turn, would have analyzed the documents and passed on the material to the relevant authorities in Dublin and throughout Ireland. This probably included the RIC in county Limerick. On September 12th, Limerick County Councilor John Aloysius Lynch travelled up to Dublin by train. He was the local Sinn Fein overseer of the Dail Loan and brought with him £23,000 to deposit with the Ministry of Irish Finance. Lynch booked into the Royal Exchange Hotel in Parliament Street and was allocated room 6, which was on the third floor. Having handed the money over to the managers of the Loan Scheme, he spent the next fortnight in the capital involved in Sinn Fein business.

In the early hours of the morning of September 23rd, three Auxiliary officers and a small group of soldiers arrived at the Royal Exchange Hotel and demanded entrance. While the hotel night porter, William Barrett, was held at gunpoint in the hotel entrance, the three Auxiliaries, wearing trench coats, military caps and goggles, looked through the hotel register to discover the room of their intended target. Then they climbed the stairs up to the third floor where they shot John Lynch. It was Neligan's belief that they had confused him with Liam Lynch, the County Cork IRA guerrilla leader. It seems more probable, though, that they knew exactly who he was. Colonel Winter was actively involved in the pursuit of the Dail Loan, as previously indicated, when he returned to the Castle one night, disguised in a "chestnut moustache and wig, trench coat..." having successfully found £4,000 of the Loan, as civil servant Mark Sturgis related in his diary. Rather curiously, neither the hotel porter nor the other guests heard the shot being fired. It would appear that a silencer was connected to the gun, or, indeed, it was of a make that made little noise. Some twenty minutes later, after their departure, a party of Dublin Metropolitan Police arrived. They claimed that they had been informed by the military that a guest had been shot. The official report of the incident claims:

> In the early hours of this morning a military party, guided by members of the Royal Irish Constabulary, went to the Exchange Hotel, Parliament Street, for the purposes of arresting a man named Jack Lynch, who was occupying No. 6 bedroom on the third floor. When the officers entered the bedroom Lynch fired at them with a revolver, the bullet striking the wall at the foot of the bed, where it was afterwards discovered. The fire was returned by a member of the party and Lynch was shot through the head. A six chamber revolver with five chambers loaded and one recently discharged was found by the police at Lynch's right hand.

The Dublin City Coroner was informed by the police that an inquest would not be permitted. Instead, the death would be investigated by a Military Court. Their verdict was that Jack Lynch had been killed in self defense. Collins was very anxious to have the assassins identified. He instructed David Neligan to find out what he could. In pursuit, Neligan wrote:

> I visited College Police Station where I found a friend on duty. He allowed me to look through the Occurrence Book, a huge volume which contained all messages and incidents reported. In it was a copy of a "phone message from a certain British military officer" stating that he and others, including Captain Baggally, with certain RIC officers had gone to arrest a Sinn Feiner at the hotel, that he had fired at them and that they had replied, killing him. I copied the message and gave it to Collins…. The same British officer figured in another murder, a fact I knew from a description of him given to Volunteers…. Tobin brought me a slip of paper and on it was written in Collins' writing: "Concentrate on Hardy." That was the name of the killer.[18]

Irish Intelligence questioned the night porter, William Barrett, about what had happened early that morning. He related that at about 3 a.m. a band of twelve men wearing khaki caps and trench coats arrived at the hotel and demanded admission. They identified themselves as military. Upon being admitted, they leveled revolvers at him, and, having checked the register, three of them went upstairs. He heard them knock at a door, but no other sound was heard. None of the other guests heard anything, either. A description of the murderers was asked for. One of them in particular stood out. He had a curious gait when walking. Collins identified him as Captain Hardy, an Intelligence Officer in the Auxiliaries, a man with an artificial leg. It seems more probable though that the one-legged man was Captain Baggallay, who had also lost a leg during the war in Europe. Baggallay was officially a courts-martial officer, but following his death, the *Illustrated London News* for December 4, 1920, listed him as "[e]xtra regimentally employed," a possible euphemism for intelligence work. Neligan reported that Baggallay had telephoned Dublin Castle telling them of Lynch's presence in the hotel. The other two men who had entered Lynch's room were later identified as Henry Angliss, alias Patrick Mahon, and Lieutenant Charles Ratsch Peel. Information for this came through "Lt. G.," or Lily Mernin. She was told, off the record, by a fellow Dublin Castle typist, at whose house the men lodged, that Angliss, when drunk, had confessed to his part in the murder.

Captain Jocelyn Lee Hardy, whom Collins so strongly believed was the one-legged man, was born in London in 1894, the son of an Ulster Protestant, Howard Hardy. Probably because of the Irish connection, Jocelyn Hardy joined the Connaught Rangers in January 1914. On August 14, his regiment arrived in France at the beginning of the World War I. Hardy, a 2nd Lieutenant in D Company, was captured in a German encirclement on August 26, 1914. After several attempts, Hardy escaped from the Germans after three and a half years as a prisoner. Upon his return to Britain, he was seconded to another Irish regiment, the 2nd Inniskillings, and sent back to serve in France. In August 1918 he won the Military Cross for bravery for rescuing a severely wounded sergeant from a "no-man's land." On October 2nd, leading a counterattack near Dadizeele, he was badly wounded and lost a leg. He was fitted with a wooden leg. Despite his attempts at disguising the fact by adopting a fast pace in walking, he earned the cruel nickname of "Hoppy" Hardy. In November 1919, he married Kathleen Hutton-Potts and she accompanied her husband to Ireland. He had been seconded on "special duties." Wearing his Connaught Rangers uniform, Hardy served as an intelligence officer with F Company of the Auxiliaries, based in Dublin Castle. There is no record of his being a member of this paramilitary force itself, and Mark Sturgis, in his diary for February 13, 1920, clearly defined Hardy's status when he recorded, "Andy [Cope] tells me that Basil Thomson's man in the Castle, Captain Hardy, has tried to intimidate witnesses…" Hardy was a Secret Service man.

Collins was anxious that Hardy should be assassinated for his supposed part in the murder of John Lynch, a man known not to carry a gun. Through his deputy, Liam Tobin, Collins instructed Neligan to identify the murderers. He discovered that Captain Hardy lived outside the Castle in a flat in Harcourt Street that he shared with his wife Kathleen. Each day he commuted to work. Squad man Joe Guilfoyle, on observation, waited at the Dublin Castle entrance with Neligan the next morning, but Hardy did not show. After some time, Neligan advised him to leave in case his presence aroused interest. Guilfoyle cycled over to Harcourt Street where fellow Squad member Paddy Caldwell was waiting near Hardy's flat. Guilfoyle told him that the job was off for the time being. Unbeknownst to them, Hardy's wife, upstairs in their flat, had seen Caldwell loitering and telephoned the Castle. As the two men began to leave, a tender full of Auxiliaries came racing down the street. They grabbed the two IRA men and bundled them aboard the lorry and took them off to the Castle for questioning. Neligan discovered for Collins that "they were interrogated, knocked about and taken for a midnight ride." Such a ride was usually associated with the stock phrase "shot while attempting to escape." Surprisingly, though, they were not. The two men were brought back to the Castle and released the next day. Their interrogators apparently believed their story: the one had been waiting for the arrival of the other, hence his apparent loitering.

On another occasion, about the first week of September 1920, Hardy turned the tables on another surveillance operation. Patrick Caldwell of Irish Intelligence had been sent by Liam Tobin to keep watch on Hardy:

> Tobin sent me up to Harcourt Street to keep a watch on a British Intelligence Officer by the name of Captain Hardy who used to visit a hotel there. I kept up this watch at certain times for a period of a couple of days. One evening, about 6 o'clock, I saw a man with a limp go into the hotel having got out of a small van. At this time I was not sure whether this was Hardy or not but Joe Guilfoyle came along and I reported my suspicions to him. We both decided to watch and make sure if these were the men we were looking for. We left the spot where we were watching and went in the direction of Camden Street via Montagu Place. When we reached an archway leading into this place a British Officer and two soldiers ordered us quietly to get inside a Crossley tender. The man who ordered us into the van was Captain Hardy who, incidentally, was the man I had seen enter the hotel a short time before that. We were taken to Dublin Castle and questioned.

Both men had incriminating papers about their person when they had been arrested.

> Joe Guilfoyle was also being searched and he had in his possession a letter from Liam Tobin to a Mr. McCabe.... The officer who was searching

Guilfoyle became quite excited when he found this note and said to Captain Hardy, who was searching me, "We have here a letter from the notorious Liam Tobbin." With that Hardy forgot all about me and directed his attention to Guilfoyle.[19]

After some questioning the two prisoners were taken to the Bridewell, a fortified police station nearby. About 3 o'clock the next morning, Hardy and a number of others took Guilfoyle away. He was taken out to the golf links at Dartry and there blindfolded. He was threatened that he would be shot if he did not give them certain information. There were no beatings; in fact, Hardy spoke in a conciliatory tone, but reminded his prisoner, "You know we have full authority to shoot any IRA man as we think fit, that we have been guaranteed immunity from any disciplinary action, no matter how extreme." Guilfoyle played dumb, and somehow got away with it. He was returned to the Bridewell. Both men were given short prison sentences.

Hardy did have a sense of decency. The war in Ireland had hardened him; he had seen colleagues killed, but one moment in time seemed to remind him of what he once was. Bill Stapleton of The Squad tells the story. He had attended a meeting, and it was now late. There was a 10 p.m. curfew, and, carrying two guns, he decided to shorten his journey home and stay overnight at the Schweppe family home at 35, Mountjoy Square. Fred Schweppe had been out in 1916 and was now a section leader in Stapleton's old company. Also, there was Paddy Kennedy, an intelligence officer:

> I was pretty jaded when I arrived and fell asleep very quickly on a sofa in the front parlour. I went to sleep fully dressed with my guns on the sofa beside me. Paddy Kennedy lay on a single bed in the same room as me. My first recollection after falling asleep is that I was being yanked across the floor.... Then I found I was surrounded by Auxiliaries with guns pointing at me.... I thought this was the end. I heard loud shouting, cursing and swearing and a British Officer came in. I think he had on an Auxiliary cap and military tunic. He was limping and stuck his head into my face and to my amazement it was Hoppy Hardy.... At this time I had no idea of the reason of the raid. They yanked me into the other room where Fred Schweppe and his family slept.... There was no sign of Paddy Kennedy anywhere. They were interrogating Fred whom they had taken out of bed as he was endeavoring to put on some clothes. They were abusing him—pushing and shoving him and using most foul language. [This was just too much for Fred, and he told them straight] "I object to you using this language in the presence of my wife and children." I thought for one moment that this was the end as Hardy made a stride forward with his gun but stopped, and stayed looking at Fred for a few seconds; then turned round and sat down. From then on there was comparative quiet.[20]

Fred Schweppe and Bill Stapleton were lifted and taken to Dublin Castle for interrogation. From there they were taken to Arbour Hill Prison. There they met IRA man Tommy Keegan and his father, who owned the Schweppes' house. Both men had been badly beaten. The raid on the house had followed on from their arrests. Stapleton, Schweppe and Tommy Keegan's father were eventually released. Tommy Keegan was sentenced to four years but was released at the Truce.

On October 1, Arthur Griffith made a shock announcement to a party of international journalists that a number of Sinn Fein leaders had been listed for assassination by British agents. "I am the first on the list," he said, "and the story is to be circulated, as it was in the case of the Lord Mayor of Cork, that I was assassinated because I was urging moderate action. The same tools are to be used as were used on Tuesday night [a] week [ago] to assassinate Mr. Lynch in his hotel." His statement to the press most likely saved his life. That Griffith was aware of what might happen to him was down to the fact that by the autumn of 1920, and possibly a little before, Irish Intelligence had penetrated Dublin Special Branch. In what was all but a throwaway comment, Liam Archer of Irish Intelligence confirms this:

> One Sunday early 1920 I decided to sleep at home. At 4 a.m. a party of military with a DMP man arrived. The search was not very intense. They behaved politely and accepted us as peaceful citizens. They missed a larger cache of mine, and papers of my sisters who worked in the office of the D. Organisation....[21]

From evidence supplied by Neligan and Broy, Collins was able to put together the timeline of the murder of John Lynch in his bed. On October 5th, he wrote to Arthur Griffith:

> At 1.35 a.m. on the morning of the murder a "phone message" was received by Captain Baggelly, General Staff, Ship St. Barracks ... to send a car. A car was sent ... members of the RIC force picked up a small party of military.... and proceeded to the Royal Exchange Hotel.
>
> At 2.15 a.m. a "phone message" passed from the Headquarters of the Dublin District to College Street Station, giving the information that the RIC had been to the Royal Exchange Hotel and shot a man named Lynch.
>
> There is not the slightest doubt that there was no intention whatever to arrest Lynch.[22]

There had been other midnight murders of prominent Sinn Feiners and Volunteers, as Charles Dalton of Irish Intelligence reported. In one case he was the intended target:

> That night I was going home just before curfew, which was then at midnight, when a large touring car passed me. I noticed that there were several men

in it, dressed as civilians. I was amazed to see the car draw up outside my house.

Immediately I scented danger. Already a number of Volunteers had been shot in midnight raids by military officers in mufti under the leadership of a Captain X. I at once retraced my steps and made for the home of a Volunteer who lived nearby, where I spent the night.[23]

Dan Breen and Sean Treacy were back in Dublin once more. Breen's "mug" was plastered on wanted notices posted throughout Ireland. There was a police reward of £1,000 on his head. On the night of October 10, 1920, Breen and Treacy decided to spend the night at the home of Seamus Kirwan at 49, Parnell Street, a place where they had stayed before. Almost as soon as they had entered the house a man rushed in and told Kirwan that the two men who had just entered had been shadowed. Breen and Treacy rushed out onto the street. As they did so, the tout who had followed them, a man wearing a bow tie, ran off. The house was no longer safe. Breen and Treacy left almost immediately, fearing a raid on the premises. Only a few days before, Breen recounted in his autobiography, he had confronted a group of the "Dublin Castle gangsters," as he called them. They recognized each other and all drew their guns but did not bring them to bear or attempt to fire. Holding his nerve, Breen walked away unmolested. As he recalled, "I was becoming obsessed with the idea that if I remained in Dublin my days were numbered. The British had touts and spotters everywhere."

When in Dublin Breen and Treacy often stayed at the home of the Flemings in Drumcondra Road in north Dublin. Michael Fleming was a veteran of the Easter Rising and was well known to them. About the second week in October 1920, Richard Mulcahy sent word to Fleming that he had received intelligence that the house was no longer safe. It was being watched. The elder daughter of the family also developed a suspicion that she was being followed by a man she had noticed hanging around the neighborhood—a man with a bow tie. On the afternoon of October 11, Miss Fleming took the Drumcondra tram into the city. She went to meet Mrs. O'Brien, the wife of Eamonn O'Brien, then in America on Sinn Fein business. As Miss Fleming disembarked, she noticed the man with the bow tie disembarking from the tram behind. At Nelson's Pillar she met Mrs. O'Brien, and the two ladies decided to visit the newly opened La Scala cinema. The cinema began to fill up with customers, and quite by chance Dan Breen and Sean Treacy came in and sat in the row in front of them. Recognizing each other they agreed to meet up after the performance, with a view to the two fugitives returning to Drumcondra for a hot meal. As they began to leave the cinema Miss Fleming noticed that "Bow Tie" had been sitting a couple of rows behind them. As they entered the foyer, Miss Fleming left the cinema by another exit from the group, to see if he would follow.[24] The four met up outside. Out on O'Connell Street she noticed the man again but said nothing. Then looking at Treacy and Breen, she realized that they, too, had spotted the man. As the party made their way towards the tram stop Breen, dawdled behind. If it came to a shootout, he did not want to endanger the ladies. At the tram stop Treacy scanned the crowd around them, looking for potential touts. Treacy and the ladies boarded the tram when it arrived; Breen hung about, being the last to board. As he did so, the tout approached with the intention of catching the tram. Breen turned and faced the man, his hand gripping his concealed gun, and stared the tout down. The man with the bow tie moved back down a side street. The tram moved off; there was no sign of their pursuer. A short time later, disembarking at Drumcondra, the little group made their way towards the Flemings' family home. What Breen did not know was that the tout caught the next Drumcondra tram, and, waiting a safe distance from the house, saw Treacy and Breen later leave and make their way to Professor Carolan's house, a five-minute walk away.

Having discovered where two of the most wanted men in Ireland were staying, "Bow Tie" telephoned Dublin Special Branch. On duty that night was Major George Osbert S. Smyth, the brother of Divisional Commissioner Gerard Smyth, who had been assassinated in Cork. The Commissioner had been killed in response to his advocating a shoot-to-kill policy. Major Smyth wrongly believed that Breen had killed his brother. In that mistaken belief, he had persuaded the military authorities in Egypt, where he was based, to release him for secondment in Ireland. Now, with a convoy of Special Branch men and soldiers, he proceeded with all haste to Drumcondra. His intention was to kill Breen.

The two fugitive Irishmen spent the night at Professor Carolan's house "Fernside" on the main Dublin-to-Belfast Road, not far from St. Patrick's Training College for Teachers:

> The house is one of the type common enough in suburban districts; a two-storeyed brick building of eight or nine apartments. A grass plot, fenced with iron railings separates "Fernside" from the roadway; on the left a door served as tradesmen's side-entrance. In an emergency an active man would have no difficulty in springing over such an obstacle. At the rear of the house is a long garden which is separated from the adjoining garden by a seven foot wall. Close to the house and directly under the bedroom window was a conservatory.[25]

They had a latchkey to the house, given to them by Carolan, so that they could let themselves in without disturbing the rest of the household. The

8. Dublin Special Branch—The Murder Gang

professor had allocated them a bedroom on the first floor at the back of the house. The fugitives arrived about 11:30 p.m. and quietly made their way up to their room. The two chatted briefly. Each had a feeling of foreboding that his time was up. Eventually they fell asleep. Breen had placed his German Mauser on a chair by the side of the bed; Treacy slept with a loaded Parabellum automatic pistol under his pillow. An hour and a half later, both men woke with a start as professor Carolan hammered on their bedroom door. Carolan had awakened to the sound of lorries coming along the road, their engines running. They came to a stop, and then there was the sound of orders being given and footsteps running along the path. It was a raid. There was a hammering at the door. Carolan rushed downstairs. Before he reached the hallway the glass panels of the front door were smashed in and the door burst open. Major Smyth, seeing Carolan, demanded to know who was staying at Fernside.

Upstairs Treacy and Breen heard noises outside. The powerful beam of a searchlight now shone through the back bedroom window. They leapt out of bed, quickly dressing. They put on jackets, trousers and socks, but did not have time enough to put on shoes. Then they heard the sound of voices in the back garden below. The two fugitives, fearing the worst, whispered farewells and shook hands. Then they grabbed their guns as they heard the sound of footsteps on the stairs outside the room. Suddenly there was the sound of two loud cracks, and bullets came whizzing through the closed door. Breen was wounded, and blood flowed from his thumb. He returned fire with his Mauser through the now opening door. There were cries of pain and the thud of falling bodies on the landing outside.

Down below, in the back garden, was Captain Jeune of D. Department Special Branch:

> As was our custom, my immediate chief, Phil Attwood, and I went round to the back of the house and waited in the garden. Suddenly we heard a volley of shots in the house, and Phil said to me, "Come on Bob, let's go in." This seemed the natural thing to do but it turned out to be a grievous mistake. At the back of the house was a conservatory, and as I saw Michael, whose surname I have forgotten, raise his pistol and fire a couple of shots. I asked him what he was firing at, and he said, "He came down from the window and I think I got him in the leg. He has gone up again."[26]

From downstairs in the garden, bullets came crashing through the bedroom window. Treacy was having difficulty reloading. Breen thought that his gun had jammed. He told Treacy to make good his escape, while he would give him cover. Another bullet entered the room and imbedded itself in the wardrobe. Then Breen dashed out onto the landing raking the darkness with his 7.36 Mauser, nicknamed a "Peter the Painter," after the infamous anarchist who used the weapon in the 1911 siege of Sidney Street in London. On the stairs he heard the sound of feet descending. As he pursued them, he was picked out by their torches, and they opened fire on him. A bullet grazed his forehead, a second pierced his thigh, two more hit him in the calves of his legs and one lodged in his right lung. Not yet aware of the seriousness of his wounds, he moved back and reloaded the Mauser. Then the bull of a man that was Dan Breen dashed after them in the belief that the best means of defense was attack. They fled before his Mauser fire, running out onto the street. Breen dashed back to the bedroom tripping over the two dead bodies of Major Smyth and Captain Alfred White; a third body, that of Corporal Worth, was writhing on the floor (he survived the shooting). Back in the room, Treacy had reloaded his Mauser. He pushed Breen towards the now-open bedroom window and told him to escape. Out he climbed, dropping onto the roof of the conservatory. He crashed through the glass and dropped down to the ground. Upstairs in the house Treacy emptied the gun over the landing staircase into the soldiers once more climbing the stairs. Then he dashed back into the room, out through the window, and down into the conservatory as Breen had done before him. There was no sign of his comrade. Treacy believed that he was dead. Meanwhile, the soldiers in the garden, hearing the prolonged shooting in the house, had rushed around to the front of the building. The garden was clear. Treacy made a run for it and made it over the low wall.

Breen, preceding him, had made his way across the garden and over its low wall and had continued into another garden. Then he scaled the walls of St. Patrick's College. Crossing the grounds, he emerged on the other side and waded the river Tolka. He had lost a lot of blood; he was confused and in danger of collapsing. He hammered on the door of a house and sought shelter. The kindly housewife summoned a neighbor who was a nurse. She stanched the blood and bandaged his wounds. Word was then sent to leading Dublin IRA man, Dick McKee, and on the following evening he sent a car for Breen. The badly wounded man was taken to the Mater Hospital, where his injuries were properly treated. Sean Treacy, Breen discovered, was alive and well, having made a successful escape. Treacy, bleeding from glass cuts to his hands and knees, had made his way towards Finglas and the home of a friend, Phil Ryan, who attended to his wounds.

Captain Jeune's account of the raid was a little less dramatic:

> What has happened in the house was that Major Smyth had opened the door of the back bedroom and walked in, with a torch alight on his belt. All the gunman, who turned out later to have been Dan Breen had to do was to

shoot Smyth through the heart. At this there was some confusion, during which Captain White, a very nice man with an excellent war record, was killed, and Cpl. Worth wounded. A little later, from the garden, I heard a single shot, which made one think that there might still be a gunman in the house. But, far from that, it was a most unfortunate accident, which involved Professor Carolan being shot by mistake while being questioned. He was taken to hospital, but died some weeks later.[27]

But not before he swore a signed deathbed statement to the effect that he had been intentionally shot through the back of the neck by a Special Branch man. In his testament, John Carolan made it clear that he had been shot after the two fugitives had fled. Carolan's statement is at odds with Jeune's:

> I admitted the raiding party on the morning of 12th October. They asked me about Dick [Mulcahy] and I replied that he had not been here for some time.
> A gun was pressed to my temple. "What do you know of the men who have fired at our Forces?" "Nothing." I was taken to the landing. Several minutes had elapsed since I had heard the crash of glass in the greenhouse. I hoped that by this time the two men had got away. A shot was fired at me point-blank. I felt a searing pain in my throat. I fell over a corpse that was lying on the corridor. I was carried to Enright's room (Enright was a harbour pilot who lodged in our house) and placed on a bed. Doctor Murray bandaged my wound.[28]

At the Mater Hospital, Breen was operated on and the bullets removed. Treacy's wounds were slight, and he was up and about the following day.

In the search of nearby houses for the fugitives, the raiding party took Michael and James Fleming in for questioning. Michael Fleming was taken back to Dublin Castle. Fearing a brutal interrogation, Michael was surprised at the good treatment he received. He was offered wine and cigars as an inducement to answer questions that would lead to the arrest of the two fugitives. He was offered a reward of £10,000 to be paid into any bank of his choice with a guaranteed safe passage abroad. When he refused, on the basis that he did not know, he was court-martialed and sentenced to three years imprisonment, a term subsequently reduced to nine months. Brother James Fleming was taken to Mountjoy Prison, where he was interrogated by Donald McLean, Chief Intelligence Officer. He was offered inducements (Egyptian cigarettes) and good advice, and despite revealing nothing, he was released.

On Thursday, October 14th, the Auxiliaries raided the Mater Hospital. They had information that a wounded man had been brought in. They believed that it was Breen. In fact, it was Volunteer Matt Furlong, who had an apparent facial resemblance to Breen. He had been seriously wounded in an accidental explosion at Dunboyne, a village about sixteen miles from Dublin. During the raid, Furlong died of his wounds, so the Auxiliaries could not question him. With a view to getting someone up from the country to identify him, the military withdrew.

Treacy became anxious lest the Auxiliaries return to the hospital and continue their search, so he sought help in having Breen removed to somewhere safe. As Treacy moved about the city, he was shadowed by a tout. On October 20, he was followed to the Republican Outfitters in Talbot Street. By now the premises were known to British Intelligence as an IRA haunt. At the shop, Treacy met Dick McKee and George and Jack Plunkett, brothers of the executed 1916 leader Joseph Plunkett. Only minutes later, IRA man Peadar Clancy, who was in O'Connell Street, witnessed an armored car and two lorries filled with soldiers heading towards Talbot Street. One minute later the military convoy, led by former Tank Corps officer, Major Frank Carew, pulled up before the shop. Treacy was standing near the door. Another IRA man out on the street made a run for it. A soldier intercepted him. Plain clothes Auxiliary Intelligence officer Francis Christian jumped down from the lorry. Straight away he knew the captured man was not their quarry. "Here is the man we want!" he called out, indicating Sean Treacy. The IRA man was attempting to escape on a borrowed bicycle. Lieutenant Gilbert Price made a grab at Treacy, and the two men grappled for Price's gun. In the melee, the soldiers in the lorry panicked and began firing. They killed both Treacy and their officer, Lt. Price. Two innocent civilians passing by were also shot. Sergeant-Major Christian was wounded but survived.[29]

Meanwhile, in order to identify the dead IRA man in the hospital, British Intelligence sent for Sergeant Roche of the Tipperary RIC. He knew Breen by sight. Roche arrived in Dublin with a colleague, Constable Fitzmaurice. Dave Neligan was detailed to accompany Roche to the hospital. The sergeant took one look at the dead man and declared, "That is not Breen. I would know his bulldog face anywhere." Neligan reported back to Collins. He ordered the killing of Roche. Neligan was horrified. Roche had not hurt anyone. As Frank Thornton of Irish Intelligence pointed out, Roche's brief was "to identify Sean Treacy's body and at the same time to visit all the hospitals with the object of trying to identify Breen." That could not be allowed to happen. Neligan was ordered to set up Roche for an assassination. The following day Neligan agreed to meet Roche and Fitzmaurice along the quays. James Slattery from The Squad described what happened next:

> A party of us went to Capel Street Bridge. Paddy Daly, Charlie Dalton and Neligan were there. When we arrived there we were told that Neligan would point out Roche and another RIC man as they stepped off the tram. We took

8. Dublin Special Branch—The Murder Gang   141

up our positions and then we saw Neligan talking to two men up near the Ormond Hotel. One of them was a stout man and looked more like a farmer than an RIC man. Joe Dolan and Frank Thornton were supposed to shoot these men, and we got the job of covering them off. We did not take any particular notice for a little while, until we saw Dolan approaching us with a gun in his hand, and the two men who had been talking to Neligan walking in front of him. When they passed us, Dolan levelled his gun and we knew that they were the men we were looking for, so we fired at them, killing Roache. The other man [Constable Fitzmaurice] escaped, although we had the place surrounded. He got away before he realised he was one of the men we were looking for.[30]

Joseph Dolan's account is succinct, almost devoid of emotion:

The two policemen were coming towards us and we let them pass. Then I took out my revolver and put six bullets into Roche when he was just in front of me in the passage-way. Tom Keogh and Jim Slattery put a few more bullets into Roche. The other policeman ran to the Castle....[31]

Neligan had been talking to Thornton when he spied the two policemen targeted for assassination. He walked down to meet them:

Roche, a huge man of burly build, was immediately shot down by the Squad. He only lived a few minutes. The Constable and I ran away. I went back to the Castle. In a few minutes I was told that the Inspector-General of the RIC wanted me at once. Entering his rooms I saw Constable Fitzmaurice and several other officers of high rank. The Inspector-General, a tough-looking fellow with an ugly face, accosted me, "Neligan," he said, "this Constable says he saw you talking to the man who shot Sergeant Roche." I replied, "He is making a mistake, Sir." "What did you do?" he asked. "Did you see the man who attacked Roche?" he continued. I told him that I had run away as I thought the shots were fired at me.[32]

The Inspector-General eventually believed him, and for the moment the incident was closed. Neligan was well aware how close he had come to being discovered, the probability of which would have resulted in torture and his own murder. Pinned to his chest would have been a little note to the effect that he had been killed by the IRA. This was a device that the "hush-hush" men had adopted to deflect the blame from themselves.

From its various police and military raids—including, no doubt, the burglary of Arthur Griffith's home—British Intelligence knew that the Minister of Finance, Michael Collins, had split up the Dail Loan and salted it away in the bank accounts of respectable businessmen and shopkeepers. George Fitzgerald, a member of A Company, 1st Battalion, was tasked with collecting money in northwest Dublin with regard to the Dail Loan. "My work generally was to ... collect the money," he revealed in his Witness Statement, "and meet the different sub organisers for the area…." One of these shopkeepers, apparently, was IRB man Peter O'Carroll, a butcher and locksmith by trade. At about 2:00 a.m. on the morning of October 16, 1920, Peter O'Carroll was shot dead at his home, and a note reading, "A traitor to Ireland—shot by the IRA," was pinned to his body.

About a fortnight earlier (a week after the death of Lynch), three armed plainclothes men raided the O'Carroll home at 92, Manor Street, in northwest Dublin. They were, according to later newspaper reports, looking for the two sons of the family who were in the IRA. The boys were not at home. Upon their departure one, of the British agents warned O'Carroll, "You are not done with us yet. Have the boys here next time, or look out."

A few days later a man called at O'Carroll's shop and asked if he could supply a replacement key for a lock that he produced. O'Carroll said that he could not help. Then the man asked if O'Carroll could cut a new key. Again, O'Carroll said that he could not. Then he realized that he had seen his "customer" before. "I seem to know your face," O'Carroll said.

"Oh, no. You never saw me before," was the reply.

"I did. You are one of the men who raided my house a fortnight ago." The stranger made an inaudible response, then left.[33]

In the early morning of October 16th, the O'Carrolls were summoned from their bed by a fierce knocking on their shop's front door. "Open the door!" came an order from down below. Mrs. O'Carroll recognized the voice as that of one of the three men who had raided the house two weeks before. Mr. O'Carroll slipped on his trousers and socks and carrying his boots went down to unlock the door before it was battered down. Mrs. O'Carroll heard the door being opened and some shouting, but she could not hear what was being said. Then there was silence. Mrs. O'Carroll, having dressed, then went down the stairs. There was a light on in the kitchen. All was quiet. The shop door was closed. She looked around, but there was no one about. She switched off the light then went back upstairs. There was no sign of her husband. She went downstairs again and walked into the shop. There she found her husband. He was dead, shot in the head. As it was curfew, she was afraid to go out onto the street and raise the alarm, so she went upstairs and shouted from the open bedroom window for help. No help arrived. No one would risk being shot during the curfew hours. At dawn a cattle drover came by, then a young boy, a neighbor, who was sent off to get a priest. One of the O'Carroll sons, arriving home, telephoned for an ambulance. The body was taken away to the city morgue.

8. Dublin Special Branch—The Murder Gang 143

Later that day a reporter from the *Freeman's Journal* questioned people living nearby to see if they knew anything about the murder. One did, and made the following statement:

> I was walking across the floor of my bedroom about 1.50 a.m. when I heard knocking at O'Carroll's door, and an order for admission. I next heard a muffled sound and remarked to my father, "That appears to be a shot." He replied that the report was not loud enough. Then there was silence. A few minutes later I saw a light in O'Carroll's shop window and heard a woman's voice calling loudly for help.[34]

Interestingly, no mention is made of the speaker in the two raids as having an English accent, which might suggest either that the interviewer did not ask or that the speaker had an Irish accent. Right from the start, Michael Collins was convinced that Captain Hardy, an Anglo-Irishman, was involved, but who were the other two men?

Having taken to serious drinking, as was the case with most of the Auxiliaries, one of the two assassins revealed himself to Miss Lil Dunne. He was Lieutenant Henry Angliss, who used the alias of Patrick Mahon in his undercover work.[35] He lodged, along with another British agent, Lieutenant Charles Peel, at the same address in Mount Street as Miss Dunne and her father, Superintendent Dunne of Dublin Castle. Feeling himself to be in safe company—all the occupants were pro–British—Angliss revealed his part in the death of Lynch. Miss Dunne worked in the Secretariat at Dublin Castle alongside Collins's secret agent, Lily Mernin. Being gregarious by nature, and wanting to be at the center of things, Miss Dunne could not help herself. She told her fellow workers all about her fellow lodgers and what they had said.

Angliss, a Dublin-born Irishman, was the son of Joseph Angliss, a Sergeant-Major in the Inniskilling Fusiliers. In 1911, at the age of nineteen, the family then being in Scotland, he enlisted in the Scottish Rifles as a private. At the outbreak of World War I, he was transferred to the Highland Light Infantry and in 1916 was promoted to sergeant. Later that same year he was further promoted to company sergeant major. In France, Angliss was awarded the Distinguished Conduct Medal for his part in a raid on the German lines and the rescuing of a wounded man. In April 1917, he was commissioned as a 2nd lieutenant in his father's old regiment, the Royal Inniskilling Fusiliers. Remaining in the army after the war, he was posted to Russia in 1919 as part of the British Expeditionary Force which was assisting the White Russians in their fight against the Bolsheviks. Returning from Russia, Angliss was recruited by Basil Thomson and trained for intelligence work in Ireland.

Fellow guest at the Mount Street lodgings, Lieutenant Peel, who worked alongside Angliss, is the most obvious candidate for being the third member of the "murder squad" that killed both Lynch and O'Carroll, using the same silenced gun. Charles Ratch Peel was born Carl Ratsch in Bournemouth, England in 1885. He was the son of a naturalized German émigré, Hermann Ratsch. Following the death of his father, his mother married John Joseph Peel in 1911. The young Carl anglicized his name at the outbreak of World War I to become Charles Ratsch-Peel and joined the Royal Navy. By 1915, he had been promoted to petty officer. Following the end of the war in 1919, Peel joined the Royal Army Ordnance Corps as a lieutenant. The *London Gazette* for August 10, 1920, lists him "to be temp. Lt. whilst specially empld." In his file in the Military Records (now housed in the National Archive, Kew) Peel is instructed to "report himself to Captain Harper Shove, Royal Fusiliers Depot, Hounslow, at 11 a.m. on Tuesday 10th August 1920." Here at the Government spy school, he was taught his new trade. By the autumn he was in Dublin, seconded to Dublin Special Branch—"The Murder Gang."

The city coroner was instructed by the Lord Lieutenant, Lord French, not to hold an inquest on Peter O'Carroll, as an inquiry would be conducted by the military authorities. Dublin Corporation, not so restricted, condemned the instruction from the Lord Lieutenant and tendered sympathy with Mrs. O'Carroll and her family "on the murder of her husband by the armed forces of England."

By now it was fairly obvious to Irish Intelligence that the names not only of prominent Sinn Feiners, but also of the people who operated below the radar, had become known to Dublin Special Branch. As Collins himself remarked, "Those fellows were going to put a lot of us on the spot." Frank Thornton from Irish Intelligence confirms Collins's belief:

> As the War developed so did the activities of the Intelligence Organisation right throughout the whole country.... During all this period it must be remembered that the enemy intelligence and activity was also very active, resulting in very serious losses to our side.[36]

On October 27, 1920, at about 6:45 a.m., the body of Secret Service officer Captain Parcell Rees Bowen M.C., DFC., was found in an alleyway between 4 and 5, Lower Merrion Street, Dublin. He had been shot by a single .45 bullet. Captain Rees Bowen of the 5th Welsh Regiment was a war veteran of the ill-fated Gallipoli campaign. In January 1918, he transferred to the Royal Air Force and served as an observer for the remainder of the war. In July 1920, he was recruited by British Intelligence. He was trained under Captain Harper Shove, at the secret spy school at the Royal Fusiliers depot at Hounslow and was sent to Dublin. His cover story was that he was an agent for a Welsh coal company. He found lodgings for "professional men," at 28, Upper Fitzwilliam Street.[37]

Curiously, none of the Witness Statements of The Squad members make any reference to him. Nor was a single shot their style. Inevitably, there would have been at least two shots—one to the body and one to the head. His death is recorded in the *Freeman's Journal* of November 6, 1920, under the heading, "Late Captain Bowen—Died while in the Secret Service in Ireland." As was usual in these cases, there was no inquest, but a secret military enquiry was held on the following Friday. The local newspapers at his home near Carmarthen, which covered his funeral, headlines their article, "Welsh Hero Murdered by Sinn Fein." But was he?

Brigadier-General Frank Crozier, who commanded the semimilitary Auxiliaries at the time, expressed his doubts in his book, *A Word to Gandhi: The Lesson of Ireland*, published in 1931. He suggested that Bowen had been shot by the British, most probably by an Auxiliary officer. Bowen was unhappy at things that he had seen and heard and threatened to take his concerns to David Davies, the Parliamentary Private Secretary to Prime Minister Lloyd George. Bowen confided in Crozier, who was also concerned over the behavior of certain Auxiliary officers, in particular Captain King, and advised Bowen to speak to Davies. Bowen revealed that he felt uneasy over his own safety. He had been threatened by a senior officer that he "would be put away, if he did not shut his mouth." Bowen was found dead in an alleyway. It would seem that the "Murder Gang" of Dublin Special Branch was turning in on itself to protect its own.

On November 14, Liam Tobin, Deputy Director of Intelligence, and assistant Tom Cullen were picked up in a nighttime raid on Vaughan's Hotel in Parnell Square. Among the raiding party were Lieutenants Peter Ames and George Bennett, both of whom Irish Intelligence had marked down for assassination. It seems probable that all four men had met before, either at Rabbiatti's Saloon or Kidds Back bar, when Broy and Neligan had passed them off as their touts. As British Intelligence lacked photographs of most of the men they sought, after some questioning Ames and Bennett expressed their assurance that the men were sound, and the conversation turned to horse racing. Cullen, who was a racing fan, even gave the Special Branch men some racing tips. After a few drinks, they all parted the best of friends. Four nights later, having realized their mistake, the Special Branch team raided Vaughan's once more, asking for Tobin and Cullen by name. By this time, the two men had taken to sleeping elsewhere. Then Frank Thornton was picked up. He was taken to Dublin Castle where he was held for ten days. He held his nerve and stuck to his cover story and again, in the absence of a photograph, and with no one able to identify him, he was eventually released. Collins himself came close to being discovered on more than one occasion. It was his belief that if he acted as if he was not on the run, then he would not be suspected. One evening, though, he and three of his colleagues in Irish Intelligence were having dinner in the Gresham Hotel. A party of Auxiliaries entered the dining room, guns in hand, and began to survey the diners. They eventually approached Collins's table; the officer in charge had a photograph of Collins in his hand. He stopped and looked at the man from Cork, ran his hand through Collins's hair, gazed again at the picture, and then moved on. On another occasion, two Auxiliaries stopped Collins in the street and proposed to take him in for questioning. Collins spoke quietly to them and told them to look around. As they did, so they noticed four men from The Squad, all seemingly holding concealed weapons, looking intently at them. After making some light-hearted remark, the Auxiliaries walked off.

The greater risk, however, was not the Auxiliaries, the foot soldiers, but the Intelligence men who led them. Collins gave orders that they, the men who operated after dark during the curfew hours, were to be identified, their addresses checked, and their movements watched and reported. They for their part, the men of British Intelligence, were making their final preparations, collecting names and addresses of IRA men and prominent Sinn Feiners. Their lists also included people they suspected but of whose guilt they could not be certain. They were getting close—so close that Collins was to remark, "Those fellows were going to put a lot of us on the spot."

9

Bloody Sunday, November 21, 1920

On November 17, Michael Collins wrote to Dick McKee, Commandant of the Dublin Brigade, "Dick, I have established the names of the particular ones. Arrangements should be made about the matter. Lt. G. is aware of things. He suggests the 21st. A most suitable date and day I think. M."

Lt. G., or "The Little Gentleman," was the alias of Lily Mernin, shorthand typist in the British Department of Defence in Dublin Castle. In her Witness Statement she wrote:

> Before the 21st November 1920, it was part of my normal duty to type the names and addresses of British agents who were accommodated at private addresses and living as ordinary citizens in the city. These lists were typed weekly and amended whenever an address was changed. I passed them on each week either to the address at Moynihan's, Clonliffe Rd. or to Piaras Beaslai.[1]

The day was suitable in that there was to be a big Gaelic football match at Croke Park that afternoon. Dublin would be crowded for most of the day, allowing The Squad and the ASU men involved to lose themselves in the crowds of supporters. Sunday, November 21, was confirmed as the date for the simultaneous assassination of all known British Secret Service agents in Dublin. There were "40 men to be executed..." as Joe Dolan of Irish Intelligence indicated. The time set was 9:00 a.m.

Before all this, Frank Thornton, who had compiled and collated all the information, presented a full report to a joint meeting of the Dail Cabinet and the Army Council:

> I had to prove that each and every man on my list was an accredited Secret Service man of the British Government. This, as everybody can realise, was not an easy task, but proves one thing, that is that our Government and Army were not going to allow any man to be shot without the fullest possible proof being produced of his guilt.[2]

With four days to go, the meeting to decide the fate of the British agents, the majority of whom were from the British Army's Dublin District Special Branch, was held at a house in Upper Dominick Street. Here Dick McKee and Frank Thornton presented their cases. Each name on the list was carefully checked. Cathal Brugha, Minister for Defence, allegedly worked through the files, rejecting those the evidence against whom he deemed insufficient. About fifteen names were rejected. In all, instructions were issued for about twenty different operations.[3]

A week before the date fixed, Liam Tobin and Tom Cullen, senior members in Irish Intelligence who were sleeping in Vaughan's Hotel, were awakened by a large party of British agents. Some they could identify, among them Bennett and Ames. These two were on their list for assassination. Both Cullen and Tobin were able to persuade the raiding party of their assumed identities after a protracted interrogation. Cullen somehow turned the conversation onto other things, including horse racing, to the extent of offering them certain winners. The raiders left, and soon after, so too, did Tobin and Cullen. Having ascertained their identities, a couple of nights later the raiders returned, asking for Tobin and Cullen by name.

With the approval of the Irish Government and Army committee, details of the operation were kept secret even from the Volunteers right up until the last possible moment, the evening of Saturday, November 20th. Then, those who needed to know, the Intelligence officers and senior Volunteer officers who were to take part, were instructed to attend a briefing. The raids were planned by Sean Russell. Each team was to consist, on average, of fifteen men: two hit men per target, an intelligence man to collect up any papers or reports, the remainder to act as cover. At any one time, there were rarely more than twenty-five men of the IRA in Dublin under arms. So, such an operation required the IRA leadership to bring in men from outside, men who were not necessarily fully trained or steeled to shoot a man in cold blood. The city was divided up into sections. The 1st Battalion would deal with agents who resided on the North Circular Road and the adjoining roads to Phoenix Park. The 2nd Battalion were allocated the area of O'Connell Street and, to a certain degree, down to Mount Street. The 3rd Battalion area was in and around Leeson Street and Pembroke Street, and the 4th Battalion, in the area around Portobello. Each team was to have at least one member of The Squad and an Intelligence Officer to identify the victim and collect up any papers within the room. The various teams were then summoned for a final briefing. Patrick Kennedy of GHQ Intelligence, formerly of D Company, 2nd Battalion, noted:

9. Bloody Sunday, November 21, 1920

On the Saturday before Bloody Sunday I was instructed to report to 100, Seville Place that night where, I was told, I would receive specific instructions regarding an operation to be carried out the following morning. When I arrived at Seville Place that night, I discovered that a number of specially selected men from my Company were present and that Paddy Moran, my Company O.C., was in charge of them.

Sean Russell took charge for that night, and he gave us our instructions for the following morning. He explained that a big swoop was to be made simultaneously on all British agents residing in private houses throughout the city and that the operation was to be carried out at nine o'clock sharp.[4]

James Cahill of D Company revealed the targets his group were allocated:

> D Company was given the task of dealing with three Intelligence Officers who were residing in the Gresham Hotel, O'Connell Street. Three groups, consisting of three men each, were detailed to carry out the shooting. The remainder of our party were given the tasks of controlling members of the hotel staff and residents, covering the exits and preventing communication with the outside during the operation.[5]

28 Upper Pembroke Street was a well-kept residence run by Mrs. Grey. It was the home to a number of British Army officers. They kept regular hours, going out each morning in their uniforms, returning home each evening for their dinner, and, when not on duty, slept the night. Two of Mrs. Grey's boarders, though, used to leave the house after dark despite the curfew, dressed in civilian clothes. Upon their return, they would sleep late into the morning. That they were British officers was confirmed to Irish Intelligence by Rosie the maid. She had seen their uniforms hanging up in the wardrobe. There were similar other cases in and around Dublin, and Irish Intelligence duly noted them. Now the briefings began.

Elsewhere, other groups also met. James Slattery and other members of The Squad, along with members of the Intelligence Section and Volunteers from individual units, were ordered to parade at the Typographical Society's offices on Middle Gardiner Street:

> We were addressed there by Dick McKee, who told us that an operation had been planned for the following morning, Sunday, at nine a.m ... I was assigned to 22, Lower Mount Street, where two enemy agents were located. One was Lieutenant McMahon, but I cannot remember the other man's name.

Frank Saurin was appointed intelligence officer for his part in the operation. The targets for his group were Lieutenants Peter Ashum Ames, an American by birth, and George Bennett, born in what is now Jakarta, Java who had served in Military Intelligence in Holland during World War I. Both men had recently changed address. Saurin adds:

The only information I had as to their whereabouts at this address was a recently captured letter to Ames and in which Bennett was mentioned. At 10 o'clock on that night I went to Upper Mount Street to locate the house. Before leaving I arranged with the squad leader, Vincent Byrne, where to meet on the following morning.[6]

Vinnie Byrne of The Squad was summoned to a meeting at Tara Hall, Gloucester Street. Here were gathered the foot soldiers of the 2nd Battalion:

> One of the senior Intelligence officers was present and explained to us the nature of the operation about to be put into action. The number present, I would say, were 20–30 men. The details as to how the groups were selected for each operation, I cannot remember, but I know that Tom Keogh was to take charge at 22, Lr. Mount St. and I was to go along with him. However, as another address came in, I was detailed to take charge of the operation at 28, Up. Mount St. I had about ten men under me, which included a first-aid man.[7]

The change of address was a last-minute notification by Intelligence Officer Charles Dalton. He had cultivated a young woman, Maudie, who was employed "in a superior boarding house in one of the fashionable streets on the south side of the city."[8] She told him about two of her boarders. They were "English gentlemen," she thought. They "looked like military officers," though they did not wear uniforms. They never went out during the day but "always at night after curfew." Lily Mernin was able to confirm that they were British Secret Service men. Then, on the day before the operation, they moved out. Fortunately, Maudie was able to give Dalton their new address. They had left it so that mail could be forwarded. Dalton informed Frank Saurin of the change.

In all, the list of targets prepared by Collins and added to by the Dublin Brigade was whittled down from thirty-five to twenty. Not all were Secret Service men. Those not on Lily Mernin's list were probably suggested by Brigade companies as being men considered to be dangerous in one way or another. No list of those to be targeted apparently still exists. Details of known places that were visited appear in Witness Statements held by the Bureau of Military History. (See Appendix III.)

At about midday on the Saturday before, Michael Collins was almost captured. Patrick Joseph Berry, a warder at Mountjoy Prison and an inside man for Irish Intelligence, had a rendezvous with Tom Cullen and Liam Tobin to exchange information. They met at Crossguns Bridge, along the Royal Canal at Phibsborough Road. As they were talking, a stranger approached. It was Michael Collins. Berry was introduced to him, and then the two men walked down to Doyle's Corner, Collins getting to know the other man more personally. At the corner,

9. Bloody Sunday, November 21, 1920

they were caught up in a street raid by the Auxiliaries, who were holding and questioning people coming from Berkeley Road and Phibsboro' churches. The two men, in their turn, were questioned. Berry took the initiative and produced an old pass to the Castle and told the Auxiliary officer armed with a gun that they were out of Mountjoy. After cursory glance at the pass, he told them, "Pass on."

On the night of November 20th, with plans for the following morning well in hand, Collins went to the Gaiety Theatre with a small group of friends. David Neligan was in that group:

> Broy, MacNamara, Tobin, Cullen, Thornton and myself attended the Gaiety Theatre on the night of the 20th November, 1920. We saw some of those, whose names we had, in a box there and they were enjoying themselves too. We cleared up some details regarding addresses. We were told that known Secret Service men and certain British Army officers, including Captain Bagally who had figured in Lynch's shooting, would be shot in their lodgings next day. Cullen said to me that he was going to Croke Park the next day to see a match. We told him to keep out of it, that it was madness to go there.[9]

After the show, Collins went to Vaughan's Hotel in Parnell Square to meet and discuss the final plans for the next day. Among those present were Dick McKee and Peadar Clancy. Also present in the hotel, but not involved in the discussion, was Conor Clune, who had come to discuss an Irish language project with Piaras Beaslai. The meeting in the hotel's smoke room broke up, and Collins left Vaughan's, as did McKee and Clancy. In truth, it was a dangerous place to hold a meeting. British Intelligence knew that it was a place of rendezvous for senior IRA figures. After the departure of the three, Piaras Beaslai remained with Clune in deep discussion. Suddenly a friend of Beaslai dashed in and told him that the place was surrounded by Auxiliaries who were about to raid the hotel. Beaslai, a wanted man, ran out through a rear exit and into the yard, where he hid in an outhouse. He had no qualms about leaving Clune. He was, after all, an innocent with no connections either to the IRA or to Sinn Fein. After examining the register, the Auxiliaries took away the innocent Clune for further questioning.[10]

That night the Auxiliaries raided the hotel for a second time and, finding nobody there, grabbed the waiter, Christy, and took him back to Dublin Castle where he was interviewed by an intelligence officer. Amidst cajoles and threats, he was offered a large sum of money. Christy was urged to slip out and telephone the Castle the next time Collins was there. Christy agreed, but upon his release, he returned to the hotel where he informed Collins of what had happened.

A Castle tout, John "Shankers" Ryan, followed McKee and Clancy the short distance from Vaughan's to a safe house, Fitzpatrick's in Gloucester

Street, where they had arranged to sleep the night. Shortly after 2:00 a.m., the Auxiliaries, with guns drawn, burst into the house. McKee, Clancy and Fitzpatrick were arrested, bundled into a truck and driven off to Dublin Castle for questioning at the hands of Captain Hardy and Major King. They arrived at Dublin Castle guardroom at 3:00 a.m. Waiting in the room for interrogation were a number of prisoners, including Clune. Amongst the prisoners was Ben Doyle, a Volunteer sometimes used by Irish Intelligence. Clancy put his finger to his lips, an indication that Doyle was not to recognize him or the alias that he was using.

Doyle, who had been chosen to take part in the assassinations, had been picked up on a raid just before noon that Saturday morning. It was at the insurance office where he worked at 30, College Green. The Auxiliaries dashed upstairs, revolvers in hand, and held up the office. All the men were searched and asked their names. Doyle was one of a small group that was taken away for further questioning. The prisoners were taken to Dublin Castle and placed in the Auxiliaries guardroom, which overlooked Exchange Court. Throughout the course of the day, more prisoners were brought in. Eventually, sometime after 5:00 p.m. Doyle was taken into the intelligence room for interrogation. An Auxiliary stood either side of him. Facing him were three Auxiliary officers, seated at a table, a revolver besides each one of them. The questioning began:

> "What is your name?" …
> "Bryan Doyle."
> "How do you spell it?" …
> "B-r-y-a-n D-o-y-l-e."
> "Do you know Ben Doyle?" …
> "No, sir."
> "Do you know Simon Donnelly?" …
> "No, sir."
> "Didn't you meet Paddy Flanagan last night in Harcourt Street?" …
> "No, sir. You must be making a mistake."

At this stage the standing Auxiliaries had their revolvers touching my cheeks and a lame-legged Auxiliary officer [Captain Hardy] said to him:

> "Don't fire till I give you the order. Do you know Sean Guilfoyle?" …
> "No, sir."
> "I'll order them to blow your bloody brains out. What's your address?" …
> "No. 11, Reginald Street."
> "We have been to that house sir," said one of the Auxiliaries besides me.
> "Did you find anything?"
> "No, sir."
> "Take him away—we'll deal with him later," said the lame-legged officer.[11]

9. Bloody Sunday, November 21, 1920

Doyle was returned to the main room to await his fate. About 2:00 a.m., Dick McKee, Peadar Clancy and Sean Fitzpatrick were pushed into the room. Recognizing Doyle, Clancy put his finger to his lips. Doyle made no move to recognize the new prisoners.

It was Sunday morning, November 21st, shortly before 9:00 a.m. "... [I]t is a fine sunny day. In the distance I hear the sound of church bells ... summoning the people, some to Mass, and others to murder." So wrote Caroline Woodcock, the wife of Colonel Wilfred Woodcock. Her husband's name was on a list of men to be executed. Some three weeks earlier, one of the men in the team that was responsible for her husband's shooting related:

> We had been engaged for the past three weeks locating the addresses of these intelligence men. Many of them were officers of high rank. They had taken up their abode in private houses in quiet residential neighbourhoods, where they lived in great seclusion, many of them under assumed names and occupations. By one means and another we had got upon their track.... By now we knew all we needed to know—their names, both their assumed names and their real ones, their appearance, habits and the nature of their occupation.[12]

Charlie Dalton of Irish Intelligence and men who were to act with him were awake and dressed by seven o'clock that Sunday morning. They breakfasted on tea and eggs. As he looked about him, Dalton observed that the other men were "examining their revolvers, seeing that they were in working order." Outwardly they appeared calm and collected, but Dalton felt that they were palpitating with anxiety, as he was. Shortly after eight o'clock they left the house, each man splitting off to meet with his assigned team. At Merrion Square, Dalton met the officer in charge of his team, which comprised of himself as intelligence officer, Paddy Flanagan, George White, Michael O'Hanlon, Andy Cooney, Leo Dunne, Ned Kelliher and Joseph O'Carroll. O'Carroll had a particular interest in the day. His father had been murdered in his shop by three British agents the month before.

As the ASU approached the entrance of number 28, Upper Pembroke Street, Colonel Wilfred Woodcock, who had hurriedly dressed upstairs, was preparing to go down to breakfast. He was to lead a Church Parade later that morning. His wife was struggling to do up the numerous little buttons of her blouse. At the bedroom window, as she struggled with the cuff, she looked out and saw a man climbing over the ten-foot-high ivy-covered garden wall. He was Leo Dunne, who had been ordered to secure the back entrance to the property and shoot any officer trying to escape that way. She drew her husband's attention to the man, and immediately he reacted. He rushed down to warn the other British officers who lived on the lower floors. Sharply at nine o'clock, the IRA team walked up the steps of the house. The front door was open. Matt, the caretaker, was shaking the mats on the steps. One of the team held him up and warned him to keep quiet. The others entered into the large hall, which had two separate flights of stairs, the result of two houses having been knocked into one. Silver-haired Mrs. Grey emerged from one of the rooms but was motioned to return by one of the gunmen. By this time, Woodcock, an officer in the 1st Battalion the Lancashire Fusiliers, had begun descending the stairs, but it was too late. The hall was full of armed men dressed in overcoats and raincoats and wearing cloth caps and felt hats. One of them ordered Woodcock to put his hands up. Then he was asked to identify himself. As he did so, perhaps knowing his probable fate, he added, "There are women in the house."

"We know it," came the reply.

As Woodcock spoke, the door behind him opened, and Colonel Montgomery emerged. Woodcock turned to warn him, "Look out, Montgomery!" he shouted. As he did so, he was shot by one of the Volunteers in the shoulder and back and fell at the foot of the stairs. Standing there on the landing, Colonel Montgomery was shot twice and fell at his wife's feet. She herself was wounded, grazed on the knee by a bullet. Lieutenant R. G. Murray, who had run down the stairs to investigate, was held up in the hall by two of the IRA, Mick O'Hanlon and Paddy Flanagan. Captain Keenlyside, who shared a room on the same floor as Woodcock, came out onto the landing and was joined by his wife. She knew that they intended to kill him. Facing the gunmen, she clung on to her husband in an attempt to save his life. Flanagan fired, and Keenlyside was hit in the arm. Luckily for him, he was only wounded. In the chaos and screams, his assailants quickly withdrew down the stairs.

The other team had ascended the other carpeted stairs. On the landing were two rooms occupied by two of the Secret Service men, Major Dowling, an officer in the Grenadier Guards, and Captain Leonard Price, previously of the Middlesex Regiment. Dalton's team divided into two groups. Simultaneously they knocked at both doors. "I have a letter for you, sir," one called out as he knocked on Major Downing's door. As the doors of the two bedrooms were opened, the Irishmen overcame the officers. They were led downstairs to join Lieutenant Murray in the hall. Irish Intelligence officer Charlie Dalton, his pockets full of captured documents, saw the Englishmen as he dashed from the house:

> In the hall three or four men were lined up against the wall, some of our officers facing them. Knowing their fate I felt great pity for them. It was plain they knew it too. As I crossed the threshold the volley was fired.[13]

9. Bloody Sunday, November 21, 1920

Murray was wounded and fell to the floor feigning death. The other two were dead. With the departure of the assassins, Colonel Woodcock crawled back up the stairs to his wife:

> The door opened, and he came in. His shoulder was covered with blood, but his first words were, "It's all right, darling, they have only hit outlying portions of me. Go back to the window.... Now I saw about twenty men running and cycling away down a lane, and I also saw the man in the garden being helped to escape by one of the servants from the flat, who came out with a key and let him out through a garage door.... I then turned to my husband, and found to my horror that he was just losing consciousness, and that the bed on which he was lying was soaked with blood. I took off his coat, and saw four bullet holes—two in his arm and shoulder, a horrible looking one in his back, and another in front."[14]

Down below in the hall, blood spatters on its walls, floors and stairs, lay the dead British officers. In all, four British officers were killed: Colonel Montgomery, Major Dowling, Captain Price, and Lieutenant Murray. Woodcock and Keenlyside eventually recovered from their wounds. Captain R. D. Jeune, who was on the team's list for assassination, was away on a mission. Due to be relieved by Dowling, he contacted Dublin Castle to enquire about the delay. He was informed by Adjutant Hyems, "I am sorry to say that there have been some raids by the Shinners and I am afraid that they have got some of our fellows." Jeune returned to his lodgings:

> In the flat next to Murray's and mine, I saw the body of my friend, "Chummy" Dowling, a grand ex-guardee, wounded three times in the war, lying full length on the floor. As he was to have relieved me he was in uniform and had obviously been shot through the heart, probably by a small Sinn Feiner because there was a bullet hole in one corner of the ceiling. In the doorway of the bathroom was Price's body. Murray had already been taken to hospital [where he died]. Colonel Colonel Woodcock, commanding the 1st East Lancs, had been shot three times, but survived. Likewise Captain Keenlyside, Adjutant of the same battalion. Colonel Montgomery had been shot on the stairs, as he came up after breakfast. He died some time later.[15]

Throughout the city there were simultaneous raids at nine o'clock. Intelligence Officer Frank Saurin accompanied O. C. Vincent Byrne, and his team moved against the British agents living at 38, Upper Mount Street. Their targets were Lieutenant Peter Ashmun Ames and Lieutenant George Bennett. Ames was an American by birth but became a British subject. He served as a junior officer in the Grenadier Guards during World War I. On June 25, 1920, his name appears in the military section of the *London Gazette* where beside his name he is listed as on "Special Appointment," a euphemism for intelligence work. Lieutenant George

Bennett, late of the Royal Army Service Corps, was also listed for special duties. He was a graduate of Magdalen College, Oxford, and served in the Intelligence Corps during World War I. Saurin's account begins:

> We gained access to number 38 without any difficulty. I asked the maid where was Mr. Bennett and Mr. Ames. When she told me, we tried the door of Bennett's room which was locked. Herbert Conroy, a member of the squad, had a sledge hammer under his coat and wanted to break in the door. I would not let him but instructed the maid to knock on the door which was opened by Bennett. We took him to a return room where Ames was sleeping, and having asked the squad for as much time as possible, as I was interested principally in the papers these Intelligence Officers might have.[16]

Vincent Byrne was the officer commanding The Squad unit at 38, Upper Mount Street. His team, in addition to himself and Saurin, included Tom Ennis, John Daly, John Doyle, Herbert Conroy, Tom Duffy, Michael Lawless, John McDonnell and William Maher. Byrne takes up the story:

> I detailed Tom Ennis to take the back room and said I would look after the other one. I gently tried the handle to open the door, and found that it was locked. The servant then said to me, "You can get in by the back parlour. The folding doors are open." ... As I opened the folding doors the officer, who was in bed, was in the act of going for his gun under his pillow. Doyle and myself dashed into the room, at the same time ordering him to put up his hands, which he did. Doyle dashed around by the side of the bed, and pulled a Colt.45 from beneath the pillows. Right behind us came Frank Saurin and he started collecting from papers etc. which was his job.[17]

Bennett was ordered out of his bed and frogmarched along the hall to Ames' room. Outside the IRA men heard firing. Then the doorbell rang. Downstairs one of the team opened the door to reveal a British soldier. He was a dispatch rider. He was allowed in, then ordered to put his hands up. Meanwhile Byrne and his men joined the other unit who had gained access to Ames' room. Byrne wrote:

> He was standing up in the bed, facing the wall. I ordered mine to do likewise. When the two of them were together, I said to myself, "The Lord have mercy on your souls." I then opened fire with my Peter [the Painter, a Mauser C96 Broom-handle]. They both fell dead.

Returning downstairs Byrne faced a dilemma. Should he shoot the dispatch rider? But then, he was not on the list, and for all that he was just a soldier. Byrne relented and told him to remain where he was for the next fifteen minutes.

Meanwhile Saurin, dedicated intelligence officer as he was, was collecting up as much paper evidence as he could:

> In my anxiety to make a thorough search I was unaware that the Squad had left and hearing some shooting in the street, I walked to the door of

9. Bloody Sunday, November 21, 1920

Bennett's room. I heard a noise and looking down the hall I saw a British soldier outside the room where the two bodies were. I wheeled to shoot but the soldier jumped into the room. At the same time Tom Ennis, who was shooting across the street from the doorstep of 38, called on me to "come on." I went to the door to see across the road another British soldier shooting down the street at the backs of our retreating squad with what appeared to be a .22 automatic. We both fired and he jumped in through a door way of his house. Afterwards we learned, much to our disappointment, that Major Carew, a much wanted Intelligence Officer, was living in the house opposite, and the soldier firing was obviously his batman.

Down the road the escaping assassins ran, keeping the house from where the firing had come from under fire as they did so. They proceeded down Mount Street and along the lane behind Holles Street Hospital. Down to the quays they continued and crossed the Liffey by an awaiting boat to safety.

Simultaneously at nine o'clock, another IRA team struck at 22, Lower Mount Street. The team consisted of Tom Keogh, Jim Slattery (the O. C.), Frank Teeling, Denis Begley, Andy Monaghan, Jim Dempsey and William McLean. Their targets were Lieutenant Henry James Angliss, also known as Patrick McMahon, and Lieutenant Charles Ratsch Peel.

Apart from the information supplied by Lily Mernin, Sean Hyde from Irish Intelligence had got to know Angliss personally. Both men shared an interest in horse racing to the extent that they exchanged tips concerning racing certainties. Angliss was a Secret Service agent—and a murderer. Of that there was no doubt. Angliss appears to have been the illegitimate son of a sergeant in the 6th Inniskillings, Joseph Angliss, and Catherine McLoughlin. The younger Angliss was brought up in England, joining the Royal Inniskilling Fusiliers soon after the outbreak of World War I. Angliss received a commission as second lieutenant in 1917 and served with the Machine Gun Corps. of the Inniskillings. Remaining in the British Army after the end of the war, he was posted to Russia in 1919, serving at Murmansk and Archangel in the secretive Allied Army giving support to the White Russians in their fight against the Bolsheviks. Relinquishing his commission in March 1920, he was sent for training as a British agent at Hounslow. He arrived in Ireland about May 1920. On September 23rd, he and two other British agents murdered a Sinn Fein Loan organizer, John Lynch, in his bed. Under the influence of drink, Angliss divulged his part in the murder to a girl at the house where he was living, Lil Dunne. Working in Dublin Castle, she relayed the story to Lily Mernin, who reported it to Irish Intelligence.

Born in 1885, Charles Peel was the son of a naturalized German-Polish man, Hermann Ratsch. He served as a lieutenant in the Labour

Corps during World War I. Peel relinquished his commission, but in August 1920, he was recruited as a Secret Service agent. In the *London Gazette's* military section, he appears with other intended secret agents under the General List:

> The under mentioned to be temp. Capts. Whilst specially empld. 6th Aug. 1920:
> Capt. E.G. Bodger, late Serv. Bn., North'd Fus.
> Capt. G. deB Wooldridge, late 8th Hamps. R. T.F.
> Lt. C.R. Peel, late Lab, Corps, to be temp. Lt. whilst specially empd. 6th Aug. 1920.

After training at the "Spy School" at the Hounslow Depot, he was sent to Ireland.

James Slattery, the officer commanding the assassination team briefed to execute Angliss and Peel narrates what happened:

> Tom Keogh and myself from the Squad, with six others from "E" Company of the 2nd Battalion, proceeded to Lower Mount Street, at the appointed hour on the morning of 21st November. We knocked at the door and a maid admitted us. We left two men inside the door to see that nobody would enter or leave the house, and the remainder of us proceeded upstairs to the two rooms, the number of which we had already ascertained. We had only just gone upstairs when we heard shooting downstairs. The housekeeper or some other lady in the house had seen a patrol of Tans passing by outside and had started to scream. The Tans immediately surrounded the house and tried to gain admission. One of our young men, Billy McLean, fired at them through the door and eased the situation for us for a little while, although he got wounded himself. I think the Tans fired first.
> We succeeded in shooting Lieutenant McMahon, but could not gain admission into the room where the other agent was sleeping.[18]

Peel, hearing the shots from outside, barricaded the door to his room with furniture. The team assigned to kill him were unable to burst in. In desperation, and in vain, they fired about twenty shots through the door in the hope of hitting him. Having failed, the gunmen descended the stairs to discover that a firefight was underway at the front of the house. They withdrew to the rear garden and began climbing over the wall. Then they came under fire. A truck full of Auxiliaries had been patrolling in the area. It stopped when hearing the sound of shots, and the occupants rushed to the front and rear of the house. A firefight developed at the front of the house. At the rear, the assassins were fired upon as they escaped over the wall. One of the team members, Frank Teeling, was wounded and dropped back down into the garden, where he sought shelter. Another of their number, Billy McLean, was shot in the hand, but under sustained return fire he and the others succeeded in getting

9. Bloody Sunday, November 21, 1920

away. At the front of the house, Tom Keogh and his men decided to rush the Auxies. "We must attack first," Keogh declared. He swung open the hall door and charged out, his men following. They succeeded in wounding or killing some of the enemy. The lorry in which the Auxiliaries had been patrolling drove off, seemingly leaving the wounded to their fate. In reality, feeling outnumbered, its driver had gone for reinforcements. The IRA men withdrew, not perceiving that Teeling had been left behind to be captured.

Slattery, in his narrative, adds information about the attack on Lieutenant McMahon:

> There was a second man in McMahon's bed, but we did not shoot him as we had no instruction to do so. We discovered afterwards that he was an undesirable character as far as we were concerned, and that we should have shot him.

John Joseph Connolly, who had been discovered in bed with Angliss, gave a little more description of the event at the court-martial of Teeling. His account was featured in a number of the Dublin newspapers at the time:

> I was awakened about 9 a.m. by someone shouting, "Hands up." When I opened my eyes I saw five men standing at the end of my bed covering me with revolvers. One of the men who appeared to be acting as leader gave the order to keep McMahon and myself covered and he proceeded to search the room. He picked up a civilian coat belonging to McMahon and said "Is this your coat McMahon?" McMahon said "No." He then put his hand in the inside pocket, took out a wallet and said, "You're a damned liar," and put the wallet in his pocket. He then said, "Where are your guns Mac?" McMahon said, "Look here we are two R[oman] C[atholic]s but the guns are in that bag." The man then walked over to the bag which was lying in a corner of the room, lifted it on to the table and burst the locks off with his hands and took out three revolvers. They were one service Colt, one Webley-Scott Automatic and one .32 automatic. He put them in his pockets.
>
> I then heard firing which seemed to come from the street and I heard a noise as if someone was trying to smash in the front door. A man's voice on the landing then shouted "Are you all right there boys. They're surrounding the house." The five men in the room then turned as if to rush out. They went a little way down the room then halted and the man who had been doing the searching raised his revolver—pointed it at the bed and fired. I saw McMahon raise his arm to cover his face and at the same time I threw myself out of the bed onto the floor. Practically simultaneously I heard other shots ring out from the other men in the room and they all rushed out of the room. McMahon was shot three times in the chest and once in the buttock.

Alerted to what was happening, two Auxiliaries, Frank Garniss and Cecil Morris, made their way to towards the sound of gunfire at 22,

Lower Mount Street. They ran directly into the path of the withdrawing IRA covering team near Mount Street Bridge. The covering team held them up, then took them into a garden, where they were shot. Meanwhile, at Beggar's Bush Garrison, alerted by the sounds of gunfire, Brigadier-General Frank Crozier himself led a truckload of men to Mount Street. The wounded Teeling was discovered in the garden of No. 22 and was sent off to the George V Military Hospital. Crozier ascended the stairs. He found James Angliss, alias Patrick McMahon, dead in a blood-soaked bed and Peel's door closed and blockaded. Calling through the door Crozier reassured Peel that he was safe. The door opened to reveal "a very scared and trembling man."

There were two targets in Lower Baggot Street: Captain William Newberry at number 92 and Captain Geoffrey Baggallay at number 119. The assassination of Baggallay was an essential. Along with Jocelyn Hardy and Henry Angliss, he was the third member in one of the British murder gangs. Baggallay was officially a courts-martial officer. As noted before, he had lost a leg as an active soldier during World War I. The team assigned to kill Baggallay comprised Matthew McDonald, Sean Lemass, James Brennan, Jack Keating, Pat McCrea and Jack Foley. Pat McCrea gives a businesslike account of the killing of Baggallay:

> The British agent in Baggot St. listed for elimination was, as far as I know, Captain Baggally, who was believed to have been one of Kevin Barry's torturers. On that Sunday morning I left home about 7.30 o'clock and made my way to the dump in North Great Charles St. I met the remainder of the men there—at least some of them. We collected our guns and got out the car. We timed ourselves to be in Baggot St. about five minutes to 9 o'clock We arrived there up to time—I think it was two or three minutes to, and within three minutes another man, who was on the job, turned up. We parked the car a little to the rear of the house on the opposite side of the street. When our men arrived there was no delay, as arranged. Three or four men entered the house, leaving one man on each side of the building as a guard for the men who had actually gone into the house. They had particulars of the agent's bedroom. When the room was entered he tried to escape through the window, but before he reached the window he was put out of action. The job was completed in the space of a few minutes. We got away without incident. We left Baggot St. and we came down Merrion Square and Westland Row. When we came into Merrion Square we picked up a few men coming off the Mount St. job—one was Herbert Conroy. We arrived back at the dump without any interference from anybody We replaced the car and dumped our guns.[19]

Baggallay was shot five times.

Captain Newberry and his wife lived in a ground-floor apartment at 92, Lower Baggot Street. It consisted of a back and front parlor. On the face of it, Newberry was a court-martial officer rather than a secret agent. He was educated at Magdalen College, Oxford, where he took Honours in Law. Newberry later served in the Queen's (Royal West Surrey Regiment) but emigrated with his wife to Canada in 1913, where he practiced law. At the outbreak of World War I, he returned to England, where he was seconded to a training depot. At the end of the war, he was transferred to Ireland as an Education Officer, and at some point after the summer of 1920, he joined the courts-martial team in Dublin.

The assassination team sent to kill him was led by Joe Leonard of The Squad. Ten men were known to have been on the mission included William Stapleton, Jack Stafford, and Hugo MacNeill. Following a knock at the door, it was opened by the housekeeper, Mrs. Stack. Leonard asked if Captain Newberry was at home. Seeing the armed men, the lady fled upstairs in terror. One of the team knocked at the front parlor door; getting no reply, they went to the back parlor. The door was opened by Mrs. Newberry. Seeing the gunmen, she attempted to close the door, but a member of the team jammed his foot in the gap. Hearing a noise from inside, another of the team fired some shots through the door and they burst in:

> ...[W]e all went into it. He was in his pyjamas, and as he was attempting to escape by the window, he was shot a number of times. One of our party on guard outside fired at him from outside. The man's wife was standing in a corner of the room and was in a terrified and hysterical condition. The operation lasted about fifteen minutes. Our line of retreat had been planned via the South Liffey Wall and ferry boat to the North Liffey Wall, and from there we were to disperse to our various homes.[20]

Captain Newberry was shot seven times and died on the open window ledge. Newberry's distraught, heavily pregnant "wife" gave birth to a stillborn baby a week later.[21]

The IRA raid on premises in Fitzwilliam Square was to target a Major O'Callaghan.[22] Captain John Scott Crawford of the Royal Army Service Corps was in bed with his wife when there was a knock at the door of their apartment. On the belief that it was one of his men delivering a message, Crawford got out of bed, put on his dressing gown, and opened the door. He found three men standing there, all armed and pointing their guns at him. Crawford was forced back into the room. He was told to raise his arms but ignored the order. "Is this a joke?" he asked. The leader of the group demanded, "Are you Major O'Callaghan?" He replied that there was a Mr. O'Callaghan living on the floor above, and two of the men went upstairs. Crawford now realized that he was talking to save his life. He engaged with them, telling them that Mr. O'Callaghan was not a major and had no connection with the BritishArmy. He himself was in charge of the Motor Repair Department. The leader of the team accused him of lying, declaring that he was a Secret Service agent. Another of the team, searching through his coat, discovered documents verifying that he was who he claimed to be. In frustration, the team leader demanded, "Why the hell did you come here? Why don't you stay and mind your own business in England?" Crawford, educated at Campbell College, Belfast, was ordered back to bed with his wife. Others of the team searched the drawers in the cupboards and bags but found nothing that would incriminate Crawford. The other two gunmen returned. O'Callaghan was not there. With a warning to Crawford, "You bloody clear out of this country in 20 hours, or we will do for you tomorrow night," the men departed. Crawford duly departed.

Elsewhere in the city at nine o'clock, Hugh Gallagher, doorman at the Gresham Hotel in Upper O'Connell Street, held the door open for a group of men. Patrick Moran entered, along with Michael Kilkelly, James Foley, Arthur Beasley, Intelligence Officer Paddy Kennedy, Michael Noone, Nicholas Leonard, Joseph Glynn, John Cullinane, William Hogan, James Cahill and Richard McGrath. Most of the men were from D Company of the 2nd Battalion, Dublin Brigade. They were targeting three British officers. Lieutenant Colonel Wilde and Captain McCormack were two of the three. Their first object was to disconnect the telephone. Then a guard was put on the people in the dining room. Moran, gun in hand, asked the doorman to take them up to rooms number 14 and 24, the numbers supplied by Lily Mernin. The assassination team split up as prearranged and proceeded towards the rooms allotted to them by Moran. The room occupied by a targeted, but unnamed British officer, was empty. Being a Roman Catholic, he had gone out to early mass. Captain McCormack of the Royal Army Veterinary Corps was sitting up in bed reading the Sunday newspapers as the unlocked door was opened. James Cahill and Nick Leonard entered the room and approached the bed. Seeing them, McCormack drew a .38 automatic and opened fire. The bullet passed between the two IRA men and buried itself in a door jamb. The two responded in the same instant, killing the British agent outright.[23]

At the same time, as another unit proceeded along the corridor. The door to one of the rooms opened. Volunteer James Cahill of D Company 2nd Battalion narrates what happened next:

> I observed a man of foreign appearance come to a bedroom door. I had a hunch that he might be one of the two other Intelligence Officers and would, if we continued on our way, take alarm, barricading himself in his room, and endeavour to call for assistance. I covered him with my gun, and asked him for his name. He promptly replied, "Alan Wilde, British Intelligence Officer, just back from Spain." At that moment Mick Kilkelly, whose group had

been detailed to deal with Wilde, came on the scene and fired, killing him instantly. The fact that Wilde was a new arrival and probably mistook us for a British raiding party would explain his readiness to give us information regarding himself.[24]

In less than ten minutes it was all over. The IRA men withdrew.

At the Shelbourne Hotel on St. Stephen's Green, an Active Service Unit and a member of Irish Intelligence raced up the stairs to the room of another British agent, as a church clock chimed nine o'clock outside. Hyped-up and full of anxiety, the leading member of the team, gun in hand, turned a corner of the stairs just in time to see a figure in the darkness approaching him. He too was armed. The young man fired a burst of his automatic first. In front of him he watched the mirror shatter. He had seen a reflection of himself. Upstairs, the targeted Secret Service man heard the shots, and, picking up his revolver, fled to an upper room of the hotel. The team burst into the officer's room on the floor below, but he was gone. The hotel was too large to search room by room, so the intelligence officer grabbed what papers he could find, and the team withdrew.

At another hotel in the city, the Eastwood Hotel at 91–2, Lower Leeson Street, the IRA team of Ned Bennett (O. C.), Christopher Byrne, Joe and Jim McGuinness, Pat O'Connor, George Dwyer and Jim Donnelly went in search of their quarry, Captain Thomas James Jennings (erroneously described as Lieutenant Colonel Jennings) and Major Callaghan. In 1915, Jennings enlisted in the Northumberland Fusiliers, and in the following year as a corporal he was awarded the Distinguished Conduct Medal for rescuing a wounded man. Bennett was sent back to England as a cadet officer and was commissioned as an officer in the West Riding Regiment in September 1918. At the end of the war, he was demobilized but taken back again for unspecified reasons. By 1920, he was in Dublin.

Christy Byrne, who headed the unit, tells the story:

> On Sunday morning at the appointed time I met all my men as arranged. I placed two of my party at the back entrance to the hotel. Donnelly and myself took up positions at the main entrance door. I detailed the remainder of the party to go into the hotel and locate the British agent, Jennings, and carry out their instructions. Ned Bennett led the party into the hotel, asked for the Manageress and inquired from her the number of the room that Jennings occupied. She said he was not there, that he had left a couple of days previously. The register was then called for and the number of the room that he had occupied was shown. The Manageress's word was not taken for it, and the party went up to the room and searched it. They saw then that he actually had left the place and there was nothing for it but to get out as quickly as possible.

I would also like to mention that Bob Byrne, who was a Company officer at the time, had also received instructions for another job on Bloody Sunday. This job was, however, called off late on Saturday evening. Knowing that I had been detailed for the Eastwood Hotel he volunteered to come with me, which he did.[25]

Jennings and Callaghan had spent the night at a local brothel, Becky Cooper's in the "Monto," a famous red-light district just off O'Connell Street. Her brother, John "Shankers" Ryan, had alerted the military to the whereabouts of McKee and Clancy; an action for which he would later pay.

Lieutenant Donald Lewis McLean, late of the Rifle Brigade, and now chief intelligence officer, lived at 117, Morehampton Road, Donnybrook. Visiting them was his brother-in-law, John Caldow. His ambition while in Ireland was to join the police force. The house was owned by a suspected informer, T. H. Smith. With him lived his wife and their three children. At nine o'clock, Jimmy Doyle, his brother Sean, and men from K Company, 3rd Battalion of the Dublin IRA approached the house. One of the children answered the knock at the door, and the six-man ASU burst into the house. Up to the bedrooms they rushed. McLean was in bed with his wife. Seeing the armed men, he knew their intention. "Not here," McLean said, "not in front of my wife."

"Get upstairs," Doyle then ordered.

Smith and Caldow were also ordered up to the floor above. The three men were pushed into an unoccupied bedroom, where they were shot. The gunmen hurried down the stairs, out onto the road, and away. With their departure, Mrs. McLean went upstairs to investigate. There she found her husband and Smith lying dead. Her brother was badly wounded. Down the stairs she ran and out into the roadway. Here she met two policemen who took her back into the house, then sent for help. Caldow survived and later returned to his home in Scotland.

An unnamed, six- or seven-man IRA team approached 28, Earlsfort Terrace. Their target was Captain John J. Fitzgerald. During World War I, Fitzgerald had served in the Royal Flying Corps, the forerunner of the Royal Air Force. Shot down, he became a prisoner of war. At the end of the war, he was repatriated. He then served as a pilot with the British Expeditionary Force in Russia. He returned to Britain in late 1919. Fitzgerald joined the RIC (Black and Tans?) in June 1920 and served as a Barracks Defence Officer. Whilst on duty in County Clare, he was kidnapped by the IRA and shot. Feigning death, he eventually escaped and was sent to Dublin for his own safety. Still apparently recovering from his injuries, he was in bed when the doorbell rang. The maid answered the door, and one of the men asked her to show them where Colonel Fitzpatrick's room was. She claimed there was no one of that name there, but there was a Captain Fitzgerald. At this point, the other gunmen entered the house and stood in the hall opposite Fitzgerald's ground floor rooms. The door was burst open, and Fitzgerald was shot four times—twice in the forehead, once in the heart, and once in the wrist, the last presumably a wound suffered as he raised his hand to defend himself. It has been hypothesized that his killing was a case of mistaken identity—Fitzgerald, when it should have been Fitzpatrick. Nevertheless, his funeral at Glasnevin Cemetery was attended by an RIC and Auxiliary guard of honor, which might suggest that Fitzgerald was something more than he appeared to be.

Lieutenant Laurence Nugent and a group of men from K Company of the Dublin Battalion met with disappointment on their mission, as Nugent himself admits:

> An incident of the operation on Sunday morning was the action in the hotel in Exchequer St. A number of the spy organisation were living at this hotel. The IRA had a list of their names, but when they examined the hotel book they found the names all right but there were no room numbers after them. The boots [a general odd-job worker] refused to give the numbers, and in order to execute the spies they would have to shoot every man in the hotel. And so the spies got off, but they left Dublin on the first available boat, and so the battle of wits was won by the IRA Intelligence Department against the great British Secret Service...[26]

Another ASU targeted the officers staying at the Standard Hotel, but none were there. They were off searching, unsuccessfully, for an IRA arms dump. There was another failure to kill a British agent up in the north of the city at 7, Ranelagh Road. The target was a known Secret Service man, Lieutenant William Nobel. Nobel—or Noble, if he was the same man, and there is some uncertainty—had served in the Notts & Derby Regiment during World War I. In 1920 he resigned his commission but was, according to the *London Gazette* of June 1, 1920, along with Messers. H.F. Boddington, Carew, E.P. Hyem, A. Thorp and P. Attwood, assigned to a special appointment on Grade GG, the accepted grade for junior Secret Service men in Ireland. Members of The Squad and others sent to assassinate him consisted of Joe Dolan, Dan McDonnell, C. S. "Tod" Andrews, James Kenny, Francis Burke, Francis X. Coughlan and Hubert Earle. Far from being an impersonal action, on the day before the shootings, one of the participants, Tod Andrews, articulated what must have been the concern of many of the young men who went out that day to kill:

> We were very excited by the assignment but the prospect of killing a man in cold blood was alien to our ideas of how war should be conducted. We neither of us relished the idea. We were apprehensive too, because it could be a

dangerous operation. We were already being affected psychologically by the terror of the Tans.[27]

On Bloody Sunday, Andrews walked to Charlemont Street Bridge where, at five to nine, he met three of the team, Francis Coughlan, Hubert Earle and James Kenny. Together they walked up to 7, Ranelagh Road and met up with the remainder of the team. Punctually at nine o'clock, Coughlan rapped at the door with his stick. A young girl of about fifteen opened it. The men dashed in and proceeded quickly up the stairs to the front room which they knew to be Nobel's. Andrews relates:

> We had our "dogs," (the name used for guns) cocked as we opened the door of the bedroom expecting to see Nobel. Our orders were to shoot him on sight as he was certain to be armed. We found the room empty except for a half naked woman who sat up in the bed looking terror-stricken. She did not scream or say a word. I was very excited but, even so, I felt a sense of shame and embarrassment for the woman's sake. I was glad to get out quickly and moved to the next room where there was a man shaving. He was literally petrified with fear. His safety razor froze in mid-air. Thinking he was Nobel, I was going to pull the trigger of my .45 when Coughlan shouted, "He's all right." He was a lodger in the house and was apparently one of our intelligence sources.[28]

Dolan questioned the woman as to the whereabouts of Nobel, but she did not know. In frustration Dolan gave Nobel's half naked mistress a "right scourging with a sword scabbard" before the team withdrew. Meanwhile, the other members of the team had searched the other rooms for any sign of Nobel, but he was nowhere to be found. The house was searched for papers, but again none were found. The team, now added to by two members of The Squad, withdrew. Andrews reflected:

> As I went back to Terenure through quiet suburban roads and lanes well known to me, I wondered whether I was glad or sorry that Nobel had not been at home. I would certainly have felt no remorse at having shot him but I found it hard to get the memory of the terrified woman and, indeed the equally terrified lodge, from my mind. We all arrived home safely and a few of us appeared prominently among the congregation leaving 11 o'clock Mass in Terenure.

Dan McDonnell, who was in the party, infers that Nobel's paramour was very lucky not to have been shot. If Nobel had been there with her, she probably would have been. In his Witness Statement (486) he relates:

> We got a very ugly mission to perform. It was to go to the house, No. 7, Ranelagh Road, where a British agent called Noble, and his paramour lived. They were both agents, and our information was that they both were the main cause of a member of our organization, named Doyle, getting a very cruel death in the Dublin Mountains.

9. Bloody Sunday, November 21, 1920

James Gleeson, in his pioneering work on Bloody Sunday, records that one Eileen Horan, whose mother ran a boarding house in Hume Street, just off St. Stephen's Green, saw a group of men emerging disappointedly from their house shortly after nine o'clock that morning. Questioning her mother, the older woman related that, "They came to shoot Mr. Clevedon, the civil servant. They ought to be ashamed of themselves, he is such a nice young man. Luckily he did not come in last night." The following day an armored car and a truck full of Auxiliaries stopped outside the house. "Mr. Clevedon," now in the uniform of a British Army officer, entered the house, packed up his clothes and left without paying.

Also absent from his Harcourt Street address was Captain William King. No mention is made of the attempt to assassinate Jocelyn, Hardy either, in any of the Witness Statements now housed with the Bureau of Military History. Major Carew was saved, having moved to 28, from 38, Upper Mount Street. Obviously, he had not filed his change of address. Secret Service man Lieutenant Jeune was on duty that night and so escaped the fate of a number of his fellow officers.

In some ways, the operations of that morning were disappointing, in that only a proportion of those men on the list, some of them most dangerous, had been killed. Though it was trumpeted as a victory of Irish Intelligence over British Intelligence, it was far from being a complete victory. There were disappointments, as Charles Dalton of Irish Intelligence reported in his Witness Statement (434):

> Although instructions were issued for about twenty different operations on the Sunday morning, several were not carried out. Later on, reports were supplied by our officers and these were examined and filed in the Intelligence Office. In some instances the excuse put forward for the non-carrying out of instructions were not considered very satisfactory; in particular, those received from the Commandant of the 1st Battalion regarding two addresses they should have visited on the North Circular Road adjacent to the Phoenix Park.

Dan McDonnell confirms Dalton's statement:

> In the 1st Battalion area there was a large number of agents who resided on the North Circular Road and the adjoining roads to the Park, and as far as I know none of those was interfered with.... Next morning we turned into Crow Street as usual and started off the routine again. We then knew the actual number of British agents who had been disposed of. We were disappointed with the result. It did achieve a purpose as most of the British agents were terrified of the place and had gone to ground.[29]

Within Dublin Castle that Sunday morning, Dick McKee Peadar, Clancy and the innocent Gaelic student Conor Clune had been separated from the other prisoners brought in on the previous night. Each of the three men was interrogated separately by Captain King, Captain Hardy and Ormonde Winter. When news of the assassinations started to come in, the interrogations became more brutal. McKee was tortured with a bayonet. Their interrogators—their torturers—demanded the addresses of GHQ officers, the names of personnel, and of all the badly wanted men in their brigade. Clune, a completely innocent man, must have wondered what sort of madness was going on. He could not answer the questions; he had no idea. His torturers were convinced that he had come up from the country to take part in the murders.

Collins, now made aware of the capture of McKee and Clancy, instructed one of his agents within the Castle, James MacNamara, a policeman and confidential clerk to the assistant police commissioner, to investigate. MacNamara could get no closer than the canteen next to the guardroom where the men were being interrogated. Here he discovered that "excited and fairly drunk Auxiliaries were threatening vengeance as they hastily swallowed their drinks."[30] Finally, frustrated at their failing to divulge what they knew, the three prisoners were taken out and killed in the narrow courtyard leading from F Company's quarters to the military guardroom. A hurriedly concocted story was dreamt up that the three men had been shot while trying to escape. The propaganda people in the Castle staged a series of photographs showing that the dead men had attempted to seize the arms of their guards but had died in the attempt. Collins was quite distraught when he heard of the deaths of McKee and Clancy—McKee especially, for the two men were friends and had worked closely together. Major Reynolds, Collins's agent within F Company of the Auxiliaries based within the Castle, sent out details of what had happened to the prisoners. Patrick Kennedy related the information in his Witness Statement:

> I do remember the nature of the information that we received from Reynolds. Reynolds reported the conversations of Auxiliaries describing how they had carried out the shootings, who carried them out and who the ringleaders were. He gave us full details as to the perpetrators of the murder of Peadar Clancy, Dick McKee and Clune. He told us that these three men were kicked and beaten first in order to extract information from them. The authorities did not succeed in getting anything from the three men, and as a result they were shot in the Castle. I believe that Captain Hardy and Captain King were two of the British gang implicated in the murders.[31]

The threatened vengeance was followed up that afternoon with the murder of a group of civilians attended a G.A.A. sporting fixture at Croke Park. The match, between Tipperary and Dublin, began at a quarter to three that afternoon. The grounds and stands were crowded, the spectators numbering between 10,000 and 15,000. Soon after the match began, an R.A.F. airplane was observed flying over the field. At about ten past three, twelve trucks full of armed Auxiliaries and Black and Tans arrived. They dispersed to four vantage points around the grounds. A machine gun was placed on the raised area along the railway end of the pitch. Both entrances in Jones's Road were forced by the police. It was alleged that some of the gate money was taken. As the police entered the stadium, an officer atop the wall fired a revolver shot. Without warning, the policemen below immediately opened fire, first into the air and then at the crowd. A little boy sitting on a branch of a tree overlooking the park fell from the tree, shot through the body. A general stampede followed. Men, women and children rushed wildly for shelter. On the pitch the players threw themselves onto the ground. Tipperary player Michael Hogan, on his hands and knees, was shot dead through the mouth. He had a second wound under his left shoulder. The youngest spectator to be shot was ten-year-old Gerald O'Leary. He died in his mother's arms. Jeannie Boyle was trampled to death by the fleeing, panic-stricken crowd. So, too, was 11-year-old William Robinson. Firing from the canal end of the pitch became intense; bullets plowed up the pitch. Others were killed, too. Bullets struck the wall at the railway end. J. Scott was killed by a ricocheting bullet. Then it was all over—fury was spent. In all, fourteen people died and sixty-two were injured, many of them seriously. Surviving spectator Miss Boyle asked an officer if the relatives would be allowed to take away the bodies. He replied, "When we are done taking in our dead, we will look after these fellows." Another Auxiliary officer declared, "Here we avenge our fallen comrades." The thousands of spectators still within the ground were ordered to put their hands up. They were formed into lines, then frisked. It was some hours later before the ground was cleared.

Dan McDonnell, Tom Keogh and Joe Dolan, who had taken part in the executions that morning, were at Croke Park that afternoon.:

> We went there ... if there was any sudden raid we would be much safer there. We parked ourselves on the famous Hill 16, and the match had just started when, as far as we could see, there was a rumble and bustle going on around the entrance at the Hogan Stand side.... We suddenly realized that the whole ground was under rifle and machine-gun fire. We scattered and separated from one another on the Hill. My hat fell off and while I was picking it up the man in front of me was shot.... I ran so fast that I was nearly the first to reach [the Ballybough gate]. The gates were not open. I jumped for the top of the gate, caught it and went over the far side.... I then went to where I lived in Infirmary Road. We had safely dumped our guns before going to Croke Park.[32]

When news of the atrocity reached the Castle, the British propaganda machine went into full production to disguise the fact of what had truly happened. An official communiqué was issued:

> A number of men came to Dublin on Saturday under the guise of attending a football match between Tipperary and Dublin. But their real purpose was to act as gunmen.
>   Learning on Sunday that a number of these gunmen were present in Croke Park, the Crown forces went to raid the field.
>   It was the original intention that an officer would go to the centre of the field and speaking from a megaphone invite the assassins to come forward. But on their approach armed pickets gave warning. Shots were fired to warn the wanted men, who caused a stampede and escaped in the confusion.

The "armed pickets" were, in fact, ticket sellers. None of them were armed. Seeing the approach of the Auxiliaries, they fled into the park for safety. Within the park, there were some armed IRA men—who wisely dropped their guns onto the ground before being searched. At no stage, though, did they fire upon the Crown forces, and there is every reason to believe them. They would have known the consequences of such an action. Sometime later, an Auxiliary officer, Major Mills, broke ranks to reveal that he had not heard any shots until the police opened fire.[33]

Earlier that morning, as news started to come in of the murders of their colleagues, matters reached boiling point in the guardroom at Dublin Castle. The Auxiliaries there started drinking heavily. There were angry words and threats to the prisoners. No one seemed to be in charge; there was no one to take control. The twenty prisoners now feared mass murder. As night descended that November 21st, the prisoners were ordered to parade in single file. They were led into the passage leading out into the Castle yard. McKee and Clune were left sitting on old beds in the guardroom. A voice called out, "Stop. Wait a minute," then a figure came down the file. It was Hardy, carrying a torch. Clancy was pulled out of line and ordered back to the guardroom. The other prisoners were then marched out into the courtyard and loaded aboard lorries and were driven to Beggar's Bush Barracks. Irish historian and author, T.P. Coogan summed up what awaited Clancy, McKee and Clune:

> McKee, Clancy and the innocent Clune would pass one of the most hellish nights imaginable. For Clune there was the terror of the uninitiated, for the others, the horror of the too well informed.[34]

At Dublin Castle the bodies of the three murdered men were handed over to their relatives and friends. The bodies of the two IRA men were dressed in uniforms of the Irish Volunteers and taken to lie in wait at the pro–Cathedral. To give credence to the death of Clune, "shot while escaping," he was described by the propaganda machine as a Lieutenant in the 1st Battalion of the County Clare IRA. The next morning, amidst tight IRA security, Collins, Cullen, Thornton and Gearoid

O'Sullivan, the adjutant-general, attended a short requiem service at the pro–Cathedral, then assisted in carrying the bodies out to the waiting hearses. Ernie O'Malley, in his account of the day, relates that a photographer took a quick snap of the occasion which appeared in the *Evening Herald*. It showed Collins and Tom Cullen at the head of the coffin. The Intelligence team, seeing a copy of newspaper photograph, organized teams to go around and quickly buy up all copies of the paper from newsagents and newsboys. Then, at the printer's, they smashed the metal die in the newspaper office, half an hour before a British intelligence-led party of Auxiliaries descended upon the office.

When Prime Minister Lloyd George heard of the assassinations, he was less than sympathetic over the loss of the British Secret Service men. "They got what they deserved. Beaten by counter-jumpers," he exclaimed to an Irish businessman, one Mr. Moylett. Winston Churchill was equally callous in his comment to Sir Henry Wilson, when he proclaimed that "they were careless fellows who ought to have taken precautions." A day after the executions, Arthur Griffith in Dublin received a message, apparently from Lloyd George, urging him, "for God's sake to keep his head, and not to break off the slender link that had been established." Tragic as the events in Dublin were, they were of no importance. These men were soldiers and took a soldier's risk. In essence, what the British prime minister was saying was that the deaths of fifteen men were collateral damage in the proposed attempts at peace in Ireland.[35]

As to the men who took part in the shooting, killing in cold blood unsettled many of them. This was especially true of men drawn from the 3rd Battalion to supplement The Squad. Lt. Lawrence Nugent expressed this concern:

> The men did not like this operation, but orders were orders and had to be obeyed. The life of every IRA man in Dublin was at stake. Nevertheless it was difficult to get details of the action as the men would not talk. Three men of K Company never returned to duty after the operation.[36]

Later explaining why the Secret Service men were killed, Michael Collins wrote:

> My own intention was the destruction of the undesirables who continued to make miserable the lives of ordinary decent citizens.... If I had another motive, it was no more than a feeling such as I would have for a dangerous reptile.... There is no crime in detecting and destroying in war-time, the spy and the informer. They have destroyed without trial. I have paid them back in their own coin.

The next day, November 22nd, Charles Dalton from Irish Intelligence was instructed to go to a house in North Richmond Street. His mission was to collect a large black deedbox containing papers. The box had been wrapped in brown paper but, due to its size, was bound to attract attention. The crown forces were everywhere. Dalton got on a tram going through Parnell Street. The box was placed on the luggage rack. Dalton sat away from it, but close enough to keep it view. As the tram moved off, he saw a military patrol holding up pedestrians. The tram came to a standstill. Dalton was now close to panic and faced with a dilemma: if the soldiers boarded the tram he would be faced with the dilemma, should he walk away and leave the box or try and bluff it? He made a third choice. He picked up the box, and with it under his arm, he left the tram, walking away from the soldiers. At every step, he dreaded that the patrol would order him to halt. Off he set, trying to walk normally. Down the road he proceeded. Then, several yards further on, he turned into an alleyway. He broke into a run, eventually reaching his destination. With relief he watched as the box was unwrapped and the tin opened. Inside were all the papers and documents belonging to the British agents who had been shot the previous day. If he had been captured with such evidence, he would have shared the same fate as McKee, Clancey and Clune.

British revenge had not been sated with Croke Park. The bodies of most of the dead British officers were shipped back to Britain. On the following Thursday, November 25th, six of the dead were given a state funeral in Westminster Abbey. Lloyd George, Winston Churchill, and Hamar Greenwood, Chief Secretary, walked up the central aisle behind the coffins. In Dublin, Michael Collins attended the Requiem Mass for McKee and Clancy. While the British newspapers condemned the killings, both of the British officers and the victims of Croke Park, Labour Party spokeswoman Miss Margaret Bondfield posed the question "...which are the reprisals, and which are the murders?"

For their own safety, British agents and their wives living outside were brought into Dublin Castle or other places of safety as the British account of the war, *Record of the Rebellion in Ireland, 1920–1921* Vol. IV, Part III: *Dublin District Historical Record* (May 1920–December 1920) demonstrated of the time:

> Officers to live in.
> Orders were issued by the Dublin District Headquarters that all officers must live within the protection of a military barracks and close to their work. Special quarters initially including three hotels, had to be commandeered to effect this order. Officers were instructed to carry arms at all times and to go out in at least twos or threes. The men were ordered to go about in parties when on pass, and to use main streets.

9. Bloody Sunday, November 21, 1920

Ironically, the British administration had become self-interned out of fear. They were forced to live in overcrowded, claustrophobic conditions. Caroline Woodcock, an officer's wife, described the situation:

> The Castle is a dreadful place, surrounded by the worst slums in Dublin. Nowadays it is like a huge rabbit-warren. Every official connected in any way, however remotely, with the [British] Government of Ireland or the police, is interned there, in many cases with their wives and families. In addition, there are innumerable military officers with their belongings, a very large number of soldiers and police. There are also numerous scores of male and female clerks, typists, & c.
>
> The accommodation is at a premium. Quite important people sleep two in a room—nay, two in a bed, sometimes. All day long motors dash in and out, orderlies scurry about with papers. About tea-time, lady clerks, jug in hand, wander out in search of milk, and exchange a few words of badinage with the waiting orderlies.
>
> Even the poor little children of some of the police officials never leave the Castle. Afternoon dances are held occasionally, at which the inhabitants stretch their cramped legs. It is the only exercise some of them get.
>
> Personally it makes one ashamed to think that the Government of the most powerful Empire in the world should allow its servants to live like this, practically as prisoners in the heart of Dublin.[37]

During the day, the military and the paramilitaries ventured forth, but only in large numbers. Their times now were the curfew hours. On Tuesday, two days after the mass killings of Bloody Sunday, a truck filled with Auxiliaries screamed to a halt outside the lodgings of IRA officer Sean Hyde. He succeeded in escaping. The raid was led by Lieutenant Charles Peel, whom the ASU had failed to locate on Sunday. British Intelligence had suffered a serious blow, but as Peel's presence revealed, it was not broken.

10

Hardy, King and Igoe

As a result of the November 21st bloodbath, there was an intensity of activity on the part of the Crown forces throughout the Dublin district. A general roundup of known Dublin Brigade members was instigated. There were, according to British reports, about 100 raids during each 24-hour period. In all, 500 arrests were made in the following week. Suspects were picked up, but identification was difficult. On Monday, November 22nd, Arthur Griffith was taken into custody—as much for his own safety as anything else. There was a fear that a rogue element within British security was intent on murdering him in retaliation for the events of the previous day. In Griffith's absence, Collins became Acting President of Sinn Fein. Evidently, over in America, Eamon de Valera was none too happy with that. Too much power was being invested in a man that he now considered to be a possible rival. As head of the IRB, some saw Collins as the legitimate successor of Padraig Pearse. In America, John Devoy, who had been subject to de Valera's high-handed attitude, referred to Collins as "Ireland's fighting chief." De Valera thought it was time to return home. Collins was obliged to make the arrangements.

Curfew restrictions in Dublin were extended to cover the period 10:00 p.m. to 5:00 a.m. As noted in the last chapter, orders were issued by the Dublin District Headquarters that all officers must live within the protection of a military barracks. Three hotels were commandeered to house those affected. Officers were instructed to carry arms at all times, and, when necessary, were ordered to go out in parties in of at least two or three people and to use only the main streets. Internment on suspicion was reintroduced, large-scale roadblocks were put up, and searches and arrests were set in motion. Captain Jeune, who had escaped the shootings, recalled that "those of us who had survived were shut up under guard in a hotel, from where it was impracticable to do any useful work." Soon after, Jeune and fellow agent W.F. Jeffries left Ireland. Jeffries later went on to take charge of Winter's London Bureau.

It is a common misconception that the events of Bloody Sunday

10. Hardy, King and Igoe

destroyed British Intelligence in Ireland. In truth, it had been paralyzed but not destroyed. What was surprising to the British authorities was the audacity and the planning of the coordinated attacks. The reality of the situation was that of the fifteen men killed, allegedly, fewer than half were Secret Service men.[1] The remainder were, according to British statements, a mixture of regular officers, courts-martial officers and civilians. Only a section of British Intelligence in Ireland had been attacked that day—the most effective part of it, the men from Military Intelligence. In the days that followed, Collins was well aware that the intelligence services, especially those of the military, still posed a serious threat. A number of their most dangerous agents, including Hardy and King, who worked hand in hand with the Auxiliaries, had survived.

Hardy, King and Igoe: the combined names sounded like an old-fashioned firm of lawyers—or perhaps undertakers might be more appropriate. Hardy and King were known; Igoe was yet to come. All three acquired a terrible reputation for brutality and murder. Not getting Hardy was a great regret for the men of The Squad. Joe Dolan summed Hardy up succinctly, "He had an artificial leg and was very vicious." An attempt had been made earlier. A source within Dublin Castle Collins learnt that Hardy was going to England on leave. A small team was assembled to assassinate him. Included in the team was Joseph Dolan of Irish Intelligence. He revealed:

> I located Hardy on the mail boat [from Kingstown]. I was better dressed than he was and I was traveling first class. I tracked Hardy all the way to London, but when we arrived there he disappeared in a taxi. I did not know what date Hardy would be returning to Ireland, but I was to watch for him at Euston Station and wire to Vaughan's Hotel in Dublin as soon as I found out the date of his return. I was to put on the wire, "Josephine traveling."
>
> Eventually when Hardy did travel I sent a wire to Vaughan's Hotel. They got the wire all right and sent out a party next morning to deal with him. Through some hitch, I think the car broke down, the party did not reach their destination and Hardy got away. He was never got.[2]

Another disappointment was the failure to assassinate Sergeant Major Hepworth. He was Hardy's NCO and had a similar reputation for brutality at Hardy's behest. Patrick Caldwell of Irish Intelligence was given the task of tracking him down. Caldwell was introduced by Tom Cullen to a Sergeant Harte of the Dublin Fusiliers. He was working for Irish Intelligence. Harte gave Caldwell a description of the target, but what was really required was a photograph. In the end, frustratingly, Hepworth was transferred away from Dublin.

Captain William Lorraine "Tiny" King was born in London in 1884, the son of a coachman. He joined the Middlesex Royal Engineers and served in South Africa during the Boer War. At the conclusion of the conflict, he joined the South African police as a first-class detective head constable. During World War I, King served with the South African Overseas Expeditionary Force, first in the Middle East and then on the western front. He fought at the Battle of Delville Wood. King was awarded the Military Cross and the Distinguished Conduct Medal, ending the war as a captain. He returned to the South African police force, but in October 1920, he joined the Auxiliary Cadets in Ireland. A tall, well-built man with an air of command, King was commander of F Company, based in Dublin Castle, from October 26, 1920, to February 12, 1921. In Dublin he met Hardy, of Military Intelligence, and together they formed an interrogation duo at the Castle's Intelligence Office.

King apparently led the raid on 36, Gloucester Street in Dublin in the early hours of Sunday morning, an assault which led to the capture of McKee and Clancy. He was involved in the interrogation that followed. Sometime between then and the next day, Monday the 22nd, following the shootings in Dublin, McKee, Clancy, and the young man, Conor Clune, who had no part in the war, were shot in the passageway leading off from the company guardroom in Dublin Castle. According to the bulletin issued, they were shot "while attempting to escape." Later, an official statement issued by the Castle, following a brief enquiry, indicated that they "attempted to grab rifles and hurl unfused grenades and were killed in action."[3] Major Reynolds, the Auxiliary officer working for Irish Intelligence, passed on the true details of the killing and the men involved.

Ernie O'Malley gave an indication of the treatment probably meted out to the three men. Under the alias of Bernard Stewart, O'Malley had been caught with a gun and notebook full of compromising material. After brief questioning, he was sent to Dublin Castle for more intensive questioning. His interrogators were Hardy and King, as previously related. In his autobiography, *On Another Man's Wounds*, O'Malley pens six pages regarding his brutal treatment. This was carried out in a room known, with a degree of black humor by The Squad, as the "Knocking Shop." After some brief questioning, to which O'Malley failed to reply to their satisfaction, King punched him in the stomach. Then:

> He struck me in the face with the full weight of his body. I fell to my knees. "Get up. Who gave you the gun?" No reply. "Are you going to answer?" "No." He struck me again in the face and blood began to flow into my mouth and to drop on to the floor.[4]

Hardy then took over attempting to gain the information, but without result. King replaced him with brutality:

"Will you answer me ?" said King. "Where do you live?" I did not answer and he hit me again and knocked me against the wall. When I stood up again he said, "Will you fight me?"

"No."

"Afraid?" sneeringly. I knew that he could knock me out in ten minutes, if not in one, but I did not want to let him have the satisfaction of thinking he had fought clean and beaten me in fair fight. If he wanted to abuse his manhood, he could do so, but he would have no excuse for it.

Hardy once more questioned him, but again getting no response, King began beating him. More questions from Hardy; then his mood changed. Hardy walked over to the stove, thrust a poker into the burning coals, then held it up to O'Malley's face:

He swung it horizontally until it was on a level with my eyes. My eyebrows were singed; the heat made my eyes burn.... My eyelashes curled up; the lids smarted. I tried to keep my eyes open. They were hurting me.... "Will you answer?" I shook my head. He raised the poker as if he was going to hit me. He put it back between the bars of the stove. "Do you think you are going to beat us?" said King. "You're going to answer questions, do you hear?" he shouted. "Where do you live" He hit me hard in a passion, smash after smash.

And so the beatings and threats continued. Then it was over.

"Wipe your face," said King. I used my hands and coat but the blood still came. "I'll see you again, Stewart, remember."

That was not to happen, though. On February 21, 1921, O'Malley with two other prisoners, Frank Teeling and Simon Donnelly, made a daring escape from Kilmainham Prison. Recently released from Kilmainham Prison himself, Volunteer Herbert Conroy went to see Oscar Traynor, newly appointed brigadier of the Dublin Brigade. He put forward a plan for the rescue of Frank Teeling, who was awaiting execution for his involvement in the Bloody Sunday killings of British Intelligence officers. In 1921, Kilmainham was a virtual fortress, with high walls and watch towers manned by British soldiers armed with machine guns. The main entrance was strongly guarded, and three massive iron gates had to be negotiated before one could even gain access to the entrance hall of the prison. The British believed that escape was impossible, and therein lay its weakness, a laxity due to the overconfidence among its staff. Conroy had noticed a degree of carelessness amongst its guards perhaps not observed by their officers. As a result of the knowledge he had gained, Conroy put forward his plan.

Each morning a group of six prisoner, guarded by a squad of soldiers, was marched from the detention section of the prison through the wings of the prison to the front hall. Their job was to collect and bring back to the prisoners' quarters the rations for the day. In order to do this, they had to be taken to the outermost door of the prison, which was naturally securely locked. The keys of this door were kept in the guardroom. This strong door and a large gate gave admission to the street by way of a small side yard.

Conroy had struck up a friendship with two British soldiers among the prison guards who were Irish. He put it to Traynor that if they were approached in the right way, they would be prepared to cooperate when they were on night duty in the guardroom. A meeting was arranged, and the two Irish guards agreed to help. With some degree of modification, the plan was prepared for a jailbreak. The idea was that the guards would get some of the prisoners into the little yard, while others outside would throw a rope ladder over the wall, using a light cord with a weight attached. The prisoners would then pull on the string to pull the rope ladder over the wall and thus escape. Twice it was tried, but the string snagged each time, and the attempt had to be abandoned. Traynor rearranged a meeting with the guards, and a new plan was formulated. What the guards had failed to mention was that within the yard there was a small gate. But the lock held a crossbolt in the locked position and the guards did not have access to the padlock key; hence, the former plan of scaling the wall.

The bolt could be cut from the inside, if only a bolt cutter could be smuggled into the prison. One of the guards agreed to smuggle it in. Bolt cutters, by their very nature, have long handles to exert pressure and thus would be noticed when brought into the prison. Michael Smyth, a 2nd Battalion Volunteer, came up with the solution. He cut the long handles in half and provided two pieces of tubular steel to fit over the remaining portions of the handles. In this way the cutter was reduced from four feet to two. Instructions were given to the guard in the correct way the tubular handles should be fitted. A wrong fitting would not provide the necessary leverage. On the night of the intended escape, the tubular handles were fitted on at the wrong angle and failed to cut the bolt. Reporting back to Smyth, the IRA men reinstructed the guard, and the following night, the guard tried again and was successful. The bolt was cut. He tried the gate, and it opened. Then he returned to the cells and led three of the prisoners—Teeling, Simon Donnelly and Ernie O'Malley, alias "Bernard Stewart"—out through the prison to the gate and freedom. Paddy Moran, who was to have been the fourth man in the escape party, refused to escape. He had been arrested in the wake of Bloody Sunday and charged with murder. However, he was not involved and had witnesses who were prepared to swear that he had been at Mass with them at the time. Moran trusted to British justice that he would be freed on the evidence. The British needed to punish someone. Moran was found guilty and hanged.

Following the ambush at Kilmichael and the deaths of eighteen Auxiliaries so soon after Bloody Sunday, the British Cabinet in London met on December 1, 1920. The ministers decided that because of "the recent outrage near Cork, which partook of a more definitely military character than its predecessors," martial law should be proclaimed in Ireland in the counties of Cork, Kerry, Limerick, and Tipperary. Major General Sir Hugh Jeudwine expressed his disappointment that Dublin had not been included. The advantages he outlined would have been:

1. Unity of command (control of police reprisals, etc.).
2. Promptitude in action and administration.
3. Heavy sentences for carrying or being in possession of arms.
4. Heavy sentences for harboring known rebels.
5. Restriction of movement.
6. Identification of individuals.
7. Control of the press.
8. Internment of suspects at discretion of the military governor.
9. Moral effect.[5]

Of all these, Jeudwine considered that unity of command to be the most important—cutting out the police, with their incompetence and indiscipline. If such procedures as indicated above had taken place in the city, then Irish Intelligence, The Squad and the ASUs would have been isolated from the people: they would fear British repercussions if discovered to be assisting the IRA. General Macready did his best to get martial law declared in Dublin, but on January 28, 1921, he was informed that the Chief Secretary was "not convinced of its necessity at present." The reason for not including Dublin would appear to be Britain's reluctance to admit that they were not in control of even the city. One thing that was conceded, following Tudor's visit to GHQ on December 11th, was that the police be placed under the orders of military governors in martial law areas. Concessions towards greater control in Dublin came into being after January 26th, when "loitering on the streets" was made an offense under ROIR. Within two months, loitering had almost been eliminated, thus reducing the ASU's chance of launching prepared ambushes on military vehicles.

About the same time that martial law was introduced in the rest of Ireland, Irish Intelligence became involved in a proposal put forward by Cathal Brugha to kidnap senior members of the British government. The notion was mooted in response to the Auxiliaries' forcing Irish M.P.s (or T.D.s) to ride in troop-carrying Lancia cars. This was to prevent Volunteers from throwing hand grenades at the vehicles. To rub salt into the wound, the vehicles carried the sign "Now bomb us." Senior Intelligence Officer Frank Thornton was dispatched to London with Sean Flood and George Fitzgerald. Their mission was to contact the Irish Intelligence section there and obtain more men to carry out their orders—the kidnapping of twelve members of the British government, Cabinet ministers, if possible. They began by following likely targets, studying their movements and their regular patterns of behavior. Thornton relates:

> After a month's check-up, during which some very interesting side-lights were disclosed on the private lives of members of the British government, we arrived at the stage where we had a definite list of twenty-five members of Parliament who did a regular thing on the same night every week.[6]

In the course of tailing likely kidnapping victims, Thornton relates:

> One day when Sean Flood and I were going out to Acton on a routine check-up on the Underground Metropolitan Railway, we ran into Westminster Station to find the lift gate just closing. Sean Flood turned round to me and said, "I'll race you to the bottom down the runway." It was a long winding passage with about three bends on it. Sean raced off in front and disappeared around the second last bend about a few feet in front of me. I heard a terrific crash and on coming around the corner I fell over two men on the ground, one of whom was Flood. We picked ourselves up and both assisted in helping to his feet the man whom Sean Flood had knocked down. To our amazement two other men who were with him ordered us to put our hands up. We more or less ignored them and started to brush down the man and apologize to him when to our amazement we discovered that the man we had knocked down was Lloyd George, the Prime Minister of England. The first act of Lloyd George was to tell his two guards to put their guns away, which they were very reluctant to do, pointing out that from our speech we were evidently Irishmen. Lloyd George's answer to this was, "Well Irishmen or no Irishmen, if they were out to shoot me I was shot long ago." ...after a few muttered apologies on our part we went on our way towards the Station, but I can tell you that we did not go to Acton. We got a train in the opposite direction and got out at the next station and made sure that we weren't being followed.
>
> In the end there were no kidnappings. The revulsion in the British press over the Auxiliaries using hostages, saw the system being quickly abandoned.

In the period between early autumn and the events of Bloody Sunday, a most audacious assassination plot was planned—the killing of Major General Henry Hugh Tudor, the man who had overseen the recruiting of 500 ex-officers to the Auxiliary Cadets. It began as an intelligence inquiry. A civilian car had been seen on a regular basis outside Kingsbridge station (now Heuston Station). Intelligence Officer Patrick Caldwell was sent to investigate. The car bore the letters XA as part of its registration. Caldwell came upon such a car bearing the same registration letters, but it had a different number. The car regularly left British military offices in St. John's Road; its passengers were obviously plainclothes policemen. Caldwell reported back to Liam Tobin, but because the numbers were not those given, Tobin appeared to lose interest. Then, a few days later, Tobin called Caldwell back to his office. "That car number you gave me now transpires to be Tudor's car and I want you to get all the information you can about its movements." Unfortunately, Caldwell was lifted when staking out Captain Hardy. Nothing concrete could be proved against him, and following a short imprisonment, Caldwell was released at Christmastime 1920. He was put back on the case. While he had been in prison, other Irish Intelligence officers had closely observed the car's movements. The route taken by General Tudor when traveling from St. John's Road to the Castle never deviated. Caldwell continued the account:

> It took me a considerable time to mark out this route as I had to take up [possible ambush] positions at various street corners along the entire route in order to make sure that I would have him routed correctly. As a result plans were made to eliminate Tudor. The attack did not come off as for some reason or other he began to change his route and took a different one each day and his visits to the Castle became irregular.[7]

Delay had resulted in a lost opportunity. Nevertheless, the plan continued. New efforts were made to ascertain Tudor's movements. An Irishman serving in the British Army, Gunner Doyle, now prompted by Irish Intelligence, made the acquaintance of Tudor's driver. Following some daily banter Doyle would enquire what the driver was up to that day, endeavoring to ascertain Tudor's movements. British security had obviously taken a hand in safeguarding Tudor, in changing his route and in other matters. The driver revealed to Doyle that he had no idea: Tudor only told him at the last possible moment.

A new plan was necessary. About the end of April 1921, Patrick Kennedy of Irish Intelligence was directed by Collins's deputy, Liam Tobin, to submit a report on the possibility of carrying out an ambush between Kingstown (Dunlaoghaire) and the city. Also, he was directed to watch and time movements of the cars carrying senior British officers from the mail boat to their barracks. Kennedy was given a list of number plates of the cars in question and selected a small team to work with. From agents inside Dublin Castle, Collins was supplied with dates and times of movements of these officers which were passed on to Kennedy.

With the truce, all plans for senior assassinations were put on hold so as not to jeopardize negotiations.

Meanwhile, the shooting of British security men and touts continued. With almost callous indifference, Paddy Daly of The Squad dictated in his Witness Statement:

> The following spies were accounted for; Pike was shot outside Fagan's public-house in Drumcondra; Brady was shot in Clontarf; two British Military Intelligence Officers were shot in the Mayfair Hotel in Baggot Street; an ex-British Army man was shot in Gloucester Street on a report from Intelligence; a Tan was shot in Domore Avenue and a Tan named Halpin, an Irishman, was shot on the canal banks at Inchicore.[8]

Squad member Joseph Byrne was involved in the killings:

> I remember an evening in December 1920, when I was instructed, with others, to proceed to Henry Street to assist in the shooting of D.I. O'Sullivan. About four of us comprised the party. A couple of us were detailed not to take part in the actual shooting but to cover off the men who were to do the job. I saw the D.I. being shot by a member of the Squad and when the shooting was over we returned to Morelands.[9]

British Intelligence was also active. On Sunday, December 12, 1920, John Joseph Hickey was shot and died two days later. At about 8:00 p.m., by now quite dark, Hickey and a friend were walking home to Kingstown (Dun Laoghaire). As they approached St. John's Home of Rest, Elm Park, two men behind them called out, "Come here!" The two men stopped and turned around. One of the two men facing them, in an English accent, ordered them, "Take your hands out of your pockets!" They immediately responded. The Englishman who had spoken took a revolver out of his pocket and pointed it at Hickey as he approached nearer. Then the gun went off, evidently unintentionally, for the gunman said that he was sorry. The gunman and his companion then moved off in the direction of Dublin. Hickey's unnamed companion described the gunmen:

> The murderer was dressed in a fawn coat and a soft peaked cap. His height was about 5ft. 9in. or 5ft 10in. He was a medium built man. He was clean shaven. The other man was 6ft. high, heavily built, wearing a fawn trench coat and similar cap to the man who fired. There was only one shot fired.[10]

Hickey, a 25-year-old bachelor, was a draper's assistant with no obvious connections to the IRA. It would seem that he was in the wrong place at the wrong time, walking along with his hands in his pockets.

The Security men were now everywhere on the streets of Dublin. Like The Squad, they acted in teams. Dan Breen experienced their threatening presence, with murder on their minds:

10. Hardy, King and Igoe

> I recognized two of the Gang on the tramcar.... I realized my predicament. I was in a tight corner. To attempt a retreat from the car would be a plain invitation to them to open fire. I sat down on the three-seater bench at the rear of the car, just at the top of the steps. Then I pulled out a packet of cigarettes and lit one. Immediately two of the Gang sat down on the same bench, one on each side of me. A third remained standing right opposite me, gripping the railings. The other two went along the centre passage to the front of the car. In all my I never felt less comfortable than at that moment. I realized my danger but saw no way out of it. Neither they nor I made any move. The car started on its journey, crowded with passengers who little realized the real-life drama that was being enacted.... All of a sudden both the man on my right and the man on my left made a simultaneous move. Their right hands went to their hip pockets. They were about to draw their revolvers. I beat them to the draw. In an instant my three would-be assassins were rushing headlong downstairs. I was at their heels with my revolver leveled. They sprang from the car on to the street...[11]

On Christmas Eve 1920, Michael Collins and senior members of Irish Intelligence went to the Gresham Hotel for dinner. Collins worked on the basis that if he did not act like a man on the run, then he would not be perceived as such by the security services. He was bold and outgoing, cycling along the streets of Dublin every day on his Raleigh bicycle, the very epitome of a young man doing his best to get ahead. Collins had a charmed life. At the time of his visit to the Gresham, he was unknown to the hotel's manager, James Doyle. It was only later, when he saw Collins at the time of the Truce, that the incident at Christmas came to mind. Doyle related the Christmas story:

> I saw him coming into the hotel on Christmas Eve 1920 with three or four others who came in for a meal. While he was here the place was raided by the military. I saw military officers approach Collins and I heard him being asked questions in the front hall. His comrades at this time were in the dining room.[12]

Collins adopted a friendly tone with his inquisitor. He gave his surname as Grace and produced papers to prove who he said he was. All the time he engaged in friendly banter. The officer questioning him had a photograph of him from an earlier period. He compared the likeness with Collins, going so far as to brush his hair to one side. With the other guests in the dining room having been briefly interviewed, the officer questioning Collins bid him a good night. The military left without arresting anyone. Collins and his party departed soon after, without partaking of the meal which they had ordered. The raid might just have been accidental, but Doyle was of the opinion that someone had identified Collins as he entered the Gresham. He was of the opinion that it was an Acting

Detective of the RIC. During the Truce, when negotiations were under way, Doyle became aware who Mr. Grace really was.

Meanwhile, the Secret Service men and the Auxiliaries continued their raids—sometimes in hope but occasionally following leads. On the night of New Year's Eve 1920, Military Intelligence showed that it was far from finished. There was a raid on the flat of one of Collins's secretaries, Miss Eileen McGrane at 21, Dawson Street in Dublin. Apparently, a Unionist sympathizer saw Assistant Director of Irish Intelligence Tom Cullen enter the house and reported it to the authorities. Cullen was not there when the raid took place, but all his papers were. The flat in Dawson Street was his temporary office. Miss McGrane, who was there, was arrested, and all the papers in her apartment were taken up. When examined, some of the papers were carbon copies of secret reports from the political section of the Detective Division.

The following day, Collins conferred with Ned Broy, from whom many of the papers had originated. Collins warned him that he should prepare a story to cover himself. The portion of papers relating to the police were handed over for investigation to the Chief Commissioner of the DMP Colonel Edgeworth-Johnstone. He set up a small investigative team. By January 21st, the Detective Sergeant in charge of the investigation was able to pin down Broy as having typed two of the reports. He interviewed Broy and showed him the evidence. Then luck, incredible luck, seemed to prove the accused policeman's innocence as he himself revealed:

> ...the copies found of these two reports had been typed by a machine which typed twelve letters to the inch instead of the usual ten, and all machines in the Detective offices at Great Brunswick Street and Dublin Castle were of the normal ten to the inch variety.[13]

Broy was not slow to point out the difference. What had happened was that Broy had typed out the report, handing over the carbon copy to Irish Intelligence. For whatever reason Collins had got Miss Moran, one of his confidential secretaries, to copy these carbon sheets on a portable typewriter with twelve characters to the inch and then had destroyed the original carbon sheets. Broy was safe for the moment. After a few days, Broy was summoned late one evening in January to the commissioner's office. This time it was a full investigation. Present were Edgeworth-Johnstone, Assistant Commissioner Barret, Mr. Magill, Secretary to the Dublin Metropolitan Police, and Superintendent Purcell. Broy continues:

> The Commissioner handed me the sheaf of captured D.M.P. reports, which numbered about one hundred, and asked me for my comments. I stated that

all closely resembled the Detective office stationery and might have been typed in the Detective office in Great Brunswick Street, except in the two cases where copies had been typed by a machine of a model that did not exist in any of the police offices, and could not, therefore, have been made in any police office. I again admitted that I had remembered typing reports which appeared to be, word for word, similar to the copies found.

Everyone appeared to agree with the logic, and Broy was allowed to go. Things dragged on until the third week in February 1921, when he was summoned once again to attend the Commissioner's office.

Here he was arrested "for giving out the documents to the Sinn Feiners." He was searched and his official pistol was taken from him. In a van, accompanied by eight guards and an inspector, Broy was taken to Arbour Hill Military Prison.

Collins was always loyal to his people, though sometimes he did not show it. With Broy's arrest, Collins was fearful that he would suffer the same fate as McKee and Clancy. Word was sent in to DMP Headquarters that there would be repercussions if he were tortured or killed. Broy was safe, though. He was in military hands, well away from Hardy and King. Coming up to his court-martial, evidence was "mislaid," and witnesses were sent away. Though much was suspected, nothing could be proved. Nonetheless, Broy was detained on suspicion and held at Arbour Hill until the Truce. Then, Collins spoke to Lloyd George's man, Andy Cope, and Broy was released. So, too, was Eileen McGrane, as part of the Truce agreement.

There was unfinished business from Bloody Sunday. Major Carew, who had been the officer commanding when Sean Treacy was shot dead outside the Republican Outfitters in Talbot Street, had escaped. On the day of the mass shootings, Dublin District "Special List" Intelligence Officer Major Frank Carew was living at 38, Upper, across the road from the targeted 28, Upper Mount Street. He had moved there without notifying the Castle. His change of address had saved his life. His new address was not on the list supplied by Lily Mernin. Carew, born in 1866, had served with distinction in the newly formed Tank Corps during World War I. He was awarded the Military Cross for bravery. Carew was serving in Ireland in April 1920, in command of the tanks, in the Dublin district. In June of that year, he was seconded to Military Intelligence and sent to London for training. His first known operation was on October 14th, a raid in which Sean Treacy was killed. On Bloody Sunday, following the shooting of Ames and Bennett, Carew and his batman fired at the retreating assassins emerging from his former lodgings. On February 2, 1921, Irish Intelligence tracked him down. He was sitting in plain clothes with a friend in the Dublin Bread Company tea shop at 33, Dame Street. A team from The Squad was sent to eliminate him. At 4:15 p.m., as he ordered tea, he was approached by a man who opened fire with an automatic. Carew was shot in the arm and passed out. The gunman did not get the chance to finish him off with a bullet to the head, as Carew's friend grabbed him. After a brief tussle, the gunman broke free and escaped. Carew was taken back to Dublin Castle, then transferred to the George V Hospital under guard. He recovered from his wound and was sent back to England to convalesce. On the evening of the shooting, Under Secretary Mark Sturgis, then in Dublin Castle, wrote in his diary:

> Wednesday 2nd February: Major Carew, a witness in tomorrow's case [the Easter Sunday shootings] was shot at tea time and wounded in the arm in a DBC tea shop. Seems a pity he was out and about but I suppose he was doing his work and its difficult to say that the moment a man becomes a witness he must be taken off his job if its an outside one and kept in cotton wool.
>
> Later, on January 5, 1922, Carew's former superior, General Boyd, included Carew in a list of seven former Secret Service men he took to Major General Sir Wyndham Childs at Scotland Yard, asking if Childs could find them jobs in England. Boyd added, "They are all good men with plenty of courage, and were the pioneers of the Secret Intelligence in Dublin, which certainly was the means of obtaining an enormous amount of valuable information for the Government."
>
> Childs did what he could and found work for Carew and the other Secret Service men in the intelligence section of the Palestine Police. Carew served in Palestine from 1922 to 1926. He returned to England where he died in January, 1943.

Carew and the other intelligence agents in Dublin greatly relied upon touts to pass on information as to the whereabouts of wanted IRA men. Collins received word from hotel worker Paddy O'Shea that a colleague, Willie Doran, the night porter at the Wicklow Hotel, was passing on information to the British. As Collins, Tobin and Cullen used the hotel from time to time to meet IRA men up from the country, Doran was an obvious threat. A message was sent to Doran, warning him of the consequences of passing information to the British. For a time, he acquiesced, but pressure from his British masters returned him to the treacherous business. Collins gave the order for his execution. Liam Tobin, Deputy Director of Intelligence, summoned Joseph Dolan and asked him to carry out the execution. Dolan chose Dan McDonnell to accompany him. McDonnell knew Doran by sight, and with a small back-up team, the two men planned the tout's execution. On the night of January 29th, the two walked into the Wicklow Hotel. As they did so, Doran came out of the dining room. Rather clinically Dolan reported:

I produced my revolver and shot him through the head and the heart, and McDonnell shot him through the stomach. We had a covering party and we had no difficulty in getting away.[14]

Whatever Doran had been telling his wife, she was under the impression that he had been working for Collins. She was convinced that he had been shot by Crown forces. Now on her own, and having to support three children, she appealed to Collins for help. Collins sent money to her with the strict instructions that she should not be told of what had really happened. The man who ordered the deaths of so many had a soft spot for the weak and vulnerable.

On January 14, 1921, William McGrath, K.C. was murdered in his home. The killing had all the hallmarks of the murder of Thomas McCurtain, Lord Mayor of Cork, and the later murders of George Clancy, mayor of Limerick, and Michael O'Callaghan, his predecessor. McGrath, his wife and children, all Roman Catholics, lived at Altona Terrace, North Circular Road in Dublin. The murder happened at about 1:30 a.m. during the curfew. There was a violent knocking at the front door before it was burst open. The noise woke the family. Despite a protest from his wife not to do so, McGrath proceeded downstairs to investigate. He called out, "Who is there?" At the first flight of the stairs, five shots rang out, and McGrath was mortally wounded but not quite dead. He had been shot in the heart, chest, stomach and legs. A local doctor and a priest were summoned, and McGrath was taken away to a private hospital nearby where he later died. Police sent to investigate found four empty cartridge cases in the hall. The stair rail was splintered, and there were bullet holes in the ceiling. In the front garden, they found a crowbar, evidently used to break into the house. A member of the family commented in a press interview that "it was neither a raid nor a robbery. They came to kill him and they did so." McGrath had no obvious Sinn Fein connections. Apart from being a lawyer (a King's Council), he also did some work for the Ministry of Labor in labor disputes. The court found that McGrath had been murdered "by a person or persons unknown." There is a possibility that his death was linked to that of John Lynch, a Sinn Fein Loan organizer.

Hardy and King continued in their raids and brutal interrogations with impunity. As head of F Company of the ADRICS based in Dublin Castle, King believed himself to be untouchable. On February 9, 1921, King and two associates, Temporary Cadets Herbert Hinchcliffe and F.J. Welsh, murdered 27-year-old James Murphy and 18-year-old Patrick Kennedy. Neither men were in the IRA but had been picked up on the street as possible suspects. They were taken to Dublin Castle for interrogation. A police witness later claimed that he had seen both prisoners being beaten, then put aboard a Ford car that drove off. Captain King, wearing plain clothes, was in the driver's seat. Just before eleven o'clock that night, a policeman out at Drumcondra heard gunshots and shortly after a Ford car drove by, heading towards the city. Kennedy and Murphy were found inside the wall of Clonturk Park. Kennedy was dead; Murphy was alive but gravely wounded. He was taken off to hospital where he died. Before he did so, he made a statement of what had happened. The two men, lined up against the wall, side by side, had buckets placed over their heads before they were shot. On the strength of Murphy's testimony, the three Auxiliaries were arrested and taken before a court-martial. Witnesses perjured themselves and claimed that the three policemen had been out on a raid with them on Leeson Street and Talbot Street. Previously it was claimed the two prisoners who had been questioned were released quite unharmed. The DMP policeman who had witnessed the beatings was discredited. It was claimed that he had been drunk at the time. Murphy's deathbed statement was declared inadmissible. The three Auxiliaries were acquitted on February 16th. Brigadier General Crozier, commander of the Auxiliaries—who was anxious to curb such undisciplined behavior and have the men punished—was overruled by his superior, General Tudor. It was said at the time that the authorities surrendered to threats from the accused men: that if they were dismissed, they would reveal the black deeds of the police in Ireland. Crozier, the only man who came out of the affair with any honor, resigned in disgust. He later stated that he had resigned "because the combat was being carried out on foul lines, by selected and foul men, for a grossly foul purpose, based on the most satanic of all rules that 'the end justifies the means.'"[15]

Released, King was transferred away from Dublin and appointed commander of D Company of the Auxiliaries, based in Galway. In November 1921, King returned to the Army. At the outbreak of World War II, he served in Nigeria in a clerical role and later as a military policeman in Egypt, where he died in 1942.

One man in particular who deserved no sympathy, in Republican eyes, was Major General Percival. He was in charge of British forces in West Cork and had a reputation for torturing and shootings. Irish Intelligence chief Frank Thornton said of him:

> ...in one particular case he tortured Tom Hales so severely that at one stage it was feared that he was going to lose his reason. In this particular case he drove splintered matches up underneath the nails but he failed to get any information from Tom.[16]

Word came into Irish Intelligence in Dublin, in March 1921, that Percival was on holiday in England. He was staying at Dovercourt on the

10. Hardy, King and Igoe

southeast coast. Collins summoned an evening meeting in Kirwin's public house in Parnell Street. Amongst those present were representatives of the West Cork flying squads. Evidence was presented for the shooting of Percival. The outcome was that on the following morning, a small team was dispatched to London to assassinate him. In London, they contacted an English-based IRA cell, and plans were put into operation. Unfortunately for them, Percival was staying in the Military Barracks at Dovercourt. There was no way they could get to him. From a friendly source within the barracks, they discovered that he would be returning to Ireland on the March 16th and would arrive at Liverpool Station in London at about three o'clock in the afternoon. Thornton made his plans, and with men augmented from the London Brigade of the IRA, he placed men in and around the railway station. At a quarter to three they saw Sam Maguire, principal intelligence officer of the London Brigade. He surreptitiously beckoned some of the assassination party to him and informed them that he had just received a tip off from a contact in Scotland Yard that a CID man had spotted some of the party, and preparations had been made to surround the station. Thornton got his men out of there as soon as possible. He remarked in his Witness Statement:

> We learned afterwards that at about five minutes to three a cordon of military and police was thrown round the station and every passenger had to pass through this cordon, some of them being held there for hours, but the birds had flown. The unfortunate part about it was that Percival was able to get back to Cork safely.[17]

British Intelligence in Ireland was not a united entity. There were two major branches of intelligence, military and police, each jealously jockeying for position. Undoubtedly, the more professional was Military Intelligence. It was certainly more successful than its police counterpart. Its officers were better organized and were trained to deal systematically with a large volume of low-grade information. They were the greater danger to the IRA, and it was Military Intelligence who lost men on Bloody Sunday. Despite the appointment of the experienced soldier, Colonel Ormonde Winter, as head of the police's Dublin District Special Branch, coordination between Military Intelligence and Special D. Branch remained poor.

Ormonde Winter had the support of the Dublin-based Black and Tans as foot soldiers, as well as. F Company of the Auxiliaries in Dublin. They, the Auxiliaries, had their own undercover men, later to be known as the Cairo Gang.

In addition to these two intelligence groups, there were also undercover men, emanating from MI5. They were answerable to Basil

Thomson in London—and to him alone. Their activities are largely unknown. Even Christopher Andrew, in his authorized history of MI5, suggests, "There was no clearly defined role for MI5."[18] It may, of course, be that Andrew was not made aware of what was available. MI5 has always been very circumspect about its dealings in Ireland. Much documentary evidence remains closed.

On December 27, 1920, British Army Intelligence suffered a setback, as far as they were concerned, when they were brought under the control of the police. This was at a time when Army Intelligence was very active, particularly in its sweeps of the city. Some 500 prisoners were in their holding cells. The transfer to police custody led to delays in communications and the authorization of actions, which led to frustration and greatly hamper the army's activities. These results led to the dispersal of Military Intelligence personnel and complications that issued from that, including the inability to identify and process prisoners quickly, which, in turn, led to congestion in the city's prisons and holding cages.

Before this takeover and following the shootings of November 21, Military Intelligence attempted to regroup, as Secret Service man Captain Jeune related:

> ...[A]bout the New Year 1921 ... the IRA were driven into the south west corner of Ireland and would have been quickly finished. But certain influences were to save them, as I learned later in London from a friend of mine, Jeffries, who had been in our show in Dublin. When this broke up he, with a staff officer, Cameron, were instructed to set up from London a proper secret service in Ireland, which was successfully accomplished.[19]

One of the new agents sent over to Dublin was Captain Cecil Lees, a former Staff Captain in France.[20] With him he brought a brutality that could match anything that King and Hardy could offer. Irish Intelligence officer Daniel McDonnell was to say:

> We did a number of trailing and following-up jobs on various people and also did other work some which failed and some that did not fail. One particular individual I was after was a Captain Cecil B. Leedes [sic]. Before he came to Dublin he was apparently a Chinese Labour Corps Commander, and he was taken over here for the one purpose of inflicting his methods of getting information on our people, which were primarily diabolical. I don't know exactly what they were, but I believe they were pretty terrible, i.e. the removal of finger nails, etc.[21]

Irish Intelligence were already onto him. They had intercepted a letter sent by him to the War Office in London. Charlie Dalton, also of Irish Intelligence, wrote:

Captain Lees had not been in Dublin very long when he wrote the letter to a friend of his in the War Office, indicating that he had been in touch with Major S.S. Hill Dillon, District G.S.O., Intelligence Branch, Dublin District, Royal Barracks. From the nature of the text it was clear that Captain Lees was a British Secret Service Agent engaged in the preliminary surveying of prospects for the murder of Irish leaders. This communication was sent to the Director of Intelligence [Michael Collins] for his instructions and was returned with the comment, "Oggs him."[22]

But they did not know where he was living. McDonnell, through his contacts in Dublin's service industries, went on to supply that information:

> I discovered him and where he lived through a contact of ours, as we had a lot of contacts with hotel waiters, boots, etc. [He was living] in a Temperance hotel, St. Andrews Hotel, Exchequer Street, Dublin. I soon learned that his general habit of going out was between 9 and 9.30 every morning. I also learned from our own Headquarters that his methods were getting cruder, and cruder, wherein they would have to be stopped.

Lees had developed a fearsome reputation as an inquisitor. As a trained agent he had been taught how to take precautions to protect himself from assassination. Founding Squad member Bernard C. Byrne revealed this in his Witness Statement and recorded the action taken by The Squad:

> Several times they thought they had him, but in fact, they had lost him completely for a period of about a fortnight prior to his actual execution.... On the Sunday night before he was shot, Tom Keogh and I were in the dress circle of the Scala picture-house, and just prior to the commencement of the programme a lady and gentleman proceeding to their seats were caught in the beam of the projector. Keogh nudged me and said, "I think that is Lees." ... After the show was over we followed him and found that he was staying in St. Andrew's Temperance Hotel in Wicklow Street. Without discussing the matter with intelligence or with any other members of our Squad, we decided that we would take up our positions on the following morning at about half-past nine, because we were aware that that was the usual time for Lees to report to the Castle. Keogh succeeded in rounding up [Ned] Bolster and Mick O'Reilly, and the four of us met at the appointed time. Bolster and myself were detailed to do the actual shooting. Lees appeared without any undue delay, and, as he was already known to me, there was no need for any further identification. He was accompanied by a lady, but we had no interest in her. We opened fire on Lees immediately, and he fell mortally wounded.[23]

Almost as a post-script, Byrne added:

> Lees was unfortunate, because roughly about three weeks before his actual execution our Intelligence people had given him up as lost as far as they were concerned. They firmly believed that lie [that] he had left the country, and were it not for our visit to the Scala picture-house he would have escaped.

In Dublin Castle, Under-Secretary Mark Sturgis noted in his diary for March 29, "One of 'O's [Ormonde Winter] people, a Captain Lease, was murdered this morning in Wicklow Street. It seems too ghastly to be even thinking of peace making with this sort of thing going on." This is what, in fact, was going on. Lloyd George's appointee Andy Cope had established contacts with Sinn Fein in a bid to end the war. Elsewhere, with no knowledge of what was going on at senior level, the intelligence war continued.

Following the arrest and murder of McKee and Clancy, the man who had tailed them, John "Shankers" Ryan, went to ground. Feeling confident that he was safe, he reemerged in Dublin, in January 1921. Having trailed the two senior IRA men to Sean Fitzpatrick's house at 36, Gloucester Street, Ryan marked the doorpost with a chalk mark, then telephoned the Castle. It would appear that one of Collins's confidants within the Castle identified Ryan from the telephone call and passed on his details to Irish Intelligence. The murder of the two men affected Collins personally, and the order went out to "Oggs" the tout. Bill Stapleton of The Squad details what happened. He begins with a description of who Ryan was:

> John Ryan was a British military policeman and was a brother of Mrs Becky Cooper of Corporation Street who ran a shebeen [and a brothel], which was a favourite haunt of many of the British Tans, Auxiliary and Army.

Stapleton continues:

> The Squad were told to have this man executed and as usual an Intelligence Officer was appointed to identify him. In this case it was Paddy Kennedy. Before the two men were detailed to carry out the execution, I asked to be allowed to take part in it as I felt very keenly about the murder of Dick McKee who was a great friend of mine with whom I fought in 1916 and served subsequently with him in the 2nd Battalion. My request was granted and the second man instructed to accompany me was Eddie Byrne. [Accompanying them as a covering party were Paddy Kennedy, Jimmy Conroy and others] About 10.30 o'clock on the morning of the 5th February 1921, our Intelligence Officer located Ryan in Hynes public house at the corner of Old Gloucester Place and Corporation St. We entered the public house with the Intelligence Officer and I saw Ryan standing facing the counter reading a newspaper and he was identified by the I.O. Before doing the job we held him up and searched him but he had no guns or papers on him. I think we said, You are Ryan, and I think he rejoined, Yes, and what about it, or words to that effect. With that we shot him. I have an idea that the chap behind the counter was one of our I.O.'s ... he made himself very scarce when we entered.[24]

James Slattery's version of the execution gives a little more detail:

10. Hardy, King and Igoe

Tom Keogh and Bernard Byrne entered the public-house by a door on the right hand side, called for two drinks, surveyed the customers. They narrowed their choice of target down to one man who was sitting on their immediate right deeply immersed in a study of the Early Bird, a racing paper. They were unable to see his features, but believed from his general build that he was the man in whom we were interested. Keogh nudged Byrne to make a move, and Byrne approached the man and asked him what they were tipping for some particular race. The man had to lower the paper. Immediately he did so they knew it was Ryan. Without any delay Keogh fired on him, with Bernard Byrne doing likewise. Ryan was dead immediately.[25]

Three of The Squad had opened fire on him. He was shot through the body, with a *coup de grace* to the head. The Auxiliaries were soon on the scene, and three possible suspects were brought before Ryan's brother-in-law, who was present at the shooting. He was unable, or perhaps unwilling, to identify them as the assailants. Further details came to light on Ryan in the newspaper reports of his death. In the *Irish Times*, he was referred to as a plainclothes corporal in the military foot police and was based in Dublin Castle. He had served in the 8th Hussars during World War I.

Alongside Jeune's new Secret Service men, a new police intelligence unit was up and running by January 1921. It was known as the Identification Branch of the Combined Intelligence Service but was known more popularly in the intelligence community as "Z" Company. Out in the countryside, large-scale military sweeps and searches had sent a lot of IRA men on the run. Being brought together, they were formed into flying columns, with devastating results at times. Other men on the run gravitated towards Dublin, where they were integrated into the various brigades. The personnel of the newly formed "Z" Company were RIC officers drawn from the various counties throughout Ireland. Their mission was to identify and track down IRA men from their own counties who were now roaming the capital.

Based in Dublin Castle, "Z" Company, upon its establishments, put in a request to the Home Office, the authority to which they nominally answered, for a supply of 100 automatic pistols and 38 revolvers. Clearly, they were not going to be a desk-bound organization. "Z" Company operated out on the streets, in plain clothes, with as many as twenty men on each surveillance, split up into smaller groups on each patrol. This secret intelligence unit was run by Colonel Ormond Winter and commanded on the streets by Head Constable Eugene Igoe, assisted by Sergeant Patrick Killeen. They became known to the Republicans as the Igoe Gang. Igoe, a tall, imposing figure of an Irishman, was from a farming family in Mayo. He had made his name as a detective in Galway before being posted to Dublin to head up the new unit. Igoe and his armed policemen soon proved quite effective. They came to be justifiably feared by the IRA. They operated in the same way as The Squad—search, find, kill.

The Igoe Gang announced their presence towards the end of 1920. Charles Dalton of Irish Intelligence briefly recounts what happened:

> A young Irish Volunteer officer by the name of Howlett, who had arrived at Broadstone railway station from the west, was waylaid and shot dead by men dressed in civilian clothes. It was inferred by the Castle authorities that this shooting was done by Sinn Fein elements.[26]

This was typical of British black propaganda, blaming the IRA for murders. It was designed to divide the community and alienate the IRA. Out in the countryside the Auxiliaries had taken to pinning notices, on the bodies of Republicans that they had killed, bearing the inscription "Spies and informers beware!" and signed "IRA."

Senior IRA Intelligence Officer Frank Thornton refers to the arrival of this new assassination gang in his Witness Statement, when he wrote, "…a new menace appeared on the scene. These were gangs of RIC drawn from different parts of the country under the leadership of Chief Constable Igoe. They wore civilan clothes, were heavily armed and moved along the footpaths on both sides of the road looking out for either city men whom they might know or Volunteers up from the country." Rumors started coming in that several county RIC members were now living at the Depot in Phoenix Park. The breakthrough in identifying who these men were came about when Maire Gleeson, the proprietress of the West End Café, Parkgate Street, opposite the entrance to Phoenix Park, got in touch with Charlie Dalton. She told him that amongst her new patrons were several plainclothes RIC men who dropped in shortly before curfew for a light supper. The men informed her that they were based in the Depot. Over the next few days, Miss Gleeson discovered that their team was headed up by Head Constable Igoe, a Mayo man. Dalton relates:

> I duly reported the facts and the Director Of Intelligence [Michael Collins] had active inquiries made through Brigade Intelligence Officers throughout the country as to the absence from their home stations of the constabulary who were engaged on political work.

News started coming in that confirmed their worst nightmares. The gang were killing not only Volunteers but also civilians. Previously at Newry, on July 6th, Igoe had personally shot four Sinn Fein sympathizers. Now he was in Dublin.

The Igoe Gang proved very effective at identifying and shooting

10. Hardy, King and Igoe

men on the run, often in broad daylight. "Shot while trying to escape" was the official verdict for such killings. Collins issued the order to track them down and finish them off—before they finished off The Squad. James Stapleton of The Squad described how the Igoe Gang operated:

> Very briefly the modus operandi of the Igoe Murder Gang was to stroll along the streets, drop into shops, pubs and restaurants, attend on the fringes of football matches etc. always on the lookout for country members of the Volunteers and on one being recognized the well-dressed members of the murder of the Murder Gang would quietly move around the individual, or individuals, and smilingly chat and talking quietly force him into a secluded spot and there, while still chatting and smiling, would interrogate him. Rarely, if ever, did they produce guns. Somwhere within 100 yards or so of the Igoe Gang there was invariably an Army Motor van and when the Gang decided to arrest an individual a whistle was blown, or a signal given, and the waiting van would arrive and take away the prisoner.[27]

This is what happened to Tod Andrews, a soldier in the Dublin ASU. When not on duty, he affected the style of a student, as he himself recalled:

> In the manner of the students of the time, many of whom cultivated a positive dandyism, I was most respectably dresses. That is to say, I wore a collar and tie and well-creased trousers.... I wore kid gloves and carried a cane. I walked down Summerhill intending to cut across Gardiner Street (now Parnell Street). I passed two tall men of whom I took no particular notice, but when I passed two more and then another pair I began to feel uneasy. My uneasiness was justified when I passed still another pair and recognized among them an RIC man from Rathfarnham named Killeen. The fourth pair of the group halted, produced revolvers and told me not to attempt to run. They asked me my name and address.[Andrews gave a false name and address, but Killeen was on to him]. They told me they were taking me to Dublin Castle. The whole squad turned in their tracks and marched me right across the city, through O'Connell Street, College Green, Dame Street into the Lower Castle yard. I realized I had fallen into the hands of the Igo[e] gang and waited for the beating and torture to begin.[28]

This did not happen though. After a few days imprisonment, he was taken into a room in the State Apartments where he was questioned by "three well-dressed civilians and one man in the uniform of an Auxiliary." Of the situation Andrews remarked:

> [T]he scene might well have been an interview board for a post in the public service. Only the civilian in the centre seat at the desk spoke. He had a marked upper-class English accent. He was quite polite in his interrogation.

In questioning, Andrews admitted that he had given a false name, as he had been arrested before and did not want any further trouble. He admitted that he was a member of Sinn Fein but not that he was not in the IRA. In the end, they seemed to accept his story. Though not imprisoned, Andrews was interned. As to why he was not brutalized, Andrews reasoned:

> I came to the conclusion that all four men in the room were Englishmen. They had, thanks to their own propaganda, formed in their minds an archetype of the IRA man wearing leggings and trench coat and cap with neither collar nor tie who was also, by definition, illiterate. I did not conform to that image. I was respectably dressed, spoke coherently and grammatically.... The fact that I was a university student added to their conception of respectability.

This is probably why Collins and the Irish Intelligence team fared so well. They simply did not look like terrorists to British eyes.

Soon Squad members came into contact with the Igoe Gang out on the street. Individual members, unrecognized by these country policemen, were pushed to one side as the gang proceeded along the street. Others were stopped and questioned but giving credible replies were allowed to continue on their way. It was only a matter of time before the gang struck lucky. Newly established, the problem that beset Collins and Irish Intelligence was that they lacked details of the Igoe Gang. Who were they? What did they look like? Some progress was made following a countrywide investigation, and the leader, Eugene Igoe, was identified. As he had served in Galway and knew Igoe personally, though not in a friendly way, a local county Volunteer Thomas "Sweeney" Newell was sent for. He was teamed up with Charlie Dalton of Irish Intelligence to seek out and locate the Igoe Gang in Dublin. Each day the two men, plus occasionally men from The Squad, patrolled the city in frustration. Then they struck lucky as Charlie Dalton recalls:

> On a weekday in January [1921] Newell rushed in to our office in Crow Street at about eleven o'clock in the morning and stated that he had seen Igoe and his party proceeding up Grafton Street in the direction of St. Stephen's Green.[29]

That morning, while Newell was making his way to rendezvous with his minder, he had seen Igoe and his gang:

> When near McBirney's I saw Igoe with about sixteen or eighteen others, in two's and three's, coming along the South Quays towards McBirney's. I stepped into McBirney's door so as to let them pass. Before reaching McBirney's they turned into one of the side streets.... I followed them up the side street into Dame Street. They crossed Dame Street into Trinity Street and into Wicklow Street.[30]

Off he went to Crow Street to report to Charlie Dalton. Dalton sent instructions to The Squad—who were standing by in the headquarters in

10. Hardy, King and Igoe

Upper Abbey Street—to rendezvous with him. Then Dalton and Newell set off in pursuit of their quarry. The Squad, fully armed, moved briskly off in twos to rendezvous with Dalton. Bill Stapleton went off with Vinnie Byrne up Anglesea Street and into Dame Street in a bid to reach the top of Grafton Street and meet the oncoming gang. Stapleton spied Dalton and Newell standing, smoking, against the wall of an insurance building, chatting to a couple of men. He and Byrne assumed that they were cautiously following the gang up Grafton Street, but this was not the case. Dalton continues:

> Newell and I proceeded to Grafton St. by the shortest route, and when we had almost reached Weir's jewellery stores in Grafton Street, I noticed that we had been passed by some men, who I instantly recognized as Igoe's party, altho' Newell had not time to confirm this. When they passed us out, they wheeled on us, and at close range said: "Don't move," which we did not, as we were unarmed. This manoeuvre took place with pedestrians passing by, unaware of anything unusual taking place.
>
> Without much delay, we were told to keep walking, and a surrounding formation of Igoe's squad kept pace with us as well as accompanying us. We walked, as directed, up Suffolk St. and down Trinity St. until we came to a building in Dame St. (No.38) which was an insurance office, where we were directed to stand against the wall. Newell was kept several paces away from me, and we were surrounded by a bodyguard on either side.
>
> Igoe, whom I had identified from his description, first questioned Newell and later questioned me, but neither of us could hear the other's answers.

While Dalton was being questioned, he saw Vincent Byrne and other members of The Squad cutting across Dame Street and going through Hely's Arch, on their way to Stephen's Green to the rendezvous. Stapleton saw Dalton and Sewell:

> On looking to the left we saw Charlie Dalton and Sweeney Newell standing, smoking, against the wall of an Insurance building and chatting to one or two others. We assumed that he was about to move towards Grafton St., behind Igoe's men. We continued across the road and up Trinity St., and eventually reached Stephen's Green.

Byrne and his group made no effort to approach them, believing them to be in conversation with some friends. Newell later recorded his version of the confrontation with Igoe in his Witness Statement. He and Dalton had

> ... proceeded into Wicklow Street and were turning into Grafton Street when I almost collided with Igoe, who was returning from Grafton Street into Wicklow Street. I had gone only a few yards when I felt a hand gripping the collar of my coat. I turned round to see who was holding me. It was Igoe. "Come on, Newell," he said, "I want you."

"My name is not Newell," I replied.

"I know you anyhow," said Igoe. Turning to one of his companions and pointing to Dalton, he said, "arrest that man." We were then turned into Wicklow Street and continued along until we were opposite the Wicklow Hotel where we halted for a few minutes. I saw several members of the Active Service Unit including Tom Ennis, Frank Bolster, Joe Dolan, Tom Keogh and --- Flood, pass along on the opposite side and turn into Grafton street.

We were again marched off into Dame Street where we were halted again. Igoe then questioned me as to who Dalton was. I said I did not know him and that he was not with me. Dalton was also being questioned. I did not hear the questions that were being put to him as we were too far apart. Igoe continue to question me. I realized the game was up and I said, "I know you, Igoe, and you know me."

Dalton meanwhile was also being interrogated a short way off:

> In reply to the questions put to me, I gave my correct name and address. I stated that I was a believer in Home Rule and that my father was a J.P. and did not agree with the Sinn Fein policy.
>
> Newell endeavored to bluff also, and we were asked how we came to know one another. I stated that he was a stranger I had met on the street who had got into conversation with me and that I was directing him somewhere or other.

When Newell lost his temper and told Igoe he knew who he was, all interest in Dalton was lost. He was told to clear off. As Dalton walked away, he was very fearful that he would be shot "while trying to escape." But the shot did not come. Dalton continued on through Trinity Street, Suffolk Street and turned into Wicklow Street. Just around the corner, he made a dash into a building and safety. He waited for five minutes, then set off back to St. Stephen's Green where he located The Squad.

Meanwhile, Newell had been marched off, two of Igoe's gang in front, one on either side of him and two behind, until they arrived at the street junction with Greek Street. Igoe questioned him once more

> ...as to how I came to be in Dublin, what was I doing there, where was Baby Duggan and many other similar questions, all of which I refused to answer. Four of Igoe's gang were beside me and two on the opposite corner. Igoe said, "run into the street," pointing to Greek Street.
>
> I said, "If you want to shoot me, shoot me where I am standing." Then he gave me a hell of a punch which sent me several yards into the street, and immediately opening fire on me. I fell and I was not able to get up as I had received four bullet wounds, one in the calf of the right leg, two in the right hip and one flesh wound in the stomach.
>
> I then saw Igoe blow a whistle. Within minutes a police van arrived. I was thrown roughly into it, and taken to the Bridewell. I was questioned as

to where I lived in Dublin. I refused to tell them. I was beaten on the head with butt ends of revolvers, four of my teeth being knocked out and three or four others broken. I was left lying on the floor for some hours and was then taken in an ambulance to King George V Hospital. I was detained in King George V Hospital until December 1921.

By the time Dalton regrouped The Squad, there was no sign of Igoe and his men. The Igoe Gang had unwittingly outsmarted The Squad. It had now become a game of cat and mouse—but who was the cat, and who was the mouse? The Squad was intelligence-led. Their targets were established, the route taken by the victim surveyed, and after having killed the man The Squad disappeared. The Igoe Gang wandered the streets in numbers in the hope of identifying a victim. Once their manner of operating was discovered, it was not difficult to pick them out—twenty well-dressed, well-built RIC men in plain clothes. They weren't fools, though. They never followed a predictable route in their meanderings; they doubled back on their random route. They constantly surveyed the faces of the people along the street. They sometimes got lucky and captured or killed the unwary IRA man up from the country.

An all-out effort was now made, using The Squad, all Active Service Units, and men from the Dublin Brigade to track down and kill Igoe and his men. The Active Service Unit was formed on January 1, 1921. Some 100 men, according to Paddy Daly of the Squad, were picked from the Dublin Brigade by its O.C. Oscar Traynor. In command of these men was Captain Paddy Flanagan. The primary function of the ASU was to carry out ambushes on military and Black and Tan lorries in Dublin. Though independent of Irish Intelligence and The Squad, the ASU sometimes acted in conjunction with The Squad, and vice-versa. Tracking the Igoe Gang was one of those combined operations. Irish Intelligence imbedded in the Castle never succeeded in identifying the individuals in the gang. What was discovered was that they were all Irishmen who had long service records in the RIC. There was one Scotsman, as Charles Dalton relates in his narrative, known as "Jock." He was, it was believed, a former member of the Black and Tans with a bad reputation for violence.

The Squad's next attempt to get the Igoe Gang occurred a few days later. Information was received that Igoe and his men were at the Depot in Phoenix Park and would be leaving there about ten o'clock that morning. The Squad and an Active Service Unit were quickly assembled and given orders to ambush the party. They were all heavily armed. Vinnie Byrnes described the armaments he and colleagues Tom Keogh and Jim Slattery used:

I collected the guns—Jimmy's long webley, Tom's Peter and short Webley, and my own Peter. Tom Keogh always carried a Webley, in case his Peter would jam. I buckled on my belt beneath my light dust coat, and slung the guns, which were all in holsters.[31]

It was believed that the Igoe Gang would walk down the north quays on their way to Dublin Castle. Charlie Byrne was the Intelligence Officer in charge. The IRA men were divided up into teams. One party was ordered to go into the licensed premises on the left-hand corner of Queen Street. Another party was sent across the road and just around the corner to wait. The remainder of the men took up positions in each doorway and shop entrance right down the quay to Arran Street West. Charlie Byrne stood near the cinema as lookout to indicate the approach of the gang. But, the gang, as unpredictable as ever, took a different route. They proceeded up Steeven's Lane. The IRA men quickly moved off to intercept them. They dashed across the quay and up Bridgefoot Street, following a similar line of ambush along Thomas Street up as far as the *Lord Edward* public house. There they waited, but there was no sign of Igoe and his men. Then they noticed in the distance a military foot patrol coming towards them. They disengaged and moved off, looking for another route that Igoe might take. The IRA men regrouped along Victoria Quay, also known as Guinness's Jetty.

Then along came a tender of Auxiliaries. The rapid movement of the vehicle mitigated against withdrawing, so the IRA units made ready to receive them. Then suddenly the tender slowed down. The Auxies must have seen them but decided against engaging so many of the enemy. They drove off rapidly. Realizing that British reinforcements would now be sent for, Charlie Byrne called off the mission and dispersed the men.

Some few days later another opportunity arose to have another go at the RIC gang. A report came in that Igoe and his men had taken to having lunch at the Ormond Hotel between 12:30 and 1:30 p.m. They broke up into smaller groups as they made their way to the hotel. This was the opportunity that The Squad was looking for. Seemingly off duty, the gang members, it was hoped, would drop their guard. Squad positions were taken up at the corner of Parliament Street and Essex Street. At about 1:00 p.m. three of Igoe's men (as they were believed to be) came rambling down the street, well–dressed, upright, and in plain clothes. As they came to the corner where The Squad men were waiting, the IRA men opened fire. Two of the three were shot dead. The third man was wounded but was able to run across Essex Street with three Squad men in hot pursuit. One of the three was Bernard Byrne, who recorded that the policeman

...had got to the opposite pavement, outside Honan's window, obviously intending to take shelter inside the shop, when the three of us fired at him. Some one of us grazed his spine with a bullet, with the result that he catapulted himself clean through the shop window, but was dead when he landed there.[32]

Three down—seventeen to go, it seemed, but the dead men were not part of the Igoe Gang. A week or so later, Irish Intelligence was informed that Igoe and his men would be traveling from Dublin Castle to an old men's home in Kilmainham, by way of Thomas Street and James's Street. An ambush site was selected, with members of The Squad taking up positions in James Street and with a further half a dozen seeking cover in the public house that was directly opposite James Street church. Two or three Squad men acted as lookouts. Outside Dublin Castle, a member of Irish Intelligence with a runner in attendance waited to let the ambushers know when Igoe departed. Time passed, and The Squad waited. Then suddenly, Vinnie Byrne dashed into the public house where one of the teams waited. Bernard Byrnes narrates the story:

"Hurry Lads and get away. We've been had." It transpired that roughly a half company of British soldiers were moving along in our direction having taken possession of every civilian whom they met in their approach, searched them, and in most cases brought them along with them for further examination. Our Intelligence Officer who should have been in front of this group was unfortunately behind them and, of course was unable to make any further progress. It appears that by some means or other, Igoe had learned that an ambush was being prepared for him and had taken steps accordingly.

We dashed out of the public house, and with about twenty yards to spare from the leading member of the British patrol succeeded in making our way down Steevens Lane. We headed for the city along the South Quays, which were practically deserted at that time except for Guinness workers at the jetty. The main body of our party crossed to the jetty side of the quay. Vinnie Byrnes and I continued along by Guinness's wall, and we were approximately half-way between the two bridges when we saw three tender-loads of Auxiliaries coming along at a very fast rate. As soon as we saw them coming Vinny and I decided that we were in a very bad position in the event of any action taking place, as our men would be firing on us as well as the Auxiliaries. We proceeded to cross the road to the jetty side to join our party, and were approximately halfway across the road when the leading tender, which was almost abreast of us, slowed down.... The tender practically stopped and we were expecting the usual "Halt, hands up," cry, when, for some reason best known to themselves, they set off in top gear and completely ignored us.

Twice now the Auxiliaries had failed to engage the IRA. One possible reason was that they feared to engage with what they perceived to be a numerically superior opposing force. The ruthless killing of seventeen Auxiliaries in two military vehicles at Kilmichael in West Cork on November 28, 1920, must have been playing on their minds. The ambush shattered the myth that the Auxiliaries were invincible supermen and raised the morale of the entire Volunteer Movement. As for the Igoe Gang, there never was a showdown. Soon after, the RIC men were brought into the Castle and thereafter only operated at night, usually partaking in large raiding parties.

Collins was anxious to engage the Auxiliaries in Dublin, as Tom Barry had been in Cork. They had had their own way for far too long, with their raids and terrorizing. Now it was time to terrorize them. An ambush was planned using The Squad, the combined four sections of the ASU, and all available men from the 2nd Battalion. Some fifty to sixty men were assembled and briefed as to the mission. The plan was to lure a large party of Auxiliaries into a killing zone at Seville Place, near the bridge over the road at Amiens Street Railway Station. Tom Cullen of Irish Intelligence let a tout know that there was to be an important meeting of the senior men of the IRB at 100, Seville Place. The tout was told that the meeting would be between 5:00 and 6:30 p.m. on the evening of February 7, 1921. The ASU took the lead in placing the ambush party. No. 100, Seville Place was taken over, the house was barricaded, and all windows manned. A large number of the men were placed on the railway bridge that crossed the street, giving them an elevated, commanding position. Across the road at the entrance to Seville Place, men took over Gilbey's Wine Merchants on the corner of Amiens Street and Portland Row. The men here were equipped with Lee Enfield rifles. Orders were given that no one was to open fire until the enemy dismounted from the cars and were in the act of raiding the house. As the enemy advanced up the steps to the hall door, the men in the house were to open fire, as were the men on the bridge and at Gilbeys wines store. A special hand grenade was prepared made from a piece of rainwater pipe, some six inches long. Vincent Byrne from The Squad, who was there, almost certainly from a nervous, but also perhaps a jocular perspective, remarked:

> To me, it was a very deadly-looking weapon and, to be truthful, I got as far away as I could from it. You can picture for yourself when you hear that the man who made it also made a shield for his face out of some sort of sheet metal, with two holes cut in it for his eyes and one for his nose. He would put you in mind of the Kelly Gang.[33]

So, there they waited with their large experimental hand grenade. After half an hour, they noticed from the railway bridge an armored car passing the top of Seville Place. Next came three or four military lorries, then a further three or four military tenders and a second armored car. They all sped by. It was thought that perhaps they might not have known where to go, but it was hoped that they would return. But they didn't. Instead, they drove further down the railway line to Clontarf Bridge. Here they climbed up to the line and set up searchlights to play along the line but came no closer. The fight that was to be a real decider was abandoned. The IRA men withdrew.

About this time, a number of Volunteers, tried by military courts, were awaiting execution. While there was little hope of rescuing them, a plan was devised to halt the executions by halting the executioners. Not considered to be soldiers, the prisoners were to be hanged. The British hangman, John Ellis, and his assistant William Willis had been summoned to Dublin to do the job.[34] Information was leaked from the Castle that Ellis would not arrive in Dublin until the day before the execution of Bernard Ryan, Frank Flood, Thomas Whelan, Patrick Moran, Thomas Bryan and Patrick Doyle. Ellis and Willis would be staying at the Gresham Hotel under an alias. From there they were to be collected, about an hour prior to the time fixed for the executions. Tom Cullen and Liam Tobin organized a watch to be kept on the hotel, noting the number of guards assigned to the hangmen. Also noted were to be what rooms, and on what floor, the two men were staying. The full Squad assembled at Oriel House early on the morning of the hangings. The British, however, had fooled Irish Intelligence. They realized that somewhere within the British administration in Dublin Castle there were spies who would pick up on the gossip and pass it on. Ellis and Willis did not stay at the hotel but were accommodated at Mountjoy Prison. They had arrived three days before the execution, the time being needed to examine the prisoners' heights and weights to ensure that their deaths would be instantaneous. The prisoners were hanged in batches of twos.

The British raids against arms dumps and individuals continued. On the night of Saturday, January 15th, in what was named "Operation Optimist," over 600 troops sealed off an area of the city between North King Street and the river Liffey. The bold venture was an attempt to capture Michael Collins. Barbed wire was used to seal off the cordon. Sandbagged machine gun posts were established along the river. Over the next two days the area was searched block by block. *Freeman's Journal* greeted the raid with some amazement or perhaps amusement. On January 17th, when the disappointed troops withdrew, its banner headline was "Dublin Siege Raised." No arrests were made. Dublin District attempted to put a positive spin on the situation, indicating that the raid had been "of great military value, and of deterrent importance in so far as the hostile population is concerned."

The next month, in February 1921, some members of The Squad were followed after an assassination. Somewhere in a laneway off North Great Charles Street, the tout following lost his quarry. He reported back to Military Headquarters. Army Intelligence were confident that there was some sort of IRA base or dump somewhere around there. A large force, complete with tanks, armored cars and hundreds of soldiers, surrounded the area from Parnell Street in the north to Summerhill in the south. The search area was increased to the North Circular Road on the east to Hill Street and Temple Street on the west. It was a poor area of the city. Most of the houses were multi-occupied tenement houses. The British systematically raided from house to house, room by room, placing guards on all the houses until the searching and interrogation had been completed. To enable them to conduct the searching thoroughly, all the occupants—male, female and children—were brought down and assembled in Mountjoy Square. While the houses were searched, other parties raided stables, sheds, and workshops at the rear of the houses, but to no purpose. The Squad dump, a headquarters dump and the 2nd Battalion dump, all within the area, remained undiscovered. As with the raid of January, the area was much too large and the cordon leaked.

The Dublin District Intelligence confirmed in its reports for the first three months of 1921 that raids were depressingly unproductive. It had become a cat-and-mouse game, with the IRA just one step ahead—one step ahead, because Dublin was their city. Further raids on bicycle shops, many reputedly also acting as munitions factories according to British Intelligence, also proved unsuccessful. Some sixty-nine shops were raided in two days. Only one proved successful—one Mills bomb and two bullets were found. While the authorities exhorted troops on raids to be more thorough, the response was that the troops were overwhelmed by the sheer number of searches:

> ...if you order a list [of raids] as long as your arm to be carried out by say next morning, Units must have several raids allotted to them to exhaust the list, and get through them as best they can.

There was a growing sense of futility amongst the British soldiers taking part. They were tired, and they simply did not want to be there.

11

IRA Active Service Units

In the west of Ireland, the men who were to become the heroes of the War of Independence were leading their flying columns against the army and the paramilitaries. As the war moved into 1921 the columns grew from 30- to 45-man units into small armies of 100 to 150-plus men. In Dublin, such large-scale operations were not possible. With thousands of British soldiers and police based in the capital, such a confrontation would inevitably have led to the utter destruction of the IRA within the city. Such a lack of response has led some revisionist historians to allege that the British had complete control of Dublin and that the IRA were afraid to confront them. This was not so, but merely a partial and incomplete interpretation of facts. Following discussions between Cathal Brugha, Minister for Defence, Chief of Staff Richard Mulcahy and Brigadier Dick McKee, Dublin's seeming inertia was dispelled by the formation of teams of Active Service Units—small three- or four-man teams of hit-and-run squads. By their actions, they created tension, apprehension, and fear amongst the Crown forces. Perhaps more importantly, as Mulcahy felt, these constant attacks were reported in the foreign press. Mulcahy, for one, and de Valera were firmly of the view that Dublin was by far the most important military area in Ireland. IRA resistance in Dublin was, from a propaganda point of view, far more important than even the outstanding achievements of the Volunteers in the southwest. If Dublin was lost, all other victories counted for nothing. The world had to see that the British forces in Dublin were in no way in control of the city. The ASUs were established to prove that. From January 1921, they attacked on an almost daily basis all over the city.

The Dublin Brigade, from which the ASUs were drawn, consisted of about 13,500 Volunteers, but they had no more than 1,000 under arms at any one time. The Brigade structure within greater Dublin comprised six battalion areas to cover the city and its suburbs:

> 1st Battalion: North of the Liffey and west of O'Connell Street.
> 2nd Battalion: North of the Liffey and east of O'Connell Street.
> 3rd Battalion: South of the Liffey.
> 4th Battalion: Southern townships beyond the city center.
> 5th Battalion: Engineers—services available to other battalions.
> 6th Battalion: Southeast County Dublin area, including Dun Laoghaire.

Each of these battalions, excluding the Engineers, was made up of six companies. From these companies were drawn the Active Service Units, dividing up into four sections: two operating north of the Liffey and two, south. They never numbered more than fifty men in total but were occasionally supplemented by dependable men drawn from their own battalions. Being full-time soldiers, those selected to serve in the ASUs were paid a salary commensurate with their former civilian pay. The ASUs were established in the autumn of 1920. Suitable candidates were selected from the battalions and invited in for an interview. George Nolan of A Company, 4th Battalion, was one:

> Some time near Christmas 1920 my Company Commander sent for me and told me that an Active Service Unit was being formed in Dublin and that it would be a full time job, adding that he had sent forward a recommendation that I would be a suitable man for it. On St Stephen's day 1920, I was instructed to report to the O/C., Dublin Brigade, at St. Laurence O'Toole Hall, North Strand. On arriving there I found about fifty men present. Oscar Traynor addressed us, stating that we had been selected to form an Active Service Unit to operate against the Crown Forces in the streets of Dublin and that our duties would be full time which would mean that we were to leave our places of employment and so make ourselves available for Volunteer work at all times. Continuing, he said that if any of us felt that we were not fit for the work we could stand down and that it would not effect us in any way. He then introduced us to our O/C., Paddy Flanagan. Following that meeting we met in the same place on at least two occasions and we were then organized into four sections. I was allocated to No. 4 Section and my Sect. Commdr. was Michael Sweeney.[1]

George White of C Company, 3rd Battalion, was instructed to attend a meeting at Oriel Hall that same day, December 26th. Again, Brigade O/C. Oscar Traynor addressed the men. He told them:

> That it would be a full time job and that we would be paid a salary of £4. 10. 0. weekly. He said that the object of the ASU was to combat the Auxiliaries and that we would commence operations immediately, and we were to work in conjunction with H.Q. Squad. Captain Paddy Flanagan was appointed O/C. Frank Flood was 1st Lieutenant, the I.O. was William Doyle, the M.O. was Paddy Flanagan.... The members of the ASU were drawn from the four battalions; it was organized into four sections numbered one to four to

correspond to the battalions with a section commander in charge of each section. Each section operated in its own battalion area.²

Sections 1 and 2 operated on the north side under Frank Flood; Nos. 3 and 4, on the south side under Paddy Flanagan. Flanagan's headquarters were at 17, Eustace Street, Flanagan's office. His section also met in Temple Bar in Fleet Street and at the shop of Jimmy Brown at 17, Great Strand. Brown was also a member of the ASU. Sections 1 and 2 met in a cul-de-sac off South Anne Street in the flat of Tom McGrath, likewise a member of the ASU. Section 4 under Michael Sweeney had several meeting places, including Mount Argus Brickworks, Keogh's of Dolphin's Barn, which also acted as their arms dump, and in Kevin Street, Dublin.

    Christopher Fitzsimons, newly appointed to Section 2, recorded his involvement in his first daylight ambush. The unit lacked any real experience, and because of that, the attack was only partially successful. It was

> an attack on a military lorry at Bachelors Walk on the 12th January 1921. Preparations were made beforehand for this attack as it was well known that it was customary for a British lorry to travel down the Quays towards Collins Barracks [then known as the Royal Barracks] from the city each morning.
>
> On the morning in question Nos. 1 and 2 Sections took up positions extending from Carson's Lane in Bachelors' Walk to Liffey Street. I was standing at the edge of the sidewalk outside Wren's furniture shop, halfway between Liffey Street and Carson's Lane, and was armed with two grenades. It was not long there when Johnnie Dunne, who was stationed at Carson's Lane, fired a grenade at a lorry of British troops which had come abreast of his position from O'Connell Street. The lorry having passed his position, came towards me. I stepped on to the roadway and fired my two grenades at it coming towards me. I withdrew immediately through Wren's auction rooms, making my escape through the Lotts. At Liffey Street Nos. 1 and 2 Sections were bunched together on both sides of the road, hoping the lorry would wheel into Liffey Street. It kept on straight, however, down the Quays for Collins' Barracks. Fire was not opened on it from Liffey Street as our men were positioned too far away from it.³

Other members of the same ASU escaped through Scannell's auction rooms while an auction with a largely female attendance was taking place. The Auxiliaries, now recovered, regrouped and returned fire. A bullet smashed through the window of Scannell's, causing screams and hysteria. Other bullets entered the interior of Walsh and Sons cabinet makers and O'Brien's public house. Surprisingly, no civilians were injured. The following day at about 4:30 p.m., along the quays at the junction of Aston Quay and Westmorland Street, two people were killed by British forces. A checkpoint had been established there to examine motor permits. Naturally, following the attack of the previous day, the soldiers were extremely nervous. Having confiscated a motorcycle and side car, a soldier dropped a rifle, which discharged accidentally. His comrades, in panic, thought that they were under attack and opened fire indiscriminately. Martha Nowlan, the 22-year-old head bookkeeper at Mitchell's Restaurant in Grafton Street, and James Brennan of Mary Street, Dublin, were killed. Seven other people, five men and two women, suffered gunshot wounds.

Volunteer George Nolan's unit carried out an attack about the same time in January 1921:

> This was an attack on an Auxiliary RIC motor car which traveled from Dublin Castle to Beggars Bush Barracks. We received instructions to attack this car on a certain morning. Three of us took up positions at Holles Street corner behind a post office letterbox and four more took up a position in the vicinity of Messers. Gough's sales yard. One of our men, better known as "Onion Quinn," was detailed to watch out for the car and signal to us when it was approaching our positions. We were about half an hour in position when Quinn walked straight across the road and took out his handkerchief which he waved to us. This was the prearranged signal. Almost immediately the private motor car came abreast of my position. We immediately opened fire with the revolvers and two hand grenades. I cannot say if we caused any casualties although it was rumored later that we did, but we didn't wait to see. I did see however, when the car had passed through our fire it zigzagged in the direction of Gough's sale yard where it was again attacked by the remainder of the section.... All of us got safely away and were none the worse of our first adventure.[4]

James Carrigan of C Company, 1st Battalion ASU was involved in perhaps the most audacious of attacks, the ambush of General Hugh Tudor, newly appointed chief of police. From his account, the action would appear to have been ordered by Michael Collins through Irish Intelligence:

> One of my first engagements with the Active Service Unit was an attack on the car of General Tudor at Charlemont Street Bridge, early in January 1921. Frank Flood knew beforehand that the car was expected at Charelmont Bridge at a certain time in or around 10 a.m. Four of us took up positions at McQuillan's public house at the junction of the canal and Charlemont Street. Frank Flood was on Charlemont Bridge opposite me. Christy Fitzsimons was in a shop on the corner of Charlemont Mall, and [John] Sliney was positioned near a GHQ Intelligence Officer that accompanied us on the crown of the bridge. After about 10 minutes delay I heard a shot fired at a touring car by the late Frank Flood. The car headed towards me, turning towards the canal and I opened fire on it. Simultaneously the other two men opened fire on it. The driver swung his car left and right away from me, upsetting a milk

van. I fired again into the car and kept on firing as I followed it. I cannot say who was in the car. I saw two passengers in the back; one was a tall gentleman and the other a tall lady. Neither can I say if we caused any casualties.[5]

Things did not always go according to plan, even with experienced ASUs. James Cahill and his 2nd Battalion unit, divided up into three teams, lay in wait to attack two lorries, only to discover there were now four. Plans had to be changed quickly. Cahill decided to leave the first two lorries to two of his team, Flood and Fitzsimons. Volunteer Dunne was to take the third vehicle and Cahill, the fourth:

> Concentrating all my attention on the last lorry I observed the alert faces of the soldiers, the muzzles of their rifles menacing the people, the fingers hooked around the triggers, and then the extending eyes of the soldiers as Flood's and Fitzsimon's grenades burst over the first two lorries. Then for me came the anti-climax, for just as I swung back my hand to throw my grenade, a van slid to a halt not more than two feet in front of me. Quickly moving round to the back of the van I found the lorry was far beyond my range and was proceeding at full speed into O'Connell Street.[6]

Then there were disasters. Frank Flood, now with some experience under his belt, was given command of an ASU. He was instructed to ambush a motorized convoy of Auxiliaries at Binns Bridge on the Drumcondra Road. As they approached the ambush position, a vehicle came along the road carrying a party of Auxiliaries. Without instruction, two of his men opened fire. The lorry drove away at speed, but at Drumcondra Bridge, it halted, and the Auxiliaries dismounted and launched a counterattack. Volunteer Michael Magee was shot dead. Flood, Paddy Doyle, Thomas Bryan and Bernard Ryan were taken prisoner after running out of ammunition. Along with two other prisoners, Thomas Whelan and Patrick Moran, the captured men were hanged at Mountjoy Prison on March 14, 1921. That night, in response to the executions, an IRA Company set forth to confront members of the British forces on the streets. Frustrated by not finding a British patrol, the Company instead attacked the DMP station in what is now Pearse Street. Alerted by the gunfire and an explosion, two Auxiliary lorries and an armored car raced to the scene. A fire fight ensued. By its end, at about three o'clock in the morning, three Volunteers had been killed and two captured. Two Auxiliaries were also killed and three wounded. Of the two dead Auxiliaries, one was a Dubliner, James O'Farrell, late of the Royal Dublin Fusiliers and latterly of the Tank Corps. Two civilians were also killed in the crossfire, Thomas Asquith and David Kelly. A 70-year-old woman, Mary Morgan, was shot in the hip.

Just as the British had prepared plans when attacked, so, too, did the ASUs while on an operation. In particular they were told to avoid prolonged action. Prolonged action was anything over three minutes. What might have tested friendships was the ASU order that one patrol was forbidden to go to the assistance of other patrols—this to avoid big formations.[7] Large groups of men standing around risked the danger of attracting attention to themselves. The British were aware that such groups could well be potential ambushers of vehicle patrols. Accordingly, orders were issued to foot patrols in January 1921 that all loiterers became liable to be searched (by proclamation). In addition, as a countermeasure, "spasmodic blocks in the main thoroughfares were established by troops or Auxiliaries, with a view to finding arms on the people." The flaw in this proposal, as the writer of the *Dublin District Historical Record* wrote, was that this "achieved little, as the arms were always handed to the women, who were immune from us"—that is, could not be searched by the soldiers.[8] The answer to this was to employ women searchers, drawn from the Women's Section of the Metropolitan Police Force in London. This did not happen until much later, though.

Nighttime attacks upon the Crown forces, while being encouraged, also had strict guidelines attached:

> All the Companies were instructed to have men posted on railway bridges crossing public roadways. The idea was to bomb the lorries as they approached the bridge. It was not intended to make a fight of it in these night attacks as to do so would require large numbers of men and curfew being so stringently operating at the time it would be particularly unsafe.[9]

The attacks continued, and the British sought further means of protecting their troops. Yet still, as the British official record of the campaign, the attacks continued:

> The rebels commenced bombing and sniping attacks on military and police vehicles in Dublin. Meanwhile, the armoring and overhead protection of lorries was being pushed on. An incomplete vehicle carrying a patrol of the 2nd Bn. Berks Regiment was, unfortunately, caught with insufficient covering at the back. Two bombs burst in the lorry, wounding one officer and seven soldiers.[10]

As a countermeasure, the British introduced armor plating and close wire mesh to their vehicles.

The ASUs responded by attaching fishing hooks to their grenades to catch in the netting. To prevent any interference, the IRA added a 2½-second fuse to the grenade. The danger, of course, was that the thrower exposed himself to being wounding by flying fragments of his own grenade should it bounce off the lorry. It became an evolving form of warfare. The attacks continued, and, if anything, became more

11. IRA Active Service Units

daring—and perhaps more desperate. Ernie O'Malley describes one such ambush in his book, *On Another Man's Wound:*

> Outside Stephen's Green I saw men attack a netted lorry and an armored Lancia of troops. Eggs [hand grenades] shattered in a tearing smash, one burst above the Lancia; automatics shot quickly, rifle reply came more slowly then the rifles merged with the swaying thresh of a machine gun. The passers by ran or threw themselves on the pavement. I lay down, watching. A man flattened on his blood in the cobbled street, two soldiers lay loosely against each other in a corner of the Lancia: up the street men tried to stop the red stains on a woman's white blouse. Women beside me were moaning and praying: "O Sacred Heart of Jesus help us." I ran for a lane beside the College of Surgeons and was soon in York Street.

The people in the area, who became familiar with the appearance of an ASU, moved quietly away from the vicinity. In a short space of time, the streets were practically deserted. The ASU waited to attack. James Cahill recorded one such wait on a winter's day:

> On an extremely cold frosty day, with occasional showers of sleet, I and six or seven of the ASU men were in ambush positions in the vicinity of Amiens Street station, awaiting a party of Auxiliaries who, our Intelligence had informed us, would pass that way, traveling in touring cars. Some of us, on arriving at the ambush position, decided to draw the safety pins from our grenades, as when attacking fast moving vehicles even a fraction of a second counts, so grasping tightly our grenades to ensure that the levers would not spring open, we stamped up and down trying to keep ourselves from freezing.
>
> When more than two hours had elapsed, and it became apparent that the Auxiliaries would not keep their appointment with us, we decided to disperse. Drawing my grenade from my pocket for the purpose of replacing the pin I discovered that the tight clasp with which I had held it, combined with the intense cold, had caused my fingers to cramp around the cold metal, and it was with great difficulty I succeeded in loosening my hold, by forcing open each finger separately.[11]

The area south of the river, which the British most feared to patrol in vehicles, they named the Dardanelles, after the Great War conflict. Stephen Keys of A Company, 3rd Battalion and his unit operated here:

> The attacks on the enemy forces were so numerous—almost a daily affair—and the casualties inflicted on the enemy were so heavy in the Redmond's Hill—Camden Street area, that the place became known as (and was commonly referred to as) "The Dardanelles."

Joseph O'Connor, also of A Company, lists forty-three attacks between January and June 1921.[12] Keys and his group were not the only ones to use the area. In his witness statement he reveals that "most of the ambushes took place in the Redmond's Hill–Camden St. area. As far as I know, the other Section Commander did the same." He goes on to explain a typical ambush:

> It was mostly soldiers in lorries that came along in the early stages. They came either down or up the street in the ordinary way, and we never let them go without attacking them. They never stopped. In my experience, they never jumped out of the cars nor did anything to try and catch the throwers of the grenades, with the result that they were an easy target going up and down Camden Street.

North of the river, the 2nd Battalion ASUs developed another form of ambush, as James Cahill elaborates:

> We adopted what was to become our normal tactics. Groups of two or three men took up positions at about thirty yards intervals, remained as inconspicuous as possible at street corners, shop windows, etc., and, on the approach of the enemy vehicles, moved on to the footpath and attacked at point-blank range.

Attacked by three units, this method of assault deterred the British from stopping to counterattack, unsure of whether they might be attacked by a further group. What the British soldiers feared was that, in their pursuit on foot of the bombers, they would be led into another ambush. While the ASUs attacked all the British forces, military and paramilitary, the favored target of the units were the Auxiliaries and the Black and Tans who brutalized the people. In respect of these paramilitaries, Keys relates:

> The Tans varied their tactics considerably. Sometimes when entering the area their tenders traveled at a very fast rate, and at other times they just crawled along. When we attacked them they stopped their cars suddenly, jumped out and shouted, "Halt, halt, halt, halt," with the result that everybody in the locality would stand because nobody knew whom they were calling on. They had the idea that, if we were there, we would halt too, but of course, that never happened.
>
> The Tans tried another plan. As they came into the area, they switched off the engine and switched it on again, causing an explosion in the silencer. Again, I think, their idea was to frighten the people off the streets. At any rate, I was very glad when they did that, because we would know when to get ready. We "hit them up."
>
> The Tans never seemed to know from where they were being "hit up." I often noticed them as they drove along looking up at the roofs and upper windows, and that is why, I think, I was so lucky never to get a crack from them. They were always watching the buildings. They never seemed to realise that they were being attacked from the streets.

At some stage, the Black and Tans did realize that the ambushes were ground attacks. They changed their tactics accordingly, as Keys found, almost to his cost:

11. IRA Active Service Units

The Tans tried another plan. They sent one tender of Tans down Camden Street, another down Heytesbury Street and a third down Harcourt Street. Both Heytesbury Street and Harcourt Street run parallel to Camden Street. The idea apparently was that when the tender in Camden Street was attacked the Tans on the other tenders would close in on Camden Street and cut off our retreat. I happened to be on duty at my favourite position—the corner of Camden Row and Camden Street—the first night they tried this plan, but, of course, was not aware of it and, therefore I was very nearly captured. We attacked the tender when it came along and, having thrown my grenade, I drew my gun and ran up Camden Row. When I reached Heytesbury Street I saw the Tans a short distance up that street. I dashed across Heytesbury Street and into Long Lane and got home safely. But it was a narrow escape.[13]

The attacks continued daily. The British authorities found it difficult to deal with them. The ASUs always had the advantage. It was they who decided when and where an attack would take place. Knowing the city, the IRA men again had the advantage, always planning their escape route in advance. A three-minute attack was over and done with before the British could react. On the downside, when the British did react, panic-stricken, innocent civilians—bystanders—were sometimes wounded or killed.

On May 10, 1921, ten men from A Company, 4th Battalion's ASU attacked a lorry at Conways, the halfway house just outside of Dublin. Patrick Collins described the action:

> As the lorry came through our position, [Michael] Sweeney, and [James] McGuinness fired hand grenades at it from the left-hand side of the road. Three men on the right-hand side of the road under good cover fired revolver shots at the driver to put him out of action and the man beside him. Almost immediately the lorry got out of control and seemed to swerve in to our position on the left-hand side. Jim Harpur and I dropped two hand-grenades into the lorry and the other three men kept on firing revolver shots. When we disposed of the hand-grenades we all simultaneously opened fire on the lorry. The British party was about eighteen strong. Of this number about sixteen were killed. The driver, who evidently was only slightly wounded and lost control momentarily, immediately recovered and drove on the lorry with its dead and wounded. The whole engagement only lasted about from ten to twenty minutes. We were unable to stop the progress of the lorry to capture the arms and equipment from it. So we withdrew and as we were withdrawing I saw that the Officer Commanding our Section, Michael Sweeney, was seriously wounded. A couple of our party took him to a doctor at a dressing station in St. Paul's Terrace. Kimmage Road, and the remainder of us made our way back to the city.

There's obviously some over exaggeration here as to casualties. The official British account, *Dublin District Historical Record,* details their losses between June 1920 and July 1921:

Casualties:
OFFICERS
Killed 13*
Wounded 9
Died of wounds 1

OTHER RANKS
Killed 9
Wounded 59
Died of wounds 2

*Though not stated, this may include the men killed on Bloody Sunday

Military Material Lost
Motor lorries 5
Crossley tenders 6
Motor cycles 1
Cycles 13
Touring cars 2

It would seem that the majority of the British soldiers were just wounded, but this is not to discount that some might have been killed. Surprisingly, the attack lasted between ten and twenty minutes. Obviously, the British had returned fire, as Sweeney was wounded, but Collins makes no mention of this. For the perpetrators of ambushes such as this, there was a mixture of fear and exhilaration. Christopher Andrews was to write of his own experiences:

> The ambush at Kenilworth [Square] produced in me a state bordering on ecstasy. I had achieved my burning ambition to fire a shot for Ireland. I felt that I could now justifiably claim a place in the ranks of those who through our successive generations had fought for Irish freedom. In terms of war or fighting the incident was trivial. Nevertheless we had risked our lives—the risk being exaggerated by our own stupidity and ignorance of what has since become known as urban guerilla warfare. We had never been trained for any such operation and acted purely on the impulse of the moment without even attempting to take cover. If it were not for the fact that the soldiers singing "I'm forever blowing bubbles" were as ill-trained as we were, we would most certainly have been killed.[14]

As the attacks on vehicles continued, the British modified their way of operating. Instructions relating to defense and counterattack were issued. Standing Orders for Armed Parties Moving by Lorry included:

> Every lorry which carries armed personnel will have the following minimum number specially told off for duty, and for immediate action:—
>   (a) A forward "look out," sitting beside the driver.
>   (b) Two side "look outs," one on each side of the lorry.
>   (c) A rear "look out" by the tail board.

All "look outs" mentioned above will have their revolvers or rifles ready for "Immediate action." In the case of rifles, "Immediate action" will mean that a round is in the chamber with the safety catch back, the rifle held muzzle pointing up, the barrel resting, if desired, on the side or tail board of the lorry.[15]

The attacks continued right up until the Truce, with new men being brought in to replace those captured or killed. This was especially true following the debacle of the assault upon the Custom House on May 28, 1921. On the whole the ASU ambushes did show to the world that Dublin had not been entirely subjugated—that Britain was not entirely in control. As a form of urban guerrilla engagement, this type of attack was successful, but it was not without its faults. Participant James Cahill analyzed the part that it played in the War of Independence:

> Looking back over that period I consider that the principal cause of failure to bring some of our missions to a successful conclusion was our leaders' inability to issue proper operation orders. Frequently our men were detailed to take up attack positions without being informed of the probable direction from which the enemy would approach, his probable strength and the number of vehicles. Information concerning such important matters as the strength and the position of the ambush party, location of covering parties, lines of withdrawal, action to be taken should additional enemy forces arrive, was frequently not issued. A check-up to ensure that each man was conversant with his task was seldom made.[16]

Yet despite the faults identified by the ASUs, the British never successfully overcame the activities of the teams operating in Dublin. Theirs was to become the model of attack for urban guerrillas throughout Europe during World War II—the assassination of Reinhard Heydrich in Czechoslovakia being perhaps the best example—and Britain's and France's colonial wars that followed. For the British, these were Palestine and Cyprus; for the French, it was the war of liberation in Algeria. The era of the big wars may now be over—who knows? But the little wars, the covert wars, have always been with us and always will be, particularly in the built-up environment.

12

Burning the Custom House

In Britain at the beginning of 1921, there was widespread opposition to the government's policies being carried out in Ireland. In Parliament, not only members of the Labour Party but also some Conservative politicians, including the rising star Oswald Mosley, were opposed to the acts of brutality and repression that featured almost daily in the newspapers. Lord Henry Cavendish-Bentinck formed the "Peace with Ireland Council." Arch Conservative Lord Robert Cecil had accepted the realism that it all had to end when he declared, "We are drifting through anarchy and humiliation to an Irish Republic. We will never settle the Irish question except in accordance with the wishes of the Irish people."[1] The trade unions also spoke out against the atrocities. The Miners' Federation called for the withdrawal of British troops from Ireland. Influential writers like George Bernard Shaw, G.K. Chesterton and Hilaire Belloc denounced the oppression of Ireland, too. Then, of course, the Americans were also making noises.

As early as the October 20, 1920, Conservative M.P. Brigadier General George Cockerill had written a letter to the influential London newspaper *The Times* proposing a truce and dialogue with Arthur Griffith. Following on from this, American journalist John S. Steele met up with Dublin businessman Patrick Moylett, a known Sinn Fein sympathizer. He presented written confirmation of Arthur Griffith's approval of the Cockerill plan. As a consequence, Prime Minister David Lloyd George announced that he was ready to discuss Ireland with Sinn Fein. By "Ireland," though, he meant some form of home rule but definitely not dominion status and certainly not an independent Irish republic. In reply Arthur Griffith indicated that he was prepared to meet accredited representatives of Britain. But as Sinn Fein was committed to an independent Republic, and Lloyd George insisted that Ireland must remain within the empire, there was little point in meeting. In the background, however, discussions continued to take place.

With Arthur Griffith in custody following the shootings of Bloody

12. Burning the Custom House

Sunday and Father O'Flanagan having replaced Michael Collins as Acting President of Sinn Fein, the priest visited London with Lord Justice O'Connor in a private attempt to negotiate peace. In a telegram to Lloyd George he wrote, "You state that you are willing to make peace at once without waiting for Christmas. Ireland also is willing. What first steps do you propose?" Talks on a higher level were instigated.

All of this was going on, seemingly, without the knowledge of Military Intelligence. Secret Service man Captain R.D. Jeune, one of the few British Intelligence Officers who had survived Bloody Sunday, stumbled upon something that he found disturbing. Elements within Dublin Castle were secretly corresponding with senior members of Sinn Fein. In an account of his wartime experiences in Ireland, written in 1972 and now housed in the library of the Imperial War Museum in London, he wrote:

> In September 1920, a raid took place, which had a significant result. It was decided to raid several houses in Drumcondra, and that we were to have the help of a detachment of the East Lancs. Particular attention was attached to the house of a man called O'Connor, known to us as an active Sinn Feiner.... There was no hostile reception, however, and the search went on. While this was happening I was standing talking to [H.F.] Boddington [a fellow Secret Serviceman], who was in charge of the raid, then a letter was brought to him, which he read and handed to me saying, "Money for jam." It was on official Dublin Castle paper and was in these words:
>
> > Dear Mr. O'Connor,
> > I am having the papers you require sent to you.
> > Yours Sincerely,
> > A.W. Cope.
>
> This was distinctly interesting. Here was the Assistant Under Secretary writing to a notorious Sinn Feiner, with whom he had obviously already been in contact.... After this I made a point of trying to find out more about this individual's doings.... Also he was one of the very few Castle officials who could safely walk about the streets of Dublin. But it was decided that no direct action could be taken against him, as it turned out that he was a protégé of Lloyd-George ... and sent him over to Ireland under Sir John Anderson in order to get a foot in the Sinn Fein camp, or, in modern parlance, to set in motion an "initiative."

If the British were in the dark over Cope, so too were the IRA. O'Connor was Judge O'Connor—"a good Irishman but a better imperialist," it was said—who had acted as an intermediary between Cope and Michael Collins, setting up a secret meeting at the home of Martin Fitzgerald of Ardnalea, Dundrum. He was the owner of the *Freeman's Journal* and a close associate of Piaras Beasley, Collins's publicity agent. Getting no joy from Collins, Cope sought other channels of approach. As one who was close to the proceedings, Lt. Laurence Nugent of the 3rd Dublin Battalion relates:

> He was not satisfied with meeting Mick Collins.... He wanted to meet Cathal Brugha, or as he called him, "the man with the quare name." It was strange that Mick carried on these talks on his own as both Dev and Cathal Brugha were available. But neither of them were members of the IRB, and it was the IRB who decided whatever peace was to be made, and men were being executed and losing their lives.²

Meanwhile, Irish Intelligence—not even they were privy to the secret negotiations—were onto Cope. He had been seen visiting Ardnalea. Mick Chadwick, an IRA officer operating in the area, asked permission from IRA GHQ to assassinate the British representative. Orders came smartly back that he was to do nothing of the sort unless he got written orders from GHQ. Cope eventually made contact with de Valera. As an inducement to begin talks, Cope offered full fiscal autonomy and other tempting offers. De Valera replied that until the offer was put on paper he could not comment. It was a small step, but contact had been made. On December 16th, Dublin Castle agreed to talk to the representatives of Sinn Fein. While these secret negotiations continued, so too did the war. Openly, British policy was to crush the IRA, while unofficially Sinn Fein was to be permitted to operate as a political party. This was to ensure that Sinn Fein participated in the forthcoming elections under the Government of Ireland Act, which was passed on December 23, 1920. The act provided for two Irish parliaments, a northern, for six counties of Ulster, and a southern for the remainder. The election was to be carried out sometime between January 1921 and March 1922. The British Government was anxious to see a cessation of violence. It considered the cost of military victory to be now too high. By March 1921, Crown casualties out in the countryside had become higher than what they had been since Easter 1916. To expedite matters, Lord French, the personification of coercion and suppression, was retired as Lord Lieutenant. He was succeeded by the first Roman Catholic to hold the post, Viscount Fitzalan. Though a Unionist in outlook, he was unhappy with the violence and the coercive policy being played out. Matters of a military nature were reaching a stalemate in Ireland. British military strength was in decline due to demobilization and the transfer of troops to Britain following industrial crises and international obligations. In the six months up to April 1921, some 9,000 experienced troops were sent home, having served their time.

In Britain there was a growing disquiet over the stories of brutality and murder by Crown forces. The Labour Party sent delegates to Ireland to investigate. Their findings were published as a *Report of the Labour*

12. Burning the Custom House

Commission in Ireland. General Thomson, the commission's military advisor, described the Army in Ireland as raw, ill-trained, with most of its officers "ignorant of their professional duties." The Auxiliaries came in for a particular slating as "the most vicious of the Crown forces" and did not "seem to recognize even the authority of Dublin Castle." Thomson put the question, "Under whom do they serve?" As for the Black and Tans, the government has, "liberated forces which it is not at present able to dominate," he wrote.[3]

Support for this view was echoed in a published article written by General Sir Hubert Gough, which argued:

> It is impossible to come to any other honest opinion (whether you excuse them or not, on account of the provocation they have received) but that the police in many cases and the soldiers in some, have been guilty of gross acts of violence without even a semblance of military order and discipline, and that these acts are not only never adequately punished, but no steps are taken to prevent their recurrence.[4]

Reports of British violence and mismanagement kept coming in. Sir Warren Fisher, sent to investigate the Dublin administration, disclosed that the whole administration system had broken down. There was no overall control. The civil, police, and military authorities had developed into separate, almost rival powers. He reported:

> Not only is the use of force not singly directed, but even as between the three elements now existing there is little evidence of effective cooperation. On the contrary there are to my mind undoubted signs of an untimely lack of sympathy and incomprehension in attitude and liaison in working.[5]

Pressure was mounting on the British Government for some sort of settlement. Certainly, things could not go on as they had. In the meantime, the elections to the northern and southern parliaments under the Government of Ireland Act went ahead. The results were declared on May 2th. In southern Ireland the Republicans were returned unopposed in all but four seats; those in the "rotten borough" and Unionist stronghold of Trinity College. Sinn Fein treated the election as constituting a second Dail. There was no chance, however, that their M.P.s would assemble as a puppet Southern Parliament.

Eamon de Valera returned to Ireland on December 20, 1920. Michael Collins had arranged his safe return. The President was met at the Custom House Dock by senior Irish Intelligence Officer Tom Cullen and Batt O'Connor. As he descended from the ship, de Valera asked Cullen how things were going. In his enthusiasm Cullen responded, "Great. The Big Fellow is leading us, and everything is going marvelous." This seemed to confirm everything that de Valera believed. Collins was trying to take over. In quiet anger de Valera responded, "Big Fellow! We'll see who's the Big Fellow." Within two weeks of his return, his prejudices were seemingly confirmed by Cathal Brugha and Austin Stack, no friends of Collins. De Valera sought to get Collins out of the way by sending him to America on a fundraising tour. In this he had the support of Brugha, Minister for Defence, and nominally Collins's superior. In a lengthy letter to Collins, de Valera outlined what was expected of him once he got there. As well as a speaking tour, he was to organize the shipment of arms to Ireland. Further, in a bid to re-assert himself as leader, and put Collins in his place, Collins was directed:

> To examine the possibilities of the U.S. from the point of view of supplying material to the Minister of Defence. To make a report and recommendations to the Minister on this head and as far as possible to execute any commissions which that Minister may give in relation to his own Department.[6]

In a less than subtle way de Valera was reasserting Brugha's position over him. This was undoubtedly an intended slight. Amongst other things, Collins realized that such an absence, away from Ireland, would see the destruction of the intelligence network that he had established. He refused to go, exclaiming, "The long hoor won't get rid of me that easily."[7] Cordial relations between the two men were clearly broken. The idea of Collins's being sent to America was eventually dropped. De Valera, however, felt the need to reassert his position as President. He was the man in charge, and he felt the need to display to others that this was the case. On March 30, 1921, de Valera gave an interview to the representatives of the *International News* and the *Universal Service* in which he reasserted his position not only as President, but the ultimate authority over the Republic's armed forces, the IRA. He declared that

> ...one of our first government acts was to take over the control of the voluntary armed forces of the nation. From the Irish Volunteers we fashioned the Irish Republican Army to be the military arm of the Government. This army is, therefore, a regular State force, under the civil control of the elected representatives, and under organization and a discipline imposed by these representatives, and under officers who hold their commission under warrant from these representatives.[8]

At a meeting of the Dail on January 25, 1921, de Valera put forward the principle of fighting a new form of warfare, one that would attract international attention. Rather than fight a number of hit-and-run ambushes, he advocated a series of battles—say 500 on either side. This, of course, was madness. It was exactly what the British wanted—to catch the IRA out in the open and destroy them. Such a series of the confrontations would see the destruction of the IRA. The British were superior in trained men, they were better armed, and they would have the support of tanks, artillery and aircraft. De Valera had learnt nothing from the failure of the Easter Rising, where 2,000 men and women were locked into static warfare and simply waited for the British forces to attack and destroy them. The suggestion received little support from those who were actually conducting the war. Nonetheless de Valera continued to push for something that would gain worldwide attention.

While de Valera, Brugha and Stack considered a possible target, Collins and his team had to deal with an informer from within their own ranks. The man in question was Vincent Fovargue, an intelligence officer of the 4th Battalion of the Dublin Brigade. He had been arrested at a meeting of the Brigade intelligence officers and sent to Dublin Castle for interrogation. Under torture he broke, and in a series of nighttime raids he led his Auxiliary captors to the safe houses used by senior IRA men. Fovargue was also used as a "stool pigeon." He was put into shared cells in Kilmainham Prison with the intention of gathering information from other prisoners. One prisoner, Sean Kavanagh, related his experience:

> I was then placed in a cell near the Birmingham Tower where I found three other prisoners whose names were Vincent Fovargue, John Noud and Green, who was an old man.... I afterwards learned that while in jail he [Fovargue] was acting as an Intelligence agent for the Castle authorities ... fellow prisoner Noud later told me that he had tried to tip me off, as he was not happy about him.
>
> Fovargue had evidently been put into my cell to see what information he could get out of me. I distinctly recall his asking me searching questions about the leaders of the IRA, including Brugha, Collins, O'Sullivan etc. Fortunately I told him nothing that was not already fairly well known.
>
> At this time it was the practice for military and police raiding parties patrolling the city to take as hostages with them prisoners from Kilmainham and other prisons. One evening about a fortnight after my transfer to Kilmainham, Fovargue was taken out as a hostage and did not return. The newspapers the following morning reported that he had escaped from the lorry when the occupants left it to chase alleged attackers.[9]

David Nelligan and Ned Broy, working for Irish Intelligence within the British administration, were most skeptical of such an escape. Neligan wrote in his book, *The Spy in the Castle:*

> Now if they had said that this man (who was completely unknown to both of us) had escaped from one I.O. it might have sounded reasonable enough. But to tell us that an unarmed man had escaped out of a motor car in the presence of three presumably armed men was imposing a strain on our credulity. Both of us thought this story too good to be true.[10]

And so it was. Colonel Winter, realizing that Fovargue's value was now at an end, whisked him away to England. Here he was given the new identity of Richard Sta[u]nton and told to infiltrate the Fulham branch of the Irish Self Determination League, the name given to Sinn Fein in England. At some point he was identified as Vincent Fovargue, kidnapped, interrogated and shot. His body was then dumped at Ashford Manor Golf Links. Pinned to his body was a note written in blue pencil, "Let spies and traitors beware—IRA."

The triumvirate of de Valera, Brugha and Stack, meanwhile, had settled on a target to draw the attention of the world to Ireland's continued struggle for independence. It was decided to attack and burn the Custom House in the heart of Dublin. Unguarded, the building was the central repository of British tax returns in Ireland. It contained records of local government and other accounts relating to the governance of the country. For maximum publicity, de Valera decided, that the attack would be during the day.

This was just suicide waiting to happen. The capital was crisscrossed with British military and police barracks whose occupants could quickly respond to any prolonged assault within Dublin. Collins did his best to avoid any involvement of The Squad, but Squad leader Paddy Daly argued that all the members should be involved. It would not be right to exclude The Squad from the inevitable fight. Daly got his way, but Collins was adamant that Irish Intelligence should stay out of it.

The man put in charge on the day was the 2nd Battalion Commandant, Tom Ennis. In all, the attacking party consisted of 50 men from the 2nd Battalion, 50 from the ASU, and 20 men from The Squad. No one from Irish Intelligence was engaged in the operation, though they did operate as observers. On the day before the assault, May 27th, Captain Tom Kilcoyne from the 2nd Battalion commandeered a large "White Rose" paraffin tanker truck. Its contents were transferred to a number of two-gallon petrol cans and distributed amongst the various units. Sledgehammers and bolt cutters were acquired to be used on locked or padlocked doors. On the day, the equipment was loaded aboard a commandeered three-ton truck and driven down the quay to the Custom House. At five minutes to one o'clock that afternoon, while The Squad and the ASU manned all the entrances, men from the battalion ran inside and proceeded to round up and evacuate the staff. The caretaker, a man by the name of Davis, telephone in hand to warn Dublin Castle of what was going on, was shot and wounded.

Ennis had seriously miscalculated how many men were required to carry out the burning duties. Some of The Squad were directed into

12. Burning the Custom House

the building to help, thus weakening the strength of those on guard duty outside. The job was to have been completed by 1:20 p.m. but evacuating the staff took longer than anticipated. Squad member Joe Byrne recalled:

> On the whole, the staff were generally submissive. Some of them, of course, objected to being held up and ordered about but when they saw that we meant business they accepted the inevitable. As far as I could see everything was going well for us until some members of the Dublin Brigade observed enemy lorries coming down Eden Quay, and thinking that their lorries were going to attack the Custom House, they opened fire immediately.[11]

Elsewhere inside the building, fellow Squad member Vinnie Byrne, with petrol can in hand,

> we proceeded to the second floor. I opened the office door and, sitting inside were a lady and gentleman, civil servants, having tea. I requested them to leave, stating that I was going to set fire to the office. The gentleman stood up and said: "Oh, you can't do that." I showed him my gun and told him I was serious. He got very worried about the whole thing. I said to him: "You had better get out at once, unless you want to be burned alive." The lady then asked me could she get her coat, and I replied: "Miss, you'll be lucky if you get out with your life." They left.[12]

Now with an empty office, Byrne removed the ledgers from the open safe and placed them upon a table in the room, along with any other papers and files. He then poured petrol all over the office's wooden floor, then on the papers. Meanwhile elsewhere in the building, his comrades were doing the same. Upon hearing the agreed signal, a series of blasts on a whistle, Byrne ignited a screwed-up ball of paper and threw it into the room. With the added accelerant, the room burst into flame. In all the other offices within the building, the same procedure occurred. The arsonists then descended the stairs and made for the exits. As Byrne reached the ground floor, he heard a burst of revolver and rifle fire. The building was surrounded by British forces, and a heavy, but brief firefight was in progress—brief because most of the Volunteers involved had barely three or four rounds of ammunition. The British discovery of an IRA's arms dump in the city a few days previously had seriously depleted stocks of ammunition.

Apparently as the IRA men entered the building and began evacuating the staff, members of the DMP, seeing what was going on, had notified Dublin Castle. Two armored cars, one containing men from F Company of the Auxiliaries, were dispatched to the site. The leading armored car arrived at about 1:25 p.m. to see the arsonists emerging from the southern side of the building. Fire was opened upon them. More Auxiliary arrivals made for the northern side of the building, where they immediately came under fire from the IRA. In the process, they suffered four men wounded. Four minutes later the F Company men were joined by Q Company, based at the north wall. They covered the eastern side of the Custom House. Consequently, the burning building was surrounded as Byrne descended the stairs. He, like the others, made for one of the exits. At this point two Auxiliaries entered, blocking Byrne's escape. Before they could react, he let off a burst of machine-pistol fire but missed both of them as they quickly withdrew. Moving to the doorway Byrne squeezed the trigger again, but to little effect. The magazine was empty. Now in the doorway, he was confronted by the two Auxiliaries. He was convinced that he was a dead man—but no, he was not killed. One of the Auxiliaries called out to him to surrender and put up his hands. Byrne dropped the pistol and raised his hands. Both Auxiliaries were covering him with their rifles. "Come over here!" one of them ordered. As he did so he was struck in the face with a rifle butt. Concussed and with a bleeding nose, he was dragged across the road to where a group of other prisoners had already been lined up. They all expected to be shot on the spot.

Elsewhere, from other exits, other IRA men made a break for it. James Slattery, one of The Squad, was among them:

> I tried to get the lads to burst out with me. A few of them did, but the Tans opened fire when we got outside the door. Sean Doyle, whose brother had been executed, broke through. He did not want to be arrested because he knew he stood no chance. When we were about half-way across the square there was a burst of machine gun fire and I was hit on the hand. I called Doyle, who was slightly in front of me, and I saw blood trickling down his chin. I told him to keep going in the direction of Gardiner Street.[13]

Slattery's injury was so bad that his hand was later amputated. Aiding Slattery's evasion, and the others who escaped, was the 17-year-old Daniel Head. From under the railway arches he ran forward and lobbed a hand grenade into a lorry full of Auxiliaries, causing casualties. He, in turn, was cut down in a hail of bullets.

With the assault over, the captured "civilians" were marshaled by the Auxiliaries into the square, their hands up in the air. Senior customs officials were asked to identify their employees, who were then released. Those remaining men were then called forth. One by one they were briefly interviewed, to be sorted out, the sheep from the goats. As he waited his turn Byrne could see all The Squad men and members of the 2nd Battalion standing prisoner under the railway arch nearby. Then British plainclothes men turned up, including a high-ranking officer, to question the prisoners in more detail. Byrne smelled the petrol on his hands. That was a dead giveaway:

I took a few cigarettes out of my pocket, wet them and rolled them very well into my hands, giving a smell of tobacco. Now it was my turn to go before the officer. I humbly asked him: "Could I go home now?" He looked at me and said: "What are you doing here?" I replied: "Sir, I was on my way to Brooks Thomas to buy some timber." He ran his hands all over me and pulled out a carpenter's rule and a few pieces of paper out of my pockets. The papers showed different sizes of pieces of timber, which I usually carried as a decoy. Handing back my rule and papers, the officer said: "Get to hell out of this." I said "Thank you, sir." I was once more clear.

On completion of the identification, about seventy "civilians" remained. Seven of them showed distinct traces of petrol or paraffin. They were all marched off under guard. The fire brigade arrived, but there was little they could do. The building was blazing fiercely. In the action, the IRA suffered five men killed: Capt. Paddy O'Reilly, his brother Lt. Stephen O'Reilly, Dan Head, Eddie Dorrins and Sean Doyle. Doyle, badly wounded, escaped, but died the next day.

That evening Michael Collins went to see the results of the attempt to destroy the Custom House. He was escorted by Joseph Byrne and Johnny Dunne, who had taken part in the action. Mingling with the assembled crowd Collins smiled when he saw that the building was still burning. He was saddened, though, because with their capture, it meant the end of The Squad as an elite unit. The trio moved off up Abbey Street and into Parnell Street, where they were confronted by a large group of Auxiliaries who were stopping and questioning the public. The three Irishmen were stopped. Totally unexpectedly, Collins turned on his inquisitor, as Byrne relates:

> I heard him abuse the Auxiliary. He said to him, "How dare you. Do you not know who I am? Give me your name and number. I'll deal with you later." The Auxiliary apologized and Collins went on his way. Apparently the Auxiliary was so excited about the incident that he let us by also.[14]

By seizing the initiative, Collins had yet again bluffed his way and escaped detection. He did not look like a terrorist. He did not dress like a fugitive, but more importantly, he did not behave as if he was on the run with a price of £10,000 on his head.

The result of the assault and burning of the Custom House drew the attention of the world's press all right, but in military terms it could only be described as a disaster. Some 100 IRA men of the Dublin Brigade were captured and detained, their weapons seized. Sir Henry Robinson, vice-president of the Local Government Board, from the British perspective, described the Custom House assault as "the stupidest thing Sinn Fein ever did." Perhaps worse for Collins, was that he now lost complete control over the Squad. Brugha, backed by de Valera, ordered the amalgamation of the Active Service Unit and the few remaining members of the Squad still at liberty. A few days following the burning of the Custom House, all sections of the Active Service Unit were mobilized for a meeting at the Plaza Hotel in Upper Gardiner Street. Present at the meeting were members of The Squad and GHQ Intelligence. Paddy Daly, now carving a new military career for himself, was put in charge of the new unit. He announced that owing to the reduced strength of the ASU, on account of arrests and other casualties, it was proposed to reorganize it. The Squad, the ASU and Irish Intelligence would merge and form one unit under his control. The new organization would follow on the lines of the old one. It would continue to consist of four sections, but the company would be divided into two halves, one to operate in the north side of the city and the other half on the south side of the Liffey. Joe Leonard would take charge of the northern half; Paddy O'Connor would command the south. To bring the unit up to strength, new replacements were found from the four Battalions of the Dublin Brigade. The strength of the new command was somewhere between eighty and one hundred men; accounts differ. From then on, The Squad only carried out operations allocated to them from headquarters.

It now became imperative to conceal the true loss in manpower sustained by the IRA in Dublin. The fear was that the British would take advantage of the situation to deal a decisive blow. Ambushes were carried out nearly every day by those few Volunteers that remained in the city. Tenders carrying troops and Auxiliaries were attacked with handguns and grenades. They were brief exchanges, barely lasting more than two or three minutes, but most creating casualties of killed or wounded.

Michael Fitzgerald of K Company, 1st Battalion lists, some of the post–Custom House attacks carried out by his men[15]:

> On 1st June, a party, under the command of Billy Bohan ambushed a military lorry near Arran Quay church. The attack was opened by two men with hand grenades that exploded on the lorry which was covered by wire netting. The attack was followed up by the officer in charge and two other men with revolver fire. Their retreat through Smithfield was covered by several other Volunteers stationed at vantage points along the line of retreat to North King Street. Our party suffered no casualties.
>
> On 3rd June, I posted a small party at the corner of Dorset Street and Blessington Street. They had just settled in position when a lorry of British troops arrived from the city. Instead of proceeding along Blessington Street as expected, it turned down towards Drumcondra. The men with the grenades decided to attack. As the grenades exploded, a Volunteer stationed at Wellington Street corner opened fire with a revolver to cover the men's retreat. It was reported that several soldiers were wounded in the

engagement. Our men retreated via Mountjoy Street and Dominick Street to Parnell Street where the guns were dumped without casualty.

An intended ambush on June 9 did not go quite to plan, as Fitzgerald narrated:

> The following week we had planned a series of ambushes on the military and Tans. Proceeding along the quays at about four o'clock on 9th June a party of twenty under the command of the company adjutant, Val Forde took up position along Ormond Quay and intersecting streets. Two men with grenades and the company adjutant with a revolver were stationed on the corner of Swift's Row. Their retreat was covered by revolver men at the corner of Liffey Street and Jervis Street, while Liffey Street, Mary Street and Capel Street were also covered, holding every possible line of retreat, while unarmed scouts maintained a communication link between each outpost.... One of the men signaled to me that a lorry was coming on the far side. A moment later I heard rifle fire, and saw the British lorry pull up near Swift's Row where our advanced party was stationed. Still the grenades did not explode; this was to have been the signal for our attack from the south quays.
>
> Realizing that something had gone wrong, and that our party could not escape along Swift's Row if the British were allowed to attack them from the quays, I shouted to our men on the south quays to take up position. They were about twenty yards from me when I issued the order. Fire! By the time I had repeated the order three times, the British had turned from Swift's Row, and were now lined along the Liffey Wall returning our fire. As bullets were hopping off the houses at my back, and knowing that we had served our purpose by giving our comrades a few minutes to retreat past the first cover party, I ordered the retreat.

The reason for the failure, it was later discovered, was the failure of the two grenades to explode. Despite this loss, the attacks continued throughout the city and were reported on by the world's press. The British did not control Dublin: that was the message that was made to the world.

On the intelligence front, the British met with some success in the city during that spring of 1921. Random and speculative raids sometimes led to a series of discoveries. On March 24th, an IRA arms dump was discovered in Mountjoy Square. Six rifles and 35 revolvers were found. Six days later, a Lewis gun, a German machine gun and nearly 6,000 rounds of ammunition were discovered at a dump in Harcourt Street. Michael Collins's office in Mespil Road was raided late in the spring of 1921. British Intelligence came very close to capturing Michael Collins himself. Details of the incident are revealed in the Witness Statement of Dr. Alice Barry. It was about 3:00 a.m. when there was a knock at the door of her home. Making herself presentable, she went downstairs and opened the door. Standing there was an Auxiliary and Patricia Hoey,

Collins's secretary. Dr. Barry was asked if she would attend Miss Hoey's sick mother. They proceeded along to the house at 5, Mespil Road, now Collins's principal office. The house was a cottage type house with a semibasement and one floor above it. Entering, Dr. Barry discovered that it was occupied by a number of Auxiliaries. They were engaged in what was known as a "sitting" raid. In essence,the raiders would surreptitiously occupy a suspected house and wait to see who would turn up. The doctor was taken by Miss Hoey to her mother's bedroom. Dr. Barry relates:

> None of the Auxiliaries accompanied us, as they evidently thought it was a case of serious illness. When I went to examine Mrs. Hoey, she said there was no need. "We merely wanted to get a message to Mick Collins who is due to arrive here at 9 o'clock in the morning. The Auxies who had arrived after curfew evidently had definite information that this house was one of Collins' offices and they had decided to remain there until he turned up. From outside there was no sign of a raid and Collins or any of his officers could easily have walked into the well-laid trap."[16]

Warned of the trap, Dr. Barry, after treating her patient's supposed illness, was escorted back to her home. From there, a message was sent out to warn Collins of the trap. It was Ginger O'Connell who finally found him proceeding along Merrion Square, shortly before nine o'clock that morning. Thus, he was saved from arrest. Later that morning, Dr. Barry was summoned to meet Collins and to receive his thanks. There was another job for her to do:

> Collins was in a state of distress because there were files of important papers secreted in the house in Mespil Road in a secret cupboard which had been constructed by Batt O'Connor. The cupboard was camouflaged by shelves constructed in front of it. He asked me to call at the house and get the papers for him. I got on my bicycle and was admitted again by the Auxies who thought it quite natural that I should wish to pay another visit to my patient. Patricia who was evidently a secretary to Collins opened the cupboard quietly and handed me the files … which would have disclosed all the IRA plans and names to the authorities. I stuck them inside my jumper and put on my coat. The Auxies were in the hall and let me pass without question.

On April 27th, an IRA arms dump in some stables in Baggot Lane was discovered. This dump provided arms for the various guerrilla groups throughout Ireland. The seizure included a machine gun, fourteen rifles, fifty-four revolvers and 12,442 rounds of ammunition. These successes were matched by an intelligence-led raid on Blackhall Place on April 29th, where forty men of the Dublin Brigade were captured.

It was time to curb the activities of the Auxiliaries, Collins decided. An action, something along the lines of Bloody Sunday, was needed. Lily

12. Burning the Custom House

Mernin had identified a large number of the cadets, who had taken to relaxing, while dressed in civilian clothes, in the cafes and restaurants along Grafton Street, South Dublin. An attack was planned for the afternoon of June 24, 1921, the time when the greatest number of Auxiliaries and other Secret Service men would be strolling in Grafton Street. Joe Dolan was on the mission:

> The idea was to nail the whole lot in one blow. These were well known to the Intelligence Section, and the Intelligence Section were on the job. The Active Service Unit were also on the job, but some of them did not arrive having been cut off by patrols. On the firing of a shot by me all were to shoot every Auxiliary seen in Grafton Street. Myself with six others were to go into Kidd's restaurant, but as I have already mentioned some of the Active Service Unit couldn't turn up to me as they were cut off by military patrols, and the same thing happened in certain parts of Grafton Street. We had arranged to have a Ford van to take away our wounded and that couldn't turn up either. It was also cut off. Because all these things happened it was decided to call the whole thing off. Just as it was called off two members of the Active Service Unit shot two Auxiliaries called Appleby and Waring.[17]

Even though a truce was in the offing, the spy game continued. Irish Intelligence continued to seek out their counterparts in British Intelligence for assassination. With so many of The Squad in custody following the Custom House debacle, men from the Active Service Unit drawn from the 3rd Battalion acted in their stead. On June 26, 1921, a six-man team was sent to execute an Auxiliary and a former Auxiliary, now believed to be working for British Military Intelligence. A member of the team, James Tully, left a brief report of the mission:

> In June 1921, we were detailed to shoot two auxiliaries who were staying in the Mayfair Hotel, Baggot Street. The party consisted of Paddy O'Connor who was in charge, Michael Stack, Peter Larkin, Jack O'Hanlon, Jim O'Neill, and myself. My job was to dismantle the telephone. At about 6.30 on a Sunday evening we entered the Hotel. The two auxiliaries with two women and a child were in a room. O'Connor, Stack, Larkin and O'Toole pushed open the door of the room and fired, killing the two auxiliaries. O'Connor took their guns. O'Neill was to have had a car running in Fitzwilliam Street to take the guns away. When I came out I put my gun in the car. O'Neill could not get the car started so it had to be abandoned and I lost my gun. The others, living in the area, had taken their guns with them.[18]

The targets were William F. Hunt, recently retired from the Auxiliaries, but still living in Dublin, and serving Auxiliary Cadet Lt. Enfield White. They were visiting their wives and Hunt's ten-year-old daughter Doris, who had recently arrived in Dublin. The ladies were staying at the Mayfair Hotel, a private hotel at 30, Lower Baggot Street. The assassination team were briefed by Frank Saurin of Irish Intelligence. He told them, as Michael Stack later recalled,

> that the maid in the hotel to which we were going was friendly and would give us all the help we required ... the door was answered by the maid. We asked her what room the Auxiliaries were in and she told us the second room on the left where they were then having lunch. I asked her where the telephone was and she directed me to it, so I told a member of the section [James Tully] to dismantle it. The section leader and myself opened the door of the dining room and fired at the two Auxiliaries seated at the table with their families, the section leader [Paddy O'Connor] taking the left-hand man and I taking the man on the right. Both men collapsed on the floor where they were then approached by the Section leader who searched them for any documents that may have been of use to us.[19]

Several shots were, in fact, aimed at the two men before the ASU men withdrew. Remarkably, though wounded three times, White survived the assault. Hunt was killed. The police were quickly on the scene and both men were taken off to Sir Patrick Dun's Hospital, where Hunt was pronounced dead. Hunt, the suspected Secret Service man, was from Watford in London. During World War I he, like Captain Hardy, had served in the Inniskilling Fusiliers. This may perhaps suggest a connection with the spy business.

Though a truce was now being talked about, the hunt for Michael Collins continued. The British sent in more agents to capture or kill their nemesis. James Doyle, manager of the Gresham Hotel in O'Connell Street, came across one such British agent looking for the Irish Intelligence chief. Doyle recalled:

> There were a lot of people coming and going visiting Collins. One incident might be mentioned. A fellow arrived at the hotel off the morning boat. He had a conversation with the porter. Amongst his inquiries he asked particulars about Mr. Michael Collins who was using the hotel a good deal at the time, and he was then, or pretended to be, on his first visit to Ireland. I recognized him as a well-known member of the Black and Tans named McIntyre. He said that he was commissioned to publish the memoirs of Michael Collins and that he had a good sum of money at his disposal for that purpose.
>
> I took an early opportunity of telling Mr. Collins what I knew of this man who left Dublin the same day without having seen Michael Collins. The next day Collins told me he had been put on the boat and warned not to return.[20]

About this same time, a two-man team of British agents arrived in Dublin. They used the aliases of Burke and Coady. The two men arrived separately. Burke had a letter of introduction, which he showed to three Cumann na mBan women who were selling flags for the Prisoners' Dependents Fund on O'Connell Street. He asked to be put in touch with the IRA. Meanwhile, he asked them if they could recommend a hotel where he could spend the night. They sent him to Fleming's Hotel to there await a contact. The next day he was collected and taken to a Squad safehouse. Burke made a good impression. He was intelligent. He wanted to work for Michael Collins, he informed them. Burke was checked out; he seemed to be genuine. It was decided to get him a job in Dublin Castle where he could act as a spy. Very soon Burke worked his way into the upper echelons of Sinn Fein. One night he even attended a reception at a house in Merrion Square, where de Valera was attending a meeting. Burke had a way about him, ingratiating himself. He was also a bit of a ladies' man. He charmed them, and they fell for him.

Some short time, later a small red-haired man name Coady arrived. He claimed that he had escaped from the internment camp at the Curragh. He, too, was taken to the safehouse. As a precaution, a check was made, which revealed that he was lying. He had never been in the Curragh. While it was being decided what to do with him, Coady and Burke appeared to develop a friendship. The supposed Curragh escapee was ill-dressed. Burke, who had arrived carrying a suitcase, offered to loan Coady his spare suit. The suit exactly fitted Coady. This was strange, for Burke was just a tad short of six feet in height, while Coady was considerably shorter. Suspicions were passed on to Irish Intelligence. Collins opted to watch them. Two surveillance teams were assembled to follow the two men. Both, however, managed to give their watchers the slip. It became obvious that they had been trained in the use of countersurveillance and took precautions to avoid being followed. John Bolger of Irish Intelligence reported that Burke's room was searched:

> Some of Burke's letters were examined, coming in, but, as these appeared to have been written in code, we found it very hard to make sense of them.
>
> On one occasion, Burke crossed the water to England. It was suggested that I should follow him there, but this idea was not pursued, as I felt I did not know England sufficiently well to go.[21]

Upon his return, both he and Coady were arrested. Burke especially was dangerous, but it was decided not to kill him, nor indeed Coady—the reason being that it might lead to complications in the negotiations then beginning. The two men were put aboard the Irish ferry and told never to return.

13

The Road to Peace

The failure of the Southern Parliament to assemble, in accordance with the terms of the Government of Ireland Act, created a dilemma. Sinn Fein, the democratically elected Irish government, had refused to cooperate with the British Government. As such, their legal standing, in British constitutional law, could only be as a Crown colony. This was totally unsatisfactory to the Sinn Fein government. The only other status, given that independence was not to be permitted, was some form of Dominion home rule as enjoyed by Australia, Canada and South Africa. Lloyd George was at first totally opposed to such status in that it would certainly lead to demands for further concessions. Then, of course, there was the IRA. No meaningful settlement was possible until they had been disarmed. But the Irish looked upon the IRA as their national army, and, as such, the IRA would have to be part of any settlement. Analysis by General Macready was that in facing an IRA resurgence in May 1921, the existing British forces in Ireland had suffered serious stress and would soon be unfit to continue. To defeat the enemy, a strong reinforcement of troops was essential. These new troops would need training, and while this was underway, British action would be no more than countering whatever actions the IRA presented.[1] In this, Macready was supported by Sir Henry Wilson, who wrote:

> There is a risk that a position of virtual stalemate may continue throughout the summer and that winter will be a decisive advantage to the rebels.[2]

One solution would be the imposition of martial law throughout Ireland. The argument in favor of this was that it would produce unity of command. The British Army would take over all functions of law and order. This would end the many police reprisals that had brought Britain into disrepute. These reprisals, including the blowing up of houses of known IRA men, had brought forward further reprisals by the IRA, which responded by burning Loyalists' big houses. The economics weighed heavily in favor of the IRA. The order to cease reprisals was issued on June 3rd. Other alternatives to regaining control were submitted, including the imposition of identity cards and the building of blockhouses across the country—as had been used in South Africa during the Boer War—and a naval blockade.

Realistically, Major Percival, who had commanded the Essex Regiment in County Cork, had seen the futility of continuing the war as it was. "If the Army had been given a free hand, and behaving as badly as the Germans had in Belgium during World War I, then the war could have been won, but at a terrible cost to the civilian population." Pressure from inside as well as outside Britain prevented such action. The only way forward was by discussion. Later, Lieutenant General A.E. Percival, in a lecture he gave to students at Sandhurst Military College, observed:

> The point I want to make here is that the rebel campaign in Ireland was a national movement backed by a large proportion of the population and was not conducted by a few hired assassins as was supposed.

On June 7, 1921, King George V traveled to Belfast to inaugurate the new Unionist-dominated Ulster Parliament. The King read out a conciliatory speech, written, it is said, by the South African leader Jan Smuts, who was in London attending a conference. The King declared:

> It is my earnest desire that in Southern Ireland there may, ere long, take place a parallel to what is now passing in this hall, that there a similar occasion may present itself, and a similar ceremony be performed. For this the Parliament of the United Kingdom has in the fullest measure provided the powers; for this the Parliament of Ulster is pointing the way.

Following a meeting of the Irish Situation Committee held on June 15th, Tom Jones, Lloyd George's most senior civil servant and secretary, wrote to the Prime Minister that Macredy, supported by John Anderson, were both of the same mind that "the policy of coercion will not succeed." It was time to talk.

On June 20, 1921, de Valera was arrested in Dublin by a patrol of the 2nd Battalion of the Worcester Regiment. He gave a false name, but after being taken in for questioning at Portobello Barracks, he revealed his real name, proclaiming that he was "President of the Irish Republic." After spending one night, being treated as an officer prisoner and being given officer's quarters, he was released the following day upon the express orders of British Prime Minister David Lloyd George. Captain Jeune was informed by fellow Secret Service officer W.F. Jeffries, now back in London, what had then happened:

> Now Jeffries told me that the following took place. Army GHQ at Kilmainham wired to his London office, "De Valera captured. Cope suggests release." This telegram arrived about 7 p.m. and Jeffries took it across to the Colonial

Office, but Hamar Greenwood had left, so Jeffries took it to Lloyd George, who rubbed his hands together, and said, "Well done the military. He must on no account be released." Taking this as settled, Jefferies left, but as soon as he had gone Lloyd George sent orders for de Valera to be released which was done.[3]

Events followed on from this release. Brigadier F. H. Viden wrote that

> ...the British Government under Lloyd George became tired of the whole affair and decided to send for de Valera, the then leader of Sinn Fein. A call from GHQ while we were at dinner one night told me to release Desmond Fitzgerald and take him immediately by car to his house in Merrion Square in Dublin. As we had not been allowed to move without an armed escort, I asked a brother officer to accompany me and we set off, each with loaded revolvers in our pockets. We arrived in Merrion Square about 10 p.m. to find a welcoming party gathered to greet Fitzgerald. Many of the Sinn Fein leaders were there including Michael Collins, on whose head up to that moment there had been a price of £20,000. We were invited in and a good time was had by all.[4]

Following the conciliatory speech of the King, in leading the way, Lloyd George felt that he could open negotiations in what would, he hoped, be perceived as a spirit of magnanimity. On June 24th, following a cabinet meeting, it was decided to send invitations to both de Valera and the Northern Ireland Minister Craig to take part in unconditional negotiations. Wily Lloyd George knew that he would hold the moral high ground if de Valera refused to meet. After an exchange of notes, de Valera, who was not to be trapped, agreed to go to London to begin talks.

It was in the interests of both sides to negotiate. From the British point of view, the war had become too costly to maintain. Public opinion in Britain was calling for an end to repression and coercion. From the Irish viewpoint, the physical defeat and eviction of British forces from Ireland was an unlikely possibility, certainly not in the near future. A truce, however, would allow time for the hard-liners to import arms to continue the war. One ship, the *Sancta Maria*, captained by Charlie McGuinness, had already secretly landed arms and ammunition in Ireland. Some 500 tommy guns had also arrived from America. Stalling for time would certainly be in the IRA's interests. Long summer days mitigated against guerrilla warfare; the darkness of winter was their ally.

De Valera took with him a delegation to London that included Austin Stack, but not, to his dismay, Michael Collins, the man that had led the country before de Valera's return. It was an obvious snub born out of jealousy. Even with his chosen delegation, de Valera chose to speak to Lloyd George on his own. The Prime Minister listed what was on offer. The new Southern Ireland state would be given the same Dominion status as Australia and Canada. It would have its own parliament, army, civil service, and control over internal affairs and taxation. However, the members of the Southern parliament would have to take an oath of allegiance to the king and his successors. A governor general would represent the king in this new Irish Free State and retain certain overriding powers. In essence, though a Dominion state, Ireland would remain little more than a colony. A truce was announced to begin on July 11, 1921, when all fighting would stop. Further negotiations would follow.

At this point, knowing full well that a republic was unobtainable, de Valera withdrew from the negotiations. In his place, he appointed Collins to continue the effort. It was a cowardly act on his part. Collins, not he, would be held responsible for the inevitable failure. After almost two months of negotiations, the British delegation presented its final offer to Collins on December 5, 1921. With it came the dreadful warning of terrible and immediate war if the proposal was not accepted. Lloyd George threatened to send a further 150,000 soldiers to Ireland. The threat was a bluff, but Collins had no way of knowing that. He signed the treaty.[5] At home the treaty was but narrowly accepted. Such words as treason were uttered before de Valera and his followers walked out of the Dail. Terrible civil war followed.

The Irish Free State, as it now became, had gained a degree of independence as a Dominion state. However, it could not be truly said that it had gained full independence. It was still subject to British oversight and had to swear allegiance to the British crown. Realistically, as Michael Collins professed, the Free State was a stepping-stone to independence. That is what it proved to be over the following two decades, when gradually British oversight was ignored and then displaced until, effectively, by 1939, the Free State was an independent republic in all but name. Ireland had shown the way, and this was to have consequences throughout the British Empire in the forty years that followed. India, Palestine, Cyprus, Nigeria, Nyasaland and the Rhodesias all gained their independence either through passive resistance or guerrilla warfare. Ireland, it could be said, was the instigator of the breakup of the British Empire.

The Republic, as it was to become, had not achieved the desired result of an independent, 32-county Irish state. Despite the fact that nearly three-quarters of the Irish population voted for independence in 1918, the country had been divided, with six of the nine counties of Ulster forming a separate government. It was a betrayal of democracy, but it was dressed up by the British as an alternative form of democracy that fulfilled the wishes of a quarter of the Irish population who wished to remain British.

From the military point of view, many British officers who had served in Ireland believed that their victory had been stolen by the British politicians who agreed to the Truce. Brigadier Frederick Clarke of the Essex Regiment voiced that notion:

> It must have been in the Autumn of 1921 that we moved back to Fort Charles. By this time we knew we were going to evacuate Southern Ireland. How we hated the idea of giving this fine old fort, which had the arms of Queen Elizabeth I carved in stone on the front wall of the officers' quarters.... Every officer and other rank felt angry and ashamed as we marched out in the dark from the fort, which had been held by British troops for about 350 years. We did not see the rabble waiting somewhere nearby to take over the fort, which they never would have captured, but the politicians had given to them.[6]

This sentiment was echoed by Major General Hawes in an unpublished autobiography that is now held in the library of the Imperial War Museum in London. He wrote:

> More and more troops were poured into Southern Ireland until there were some 100,000 of them. Techniques for quelling the rebellion were perfected and the rebellion was being subdued. HM Government chose this moment to give in. All the casualties we suffered were wasted. While it might have been wise to give Southern Ireland independence, I feel this might well have been done much earlier or kept until we had made it quite clear that we were acting from a position of strength.

Hawes and other senior officers genuinely believed that they were on the verge of victory over the IRA when the Truce was declared in July 1921. Others at the time, the politicians especially, saw the situation more clearly, for Britain had neither the coercive capability nor the political will to carry on the campaign to finality. British policy towards Ireland in the 1914–21 period had proved inept and consisted largely in refusing to take difficult decisions until forced to do so by events. The British government had failed to deliver a form of home rule acceptable to the majority of the population of Ireland, post–1918. It took far too long for them to accept that Sinn Fein was the legitimate government in the eyes of the world and that the IRA was its army. The IRA enjoyed the decisive advantage of popular support amongst the majority of the population, with the exception of six counties in Ulster and parts of County Cork, whose people were, for one reason or another, pro–British in their stances.

British Intelligence in Ireland during the period from 1914 to 1921 was a failure—though not a complete failure. It had its moments, but these were all too few. In particular was Winter's Dublin District Special Branch, which did have successes, particularly in their targeted raids which often produced a paper trail. The two police forces, the RIC and the DMP, never succeeded in obtaining worthwhile information.

Both forces failed to penetrate the armed movement as they had in the past.

The RIC did collect information during the earlier part of the war, but the intelligence was never analyzed at a local or national level and acted upon. Following the boycott of the RIC, information dried up almost completely out in the countryside. In Dublin, only a small section of the DMP's "G" Department was involved in gathering political information. Once it was destroyed by assassination and the threat of assassination, this source of information also ceased. Everything had to be relearnt by British Army Intelligence and Colonel Winter's Special Branch. Lacking experience, and being driven by time constraint to acquire intelligence, the paramilitary police resorted to brutality. Once this brutality was revealed to the British public, it brought forth a feeling of revulsion and a demand for talks.

While it is true to say that the IRA held the upper hand in intelligence during the war of independence—without it the war could not have been sustained—they had the considerable advantage of popular support for their aims, if not always for their methods, and their intelligence work was efficiently conducted. But there is also strength in numbers. The British had many thousands of troops and police to hand, and although the swarms of undercover agents in Ireland achieved little, the lack of adequate information could partly be remedied by large-scale sweeps and searches. This was how most IRA men and documents were captured and worthwhile intelligence, gathered. By the time of the Truce in July 1921, the rebels, both in Dublin and out in the country, were under extreme pressure as a result of such operations. Though it has to be said that the prospects for a decisive British victory were as slim as ever, it could be argued that the IRA, both out in the countryside and in Dublin, had won by not being defeated.

Appendix I

Intelligence Staff and The Squad

(Source: Vincent Byrne, Member of The Squad, 1919–1921, Witness Statement 423, and others.)

Intelligence

Director of Intelligence: Michael Collins
Deputy Director of Intelligence: Liam Tobin
2nd Deputy Director of Intelligence: Tom Cullen
3rd Deputy Director of Intelligence: Frank Thornton
Members: Joe Dolan, Frank Saurin, Ned Kelleher, Joe Guilfoyle, Paddy Caldwell, Paddy Kennedy, Charlie Dalton, Dan McDonnell, Charlie Byrne.

The Squad

First part-time Squad—Mick McDonnell, Tom Keogh, Jimmy Slattery, Paddy Daly, Joe Leonard, Ben Barrett, Vincent Byrne.

First full-time paid Squad—Mick McDonnell, Tom Keogh, Jimmy Slattery, Paddy Daly, Joe Leonard, Ben Barrett, Vincent Byrne, Sean Doyle, Paddy Griffin, Eddie Byrne, Mick Reilly, Jimmy Conroy.

After some time, The Squad was strengthened by the following members—Ben Byrne, Frank Bolster, Mick Keogh, Mick Kennedy, Bill Stapleton, Sam Robinson.

Other men who were out on occasions with The Squad—Dan Breen, Seamus Robinson.

Members of the Tipperary Flying Column—Sean Treacy, Sean Hogan, Mick Brennan of Clare

In 1921, The Squad numbers were brought up to twenty-one with the inclusion of Patrick Lawson and Tom McKenna. The Squad was then divided into three teams headed by Joe Leonard, Tom Keogh and Jim Slattery, with Paddy Daly in overall charge under Collins. Following the burning of the Custom House, The Squad was brought up to fifty members recruited from the Dublin ASU and was then renamed The Guard.

Active Service Units: Known Members

No. 1 SECTION	*No. 2 SECTION*	*No. 3 SECTION*	*No. 4 SECTION*
D. O'Sullivan	T. McGrath	J. Gibbons	J. McGuinness
C. Quinn	G. Gray	G. White	J. McGuinness
F. Flood	J. Heery	J. Browne	P. O'Connor
P. O'Connor	J. Gilhooly	P. Quinn	P. Rigney
J. Foy	P. Evers	C. Downey	J. Tully
J. Sliney	J. Cahill	F. Downey	I. Lillis
E. Breslin	J. Muldooney	J. Dolan	P. Mullen
S. Burke	C. Fitzsimons	M. Dowling	G. Nolan
C. Maxwell	R. Purcell	J. Hanlon	P. Collins
P. Ratcliffe	J. Gillan	P. Brunton	J. Harpur
J. Kerrigan	P. Drury	J. Doyle	M. Walshe
F. Flood	J. Caffrey	D. Jervins	I. Leigh
I. Ryan	W. Gannon	J. Carrol	M. Stack
B. Ryan	T. Bryan	W. Corry	S. McEnerney
P. Doyle	G. Nolan	W. Philips	M. Sweeney
M. McGee	J. Brown	M. Stapleton	G. Murphy
C. O'Malley		P. Larkin	A. O'Toole
M. Dunne			L. Fitzgerald
J. Carrington			P. Morrisey
M. Kerrigan			
P. Flanagan			
J. O'Connor			

Appendix II

Known or Suspected British Agents

A list compiled from entries in the *London Gazette*, and new pay grades awarded (Class II) to officers "specially employed." Based, with some slight amendments, on David Grant's david@corisande.com website, for which the author duly acknowledges this source of information.

The establishment of D. Branch consisted of:

1 District Agent, Grade FF—20 shillings per day
5 Chief Agents, Grade GG—15 shillings per day
3 Departmental Agents, Grade GG—15 shillings per day
15 Sub Agents Grade HH—12shillings & 6 pence per day
75 Agents, Grade II—10 shillings per day.

Senior Staff in Ireland

Brigadier General J. E. S. Brind, GHQ Intelligence Staff, Dublin Castle
Colonel S. Hill-Dillon, Assistant Chief of GHQ Intelligence Staff
L.H. Kitton, GHQ Staff
R.T. Lee, GHQ Staff
L. G. Whistler, GHQ Staff
Major General Hugh Tudor, Chief of Police
Brigadier General Ormonde Winter, Deputy Chief of Police
Colonel H. E. Rawson, Military Intelligence
Lieutenant W. Wilson, Chief of Special Branch, Dublin

Junior Officers

Shrove, FH	Boddington, HF	Arrowsmith, CF	Attwood, P.	Carew, H.
Carpenter, PWH.	Hyem, EP	Newton, CB	Noble, W.	Thorp, AF

Kershaw, JV	Porters, AG	Whistler, LG	Bell, JW	Bennett, G
Blake, FAA	Cust, LGA	Halestrap, AE	Michael, T deW	Price, GA
Small, EA	Stokes, LES	White, AP	Woolley, J	Young, SCG
Adcock, –	Alexander, CB	Ames, PA	Anderton, A	Barclay, Lrde
Barclay, Shaw	Bessell, JH	Biggs, TW	Bodger, EG	Breen, EG
Buckton, FE	Carruthers, GJ	Casey, GH	Carter, AH	Coles, WT
Colley, CH	Coltman, JR	Curtis, DCM	Deacon, WH	Debny, RM
DeSarigny, V	Dowling, CMC	DuBouley, GGH	Feary, S	Fitzpatrick, CP
Fitch, CG	Foley, CP	Gallaher, WM	Garrad, FW	Griffin, LTM
Gunnis, RGS	Haywood, J	Howell, E	Jameson, ARL	Jeune, RD
Jeffries, WF	Langrishe, TH	Lawes, EH	Leigh-Bennett, R	LeGrand, CW
leGrand, WS	Leeming, TS	Lewis, WA	Licence, JH	Maclean, DL
MacSweeney, D	Melville, BD	Minish, HW	Montmorency, H	Mules, PA
Murray, RG	O'Donnell, D	Osborne, HE	Palmer, LSN	Peel, CR
Price, LP	Rogers, JDS	Rhodes, BB	Sarigny, VMCB	Searle, CJB
Shiner, EEJ	Stubbs, EE	Sugden, GT	Tanqueray, JFD	Taylor, GS
Tew, CCB	Tottie, R	Ward, FJ	Ware, WIB	Williams, S
Wooldridge, GdeB	Lees, CHE			

Appendix III

Known or Suspected Touts

Officers Killed or Wounded by the IRA

(Percy) William Straw was killed on October 21, 1920. An Englishman of no visible means of support, he was lodging in rooms above a fish shop in Quay Street, Balbriggan. On the night of September 20, 1920, two Black and Tans, District Inspector Burke and his brother Sergeant Burke, were killed by a unit of the North Dublin Brigade as they left Smith's Bar in the Square, Balbriggan. As a reprisal, the Tans burnt the town. Straw was seen to direct them. It was claimed that he pointed out the houses of families connected with IRA members. Two suspected IRA men, James Lawless and John Gibbons, were murdered. Straw was picked up by the IRA and taken to nearby Dempsey's mill where he was court-martialed and shot by Volunteers Dan Brothy and Joe Kelly. Prior to his execution he was asked if he had anything to say. He replied, "No, when I undertook this mission I was fully aware of what the end might be and now I accept my fate without complaint." To prevent Black and Tan reprisals, his body was buried in a shallow grave. Following heavy rains his body was exposed and recovered. He had been shot in the body and in the head. Straw had served as a captain in the British Army during World War I. Joe Leonard of The Squad, in his Witness Statement, gives a full account of the events leading to his execution. It is possible that Straw was more than just a tout.

John Ryan, was killed on February 5, 1921. A former lance corporal in the British Army, Ryan, in the notices of his death in the newspaper, is referred to as a "military foot policeman." He had followed Dick McKee and Peader Clancy, then notified British Intelligence where they were staying, information that lead to the arrest, torture and murder of both. About 10.30 a.m., February 5th, Ryan was tracked down to Hynes' public house in Old Gloucester Place. A team from The Squad—Bill Stapleton, Eddie Byrnes and Paddy Kennedy—entered the pub, where they saw Ryan reading a newspaper. He was held up and asked his name, which he confirmed was Ryan. With that he was shot dead. Bernard C. Byrne in his Witness Statement gives a detailed record of events.

Patrick O'Neill, an ex–British Army captain, was wounded but survived the attack at his lodgings at 38, Heytesbury Street, off the South Circular Road not far from St. Stephen's Green. The attack happened shortly before 10 a.m. on April 15, 1921. O'Neill was living in a basement room of the house. An unidentified IRA man knocked at the door of the house and requested to see Captain O'Neill. As the landlady went off to find him, the gunman descended the steps to the basement. As O'Neill looked out from the window, the gunman fired and wounded him in the shoulder. O'Neill was taken to King George V Hospital where he recovered.

Peter Graham, a 23-year-old from Kingstown (Dun Laoghaire), was shot and killed on the golf links at Killiney, County Dublin on May 15, 1921. Attached to his body was a sheet of paper with the words "Convicted spy, tried and found guilty by IRA." He was shot five times to the head and body. The perpetrators, five in number, left by a car. His family were awarded £500 compensation.

Patrick Joseph Dunney, a corporal, invalided out of the Machine Gun Corps, was shot on May 18, 1921. He had been gathering intelligence in Wicklow, having established contact with both Cumann na mBan and the local branch of Sinn Fein. His information was relayed to a "Mr. Cross in Ballycorus." Suspected of being a spy, a friendly soldier by the name of Roper revealed to IRA man Patrick J. Brennan that Dunney was a sergeant of the Royal Garrison Artillery stationed at Tallaght, Co. Dublin and was living at Inchicore. "He said he never wore uniform and he understood that he had a telephone in the house. I had the information about this man conveyed to Michael Collins direct and, to the best of my knowledge, he was found shot some time later in a field at Inchicore." He was executed by members of 4th Battalion ASU. The local newspapers revealed that, "There were bullet wounds in the head and chest, and a handkerchief had been tied over the eyes."

Stephen Arthur Bardon, a single man, aged 40, was the son of a policeman. He was shot dead near Featherstonehaugh while riding his bicycle on the way to work at the Guinness brewery on May 19, 1921.

He suffered several bullet wounds to the head.

Leslie Fraser was an ex-Irish Guardsman. He was shot on May 22, 1921, outside Walsh's public house in Stoneybatter, Dublin. He was 24 years old. Leaving the pub with a drinking companion, he was confronted by a young man, who told the companion to go away. The young man then drew a revolver and shot Fraser several times in the body and then to the head. The gunman was assisted in his getaway by several companions. Still alive, Frazer was taken to Richmond Hospital, and an armed guard was placed around the building. Frazer died later that night.

John Ellard Brady and Thomas Halpin, both former soldiers in the British Army. They were killed on June 4, 1921. In his Witness Statement, Frank Saurin of Irish Intelligence recorded:

> Brady and Halpin were shot in Clontarf just before the Truce. This was an F Company, 2nd Battalion job. Brady ...[who] had been in the sacking of Balbriggan was the principal target ...Brady was sitting on the sea wall opposite St. Lawrence Road, Clontarf, in company with two men, Halpin and Denver, when the F Company man cycled up and shot dead both Brady and Halpin. Halpin was an ex–British Navy A.B., and it is open to question whether he deserved to be shot. To the best of my recollection Brady was concerned in getting local information for the Black and Tans.

Charles Dalton of Irish Intelligence added: "They had been acting as touts in conveying information to the Crown forces."

Robert Pike, alias "Bow tie," was shot outside Fagan's public house, Drumcondra, on June 18, 1921. Charles Dalton wrote of him:

> He was a member of the tinker class and lived in Tolka Cottages, Drumcondra. I believe he was an ex-soldier who had been in the world war, and he was conveying information to the Crown forces. There was an unconfirmed statement that he had reported on Dan Breen's and Sean Treacy's movements from Fleming's of Drumcondra to Fernside.

Andrew Knight, a tramway inspector operating on the line to Dalkey, County Dublin. He was taken off a tram and led away to Killiney Golf Course, where he was executed on July 7, 1921. He was shot to the body and the neck. In his Witness Statement to the Bureau of Military History, Constable Patrick Mannix of the DMP, working for Irish Intelligence, recorded:

> I supplied information that Andrew Knight, a tram Inspector on the Dalkey line was a very active anti–IRA and that he was supplying information about IRA activities to the British military. As a result of the information supplied, he was taken off a tramcar by the IRA and taken out to Killiney Golf Links, where he was shot. In his pockets were found cheques for information he had given to the British. A search was made in his residence in Clarinda Park and in his box was found a list of names of members of the IRA.

The British Government awarded £1250 to Knight's family in a compensation claim.

Appendix IV

British Secret Service Men and Others Assassinated or Wounded on November 21, 1920

A list compiled from Frank Thornton's Witness Statement (W.S. 615), and other Witness Statements of those who took part. The names of known Secret Service agents are starred (*).

Gresham Hotel, Upper O'Connell Street
Targets: Captain Patrick McCormack and Lt. Leonard Aidan William Wilde
IRA team: Patrick Moran (O.C.), Michael Kilkelly, James Foley, Arthur Beasley, Paddy Kennedy, Michael Noone, Nicholas Leonard, James Cahill, Joseph Glynn, John Cullinane, William Hogan, Richard McGrath.
Killed: Capt. McCormack and Lt. Wilde*.

28, Earlsfort Terrace
Target: Captain John Fitzgerald.
IRA team: Seven men (names unknown).
Killed: Capt. Fitzgerald.

Fitzwilliam Square
Target: Major O'Callaghan.
IRA team: Unknown.

38, Upper Mount Street
Targets: Lt. Peter Ashmun Ames and Lt. George Bennett
IRA team: Vincent Byrne (O.C.), Frank Saurin (I.O.), Tom Ennis, John Daly, John Doyle, Herbert Conroy, Tom Duffy, Michael Lawless, John McDonnell, William Maher.
Killed: Lt. Ames* and Lt. Bennett*.

22, Lower Mount Street
Targets: Lt. Henry James Angliss (A.K.A. Patrick McMahon) and Lt. Charles Ratsch Peel
IRA team: Tom Keogh, Jim Slattery, Frank Teeling, Denis Begley, Andy Monaghan, Jim Dempsey, William McLean.
Killed: Lt. Angliss*.

92, Lower Baggot Street
Target: Capt. William Frederick Newberry
IRA team: Joe Leonard (O.C), William Stapleton, Jack Stafford, Hugo MacNeill.
Killed: Capt. Newberry.

119, Lower Baggott Street
Target: Capt. Geoffrey Thomas Baggallay
IRA team: Matthew McDonald, Sean Lemass, James Brennan, Jack Keating, Jack Foley
Killed: Capt. Baggallay.

117, Morehampton Road
Targets: Lieutenant Donald Lewis MacLean, Thomas Herbert Smith and John Caldow.
IRA team: Six men from K Company, 3rd Battalion, including Jimmy & Sean Doyle.
Killed: Lt. MacLean* and Thomas Smith.

28, Upper Pembroke Street
Targets: Colonel Montgomery, Colonel Woodcock, Major Charles Milne Dowling, Capt. Leonard Price, Capt. Keenlyside, Lt. Murray.
IRA team: Paddy Flanagan, Charles Dalton (I.O.), George White, Michael O'Hanlon, Andy Cooney, Leo Dunne, Ned Kelliher, Joseph O'Carroll
Killed: Col. Montgomery, Major Dowling* and Capt. Price*.

Eastwood Hotel, 91-2, Lower Leeson Street
Target: Lt. Colonel Jennings.
IRA team: Ned Bennett (O.C.), Christopher Byrne, Joe McGuinness, Jim McGuinness, Pat O'Connor, George Dwyer, Jim Donnelly.

7, Ranelagh Road
Target: Lt. William Noble.
IRA team: Joe Dolan, Dan McDonnell, Todd Andrews, James Kenny, Francis Burke, Francis X. Coughlan, Hubert Earle.

Hume Street off St. Stephen's Green.
Target: "Mr. Clevedon."
IRA team: Unknown.
Details are taken from James Gleeson's *Bloody Sunday*.

Collateral Damage
Lt. Frank Garniss and Cecil A. Morris, Auxiliary R.I.C., taken prisoner and shot in the garden of 16, Northumberland Road. John Caldow (a civilian?), wounded at 119, Morehampton Road.

Known Additional Addresses Visited

Church Road
Men from the 2nd Battalion. Target not there.

Exchequer Hotel, Exchequer St.
Men from the 4th Battalion. Unable to find target.

Fitzwilliam Square
Major Cecil Callaghan, the target, was not at home. Captain John Scot Crawford, who was there, was not shot because he was not on the List.

Harcourt St.
Captain Jocelyn Lee Hardy was not at home.
Major William King not at home.

84, Lower Baggot St.
Men from 2nd Battalion. Targets not there.

North Circular Rd.
Two targets, but mission aborted.

Northumberland Rd.
Men from 3rd Battalion. Targets not there.

Shelbourne Hotel
Mission aborted.

Standard Hotel
Men from the 4th Battalion. Targets not at home.

Appendix V

Members of G. Division, Dublin Metropolitan Police, Shot and Killed by The Squad

1. July 30, 1919: Detective Sergeant Patrick Smyth, shot near Drumcondra, Dublin.
2. September 12, 1919: Detective Sergeant Daniel Hoey.
3. October 19, 1919: Detective Michael Downing.
4. November 29, 1919: Detective Sergeant John Barton.
5. January 21, 1920: RIC District Inspector William C. Forbes Redmond, seconded to G. Division, DMP.
6. April 14, 1920: Detective Constable Harry Kells, Camden Street, Portobello, Dublin.
7. April 20, 1920: Detective Laurence Dalton.

Chapter Notes

Introduction

1. G. Division, Dublin Metropolitan Police, was divided into three sections—political, routine crime, and transport. It was run from two offices, one at 1, Great Brunswick Street (now Pearse Street), and the other at Dublin Castle. The political section existed for the countering and supervision of all national movements directed against the British administration. Methodical observations were kept on all suspects deemed as being disloyal to Britain. Their files were marked with a large "S" denoting suspect. The total strength of G. Division was about forty, the majority of whom were married and living out in the city. Those unmarried resided in the barracks at No. 1, Great Brunswick Street. G Men were selected from the uniformed service from those who had at least three years' service. If several suspects were to be arrested at the same time, G. Division called upon the assistance of the uniformed police; for very big operations, the British military were called upon. At the end of 1915, G. Division evacuated their premises at Exchange Court and moved to a new building at No. 1, Great Brunswick Street, occupying the end portion of the building nearer D'Olier Street, while the remainder of the building was occupied by B. Division, the uniformed service. In 1919, the political branch moved into Dublin Castle.

2. The officer in charge of the G Men, who removed the Volunteer leaders from the ranks, was Owen "Butt" Brien. "Brien was about five feet high and perhaps three in girth. He had a round closed pussy-cat's face and little piggy eyes. Weighing about fourteen stone he had suave oily manners.... Seeing that G-men were recruited solely from uniform it was astonishing how he got in owing to his lack of height and more astonishing that he had attained his present rank." David Neligan, *The Spy in the Castle*, p. 59.

3. Colonel Eamon Broy, Intelligence Agent, Witness Statement 1280, p. 50.

4. Tim Pat Coogan, *Michael Collins: A Biography*, p. 81.

5. Joseph Good, Kimmage Garrison, Bureau of Military History, Witness Statement 388.

6. Margaret Skinnider, *Doing My Bit for Ireland*, p. 25.

7. Seumas Daly, Volunteer, 2nd Battalion, Witness Statement 360.

8. Mulcahy Papers P7/D/60.

9. Dorothy Macardle, *The Irish Republic*, p. 234.

10. Eamon Broy, Witness Statement 1280, p. 71.

11. Tom Barry, *Guerilla Days in Ireland*, p. 81.

12. Dan Breen, *My Fight for Irish Freedom*, 1964, pp. 55–6.

13. *An tOglach,* January 31, 1919.

14. James Gleeson, *Bloody Sunday*, p. 36.

Chapter 1

1. Nicholas Laffan, Witness Statement 203.

2.

3. George Fitzgerald, Witness Statement 684.

4. Edward Dolan, Witness Statement 1078.

5. Tom Scully, Witness Statement 491.

6. Gary Houlihan [Holohan], Witness Statement 328.
7. George Fitzgerald, Witness Statement 684.
8. Evelyn Lawless, Witness Statement 414.

Chapter 2

1. Report by Basil Thomson, "On the Organization of Intelligence in Ireland." *French Papers*, 75/46/12, Imperial War Museum.
2. House of Lords Record Office, G.O.C. *Ireland to Prime Minister*, 79/Irish/195 War Office 32/4307.
3. *Parliamentary Papers* (1921), pp. xxix, 444–51.
4. House of Lords Record Office, *Strachey Papers*, S/21/2/6 p.366.
5. Military Intelligence Report, Nov. 1917, National Archive, C.O 904/157.
6. *French Papers*, Imperial War Museum, 75/46/3.
7. *Ibid.* 75/46/13.
8. Military Intelligence Report, October 1917, C.O. 904/157.

Chapter 3

1. As early as May 1918, Michael Collins was involved in parallel intelligence gathering. Piaras Beaslai states, "But Michael Collins still continued working in the same direction, though he was at the time adjutant general and director of organisation—two most exacting positions." *How It Was done—IRA Intelligence* (Dublin's Fighting Story, p. 378).
2. The Dail Loan Scheme was inaugurated to finance Dail Eireann and the services it provided. The British government viewed it as illegal in that it was financing an illegal government in opposition to the British government.
3. Colonel Eamon Broy, Witness Statement 1280, p. 70.
4. Eamon Duggan (1874–1936) went on to become Judge Advocate General. He was arrested by the Auxiliaries on November 25, 1920. Duggan was later part of the Irish negotiating team at the time of the Treaty. Mulcahy described him as a "logical negotiator."
5. Joe Leonard, Squad Member, Witness Statement 547, p. 8.
6. David Neligan, *The Spy in the Castle*, p. 71.
7. Frank Thornton, Deputy Assistant Director of Intelligence, Witness Statement 615, p. 1.
8. Charles Dalton, *With the Dublin Brigade*, p. 206. Colonel J. V. Joyce of Beggar's Bush Barracks also drew up a list of those employed in the Irish Intelligence Branch in his 1959 Witness Statement (W.S. 1,762). See Appendix 1.
9. Charles Dalton, pp. 94–5.
10. Patrick Kennedy, Irish Intelligence, Witness Statement 499, p. 1.
11. Piaras Beaslai, pp. 379–80.
12. Frank Thornton, pp. 3–4.
13. The Auxiliaries arrived in Ireland in July 1920 to supplement the existing British forces. They were a *corps d'elite* of ex-officers and were paid £1 a day. They were divided up into fifteen companies of one hundred men each and spread throughout Ireland. Five companies, C, D, E, F, and Q, were based in Dublin.
14. Frank Saurin, Intelligence Officer, Witness Statement 715, p. 2.
15. Eamon Broy, Witness Statement 1280, p. 74.
16. *Ibid.*
17. Broy, p. 97.
18. Broy, Witness Statement 1285, pp. 16–17.
19. Tom Barry, *Guerilla Days in Ireland*, p. 178.
20. Charles Dalton, *With the Dublin Brigade*, p. 125.
21. Beaslai, p. 378. Tim Pat Coogan, *Michael Collins*, p. 107.
22. Coogan, p. 82.
23. Lily Mernin, Shorthand Typist, Dublin Castle, Witness Statement 441, p. 1. Elizabeth Mernin (Lily) was born in Dungarvin, Co. Waterford, on November 16, 1886. She proved to be one of Collins' most important agents within Dublin Castle. She was known to other members of Irish Intelligence under her alias of the "Little Gentleman." Mernin was the cousin of Piaras Beaslai and worked closely with Frank Saurin and Tom Cullen. She identified the names and addresses of the British agents assassinated on November 21, 1920. Undiscovered, Mernin continued to work as a shorthand typist for the British up to February 1922. She was then employed by

the Irish Army from July 1922 until her retirement in February 1952. Mernin was awarded a military service pension for her work for Irish Intelligence between 1918 and 1921. Although unmarried, she gave birth to a son in London in June 1922. Circumstantial evidence suggests that the father was Piaras Beaslai. Lily Mernin resided at 167, Mangerton Road, Drimnagh. She died in Dublin on February 18, 1957. See: Marie Coleman's entry for her in the Royal Irish Academy's *Dictionary of Irish Biography.*

24. Richard Bennett, in his 1959 (reprinted in 2007) book, *The Black and Tans*, p. 102, not having the benefit of the later released Witness Statements, believed "Lt. G" to be a "mysterious British Intelligence officer."
25. Mernin, p. 2.
26. Mernin, p. 4.
27. David Neligan, G. Division, DMP, Witness Statement 380, pp. 2–3.
28. *Ibid.*, p. 4.
29. Peter Forlan, Head Constable RIC, Witness Statement 316, pp. 7–8.
30. Statement of Sergeant Mannix which appears in Frank Thornton's Witness Statement, 615, p. 18. See also, Mannix's Statement 502, p. 2, for a less detailed account.
31. *A Record of the Rebellion in Ireland in 1920–21, and the Part Played by the Army in Dealing with It (Intelligence)*, Sir Hugh Jeudwine Papers, 72/82/2. Imperial War Museum. See also: *Irish Narratives*, edited by Peter Hart, 2002. p. 45.
32. Charles Dalton, *With the Dublin Brigade*, p. 96.
33. Sean Kavanagh, Schoolteacher, Witness Statement 524, p. 2.
34. Kavanagh, p. 2.
35. Liam Archer, GHQ Intelligence, Witness Statement 819, p. 18.
36. Frank Thornton, p. 8.
37. Patrick Kennedy, GHQ Intelligence, Witness Statement 499, p. 3.
38. Joseph Dolan, GHQ Intelligence, Witness Statement 663, pp. 3–4.
39. Charles McQuaille, Witness Statement 276, pp. 4–5.
40. Vincent Byrne, The Squad, Witness Statement 423.
41. Kennedy, p. 4.
42. Liam Archer, Irish Intelligence, Witness Statement 819, p. 19.
43. Sister Eithne (Eveleen Lawless), Secretary to Michael Collins, Witness Statement 414, p. 5.
44. Coogan, p. 122.

Chapter 4

1. Bernard C. Byrne, Member of the Squad, Witness Statement 631 p. 2.
2. Broy, p. 80.
3. Paddy Daly claimed that Collins initially appointed four full-time Squad members, Daly himself (as leader), Joe Leonard, Ben Barrett and Sean Doyle. Daly was, in fact, appointed as leader of the later reformed, salaried Squad. Vincent Byrne (Witness Statement 423, p. 33) lists the original and the second, full-time Squad. The names are at variance with Daly's listing. See Appendix 1.
4. James Slattery, F Company, 2nd Battalion, Dublin Brigade, Witness Statement 445, p. 2.
5. Vincent Byrne, member of the Squad, Witness Statement 423, pp. 34–5.
6. William Stapleton, The Squad, Witness Statement 822.
7. Lt. Patrick Lawson, The Squad, Witness Statement 667, p. 12.
8. Commandant Frank Henderson, Witness Statement 821, p.62.
9. Broy, p.80.
10. Neligan, David, *The Spy in the Castle*, pp. 49–50.
11. Liam Archer, Irish Intelligence, Witness Statement 819, p. 20.
12. Bernard C. Byrne, Member of the Squad, Witness Statement 631, pp. 32–3.
13. *Ibid.* p. 33.
14. Vincent Byrne, Witness Statement 423, p.44–45.
15. Ulrick O'Connor, *A Terrible Beauty Is Born*, p.124.
16. Slattery, p. 5.
17. Eamon Broy, DMP., Witness Statement 1280, p. 82.
18. *Freeman's Journal*, August 12, 1919.
19. Tim Pat Coogan, *Michael Collins: A Biography*, p. 118.
20. James Slattery, Witness Statement 445, p. 6.
21. Neligan, p. 51.
22. *Irish Times*, September 9, 1919.
23. Sister Eithne (Eveleen Lawless),

Secretary to Michael Collins, Witness Statement 414, p. 2.
24. Broy, Witness Statement 1285, p. 24.
25. William Stapleton, The Squad, Witness Statement 822.
26. The quote is taken from T. Ryle Dwyer's book, *The Squad*, p. 61. In his bibliography he lists the Witness Statements of Patrick O'Daly, 220 and 368. W.S. 220 only goes up as far as the Easter Rising. W.S. 368 is that of Sean McGarry. Michael T. Foy, in his *Michael Collins's Intelligence War*, lists his source as Paddy Daly W.S. 814. This reference relates to another Paddy Daly, who was an IRA gunrunner in Liverpool and Glasgow. A search through the Witness Statements has failed to discover the source of the quote. The friendly detective may well have been Sergeant Joseph Kavanagh.
27. Joe Leonard, Witness Statement 547, pp. 3–4.
28. Vincent Byrne, The Squad, Witness Statement 423, p.12.
29. Bernard C. Byrne, Witness statement 631, pp. 2–3.
30. *Ibid.*, p.14.
31. Bernard C. Byrne, The Squad, Witness Statement 631, p. 4.
32. *Ibid.*
33. Eamon Broy, Witness Statement 1285, p. 22.
34. *Irish Times*, December 22, 1919.
35. The gang are credited with having fired the first shots of the War of Independence. Richard Mulcahy was appalled at the operation. Michael Collins appeared to be grateful that the war had begun. He was always on good terms with Dan Breen.
36. Vincent Byrne, pp. 17–18.
37. Charles Dalton, *With the Dublin Brigade*, p. 76.
38. Neligan, p. 64.
39. Frank Thornton, Witness Statement 615, p. 36.
40. Joseph Dolan, Witness Statement 663, p. 2.
41. Sister Eithne (Eveleen Lawless) Secretary to Michael Collins, Witness Statement 414, pp. 6–7.
42. Liam Archer, GHQ Intelligence staff, Witness Statement 819, pp. 18–19.
43. Neligan, pp. 68–9.
44. Vincent Byrne, Witness statement 423, p. 42.
45. Byrne, p.43.
46. Dan Breen, *My Fight for Irish Freedom*, pp. 126–7.
47. Gleeson, *Bloody Sunday*, pp. 102–3. "Private source." There's a strong probability that the spy was G. Man Ned Broy, though he makes no claim to the killing in his two Witness Statement Accounts to the Bureau of Military History.
48. Neligan, p. 107.
49. Caufield, Max, *The Easter Rebellion*, p. 354.
50. Tim Pat Coogan, *Michael Collins: A Biography*, p. 45.
51. Eamon Dore, Witness Statement 153, p. 7.
52. Edward Balfe, Acting O/C, Wexford Brigade, Witness Statement 1373, p. 9.
53. Frank Thornton, Deputy Assistant Director of Intelligence, Witness Statement 615, p. 43.
54. Balfe, pp. 8–9.
55. Townsend, Charles, *The British Campaign in Ireland 1919–1921*, pp. 41–2.

Chapter 5

1. David Neligan, *The Spy in the Castle*, p. 93.
2. Imperial War Museum, *French Papers*, MSS/45/12.
3. *A Record of the Rebellion in Ireland in 1920–21 and the Part Played by the Army in Dealing with It* (Intelligence). Sir Hugh Jeudwine Papers, 72/82/2. Imperial War Museum. Featured in Peter Hart [ed], *British Intelligence in Ireland 1920–21*, p. 58.
4. Hart, p. 23.
5. For more on this campaign see: Joseph McKenna, *The Irish-American Dynamite Campaign*.
6. Long Papers, 947/348.
7. *Report of the Committee of Inquiry into the Detective Organisation of the Irish Police Forces 7th Dec. 1919.*, French Papers, 75/46/12.
8. For a list of touts discovered and shot in Dublin, see Appendix.
9. Neligan, p. 64.
10. Tim Pat Coogan, *Michael Collins: A Biography*, suggests a different wartime history for Byrne: "He had worked in intelligence in India before the First

World War and during it somehow managed to elude detection in Germany."

11. Frank Thornton, Irish Intelligence, Witness Statement 615, p. 38.

12. Isham appears to have been dismissed and reduced in rank from Lieutenant Colonel, to his former rank of Lieutenant, with the commensurate reduction in pay. Senior Civil Servant Mark Sturgis, appears to be referring to him in a diary entry July 27, 1920: "No. 37, whom I saw in London, is giving trouble and I tackled 'O' about him. The Army has done with him and they say over paid him and 'O' doesn't want him at any price so he is turned off." 'O' is the code-name of Brigadier General Ormonde de l'Epee Winter, Chief of Police and Director of Intelligence in Ireland from May 1920.

13. Bell's report, PRO. CO 904/188/1

14. Bell's report, PRO, CO 904/188/1

15. Frank O'Connor, *My Father's Son*, p. 116.

16. Joseph Dolan, GHQ Intelligence, Witness Statement 663, p.10.

17. Tim Pat Coogan, *Michael Collins: A Biography*, pp. 130–1.

18. Dolan, p. 11.

19. In his official records—his "Soldiers Effects"—his father's name is given as James McNulty. Molloy might also have been operating under the alias of "Private Smith," the name given of a man shot in Dublin on March 24, 1920, the same day as Molloy.

20. Neligan, p. 2.

21. Vincent Byrne, Member of the Squad, Witness Statement 423, p. 37.

22. *Ibid*.

23. Neligan, p. 72.

24. Byrne, p. 46.

25. James Slattery, The Squad, Witness Statement 445, p. 9.

26. Michael Hopkinson [Ed.], *The Last Days of Dublin Castle*, p. 15. George Frank Brooke, shot dead on July 30, 1920, was Chairman of the Dublin & South-Eastern Railway. He had been a member of Lord French's Advisory Council, and a member of the Irish Privy Council. The implication was that he was also apparently part of a three-man team, consisting of himself, Alan Bell, spymaster appointed by Basil Thomson, and Detective Inspector W. C. Forbes Redmond, who arranged the assassination of Sinn Fein organizers.

Chapter 6

1. William Sheehan, *British Voices*, Dublin District Historical Record, p. 11.

2. *Dictionary of National Biography*, Sir John Anderson's entry written by Lord Salter.

3. Sheehan, p. 151.

4. Michael Noyk, solicitor, Witness Statement 707. Colonel Herbert Edward Rawson (1852–1924) was born in Port Louis, Mauritius, in September 1852. He was educated at Winchester College before attending Sandhurst. He was commissioned into the Royal Engineers and saw service in South Africa during the Boer War. Rawson played football for his regiment against Oxford University in the 1874 F.A. Cup Final, his team losing 2–0. In 1875, Rawson, alongside his brother William, was selected to play for England against Scotland, resulting in a 2–2 draw. Rawson served in the Royal Engineers during World War I. He appears to have been seconded to Military Intelligence and served in Ireland. Rawson died in England in October 1924.

5. K. Strong, *Intelligence at the Top: Recollections of an Intelligence Officer*, p. 5.

6. *Captain R. D. Jeune Papers*, Imperial War Museum.

7. Cameron and his wife Ruby were jailed for three years in May 1911 for fraud, regarding the alleged theft of a pearl necklace, recently insured for £6,500. Released in September 1914, Cameron rejoined the British Army, serving in France during World War I, gaining prominence in Military Intelligence by 1918. After service in Ireland, he retired due to ill health and committed suicide on August 18, 1924.

8. Sheehan, pp. 187–8.

9. *The Diary of Private J. P. Swindlehurst*, Imperial War Museum. Reprinted in William Sheehan, *British Voices*, p.2 6. "Tommy," short for Tommy Atkins, was the nickname for the lower ranks of the British Army. The name first appeared about 1743.

10. Kathleen Napoli MacKenna, unpublished memoir. Tim Pat Coogan, *Michael Collins: A Biography*, p. 150.

11. The Auxiliary's Story, in James Gleeson's *Bloody Sunday*, p. 77. The Auxiliary officer has been identified as William Munro.

12. Swindlehurst Diary, January 16, 1921.
13. Uinseann MacEoin, ed., *Survivors*. Argenta, Dublin, 1987, p. 317.
14. Ernie O'Malley, *On Another Man's Wound*. Anvil Books, 2002, p. 273.
15. Frank Thornton, Deputy Assistant Director of Intelligence, Witness Statement 615. John Shaw Reynolds, formerly a captain in the South Staffordshire Regiment, later went on to become a colonel in the Irish Free State Army.
16. Patrick Kennedy, Irish Intelligence, Witness Statement 499.
17. There is confusion over the "Cairo Gang," the origin of the name, and the men assassinated on Bloody Sunday. The men in the photograph are the Intelligence section of F Company of the Auxiliaries based in Dublin Castle. They are not the same men targeted on Bloody Sunday who were from British Military Intelligence. It seems more likely, given that two members of F Company were targeted near Café Cairo, on June 24, 1921, that this is the origin of the name, first put forward in the 1950s. The two men were L. G. Appleford, No. 6 in the photograph, who was wounded, and George Warnes, not included in the photograph, who was killed. Irish Intelligence at the time referred to these Auxiliaries as "the Special Ones."
18. Lily Mernin, Witness Statement 441.
19. Kathleen Napoli MacKenna, *Capuchin Annual*, 1970.
20. *A Record of the Rebellion in Ireland in 1920–21, and the Part Played by the Army in Dealing with it (Intelligence)*. Sir Hugh Jeudwine Papers, Imperial War Museum 72/82/2. Reproduced in *Irish Narratives*, edited by Peter Hart.
21. *Ibid*. p. 23.
22. *A Record of the Rebellion*, pp. 45–6.
23. George Fitzgerald, A Company, 1st Battalion, Dublin Brigade, Witness Statement 684, p. 34.
24. Wilson Diary, 7th July 1920, Wilson Papers, Imperial War Museum.
25. Charles Townsend, *The British Campaign in Ireland 1919–1921*, p. 101.
26. The Customs House contained the records relating to the financing and administration of British government departments in Ireland. Authorized by Eamon de Valera, on May 25, 1921, it was attacked by a large party of IRA and Irish Citizen Army men and set on fire. Desperately short of ammunition—the covering party had barely five rounds each—they came under attack from several units of the Auxiliaries. In the battle that followed six IRA men were killed, twelve were wounded, and some seventy men were captured.

Chapter 7

1. Michael Hopkinson, *The Last Days of Dublin Castle: The Diaries of Mark Sturgis*, p. 32.
2. "Periscope," *The Last Days of Dublin Castle, Blackwood's Magazine*, August 1922, pp. 166–7.
3. William James Stapleton, The Squad, Witness Statement 822.
4. Incredibly, at first, serving officers seconded intelligence work in Ireland were listed in the official section of the *London Gazette* with "Special Appointment" added to their name.
5. *A Record of the Rebellion*, p 6.
6. "It is not, however, easy to recruit people for this work and, during a period of some eight or nine months, only sixty, in all, were obtained and transported to Ireland. Of these, many proved unsatisfactory and had to be discarded. One, the notorious Mr. Digby Hardy, had proved himself a villain of the first water… Michael Collins, who denounced him, in front of a lot of journalists, as "the spy unmasked." Ormonde Winter, *A Report on the Intelligence Branch of the Chief of Police, Dublin Castle*, p. 79. F. Digby Hardy's real name was J. L. Gooding. He was a career criminal usually specializing in fraud. While serving a five-year sentence he wrote to Lord French offering to work as a secret service man against the IRA. He was released, then sent for training at the London spy school, before being sent to Ireland. He was put in touch with Arthur Griffith and offered to lure Sir Basil Thomson to Kingstown where he could be murdered. Griffith asked him to attend a secret meeting where he was exposed as a British spy.
7. Captain Leslie Holbrook Kitton M.C. (1894–1978), Royal Scottish

Regiment. On January 28, 1920, he temporarily relinquished his commission while he was "specially employed" (a euphemism for Intelligence work). In the New Year's Honours of 1923, he was awarded the MBE. He is listed in the Irish section of the recipients of honours, which seems appropriate.

8. Bernard C. Byrne, Squad member, Witness Statement 631, p. 25.
9. Hopkinson, p. 60.
10. Ernie O'Malley, *Bloody Sunday*, in *Dublin's Fighting Story*, p. 292.
11. Mark Sturgis, *Diaries*, p. 180.
12. *British Voices*, p. 21.
13. Joseph McGuinness ASU 4th Battalion, Witness Statement 607, p. 10.
14. George Nolan, ASU 4th Battalion, Witness Statement 596, p. 5.
15. Hopkinson, p. 184.
16. *Winter's Tale*, p. 304.
17. *A Record of the Rebellion*, p. 35. The IRA Director of Intelligence referred to was, in fact, the former intelligence chief, Eamonn Duggan. At various times Liam Tobin, Tom Cullen and Frank Thornton were all detained or arrested, but later freed through lack of evidence, and more particularly through lack of photographs or informers to identify them.
18. M. S. Allen, *The Pioneer Policewomen*, Chatto & Windus, London, 1925, p. 60.
19. Richard Bennett, *The Black and Tans*, p. 44.
20. *A Report of the Intelligence Branch of the Chief of Police*, p. 65.
21. *Ibid.* pp. 86–7.

Chapter 8

1. Lt. Col. Wilson's original Special Branch team consisted of Major Carew, Captains: H. F. Boddington, P. Carpenter, and A. Thorpe; Lieutenants: W. Noble, P. Atwood, and P. Hyem.
2. Neligan, *The Spy in the Castle*, p. 91. The name "Count Sevigne" was the *nom de guerre*, as Neligan reveals in his Witness Statement (380, p. 20) of Major Benjamin Handley Geary V.C. It would seem that he was the MI5 head of station in Dublin. Christopher Andrew in his authorized history of MI5, *The Defence of the Realm*, makes no mention of him in any form. Geary was born in 1891 at Marylebone, London, and educated at Dulwich College and Keble College, Oxford. At the outbreak of World War I, he was commissioned as a 2nd Lieutenant in the East Surrey Regiment. He was awarded the Victoria Cross in 1915 for bravery at Ypres. During the action, he was shot in the head and lost the sight in his left eye. Upon recovery, he was temporarily seconded to the Royal Flying Corps on ground duties before returning to his old regiment then serving in Italy. In January 1918, the regiment returned to France, where Geary was again wounded. He left the Army in 1919 and was apparently recruited into the Secret Service and sent to Ireland as an acting major. In the late 1920s, he took Holy Orders in the Church of England and served as an army chaplain. He emigrated to Canada, where he died in 1976.
3. Frank Thornton, Deputy Assistant Director of Irish Intelligence, Witness Statement 615, p. 23.
4. Christopher Andrew and David Dilks [Eds.], *The Missing Dimension: Eunan Halpin, British Intelligence in Ireland, 1914–1921*.
5. Captain R. D. Jeune. William Sheehan, *British Voices*, pp. 84–5.
6. *Ibid.*, p.85.
7. Richard Bennett, *The Black and Tans*, p. 183.
8. Wilson's Diaries, details from Charles Townsend's, *The British Campaign in Ireland 1919-1921*, p.1 16.
9. *Ibid.*
10. Patrick Kennedy, Irish Intelligence, Witness Statement 499, p. 1.
11. Lieutenant Joseph Kinsella, Intelligence Officer, IRA, Witness Statement 476, p. 9.
12. Martin Finn, Section Leader, C Company, 1st Battalion, Witness Statement 921, p. 7.
13. Volunteer Christopher Crothers, Witness Statement 1759, pp. 1–2.
14. Lily Mernin, shorthand typist, Dublin Castle, Witness Statement 441, pp. 4–5.
15. *Ibid.*, p. 5.
16. Frank Thornton, Witness Statement 615, p. 21.
17. *Ibid.*, p. 23.
18. David Neligan, Detective Branch, DMP, Witness Statement 380, p. 7.

19. Patrick Caldwell, Irish Intelligence, Witness Statement 638.
20. William James Stapleton, The Squad, Witness Statement 822.
21. Liam Archer, Irish Intelligence, Witness Statement 819, pp. 20–21.
22. Tim Pat Coogan, *Michael Collins: A Biography*, p. 158.
23. Charles Dalton, *With the Dublin Brigade*, pp. 90–91.
24. Charles Dalton in his Witness Statement (W.S. 434) identifies "Bow Tie" as a tout called Robert Pike, a former British soldier. For his part, Pike was shot dead on June 18, 1921.
25. Dan Breen, *My Fight for Irish Freedom*, p. 137.
26. Jeune, p. 87.
27. *Ibid.* p. 88.
28. Part of Carolan's death bed statement appears in the Anvil Book edition of Breen's book, published in 1964, p. 191.
29. In Breen's account of the struggle, Treacy killed Price and wounded Christian. A third intelligence officer, from a distance of about five yards, then shot and killed Treacy. Breen, it should be added, was not an eyewitness to the shootings. The British account, which appears in the Dublin District Historical Record (*Record of the Rebellion in Ireland (Vol. IV, Part III)*, National Archives, Kew, is more succinct:

> Talbot Street on 14 November, on receipt of information that a Republican meeting was in progress at the Republican Stores, Talbot Street (Dublin), one officer, twenty other ranks (1st Lancashire Fusiliers), with an armored car, were sent at once from the Castle to raid the place. On arrival the alarm was given, and it has since been ascertained that one of the rebels deliberately exposed himself in the street, opening fire to divert our attention. Fire was also opened from the house. This man (Treacy) was killed, and also several other civilians. Of the Crown forces, one was killed and three wounded. The Stores were searched, but by this time the meeting had broken up. All the IRA leaders had been present.

30. James Slattery, The Squad, Witness Statement 445, p. 10.
31. Joseph Dolan, Irish Intelligence, Witness Statement 663.
32. Neligan, Witness Statement 380, p. 10.
33. This conversation is taken from *The Freeman's Journal*, October 18, 1920.
34. *Ibid.*
35. Lily Mernin, Witness Statement 441, p. 3., and Richard Bennett, *The Black and Tans*, p. 103.
36. Frank Thornton, Irish Intelligence, Witness Statement 615.
37. *Record of the Rebellion in Ireland*, Headquarters of Dublin District Intelligence W.O. 35/71.

Chapter 9

1. Lily Mernin, Witness Statement 441, p. 2.
2. Frank Thornton, Witness Statement 615, p. 24. Regarding those men listed for execution, Thornton was adamant that those on the list prepared by him were Secret Service men, regardless of their "official" status. He wrote:

> In various statements made by English writers dealing with this particular incident, i.e., Bloody Sunday, it has been suggested that the officers shot on that particular morning were court-martial officers. This is completely inaccurate. As I have already intimated in the foregoing paragraphs, great care was exercised in checking up on the activities of all these men and the Cabinet and Army Council had to be satisfied that they were actually employed on Secret Service work here in Ireland before they would agree to their execution. These men were a very definite Secret Service organization operating outside the various Barracks or Headquarters in Dublin and were established with the main object of destroying our Headquarters and army organization and the fact that we, who became aware of their activities earlier on, and smashed them by one military operation on Bloody Sunday, is sufficient answer I think to those who would try and confuse the issue by suggesting that they were shot purely because they had acted in the capacity of court-martial officers on some of our comrades. There is no doubt whatsoever but that they were active members of a very active Secret Service Organisation and were dealt with accordingly [p.26].

3. Frank Dalton Witness Statement 434.
4. Patrick Kennedy, GHQ Intelligence,

formerly of D Company, 2nd Battalion. Witness Statement 499, p. 4.

5. James Cahill, D Company, 2nd Battalion, Witness Statement 503, p. 6.

6. Frank Saurin, GHQ Intelligence, Witness Statement 715, p. 7.

7. Vincent Byrne, The Squad, Witness Statement 423, p. 53.

8. In his 1929 book, *With the Dublin Brigade*, Dalton refers to her as "Rosie." No doubt the change of name was to protect her.

9. David Neligan, Witness Statement 380, p. 1.

10. Vaughan's Hotel in Dublin had long been a favorite meeting place for the Intelligence Department and senior IRA officers. This became known to Dublin Special Branch agents who raided the hotel periodically after being informed of their presence by "touts." Collins appears to have ignored the advice offered to him by "Lt. G." (Lily Mernin), who contacted him after one visit—"Don't overdo. The road to Parnell Square is too well trod. Fifteen men, including you, went there to Vaughan's Hotel last night between 9 and 11 p.m." [Unattributed source: Richard Bennett, *The Black and Tans*, p. 102.]

11. Gleeson, pp. 160–161.

12. Charles Dalton, *With the Dublin Brigade*, p. 114. See also: Dalton's Witness Statement 434.

13. *Ibid.*, p. 118.

14. Caroline Woodcock, *An Officer's Wife in Ireland*, p. 65.

15. William Sheehan, *British Voices: Captain R. D. Jeune*, p. 89.

16. Frank Saurin, Witness Statement 715.

17. Vincent Byrne, Witness Statement 423.

18. James Slattery, Squad member, Witness Statement 445.

19. Pat McCrea, 2nd Battalion, Witness Statement 413.

20. William Stapleton, 2nd Battalion, Witness Statement 822.

21. David Grant on his website, www.bloodysunday.co.uk/murderedmen/newberry.html, argues convincingly that the woman in Newberry's apartment was his Irish mistress rather than his wife Hettie, who was living in north London. The almost throwaway reference to her being his wife would no doubt have been to protect his (and the government's) reputation.

22. Possibly an Irishman, Major J. C. O'Callaghan, formerly a major in the Royal Field Artillery during World War I, though this is in no way a certainty. A number of the senior officers in responsible positions in the Irish Administration at the time were Artillery men. There is no record of his being transferred to special assignments.

23. There was a considerable controversy over the shooting of Captain McCormack. The official version of his being in Dublin was that he, a military vet, though no longer on the Army List, was buying ponies for a Cairo polo club. His mother protested that he was not a Secret Service man. With influence within the old Parliamentary Party and Sinn Fein, pressure was brought to bear upon Collins, who was obliged to deny that McCormack was a spy and that he had been shot because he was a British Army officer. Evidence would seem to suggest that McCormack was indeed a spy. Dublin Castle official Mark Sturgis wrote in his diary for Sunday night, November 21st: "...at least a battalion of the IRA, perhaps more, systematically raided the houses occupied by Military officers—mostly either those who have been employed in Courts Martial or Secret Servicemen—in pairs of twelve and upwards at 9 a.m. this morning...These murders took place in nine private houses... except two Secret Service men assassinated in the Gresham Hotel and two Auxiliaries who were killed out of doors."

Caroline Woodcock in *An Officer's Wife in Ireland* acknowledges that, "Among the dead were two officers who had dined at our house on the Saturday night. These men were Roman Catholics, and, I was told, had taken up special service work from a sense of duty." Among the group of Secret Service men targeted that day, four were Roman Catholics—Henry Angliss, John Fitzgerald, Patrick McCormack and the unnamed officer at the Gresham, who had gone off to early morning Mass. As Angliss and Fitzgerald lived at separate addresses, it would perhaps be more logical that the two who lived together at the Gresham were the guests of the Woodcocks. James Cahill was in no doubt that

McCormack was a Secret Service man: "The possession of a gun in that period and his readiness to use it, completely refutes statements which have been made from time to time that he was not a British Agent, and that our Intelligence erred in including him amongst those to be executed" (W.S. 503). Regarding Wilde, James Doyle, manager of the Gresham Hotel, in his Witness Statement was to write: "Mr. Wilde had been here for a considerable time before Bloody Sunday. When Archbishop Clune visited this hotel again subsequently, I mentioned the shootings to him and he told me that Wilde had been put out of Spain; that he was well-known there as a British agent."

24. James Cahill.
25. Christopher Byrne, Witness Statement 642.
26. Laurence Nugent, Lieutenant, K Company, 3rd Battalion, Witness Statement 907.
27. C.S. Andrews, *Dublin Made Me*, p. 160.
28. *Ibid.*, pp. 162–3.
29. Dan McDonnell, the Squad, Witness Statement 486.
30. Ernie O'Malley, "Bloody Sunday" in *Dublin's Fighting Story*, p. 291.
31. Patrick Kennedy, Irish Intelligence, Witness Statement 499.
32. McDonnell, Witness Statement 486.
33. James Gleeson, in *Bloody Sunday*, p. 150, revealed that "It was not until some years later that a high ranking officer of the Auxiliaries divulged that the Auxiliaries could not make up their minds that Sunday whether to burn and sack O'Connell Street—Dublin's main thoroughfare—or raid the football match, so they tossed up for it and Croke Park lost." A military enquiry was held to look into the incident. It was headed by a three-man team consisting of Major R. Bunbury, president, Lieutenant S. H. Winterbottom of the 1st Lancashire Fusiliers and Lieutenant B. J. Key of the 2nd Worcester Regiment. The enquiry was held in camera under the Defence of the Realm Act, in lieu of a coroner's enquiry. Over 30 people were questioned, most of whom were from the RIC (Black and Tans) and the Auxiliaries. Predictably, the outcome, delivered on December 8, 1920, decided that the firing was begun by members of the IRA within the crowd. At variance to this was the statement of three members of the DMP who contradicted this evidence. The enquiry found that a total of 228 rounds of small arms ammunition were fired by the RIC (including the Auxiliaries), and 50 rounds were fired from a machine gun at the St. James Avenue exit. For more details, see the report now housed in the Public Record Office at Kew (WO 35/88).
34. Tim Pat Coogan, *Michael Collins: A Biography*, p. 159.
35. Maye, Brian, Arthur Griffith, Dublin, 1997, p. 149.
36. Lt. Lawrence Nugent, 3rd Battalion, Witness Statement 907.
37. Caroline Woodcock, *An Officer's Wife in Ireland*, p. 89–90.

Chapter 10

1. Frank Thornton of Irish Intelligence questioned this breakdown of the men killed. See his statement, Note 2 of Chapter 7. British propaganda would no doubt have sought to defame the "murderers" of innocent officers.
2. Joseph Dolan, Irish Intelligence, Witness Statement 663.
3. *Register of Secret Documents*, Dublin District WO35/174.
4. Ernie O'Malley, *On Another Man's Wound*, pp. 273–9.
5. *Jeudwine Papers*, December 1, 1920.
6. Thornton, Witness Statement 615.
7. Patrick Caldwell, Irish Intelligence, Witness Statement 638.
8. Paddy Daly, The Squad, Witness Statement 387.
9. Joseph Byrne, The Squad, Witness Statement 461.
10. Notes from the Military Court of Enquiry held on December 16, 1920. Major T. F. K. Dunns, presiding. It is tempting to suggest that the other British agent, "6ft. high, heavily built," was Captain King.
11. Dan Breen, *My Fight for Irish Freedom*, pp. 131–2.
12. James Doyle Witness Statement 771.
13. Eamon Broy, Witness Statement 1280.

14. Joseph Dolan, The Squad, Witness Statement 663.
15. "The Kerryman," March 1938, from Crozier's *Unpublished Memoirs*.
16. Thornton, Witness Statement 615.
17. *Ibid.*
18. Andrew, Christopher, *The Defence of the Realm: The Authorised History of MI5*, p. 90.
19. Captain R. D. Jeune, p. 90.
20. Cecil Lees was heir to the Lees Baronetcy of Blackrock, County Dublin. He was born in France in 1873, while his father was serving as a British consul. During the Boer War he served, first of all, as a trooper, then later as a lieutenant in the Cape Mounted Rifles. While pursuing a small party of Boer horsemen, he and his men were lured into a trap and captured. He was released at the end of the war. Lees remained in South Africa, working in the South Africa Civil Service, regulating the importation of Chinese mine laborers. In this work, he developed an expertise in fingerprinting in order to identify the work force. Lees assisted in the transport of Chinese workers to act as laborers on the Western front on the outbreak of World War I. He joined them in 1917 as Captain Lees. He was demobilized in France in March 1920. The *London Gazette* for November 29, 1920, lists him as, "Specially Employed," a euphemism for intelligence work. At the time of his death, Lees was living in Dublin with a Frenchwoman, Miss Annette Wolff of Paris. He had a wife, Jeannie King Paterson, and three children from an earlier marriage who lived in Natal, South Africa.
21. Daniel McDonnell, The Squad, Witness Statement 486.
22. Charles Dalton, *With the Dublin Brigade*, p. 210.
23. Bernard C. Byrne, Witness Statement 631.
24. William Stapleton, The Squad, Witness Statement 822.
25. James Slattery, The Squad, Witness Statement 445.
26. Charles Dalton, *With the Dublin Brigade*, p. 227.
27. Stapleton, Witness Statement 822.
28. C.S. Andrews, *Dublin Made Me*, pp. 177–80.
29. Charles Dalton, *With the Dublin Brigade*, p.224.
30. Thomas "Sweeney" Newell, Witness Statement 698.
31. Slattery, Witness Statement 445.
32. Bernard C. Byrne, Irish Intelligence, Witness Statement 631, O'Malley Notebooks, b76 and 116.
33. Stapleton, Witness Statement 822.
34. C.S. Andrews, *Dublin Made Me*, pp. 177–80.

Chapter 11

1. George Nolan, A Company, 4th Battalion, Dublin Brigade, Witness Statement 596.
2. George White, C Company, 3rd Battalion, Witness Statement 596.
3. Christopher Fitzsimons, F Company, 2nd Battalion, Witness Statement 581.
4. Nolan, Witness Statement 596.
5. James Carrigan, ASU C Company 1st Battalion, Witness Statement 613.
6. James Cahill, ASU, D Company, 2nd Battalion, Witness Statement 503.
7. Joseph O'Connor, A Company, 3rd Battalion, Witness Statement 487.
8. Dublin District Historical Record, Summary of events in Dublin, Period: December 1920 to July 1921 (Truce). *Record of the Rebellion in Ireland, 1920–1921, Vol. IV, Part II*. British National Archives, Kew.
9. Joseph O'Connor.
10. Dublin Historical Record.
11. James Cahill, ASU, D Company, 2nd Battalion, Witness Statement 503.
12. Joseph O'Connor, A Company, 3rd Battalion, Witness Statement 487, lists 43 attacks carried out by his unit between January and June of 1921:

Clare Street	January 1921	Pearse St	29. 4. 21
Mespil Road	"	Wexford St.	5. 5. 21
Nassau St. & Merrion Square	February 1921	Grafton St	12. 5. 21
Bishop St. & Aungier St. corner	"	Clare St	18. 5. 21
Merrion Square	6.2.21	Mount St	23. 5. 21

Location	Date	Location	Date
Camden St	6.2.21	Stephen's Green area	24.5.21
Merrion Square	13.2.21	Custom House	25.5.21
Lower Mount St	16.2.21	Stephen's Green	29.5.21
Camden St	28.2.21	Trinity College	8.6.21
College Green	1.3.21	Pearse St	8.6.21
South Richmond St	2.3.21	Ringsend	9.6.21
Pearse St.*	14.3.21	Northumberland Rd	10.6.21
Merrion Square	16.3.21	Stephen's Green	10.6.21
South Richmond St	18.3.21	St. Vincent Hospital	13.6.21
Aungier St.	20.3.21	Grafton St.	14.6.21
Grand Canal Bridge	22.3.21	Merrion Square	14.6.21
Camden St	28.3.21	Ringsend Rd	16.6.21
Merrion Square	30.3.21	Dartmouth Square	21.6.21
Grafton St.	18.4.21	Grafton St.	24.6.21
Sandford Rd	19.4.21	Baggot St.	26.6.21
Redmond's Hill	27.4.21	Ringsend Coastguard	30.6.21
Lower Baggot St	28.4.21		

*At the time this would have been Gt. Brunswick St. It was renamed Pearse St. after Independence.

13. Stephen Keys, A Company, 3rd Battalion, Witness Statement 1209.
14. C. S. Andrews, *Dublin Made Me*, Lilliput Press, Dublin, 2001, p. 175.
15. *Record of the Rebellion in Ireland, 1920–21*.
16. James Cahill, Witness Statement 503.

Chapter 12

1. Richard Bennett, *The Black & Tans*, p. 53.
2. Lt. Laurence Nugent, K Company, 3rd Battalion, Witness Statement 907.
3. Labour Party, *Report of the Labour Commission to Ireland*. London, 1921.
4. General Sir Hubert Gough, "The Situation in Ireland." *Review of Reviews*, February 1921.
5. "Report of a Visit to Ireland by Sir Warren Fisher." February 11, 1921. *Lloyd George Papers*, F17/9, Quoted in Charles Townsend, *The British Campaign in Ireland, 1919–1921*, p. 61.
6. Tim Pat Coogan, *Michael Collins: A Biography*, p. 230.
7. *Ibid.*, pp. 204–5.
8. Dorothy Macardle, *The Irish Republic*, p. 402.
9. Sean Kavanagh, Kilkenny, Witness Statement 524.
10. David Neligan, *The Spy in the Castle*, p. 129.
11. Joseph Byrne, The Squad, Witness Statement 461.
12. Vincent Byrne, The Squad, Witness Statement 423.
13. James Slattery, The Squad, Witness Statement 445.
14. Joseph Byrne, The Squad, Witness Statement 461.
15. Michael Fitzpatrick, "British Forces in Scene of Confusion," *Dublin's Fighting Story, 1916–21*, pp. 322–326.
16. Dr. Alice Berry, Witness Statement 723.
17. Joseph Dolan, Irish Intelligence, Witness Statement 663.
18. James Tully, ASU, Witness Statement 628.
19. Michael Stack, ASU, Witness Statement 525.
20. James Doyle, Manager of the Gresham Hotel, Witness Statement 771.
21. John Bolger, Irish Intelligence, Witness Statement 1745.

Chapter 13

1. Memo by G.O.C. Ireland, 23rd May 1921, C.O. P. 2965, Cab. 24 123.
2. *Ibid.*
3. *Captain Jeune Papers*, The Library, Imperial War Museum.

4. William Sheehan, *British Voices*, p. 50–1.

5. The incapability for Lloyd George to deliver on his threat of immediate and terrible war is indicated in the table below. The number of soldiers in the Army establishment, including Reserves and the Territorial Army, as of 18th April 1921, was 341,000 This figure was expected to fall during the year to about 235,000 with demobilization. *Whitaker's Almanac* for 1921 gives a breakdown of the displacement of British troops:

Distribution of British Forces

Home	140,523
Colonies	12,290
Rhine & Plebiscitary Areas	14,200
Constantinople	4,300
Egypt	10,300
Palestine	4,500
Mesopotamia (Iraq)	14,300
Total	**200,413**

In short, Lloyd George could not supply the troops threatened. No doubt aware of the figures, it was Collins's intention, following the withdrawal of British troops from the Free State, to launch an assault against Ulster using the constituted Irish Army, as per the treaty, and elements of the IRA flying columns, on the same basis that Lloyd George could not, or would not, send additional troops to the North. Events, however, prevented the plan from being put into play.

6. *Brigadier Frederick Clarke Papers*, Liddell Hart Centre for Military Archives, King's College, London.

Bibliography

PRIMARY SOURCES

United Kingdom
Imperial War Museum, Dept. of Documents:
Major General Hawes.
Lt. General Jeudwine Papers.
Captain R.D. Jeune Papers.
Field Marshall Sir Henry Wilson Papers.
Lord John French Papers.

King's College, London:
Liddell Hart Centre for Military Studies, Brigadier Frederick Clarke Papers.

U.K. National Archive, Kew:
British Army Medal Index Cards W.O. 372.
British Army Officers' Service Records.
Colonial Office Papers C.O. 903–6 and CAB 24 123.
Dublin District H.Q. File and War Diary W.O. 35.
Files on Sinn Fein and Republican Suspects C.O. 904/193–216.
Inquiry into the Events of Bloody Sunday WO 35/88.
Intelligence Officers' Reports, 1916–1918 C.O.904.
MI5 G Branch history KV 1/42.
Record of the Rebellion in Ireland, 1920–1921 (Vol. IV, Part III).
RIC Inspector General's Monthly Reports C.O. 904/101–156.
Sir John Anderson Correspondence HO 317.
Table of Secret Service Expenditure, HO 317/59.
War Office, Army of Ireland, W.O. 35/214.

University of Cambridge:
Quinlan, Kevin, *Human Intelligence Tradecraft and MI5 Operations in Britain 1919–40* (Ph.D. Dissertation).

Wiltshire Record Office:
Long Papers.

Ireland
Bureau of Military History:
Witness Statements (See Chapter Notes for Details).
Dublin Metropolitan Police Bi-weekly Reports.

National Library of Ireland:
American Commission on Conditions in Ireland.
Michael Collins Papers.

University College Dublin Archives:
Mulcahy Papers.
Ernie O'Malley Papers and Notebooks.

SECONDARY SOURCES
Books
Allen, M.S., *The Pioneer Police Women*. London: Chatto & Windus, 1925.
Andrew, Christopher, and David Dilks, eds. *The Missing Dimension*. London: Macmillan, 1985.
_____. *Secret Service: The Making of the British Intelligence Community*. London: Guild Publishing, 1985.
_____. *The Defence of the Realm: The Authorised History of MI5*. London: Penguin Books, 2010.
Andrews, C. S. *Dublin Made Me*. Dublin: Lilliput Press, 2001.

Barry, Tom. *Guerrilla Days in Ireland*. Dublin: Irish Press, 1949.

Bartholomew. *Dublin Streetfinder*. London: N.p., n.d.

Beaslai, Piaras. *Michael Collins and the Making of a New Ireland*. London: Harrap, 1926.

Bennett, Richard. *The Black and Tans*. Stroud: Spellmount Ltd., 2007.

Boyce, D. G. *The Irish Question and British Politics, 1868–1996*. London: Palgrave Macmillan, 1996.

Boyne, Sean. *Emmet Dalton*. Kildare: Sallins, 2015.

Breen, Dan. *My Fight for Irish Freedom*. London: Anvil Books, 1964.

Callwell, Major General Sir C. E. *Field Marshall Sir Henry Wilson: His Life and Diaries*. London: Cassell & Co., 1927.

Coogan, Tim Pat. *Michael Collins: A Biography*. London: Hutchinson, 1990.

____, *The Twelve Apostles*. London: Head of Zeus, 2016.

Costello, Francis, ed. *Michael Collins: In His Own Words*. N.p: London, 1997.

Crozier, F.P. *Ireland Forever*. London: Jonathan Cape, 1932.

Dalton, Charles. *With the Dublin Brigade*. Cork: Mercier Press, 2014.

Deacon, Richard. *A History of the British Secret Service*. London: Frederick Muller, 1969.

Dwyer, T. Ryle. *The Squad*. Cork: Mercier Press, 2005.

Foy, Michael T. *Michael Collins's Intelligence War*. Stroud: Sutton Publishing, 2006.

Gleeson, James. *Bloody Sunday*. Guilford, CT: The Lyons Press, 2004.

Grob-Fitzgibbon, Benjamin. *Turning Points of the Irish Revolution*. New York Palgrave Macmillan, 2007.

Hart, Peter, ed. *British Intelligence in Ireland, 1920–21: The Final Report*. Cork Cork University Press, 2002.

Hittle, J.B.E. *Michael Collins and the Anglo-Irish War: Britain's Counterinsurgency Failure*. Washington, DC: Potomac, 2011.

Holmes, Richard. *The Little Field Marshal: A Life of Sir John French*. London: Cassell, 2005.

Hopkinson, Michael, ed. *The Last Days of Dublin Castle: The Diaries of Mark Sturgis*. Dublin: Irish Academic Press, 1999.

Jeffery, Keith. *The Official History of the Secret Intelligence Service 1909–1949*. London: Bloomsbury, 2010.

Jones, Thomas. *Whitehall Diary, Vol. 3*. Edited by Keith Middlemas. Oxford: Oxford University Press, 1971.

Johnston, Roy H.W. *Century of Endeavour*. Dublin: Lilliput Press, 2006.

Kee, Robert. *The Green Flag, Volume III: Ourselves Alone*. London: Penguin Books, 1989.

Labour Party. *Report of the Labour Commission to Ireland*. London: Labour Party, 1921.

Macardle, Dorothy. *The Irish Republic*. London: Corgi, 1968.

Macready, General Sir Nevil. *Annals of an Active Life*. London: Hutchinson & Co. Ltd., 1924.

McKenna, Joseph. *Guerrilla Warfare in the Irish War of Independence, 1919–1921*. Jefferson, NC: McFarland, 2011.

McMahon, Paul. *British Spies and Irish Rebels*. Woodbridge: Boydell Press, 2011.

Neligan, David, *The Spy in the Castle*. London: Prendville Publishing Ltd., 1999.

O'Brien, Paul. *Havoc: The Auxiliaries in Ireland's War of Independence*. Cork: Collins Press, 2017.

O'Conchubhair, Brian, ed. *Dublin's Fighting Story*. Cork: Mercier Press, 2009.

O'Connor, Frank. *My Father's Son*. London: Pan Books, 1971.

O'Malley, Ernie. *On Another Man's Wound*. Dublin: Anvil Books, 2002.

O'Neill, H. C. *The Royal Fusiliers in the Great War*. London: Naval & Military Press, 1920.

Pachenham, F. *Peace by Ordeal*, London: Sedgwick & Jackson, 1972.

Ryan, Meda. *Michael Collins and the Women Who Spied for Ireland*. Cork: Mercier Press, 2006.

Seligmann, Matthew S. *Spies in Uniform: British Military and Naval Intelligence on the Eve of the First World War*. Oxford: Oxford University Press, 2006.

Sheehan, William. *British Voices*. Cork: The Collins Press, 2005.

____. *Fighting for Dublin*. Cork: The Collins Press, 2007.

Strong, Kenneth. *Intelligence at the Top: The Recollections of an Intelligence Officer*. London: Doubleday, 1968.

Sturgis, Mark. *The Last Days of Dublin Castle: The Diaries of Mark Sturgis*. Dublin: Irish Academic Press, 1999.

Townsend, Charles. *The British Campaign in Ireland, 1919–1921*. Oxford: Oxford University Press, 1975.

———. *The Republic: The Fight for Irish Independence*. London: Penguin, 2014.

Valiulis, Maryann Gialanella. *Portrait of a Revolutionary: General Richard Mulcahy*. Dublin: Irish Academic Press, 1992.

Walsh, Maurice. *Bitter Freedom*. London: Faber & Faber, 2015.

Winter, Brigadier General Sir Ormond de L'Epee. *Winter's Tale*. London: Richards Press, 1955.

Woodcock, Caroline. *An Officer's Wife in Ireland*. London: Parkgate Publications, 1994.

PERIODICALS, NEWSPAPERS AND ANNUALS

Army Lists (British)
Army Quarterly
Blackwood's Magazine
Capuchin Annual
Contemporary Review
An Cosantoir
Daily Herald
English Historical Review
European Studies Review
Hansard: *Commons*
Hansard: *Lords*
Historical Journal
Irish Historical Studies
Irish Independent
Irish Times
Journal of Contemporary History
Kelly's Directories of London
London *Gazette*
Review of Reviews
The Times

Index

Active Service Units 199, 205 passim, 229
Allen, Miss M.S. 119
American Expeditionary Force 11
Ames, Peter Asham 129, 145, 148–9, 155, 156
An tOglach 10, 15, 22, 39, 92
Anderson, Sir John 122, 123, 233
Andrew, Christopher 190
Andrews, C.S. "Tod" 165, 166, 195–6
Angliss, Capt. Henry 131, 143, 157
Antient Concert Rooms 34, 51
Appleford, L.G. 103
Archangel 157
Archer, Liam 44, 54
Army List 30
Ashe, Thomas 9
Asquith, Herbert 25
Asquith, Thomas 209
Attwood, P. 165
Aud 24
Austro-Hungary 27
auxiliaries 35, 99–101, 104, 108, 129, 151, 188, 201–2, 209, 212, 223, 224, 227–8

Baggallay, Capt. 131, 151, 160
Balfe, Edward 76
Balfour, Arthur 97
Bardon, Stephen 244
Barrett, Ben 85
Barrett, Michael 42
Barry, Dr. Alice 227–8
Barry, Tom 12, 37, 100
Barton, Det. Sgt. John 54, 61, 62, 78, 249
Beaslai, Piaras 15, 37, 39, 40, 151, 217
Beesley, Arthur 162
Beggar`s Bush Barracks 160
Begley, Denis 157
Bell, Alan 80, 83–4, 87–9
Bennett, Lt. George 127, 145, 148–9, 155–6, 157
Bennett, Ned 163
Bennett, Richard 120
Bere & Spike Islands 108
Berry, Patrick J. 150

"Big Fellow" *see* Collins, Michael
Birkenhead, Lord 97
Birrell, Augustine 24
Black & Tans 97–8, 212–13
Blackwood's Magazine 111
Bloody Sunday 148 passim, 174, 175, 177
Blythe, Ernest 59
Boddington, H.F. 165
Boer War 6
Bohan, Billy 226
Boland, Harry 12, 14, 16
Bolster, Ned. 191
"Bow Tie" 135–6; *see also* Pike, Robert
Bowen, Capt. Rees 144–5
Boyd, Maj. Gen. 94, 125
Brady, John E. 245
Breen, Dan 14, 15, 64, 65, 73, 74, 135, 136–8, 182–3
Brennan, James 160
Breslin, Peadar 18
Brind, Gen. J.E.S. 94
British Socialist Party 82
Brooke, Frank 89–90
Broy, Eamon (Edward, Ned) 3, 31, 35, 36, 41, 45, 56, 63, 120, 134, 184–5, 220
Brugha, Cathal 14, 15, 74, 148, 179, 205, 220
Bruton, Sergeant 58
Bryan, Thomas 209
Burke (British agent) 230–1
Burke, Francis 165
Burke, Tom 17
Burton, Maj. Stratford 39
Byrne, Barney 50, 61, 62, 115–6, 191, 192, 193, 201
Byrne, Charlie 33, 200
Byrne, Christopher 163
Byrne, Brig.-Gen. J.A. 13, 28
Byrne, John Charles *see* Molloy, Brian Fergus
Byrne, Joseph 225
Byrne, Sgt. Matt 42
Byrne, Vinnie 47, 48, 55, 51, 57, 58, 61, 64, 65, 71, 86, 150, 155, 156, 197, 201, 202, 223, 224, 225

269

Index

Café Cairo 86, 103
Cahill, James 148, 162, 209, 212, 215
Cairo Gang 118
Caldow, John 164
Caldwell, Paddy 33, 132, 133, 175181
Callaghan, Major 163, 164
Cameron, Cecil A. 96
Carbery, Christopher 30, 102
Carew, Maj. Frank 157, 165, 167, 185–6
Carolan, Prof. John 136–7
Carson, Sir Edward 6
Casement, Sir Roger 9, 12, 24, 27
Cavendish-Bentinck, Lord Henry 216
Cecil, Lord Robert 216
Central Raid Bureau 119
Chadwick, Mick 218
Childers, Erskine 93
Childs, Gen. Wyndham 186
Christian, Sgt.-Maj. Francis 140
Christy the porter 151
Churchill, Winston 97, 172
Clancy, George 187
Clancy, Peadar 50, 152, 153, 167–8, 170, 176
Clann na Gael 26
Clare, County 8
Clarke, Basil 93
Clarke, Brig. Frederick 236
Clarke, Tom 3, 7
"Clevedon, Mr." 167
Clonakilty 4
Clontarf 13
Clune, Connor 151, 152, 167–8, 170, 176
Coady (British agent) 230–1
Cockerill, Brig. Gen. 216
Coffey, Det. Denis 71, 72
Coles Brothers 18
Collins, Hannie 4
Collins, Marianne 4
Collins, Michael 4, 5, 7, 9, 10, 12, 14, 15, 19, 22–23, 30, 31, 32, 35, 40, 44, 58, 61, 91–2, 102, 115, 120, 125, 14, 150, 170–1, 174, 219, 220, 225, 227, 230, 234, 235
Collins, Patrick 213
Collinstown Aerodrome 20–21
Connaught Rangers 100, 131
Connolly, James 6
Connolly, John Joseph 159
Conroy, Herbert 156, 160, 177–8
Conroy, James 192
Conscription Crisis 11
Coogan, Tim Pat 37, 57, 170
Cooney, Andy 153
Cooper, Becky 164
Cope, Alfred "Andy" 93, 107, 131, 185, 192, 217
Cosgrave, William 9
Coughlan, Francis X. 165, 166
Craig, Sir James 234
Crawford, Capt. J.S. 161, 161–2

Croke Park 147, 168–70
Crothers, Christopher 127
Crow Street 34
Crozier, Brig.-Gen. 100, 145, 160, 188
Cullen, Tom 32, 40, 55, 73, 82, 83, 103, 104, 129, 134, 145, 148, 170–1, 202, 219
Cullenswood House 91, 120
Cullinane, John 162
Cumman na mBan 9, 121
Custom House, Dublin 220 passim

Dail Eireann 9, 13, 15, 51
Dail Loan 23, 46, 84, 87, 130
Daily Telegraph 125
Dalton, Charles 33, 37, 43, 59, 66, 134–5, 140–1, 150, 153, 171–2, 194, 196–7, 198
Dalton, Det. Constable Laurence 71, 249
Daly, John 156
Daly, Paddy 51, 53, 60, 68, 70, 85, 89, 140–1, 182, 221
Daly, Seamus 6
"Dardanelles" 211–12
Dempsey, Jim 157
Denham, Godfrey 95, 96
DeValera, Eamon 8, 12, 15, 31, 205, 218–21, 233, 234
Devlin's pub. 37
Dodd, Joe 17
Dolan, Edward 18
Dolan, Joe 68, 71, 85, 102, 141, 147, 169, 175, 186, 229
Dolan, John 165
Dominion Home Rule 232
Donnelly, Jim 163
Donnelly, Simon 177
Doran, Willie 186–7
Dore, Eamon 75
Dorrins, Eddie 225
Dowling, Maj. "Chummy" 154, 155
Dowling, Joseph 12, 27
Downing, Constable Michael 59, 145, 249
Doyle, Ben 152
Doyle, Gunner 181
Doyle, James 164, 183, 230
Doyle, Paddy 209
Doyle, Sean 156, 164, 225
Doyle, William 206
Doyle's Corner 150
Dublin Bread Co. 67, 185–6
Dublin Castle 9, 28, 33, 72, 145, 152, 201, 218, 220, 231
Dublin District Special Branch 94, 116, 136, 144, 145, 148, 204, 210, 213–4, 236
Dublin Metropolitan Police 3, 24, 25, 30, 32, 91
Duffy, Tom 156
Duggan, Eamon 12, 30, 35
Duggan, G.C. 111
Duke, Henry 11
Dun Laoghaire 6, 120

Index

Dunne, John 207, 225
Dunne, Leo 153
Dunne, Lilly 40, 143, 157
Dunne, Superintendent 40
Dunney, Patrick 244
Dwyer, George 163

Earle, Hubert 165, 166
East Cavan 12
Easter Rising 3, 7, 9
Eastwood Hotel 163
Edgeworth-Johnstone, Col. 184
Ellis, John 203
Ennis, Tom 51, 154, 157, 221
Exchange Hotel 130

Fernside 136
Finn, Martin 127
Fisher, Sir Warren 107, 219
Fitzgerald, Desmond 234
Fitzgerald, George 17, 20, 21, 106, 107, 141–2, 180
Fitzgerald, Capt. John J. 164–5
Fitzgerald, Michael 226, 227
Fitzmaurice, Constable 140
Fitzpatrick, Sean 192
Fitzsimons, Christopher 207, 208
Flanagan, "Rabbit" 48
Flanagan, Fr. Paddy 42, 153, 154, 206–7, 217
Fleming family 135, 139
Fleming's Hotel 231
Flood, Frank 203, 206, 208, 209
Flood, Sean 180
Foley, Dick 102
Foley, Jack 160
Foley, James 162
Foley, Michael 36
Ford, Val. 228
Fovargue, Vincent 220–1
Fowler's shop 34
Fraser, Leslie 244–5
Freeman's Journal 145, 203, 217
French, Lord John 11, 64, 65, 66, 67, 78, 80, 84, 93
Frongoch 6
Furlong, Matt 139

G-Men 3, 19, 22, 31, 236
Gaelic Athletic Association 4, 10
Gaelic League 9
Gaiety Theatre 151
Galway, Bishop of 57
Garde, Colonel 106
Garnis, Frank 159–60
Gay, Thomas 31, 36, 41
General Election 13, 28–29
General Post Office 47
George V 233
George V Military Hospital 160

German Gymnasium 5
German Plot 12, 27, 79, 91
Germany 14
Gibney, Det. William 61, 62, 63
Gifford, Nellie 5
Gilby's Wine Merchants 202
Glasnevin Cemetery 165
Gleeson, James 167
Gleeson, Maire 194
Glynn, Joseph 162
Good, Joe 5
Gorey, Wexford 76
Gough, Gen. Sir Hugh 215
Government of Ireland Act 218
Grafton Bar 86
Grafton Street 229
Graham, Peter 244
Gray, Mrs. 148, 154
Greenwood, Sir Hamar 93, 172, 234
Gresham Hotel 146, 148, 162, 183, 230
Griffith, Arthur 8, 11, 13, 69, 125, 129, 141, 174, 216
Guilfoyle, Joe 33, 102, 132, 133

Hall, Admiral Reginald 27
Halley, Det. Nicholas 65
Halpin, Thomas 245
Hardy, Frank Digby 114–5
Hardy, Capt. Jocelyn 100, 102, 103, 131–2, 133, 143, 152, 160, 167, 175–6, 187
Harper, Captain 95
Harrell, W.V. 27
Hawse, Maj. Gen. 236
Head, Dan. 224, 225
Hegarty, Diarmuid 22, 58
Henderson, Frank 53
Henderson, Leo 50
Hepworth, Sergt. Maj. 175
Hickey, John J. 182
Hill Dillon, Col. S. 39, 78, 86, 94, 107, 191
Hinchcliffe, Herbert 187
Hoey, Det. Daniel 31, 54, 56, 57, 78, 249
Hoey, Patricia 228
Hogan, Michael 169
Hogan, Sean 14, 64
Hogan, William 162
Home Rule 5, 8, 10
Houlihan, Gary 19, 20
Hunt, William F. 229–30
Hurley, Sean 5
"Hush-hush men" 124
Hyem, E.P. 165
Hynes Public House 192

Igoe, Head Constable Eugene 175, 193–4
Illustrated London News 131
International News 220
Irish Bulletin 115
Irish Free State 235
Irish Parliamentary Party 7, 13

Irish Republican Army 109, 123
Irish Republican Brotherhood 4, 5, 7, 8
Irish Times 193
Irish Volunteers 4, 5
Irish Woodworkers 61
Isham, Ralph Heyward 81

Jammets 35
Jeffries, William F. 96, 233–4
Jennings, Capt. T.J. 163, 164
Jeudine, Maj. Gen. 94, 179
Jeune, Capt. Robert 125, 129, 137, 138, 155, 174, 190, 217
Johnstone, Col. 40
Jones, Tom 36, 233

Kavanagh, Joseph 30
Kavanagh, Sean 41, 43–4
Keating, Jack 160
Keegan, Tommy 134
Keenlyside, Capt. 154
Kell, Col. Vernon 79
Kellegher, Ned 33, 153
Kells, Det. Henry 70, 71, 249
Kelly, David 209
Kelly, J.J. 7
Kelly Gang 202
Kennedy, Mick 56
Kennedy, Paddy 33, 42, 48, 133, 148, 162, 168, 187–8, 192
Kenny, James 165
Keogh, Tom 47, 51, 52, 56, 61, 62, 64, 65, 68, 71, 87, 88–90, 150, 15, 158, 159, 169, 191, 193, 200
Kerr, Sergeant 38
Kidd's Buffet 129, 145
Kilcoyle, Tom 85, 221
Kilkelly, Michael 162
Killeen, Sgt. Patrick 193
Kilmainham Prison 234
Kilmichael battle 100
King, Capt. William L. 100, 102, 103, 127, 145, 152, 167, 175, 187, 188
Kingstown *see* Dun Laoghaire
Kinsella, Joseph 126–7
Kirwan, Seamus 135
Kitton, Capt. 116
Knight, Andrew 245

Laffan, Nicholas 17
Larkin, Peter 229
La Scala Cinema 135
Lawless, Evelyn 22, 58, 68, 69
Lawless, Michael 156
Lawson, Patrick 53
Lea-Wilson, Percival 75–6
Lee-Enfield rifles 19
Lees, Capt. Cecil 190–1
Lemass, Sean 160
Leonard, Joe 31, 51, 60, 64, 160, 226

Leonard, Nicholas 162
Lincoln Gaol 14
Lloyd George, David 11, 16, 92, 99, 107, 108, 125, 171, 172, 180, 216, 233–4
Logue, Cardinal 64
London Gazette 144, 155, 165
Londonderry, Lord 78
Long, Walter 11, 27
Love, Det. Insp. 58
"Lt. G." *see* Mernin, Lily
Ludendorff, General 11, 13
Lynch, Diarmuid 49
Lynch, John 117, 129–30, 134, 157
Lynch, Patrick 8

MI 5, 26
MacDiarmada, Sean 3
MacKenna, Kathleen Napoli 105
MacMahon, Sean 10
MacNeill, Eoin 70
MacNeill, Hugo 70, 161
Macready, Gen. Nevil 94, 111, 122, 123, 179, 232, 233
Magee, Michael 209
Maguire, Sam 4
Maher, Sergeant 43
Maher, William 156
Mahon, Sir Bryan 11
Mahon, Patrick *see* Anglis, Henry
Malone, Ainne 102
Manchester Guardian 8
Mannix, Patrick 42, 43
Mansion House, Dublin 11, 13
Markham, Thomas 3
Markievicz, Constance 5
Martini-Henry rifles 19
Mason, Jenny 58
Mater Hospital 139
Maxwell, Sir John 25
McCarthy, Sergt. 67
McCormack, Capt. 162
McCrae, Pat 48, 51, 160
McCrane, Tommy 18
McCurtain, Thomas 187
McDonald, Matthew 160
McDonnell, Dan 166, 169
McDonnell, James 14, 15
McDonnell, John 156, 165
McDonnell, Mick 50, 56, 64, 67, 71
McFeely, Inspector Neil 22–23, 58, 59, 69
McGee, Peter 33
McGraine, Eileen 121, 184
McGrath, Richard 162
McGrath, Sean 82
McGrath, William 187
McGuinness, Charlie 234
McGuinness, James 213
McGuinness, Joseph 8, 118, 163
McKee, Dick 50, 70, 138, 147, 148, 152, 153, 167–8, 170, 176, 192

McKenna, Patrick 8
McLean, Billy 157, 158
McLean, Lt. Donald 139, 164
McMahon, Sir James 39
McMahon, Lt. 159–160
McNamara, James 30, 41, 67, 83, 168
McPherson, Ian 92
McQuaille, Charles 47
Mernin, Lily 39–40, 86, 104, 127–8, 131, 143, 14, , 150, 157, 162, 229
Merrigan, Tom 21
Messines Ridge 8
military intelligence 91
Molloy, Brian Fergus 81, 82, 84, 85, 86, 87
Monaghan, Andy 157
Montgomery, Bernard 93
Montgomery, Col. 154, 155
Monto 164
Moran, Michael 162
Moran, Paddy 33, 178–9, 203, 209
Moreland's Cabinet Makers 52
Morgan, Mary 209
Morris, Cecil 159–60
Mosley, Sir Oswald 216
Moylett, Patrick 216
Moynihan, Capt. Pat 39, 46
Mulcahy, Richard 7, 8, 10, 12, 14, 15, 50, 92, 106, 120, 205
Murder Gang 117, 124, 144, 195
Murmansk 157
Murphy, Fintan 22, 58
Murphy, James 187–8
Murphy, Kate 127
Murray, Jimmy 19
Murray, Lt. R.G. 154

National Aid Assoc. 7
Neligan, David 32, 40, 41, 54, 57, 67, 7, 78, 81–21, 84, 100, 123, 13, 140–1, 220–1
New Ireland Assurance 32, 83
Newberry, Capt. William 160–1
Newell, Thomas "Sweeney" 196–7, 198
Noble, Lt. William 165, `66
Nolan, George 118, 206, 208
Noone, Michael 162
Noyk, Michael 94
Nugent, Lt. L. 165, 171, 218
Nunan, Sean 38

O'Brien, Art 82
O'Brien, Det. Denis 54
O'Brien, Eamon 135
O'Brien, Nancy 39
O'Callaghan, Major 161
O'Callaghan, Michael 187
O'Carroll, Joseph 153
O'Carroll, Peter 117, 142–3
O'Connell, Ginger 22
O'Connell, Patrick 14
O'Connor, Batt 82, 83, 219

O'Connor, Joe 19, 211–12
O'Connor, Judge 217
O'Connor, Pat 163, 226, 229, 230
O'Connor, Rory 10
O'Donahue & Smith 34
O'Farrel, James 209
O'Hanlon, Gertrude 60
O'Hanlon, Jack 229
O'Hanlon, Michael 153, 154
O'Hanrahan, Harry 31
O'Malley, Ernie 101, 102, 116, 171, 176–7, 178, 211
O'Muirthuile, Sean 70
On Another Man's Wounds 101, 211
O'Neill, Jim 229
O'Neil, Patrick 244
Operation Optimist 203
O'Reilly, Joe 17, 84–5
O'Reilly, Paddy 225
O'Reilly, Stephen 225
O'Reilly, Mick 191
Ormond Hotel 200
O'Shea, Paddy 186

Parkgate 86
Pat Sheerin's Dairy 48
Peel, Lt. C. Ratch 143–4, 157, 158, 173
Percival, Maj.Gen. 93, 188–9, 233
Periscope 112
Pike, Robert 245
Pioneer Policewoman 119
Plunkett, Count Horace 7, 9
Plunkett, Joseph 6, 7
Price, Insp. Ivon 24
Price, Capt. Leonard 154, 155

Quinlisk, Henry 68–9

Rabbiatti's Saloon 145
Rawson, Col. H.E. 94
Record of the Rebellion 43, 77, 105, 106, 109, 110, 172
Redmond, John 5, 8, 10
Redmond, W.C. Forbes 67, 68, 81, 249
Redmond, Willie 8
Report on the Intelligence Branch of the Chief of Police 122, 123
Report of the Labour Commission 218–9
Restoration of Order in Ireland 97, 107
Revelle, Det. Sgt. 72–3
Reynolds, Maj. John 102, 168, 176
Roberts, Inspector Albert 55
Robinson, Sir Henry 225
Robinson, Seamus 14, 64
Robinson, William 169
Roche, Sergeant 140–1
Roman Catholic Church 10, 28
Roscommon 13
Rosie the maid 148
Royal Barracks 107

Index

Royal Irish Constabulary 4, 15, 97, 24, 25, 32, 79, 194
Russell, Sean 148
Russian Revolution 11
Ryan, Bernard 203, 209
Ryan, John "Shankers" 151, 192–3, 343–4

St. Andrew's Hotel 191
St. Patrick's Training College 136
St. Stephen's Green 163
Sancta Maria 234
Saurin, Frank 33, 35, 104, 128, 148, 155, 156
Savage, Martin 64, 65
Scannell's Auction House 207
Schweppe family 133–4
Scotland House 119, 123
Scott, J. 169
Shanaghan's pub 18
Sharkey, Paddy 64
Shaw, Sir Frederick 11, 93
Shelbourne Hotel 35, 81, 106, 163
Shortt, Edward 11
Shove, Capt. Harper 144
Sinn Fein 6, 8, 9, 10, 11, 13, 14, 27, 28, 29, 57, 60, 79, 84, 174
Skinnider, Margaret 6
Slattery, James 51, 56, 61, 71, 89–90, 157, 158, 192, 200, 224
Smart, Maire 35
Smith, T.H. 164
Smith-Cummings, Mansfield 80–1
Smuts, Jan 233
Smyth, Maj. George 136–7
Smyth, Michael 178
Smyth, Det. Patrick 54, 56, 57, 78, 249
Smyth, Lt. Col. S.F. 99
Soloheadbeg 14
Soloheadbeg Gang 64
Southern Parliament 232
Special Gang 103
Special (Irish) Branch 79–80
Spy in the Castle 220–1
Spy School 95–6, 144, 158
The Squad 66, 192, 199, 204, 221, 226
Stack, Austin 9, 106, 220, 234
Stack, Michael 229, 230
Stack, Mrs. 161
Stafford, Jack 161
Standard Hotel 165
Stapleton, Bill 51, 52, 53, 55, 59, 133, 161, 192, 195, 197
Steele, John S.
Straw, Percy 243
Strong, Kenneth 95
Sturgis, Mark Beresford 93, 111, 117, 131, 192
Sweeney, Michael 206, 213, 214
Swindlehurst, J.P. 98, 101, 117

Tara Hall 150
Taylor, Sir John 80
Teeling, Frank 157, 158, 177
Tegart, Charles A. 95, 96
Thomson, Basil 27, 79, 81, 94, 112
Thomson, General 219
Thornton, Frank 32, 34, 42, 49, 67, 76, 82, 83, 103, 126, 141, 144, 145, 147, 148, 170–1, 180, 189, 194
Thorp, A. 165
The Times 13, 216
Tobin, Liam 32, 55, 67, 71, 73, 75, 82, 85, 87, 104, 129, 132, 145, 148, 181, 203
Tracy, Patrick 12, 31
Treacy, Sean 14, 15, 64, 73, 74, 135, 137–8, 140
Trinity College 62
Tudor, Maj. Gen. Hugh 94, 99, 100, 108, 126, 180, 181, 208–9
Tully, James 227
Turkey 14

Unionists 10, 13
Universal Services 220

Vaughan's Hotel 37, 151, 175

Walsh, Captain 107
Walsh, Maud 106–7
Walsh & Sons 207
Walshe, Det. Constable 63
Warnes, George G. 103
Wharton, Det. Sgt. 59–60
Whelan, Thomas 203, 209
White, Capt. Alfred 138
White, Lt. Enfield 229–30
White, George 153
Who's Who 30
Wilde, Lt. Col. 162
Willis, William 203
Wilson, Sir Henry 11, 125–6, 232
Wilson, Lt. Col. W. 94, 108, 123, 125
Wimberley, Maj. Gen. 98
Wimborne, Lord 11
Winter, Ormonde 94–95, 105, 109, 111–14, 125, 130 118, 119, 120, 121, 122, 189, 192, 193, 221, 236
Winter's Tale 112
Woodcock, Caroline 153–4, 173
Woodcock, Lt. Col. W. 153–4, 155
Woods, Tony 101
Worcester Regiment 233
A Word to Gandhi 145
Worth, Corporal 139
Wren's Hotel 70
Wylie, W.E. 108

Z Company 193